THE HUDSON RIVER BASIN

Environmental Problems and Institutional Response

VOLUME 1

1979

ACADEMIC PRESS

A Subsidiary of Harcourt Brace Jovanovich, Publishers

New York   London   Toronto   Sydney   San Francisco

ACADEMIC PRESS, INC.
111 Fifth Avenue, New York, New York 10003

United Kingdom Edition published by
ACADEMIC PRESS, INC. (LONDON) LTD.
24/28 Oval Road, London NW1 7DX

Library of Congress Cataloging in Publication Data
Main entry under title:

The Hudson River Basin.

Includes index.
1. Regional planning—New York metropolitan
area. 2. Regional planning—Hudson River Valley.
3. Environmental policy—New York metropolitan
area. 4. Environmental policy—Hudson River
Valley. I. Richardson, Ralph W. II. Tauber,
Gilbert.
HT394.N5H83   309.2'5'097473   78–19999
ISBN 0–12–588401–X

THE
HUDSON RIVER
BASIN

Environmental Problems and Institutional Response

VOLUME 1

Edited by

RALPH W. RICHARDSON, JR.

GILBERT TAUBER

Natural and Environmental Sciences Division
The Rockefeller Foundation
New York, New York

Contents

Foreword

The Hudson Basin displays a wide array of environmental problems that are sufficiently serious or complex to have become public issues. That so many of these problems have escalated to the level of issues is not so much an indication of the poor state of the environment itself as it is a reflection of the inadequacy of existing institutions.

Most of the environmental problems in the Hudson Basin today are the result, direct or indirect, of the tremendous population and economic growth in the 25 years following World War II. The physical development required to accommodate that growth was often poorly planned and placed tremendous stress on environmental resources. During the same 25-year period, there also were major movements in population and shifts in industrial location. These eroded the fiscal base of the region's older cities and placed a great strain on the governmental and social institutions of both the central cities and the developing suburban areas. In the 1970s there has been increasing recognition of the environmental problems generated in the two previous decades. But because the region's economy has also slackened in this decade, the money needed to repair existing environmental damage is not currently available. Therefore, present efforts must focus on preventing further damage.

Natural systems in the Hudson Basin have been heavily impacted by man, not only since World War II but also over several generations. When, however, one considers the region's huge concentrations of population and economic activity, its natural systems are still quite productive. Nevertheless, we have no grounds for complacency. Relatively little is known about the underlying dynamics, and therefore the carrying capacity, of the basin's natural systems, including their ability to assimilate pollutants and to recover from other types of stress caused by human activity.

The Project's ten task groups presented numerous case studies of environmental controversies or "problem situations" in the Hudson Basin. Most of these problem situations illustrate one or more of the following:

- Multiple effects of siting large-scale energy-producing facilities
- The lack of land use control above the local level
- The lack of local capacity to control the effects of large-scale initiatives that induce development or otherwise influence land use
- Inadequate legislation leading to court battles in which diffuse environmental interests are pitted against highly focused economic interests
- The "taking issue," i.e., the lack of clarity and consensus on how far the public can assert an interest in private land before it becomes a "taking" which must be compensated
- The neglect of existing rail freight facilities while public investment encourages increased reliance on truck transportation
- The inadequacy of scientific and institutional capacity to allocate water resources among competing uses in the Hudson Basin
- The difficulty of controlling pressures that are accelerating the withdrawal of land from agricultural use
- The distorting effects of the property-tax system on land use
- The inadequacy of existing procedures for assessing the costs and benefits of environmental decisions

The environment management needs of the Hudson Basin are manifold. Based on the work of the Project's task groups, the following appear to need the most attention:

- The rehabilitation of the inner-city environment and the control of urban sprawl
- The reduction of health hazards in the work and home environments
- The improvement of institutional capacity for regional water management
- The filling of the gaps in land use planning and regulation
- The moderation of solid-waste generation and the improvement of disposal techniques
- The protection of ecologically significant land and water resources
- The integrated planning of transportation modes and land use
- The moderation of energy demand and the augmentation of supply
- The improvement of the management of interstate air quality

- The optimization of public and private investment policies affecting the environment

States and many of their constituent units of local government have assigned most of their functions to single-purpose agencies and departments. The most fundamental weakness of the single-purpose unit is the limited scope of its mandate, mission, authority, expertise, and funding, which results in the inability to manage the consequence of its actions. The need to strengthen environmental management institutions has been identified by the Hudson Basin Project as the most important underlying problem in the study area. The measures needed to correct present deficiencies can be summed up as follows: Improve information management. Broaden assessment processes. Increase and strengthen arenas for conflict resolution. Improve the substance and explicitness of policy. Strengthen institutional capacity to formulate and execute policy.

The above steps, if pursued over time by all affected interests, would strengthen the public's perception and its will to act on the primary need to improve institutional capacity for environmental decision-making. As a next step, it is proposed that a new organization be created to involve environmental research producers, funders, and users in the pursuit of the recommendations outlined in Volumes 1 and 2. The organization's primary task would be to develop and execute projects and programs that lead to more effective decisions about specific environmental problems in the basin. Concurrent tasks would include basic research, the development of a regional research agenda, and information transfer.

Chapter 1, originally published as the Project's final report, is the product of a collaborative effort of a staff and consultant team consisting of Leonard B. Dworsky, Chadborne Gilpatric, Caroline F. Raymond, Gilbert Tauber, Anthony Wolff, and the undersigned. A complete list of Project participants and a brief history of the Project are included in the appendixes to Volume 2. Although the analysis, conclusions, and recommendations presented here represent the sense of what can be fairly drawn from the Project's work, it does not necessarily reflect a consensus of all participants. Therefore, responsibility for the final form, substance, and emphasis of this report must rest with the undersigned.

For the contributions and assistance so unstintingly tendered by all—The Rockefeller Foundation, the Advisory Panel, task group members, consultants, and Project staff—deepest appreciation is extended.

C. David Loeks

Preface

These two volumes are drawn from the work of the Hudson Basin Project, a three-year study of environmental problems and issues and of the institutions that are attempting to manage them. The Project, initiated in 1973, was funded by the Rockefeller Foundation and carried out by Mid-Hudson Pattern, Inc., a nonprofit regional planning organization, under the direction of C. David Loeks.

Some of the environmental issues analyzed in the Project have been resolved; others are still being debated. However, the Project's contribution to environmental policy analysis goes beyond specific issues or the boundaries of a specific region.

The Project's innovative approach begins with the delineation of its study area, which comprises the New York metropolitan region plus that portion of its hinterland within the Hudson River watershed. It is an area large enough to reveal the interrelationships of environmental problems, yet small enough to be comprehended in concrete terms. Within this area, the Project was able to examine the very broad range of issues resulting from long-term interaction between human settlement and its surrounding natural resource base.

Another distinctive feature of the Project was the division of "the environment" into ten "policy sectors." An interdisciplinary task group was asked to view the basin's environment from the standpoint of a given policy sector and to examine the interactions between its sector and each of the other nine. At the outset, the participants were asked to suspend temporarily their preconceptions about what constitutes "the environment." As the reader will soon note, the definition that emerged was very broad indeed.

Approximately 125 people contributed to the Hudson Basin Project. They produced over 4000 pages of memoranda, working documents, and reports. The Project's final report and the ten task group reports were published in "working paper" format by the Rockefeller Foundation in 1976 and 1977.

Early in 1978, Academic Press proposed that the report series be edited for publication as a book, thereby making the material available to a larger audience and in a more permanent form. Chapter 1 of the present work is a summation of the entire Project as presented in the final report. Chapters 2 through 11 are drawn from the work of the individual task groups concerned with the ten policy sectors.

In editing the earlier report series for publication in these two volumes, it was necessary to condense some of the reports and to omit several detailed background papers prepared by individual task group members.

We hope we have succeeded in retaining essentially all of the material of long-term interest to students of environmental management and policy analysis, and hope also that we have done justice to the many people who gave so generously of their time and talents. If any errors of commission or omission have been made in editing the present volumes, the responsibility lies with the undersigned, rather than with the task group members or with the Project's director.

Ralph W. Richardson, Jr.
Gilbert Tauber

Contents of Volume 2

THE
HUDSON RIVER
BASIN

Environmental Problems and Institutional Response

VOLUME 1

Chapter 1

ANATOMY OF AN ENVIRONMENT

1.1 Introduction

Environment, in its broadest sense, denotes the totality of things, forces, or conditions that act upon or influence an organism or a group of organisms. However, when we speak of *an* environment, we are necessarily referring to the array of influences on a particular organism or group of organisms. The operative phrase in our definition is "act upon or influence." We are concerned with the environment not just because it is there, but because it acts upon and influences the people of a region.

To a greater extent than most other species, man lives in an environment of his own making. Some of the changes that man makes in his environment are deliberate; others are unintended (but predictable) consequences of purposeful action. Still other changes are inadvertent—i.e., neither intended nor predictable—but even these are nearly always the consequences of some purposeful action.

This comment brings us to the concept of management, which can be defined as the activity—more or less skillful—of controlling or handling something. As a species, man is unique in the degree to which he is able to manage his environment. Most environmental management is collective in the sense that it is governed by institutions. In our society we tend to think of institutions in terms of formal organizations, but the term can refer to any

1

well-established social arrangement or practice, even if it is not formally embodied in law or in a particular organization.

Are institutions parts of the environment? Certainly. As much or more than the physical environment, they are among the things that act upon and influence man. So, too, are the values and attitudes embodied in institutions, since these shape our perceptions of the environment in relation to ourselves. Thus, our environment, any environment, is a dynamic and infinitely complex network of interacting influences, both physical and nonphysical. Issues that are generally regarded as "environmental" may revolve around questions of economics, ethics, or social policy, as well as around the validity of scientific data or concepts about the physical world. Nevertheless, whatever the focus of conflict, environmental issues ultimately tend to involve rights or interests in physical things.

The Study Area

The Hudson Basin study area as defined by this Project includes the tristate New York metropolitan region and the portion of its hinterland within the Hudson River watershed (Fig. 1-1). The region comprises 44 counties in an area of just over 25,000 square miles. It contains only 0.7% of the area of the United States, but its 20.5 million people represent nearly 10% of the nation's total population.

To our knowledge this is the first study of environmental problems at a regional scale that includes a large metropolitan area *plus* much of its associated hinterland, yet the Hudson Basin study area is only one (albeit the largest in population) of 33 such major metropolitan–hinterland regions in the United States. Nearly half the nation's people live and work in these high-population areas.*

Three prominent topographical features that have shaped the region's development are clearly discernible in satellite photographs: the extended coastal areas; the great natural harbor of New York; and the long corridor of the Hudson and Mohawk rivers bounded by the Catskills to the west, the Adirondacks to the north, and the Taconic and Green mountains to the east. These high elevations are crucial to the region's water and air resources. Water assets include the marine environments in the coastal areas, a half-dozen rivers and their numerous tributaries, hundreds of thousands of acres of biologically fertile wetlands, and over 6200 lakes and ponds.

Four-fifths of the study area is in New York State. Of this portion, 21% (2.7 million acres) is protected in state parks and forests, the largest amount and

---

*See Appendix D for list of Standard Metropolitan Statistical Areas (SMSAs) of over 1,000,000 population.

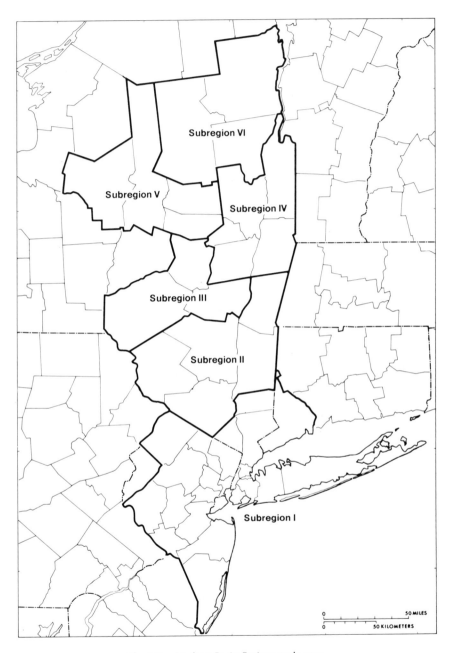

Fig. 1-1. Hudson Basin Project study area.

proportion of state-controlled land serving a metropolitan area in the United States. New Jersey and Connecticut also have extensive state-owned, undeveloped tracts in this region. By contrast, less than one-tenth of the basin's land area is urbanized.

To distinguish significant socioeconomic variations and environmental features, the study area was divided into eight subregions (Appendix E). Three of these make up the tristate New York metropolitan region, which has 18 million inhabitants—75% of New York State's population, 80% of New Jersey's, and 25% of Connecticut's, or 89% of the study region's total. Much of the economic and institutional power of the Hudson Basin is concentrated in this metropolis, which continues to exercise national and international influence. Through three and a half centuries of growth, abetted by a beneficent environment, it has become one of the most highly developed urban centers in the world in terms of its physical plant, socioeconomic infrastructure, civilization, and complexities of government.

A close look at the Hudson Basin region in the mid-1970s finds much of its environment still favored and generally satisfactory. At the same time, however, the region is experiencing the kinds of environmental problems that typically emerge from the interaction of dense and highly developed human settlement with the "natural" environment.

Growth Trends

The region's current environmental problems can be accounted for at least in part by the spectacular growth it experienced during the two decades after World War II. In the 20 years from 1950 to 1969, as shown in Fig. 1-2, population in this region grew by 29%; in 21 suburban counties the population nearly doubled, adding 4.5 million people; housing units increased 43%; electricity consumption more than tripled; and the number of motor vehicles nearly doubled.

Such massive growth had pervasive impacts on the basin's environment. Notably, there was a widespread increase in air and water pollution, open space was built over and fouled, and the region's domestic and imported resources were consumed at an alarming—and increasing—rate.

One major consequence of this evident environmental degradation was a general social awakening to the need to bring natural environmental issues under better public management. This concern and its political expression grew in the late 1960s, culminating at the end of the decade in the passage of the National Environmental Policy Act.

During these decades of expansion we have come to recognize at least two distinct kinds of growth. The first and more dramatic involves major projects and situations that are characteristically large in scale and highly

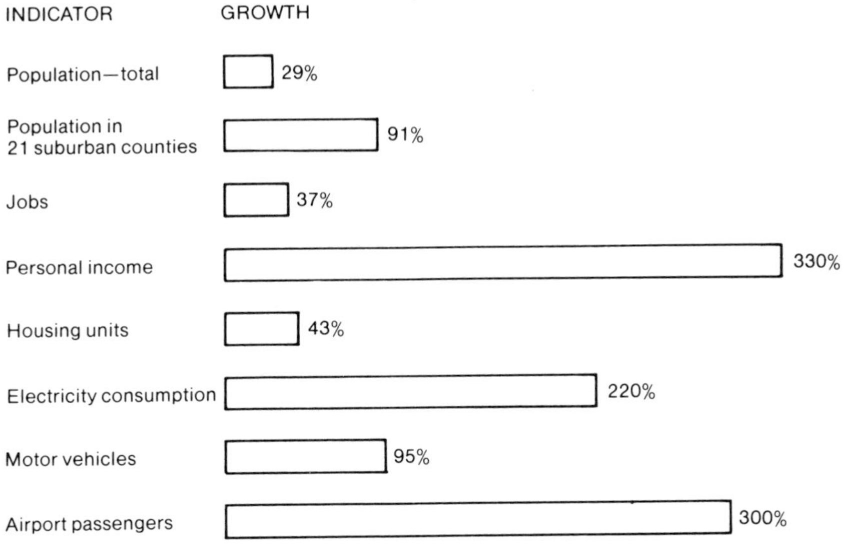

INDICATOR	GROWTH	
Population—total	29%	
Population in 21 suburban counties	91%	
Jobs	37%	
Personal income		330%
Housing units	43%	
Electricity consumption	220%	
Motor vehicles	95%	
Airport passengers		300%

Fig. 1-2. Indicators of growth in the Hudson Basin region, 1950 to 1969.

complex, with serious environmental impacts that in turn often entail second- and third-generation effects of serious proportions. The controversial proposed pump-storage electric generating plant at Storm King Mountain on the Hudson River, the New York State Thruway, and the proposal to expand Stewart Airport in Orange County into the region's fourth jetport are examples.

The public's preoccupation with major projects often distracts attention from the fact that most growth and change affecting the environment occur in diffused and relatively small increments that seldom make the headlines. This kind of growth, and the seemingly minor concomitant issues that it raises in specific situations, assumes major importance when viewed from regional perspective. Because of its cumulative impact, new institutional arrangements are often required for the effective resolution of the issues involved.

In the decade of the 1970s the public is becoming aware of a markedly different development scenario in the Hudson Basin, a scenario that points to a less expansive future. Average annual rates of change in key indicators for the region have declined significantly, sometimes sharply, from the 1950–1969 period.

Population growth has slackened, employment is virtually static, and indicators such as personal income and electricity consumption are increasing at much slower rates.

The Demographic and Economic Context*

The environment of the Hudson Basin cannot be considered in isolation from the people who live and work in it. Changes in that population—its numbers, its composition, its spatial distribution—have profound effects on the environment. So, too, do changes in economic conditions, for they influence the nature and extent of demands on environmental resources, as well as the fiscal base that can be drawn upon to protect the environment and meet other social needs.

The two major components of population change are natural increase—the difference between births and deaths—and migration. The decline in births in the region reflects a nationwide trend, but zero natural increase will be reached sooner here because of the Hudson Basin's traditionally lower fertility rate and its older population.

Until recently, the region's lower rates of natural increase were more than made up by a steady influx of migrants from other parts of the United States and from abroad. Today, migration has slackened and more people are moving out of the region (mainly to the South and West) than are moving into it. The net out-migration in the early 1970s was largely accounted for by retirees and those of college or draft age. However, the region's current economic situation portends further out-migration, particularly among the more highly skilled, young, better educated, and more mobile middle-class labor force.

Despite the prospect of zero population growth or actual population loss, there will be continued growth-related demands on the region's resources on account of shifts in the age structure and relocation of activities within the region. Barring a substantial increase in out-migration, current levels of need for employment and housing are expected to continue well into the 1990s, when the lower fertility of the past 10 years will be reflected in corresponding reductions in the labor force and rates of household formation. The region's present working-age population, roughly ten million, has grown nearly twice as fast in the 1970s as in the preceding decade, because the children of the postwar baby boom have reached young adulthood.

Decentralization of Population and Employment

As population growth within the region has slowed, its people have been moving outward from the cities to the suburbs and exurbs. This spreading pattern of development is in large measure the outcome of public policy reinforcing social preference. Such policies, though seldom explicit, have manifested themselves over the last few decades in a wide range of programs and fiscal considerations to which consumers have responded.

*See Armstrong (1975).

Since 1970, white out-migration from New York City has risen, even as the base of the suburbanizing population has shrunk. The core now contains over 80% of the black and Hispanic population of the New York metropolitan area, but less than 50% of the white population. Restrictive zoning has fostered the exclusion of minorities from the suburban areas, whereas federal and state aid programs, especially the poverty-linked programs of the sixties, which focused on central city areas, encouraged the concentration of low-income population in those areas.

Given present population conditions and the continuation of public policies influencing internal migration, the region's central cities will continue to lose population to their peripheries. The cities will probably, under current policies, continue to contain a disproportionate share of low-income families.

Outlying areas such as Suffolk, Monmouth, and Ocean counties in New Jersey and the mid-Hudson counties in New York continue to receive out-migration and employment growth in the New York–New Jersey metropolitan area. Saratoga and Greene counties are likely locations for suburbanization from the Albany–Schenectady–Troy metropolitan area, while linear development will characterize much of the future growth in Schoharie and the Mohawk Valley counties. In the less accessible rural and recreational areas, such as the Catskills and the Adirondacks, population may increasingly be drawn from those seeking rural lifestyles.

Economic Activity Patterns

The major types of economic activity show separate patterns of location within the basin. Extractive industries are concentrated in the Catskill, mid-Hudson, Mohawk, and Adirondack districts. The low metropolitan share of agriculture and mining employment is mainly in administrative offices. Goods-producing activities are only slightly underrepresented in the New York metropolitan area, although patterns of distribution within the area strongly favor inner suburban locations. Elsewhere in the basin, goods production is a large share of the Mohawk industrial base but is underrepresented in the Capital and mid-Hudson areas. The service sector clearly dominates job opportunities in the New York metropolitan and Capital districts, with finance playing the leading role in the former and government in the latter.

Because of its strong white-collar and service orientation, the economy of the Hudson Basin is structurally more advanced than many regional economies elsewhere in the nation. Traditionally, it has been less sensitive to business-cycle fluctuations. The region exports national and international office functions from its vast concentration of major headquarters; financial, legal, service, quasi-public, and public institutions; as well as specialized manufactured products, the arts, communications, research, and technology. These activities are not heavily dependent upon energy and raw-material input. The region's lower share of the extractive industries and industrial production, however, means that it must import the bulk of its food and its fuel.

During the sixties, the region had a competitive advantage in the nation-wide shift toward office and service activities. About 1.3 million jobs were created in white-collar and service occupations, and even the region's man-ufacturing industries gained marginally in total employment.

Decline in Employment

The picture for employment has changed drastically in this decade. There has been a net loss of about 54,000 jobs in the seventies. About 90.6% of the region's job opportunities are still concentrated in the New York metropoli-tan area. Within that area there has been a striking decentralization of em-ployment. The core lost 280,000 jobs during the 1970 recession but the outer suburbs gained 30,000 jobs. In Manhattan, which contains about one-quarter of all the jobs in the region, the gains of the sixties were entirely erased.

The loss of nearly one-quarter of the core's industrial base since 1960 is not unexpected, considering the costs and inefficiencies that most kinds of industrial production must endure in a high-density setting with an aging physical plant. However, the more northerly districts and the basin in gen-eral must also expect further losses in manufacturing employment. Nation-wide trends favor shifts toward growing market areas. Moreover, the nation's overall industrial labor requirements are declining as a result of capital-intensive technology, resource scarcities, and dampened demand due to smaller family size and rising service consumption.

The prospect of stagnant or slow growth in the region's service sector, and of mounting white-collar unemployment at the core, is more ominous than the decline in manufacturing employment. Many elite office functions of the white-collar industries require high-density work environments that allow intensive personal interaction, access to varied specialized services, and a large, diversely skilled work force. Although headquarters are also decen-tralizing to campus and suburban locations, the region's competitive advan-tage in attracting national office functions is anchored in Manhattan's mas-sive office agglomeration.

Labor-saving changes in the white-collar industries, as well as decen-tralization of their operations, have weakened some of the important loca-tional ties to the region's major business center. A further reduction in the office function would jeopardize Manhattan's vitality. The economy of New York City and the region would suffer; severe social effects would occur; the viability of public transportation would be undermined; auto dependency would be heightened; and energy consumption would be increased at a time when the future demands a more efficient, resource-conserving environment.

Although population growth has been relatively static since 1970, the region's labor force has increased by one-third million. The bulk of this growth consists of jobless people seeking work. If there is no growth in job opportunities, out-migration could reduce this region's population by more than 500,000 before 1980, with 300,000 more unemployed. Achieving full employment with no out-migration, plus accommodating the potential growth in the resident labor force, would require about 650,000 new jobs over the remainder of the decade.

Summary

There have been serious retrenchment and uncertainty in the economic and social scene earlier than but not widely recognized until 1974. This slowdown, accompanied by rising unemployment and capital shortages, has included a decline in the number of new construction projects, and thus in the stress such projects impose on the environment.

But the abrupt easing of pressures on the natural environment should not be assumed to signal permanent change in the accommodation between man and the life-supporting environment. Renewed economic vigor and social change will bring with them new programs to alter the environment. Meanwhile, hard times provide convenient justification for some to ignore constraints posed by the natural environment. And there remain more than a few "quiet" environmental crises, small in scale and diffuse, that if not managed well and properly solved will add to the erosion of the man-made and natural environment.

1.2   Overview of the Policy Areas

An initial objective of the Hudson Basin Project was to develop an overview of the area's environment, considering both natural and man-made components. Although the very word "environment" connotes unity, to understand the environment in that sense it was necessary in the initial analysis to separate the topic into subjects of more manageable size. This task was approached in terms of *policy areas*. These are broad areas of public decision-making, each of which can be related to a system of institutions, public and private, whose activities affect the quality of the environment.

To obtain such an overview, interdisciplinary task groups averaging five persons each were established for ten broad sectors of environmental policy. These were Land Use/Human Settlement, Transportation, Environmental Service Systems, Energy Systems, Land Use/Natural Resource Management, Biological Communities, Water Resources, Air Resources, Human Health, and Leisure Time and Recreation. The boundaries between policy sectors were by design not sharply defined. This provided a certain amount of built-in overlap that helped ensure full coverage of the subjects.

This section summarizes the background information and the more salient findings about each of these policy areas drawn from the work of the task groups, consultants, and other Project participants.

Land Use/Human Settlement

The earliest European settlements in the Hudson Basin were oriented to trade rather than to agriculture. The first two, the progenitors of today's New York and Albany, were strategically placed at the mouth of the Hudson River and near its head of navigation. The importance of these and other early settlements along the region's waterways was reinforced by subsequent transportation improvements—post roads, canals, railroads—that tended to follow water-level routes. The region's upland areas, though vast, were of limited value for agriculture and remained thinly settled.

The Regional Settlement Pattern

Today, the study area contains two major metropolitan complexes, centered on New York and Albany, as well as the eastern edge of a third metropolitan complex that includes the cities of Utica and Rome at the headwaters of the Mohawk River.

Major corridors of development follow the historic water routes. The mid-Hudson and Mohawk corridors link the three metropolitan complexes. The Champlain corridor extends from the Albany area northward toward Montreal. Bounding the corridors are three major upland zones of hilly to mountainous terrain, the Adirondacks, the Catskills, and the Taconics.

The broad regional pattern of metropolitan zones, corridors, and uplands was set long ago and is not likely to change in the foreseeable future. But on a somewhat finer scale, that of the community or even of the county, patterns of settlement have been sharply altered since World War II.

The Urban Centers

In 1945, after 15 years of depression and war, millions of people in the region were living in overcrowded and deteriorated housing. Peace brought a boom in car ownership and suburban homebuilding, followed by massive new highway construction, the shifting of freight traffic from rail to rubber, and the outward movement of industry to highway-oriented sites.

The people who left for new homes in the suburbs were mainly white and middle-income. There were people waiting to take their places, but they were poor, mainly black and Hispanic, and they were moving into the city just when the jobs were moving out.

The bad housing got worse, the old industrial plants stood empty, the tax base withered, and the physical blight was accompanied by growing social disarray. For many communities in the region there was hope in urban renewal. There was also a lot of money to be made in ambitious redevelopment projects which, in some cases, offered publicly subsidized means of containing minority neighborhoods that were encroaching on white ones.

Scores of cities and villages in the Hudson Basin chose to excise their ulcerated middles. It was drastic surgery, and many of them have not yet recovered. A number of sites cleared for urban renewal in the sixties, especially sites designated for commercial use, are still vacant and waiting for sponsors. Some of the housing built in urban renewal areas has been quite good, but it does not begin to replace the housing that was torn down and rarely shelters the income group it displaced. Rentals for new, publicly assisted housing in New York City are frequently beyond the reach of most of the taxpayers who are subsidizing them.

Meanwhile, sound older housing is being lost faster than new housing can be built. The reasons for this are not hard to find. Maintenance and fuel costs are high, and so is the cost of money to finance repairs. Moreover, landlords of older buildings are confronted by an archaic property tax system that makes it far less profitable to maintain buildings than to allow them to run into the ground. In recent years, there has been a noticeable shift in the emphasis of housing agencies from programs of subsidizing new construction to programs aimed at encouraging the maintenance and rehabilitation of existing housing. Because of the recession and money-market conditions, the impact of these programs so far has been modest.

The Dispersion of Employment and Residential Development

Outside of the old urban centers, the pattern of land use has been radically altered by the high-speed, limited-access highways built since the 1950s. Like earlier improvements in passenger transportation—trolleys, commuter railroads, parkways—the interstates initially broadened the area of residential settlement around large cities. But the new roads also radically improved the movement of goods by truck, thereby freeing industry from older urban locations served by rail and waterways.

During the 1960s, scores of large employers moved from the old riverfront cities to new locations out on the highways where they could obtain the large, level sites required by modern production lines and materials-handling techniques. If truck transportation costs were higher than rail costs at the old locations, trucks offered greater speed and flexibility.

The departure of industries from the old centers raised costs for those who remained. As industries moved out to highway-oriented sites, they were followed by warehouse and service activities, and even by corporate headquarters.

The dispersion of employment has generated new, low-density residential development in locations entirely unrelated to the old paths of commuter travel—whether by rail or highway. The result is no longer even urban sprawl, but scatteration. Because development in this new pattern is oriented to multiple employment centers, with multiple, large, and overlapping commutation areas, it is hard to predict just where growth will occur. In fact, it tends to occur where it is least expected, since that is where land is cheapest.

One reason land is cheap in undeveloped areas is that there has been little or no public investment in infrastructure, such as streets and sewers. Cheap land permits houses on large lots, but large lots entail more cost per house for virtually every kind of public service and facility—more miles of roads and sewer lines, more school-bus mileage, more firehouses.

The low density of these areas virtually precludes any alternative to the private automobile for travel to work. The higher cost of energy may shorten acceptable commutation distances to a given workplace, but with business locations so dispersed, the broad pattern of random development can be expected to persist.

Housing Supply

A generation after World War II, there is still a severe housing shortage in the Hudson Basin. As of 1970, the region had nearly 7 million dwelling units and 6.6 million households, but the difference of 400,000 should not be construed as surplus housing stock. Only a third of it was actually vacant and available for sale or rent. About half the total consisted of second or seasonal homes; the balance was unfit for occupancy. The current regionwide vacancy rate is well under the 4% norm that ensures ease of entry and adequate choice in the housing market, and the situation has been getting worse rather than better.

In the last 25 years, over 2.6 million new housing units have been built in the region. But in that same period more than 600,000 units of existing housing have been lost through demolition, fire, or other causes, while the total number of households in the region has increased by 2.3 million. Moreover, housing production in the region has been declining since the mid-1960s, initially as capital was diverted into the nonresidential boom that peaked in 1969, and then as tight money combined with the area's high construction costs to drive housing prices upward beyond the means of all but the most affluent.

Household Formation and Housing Needs

The rate of household formation has slackened since 1970, but it can be expected to rise again because of the large numbers of people who are now entering the critical house-buying age group of 30 through 34. Average household size, which has already fallen below three persons per occupied unit, will probably continue to decline because of changes in life styles and dwindling birth rates. For the rest of this century, however, the numbers of people in the house-buying age group will continue to increase as a legacy of the fecund fifties and sixties.

From now through 1985 the housing production requirement for the Hudson Basin region will be on the order of 250,000 units per year, apart from the upgrading or replacement of substandard units. This estimate assumes no substantial net out-migration. On the other hand, the inability of breadwinners to find adequate housing at reasonable prices may well be contributing to out-migration.

Transportation

Transportation has been the most important single determinant of human settlement in the Hudson Basin, but the relationship between settlement and transportation is a reciprocal one. People's daily activities create demands for the movement of both people and goods. These demands are channeled through different transportation systems, creating flows of vehicles. Traffic flows create congestion, which modifies both demand for travel and the location of human activities. At the same time, transportation facilities, by providing faster (or slower) transportation, change the accessibility levels of different parts of a region, and so modify the locations of housing, workplaces, and other human activities.

Transportation systems in the Hudson Basin are highly developed in comparison with other areas in the United States. The energy-efficient modes of water and rail transport reached maturity some time ago. During the last 50 years, and especially in the last 25, the overwhelming development has been in air and highway transportation.

Waterways

The basin's primary inland waterway is, of course, the Hudson River, which is navigable to ocean-going vessels as far north as Albany. The Upper Hudson is linked to the Great Lakes via the Erie Canal and via the Champlain Canal to Lake Champlain and the St. Lawrence. However, the canals are closed during the winter months. The "back door" of the Hudson Basin area is accessible via the Delaware River.

Petroleum accounts for the largest share of tonnage on the region's inland waterways, followed by stone, sand, and gravel. There are no petroleum pipelines serving the Hudson's main stem or the lower Mohawk. Barges and seagoing tankers deliver to waterside terminals or "tank farms," from which the fuel is distributed to dealers and retail customers by truck.

Freight traffic on the inland waterways has been fairly stable in recent years. Lock records show declining usage by recreational craft since 1966. This decrease may be due to adverse weather conditions and the 1970 Holding Tank Law, as well as higher fuel costs.

In the port of New York, general cargo has deserted the finger piers of the Hudson and East rivers for container facilities at Port Newark, Port Elizabeth, and elsewhere in New Jersey. Bulk cargoes have also been shifted to specialized terminals well away from Manhattan Island. Transatlantic passenger service has all but disappeared, but cruise ships have been making heavy use of the new passenger ship terminal on Manhattan's West Side.

Railroads

The rail system in the basin is a very mature one; some of its routes were laid out more than 125 years ago. Freight traffic on the system has stabilized in recent years, but passenger traffic has declined sharply since the 1940s. Even with increased Amtrak service—unlikely in the foreseeable future—and higher driving costs, rail passenger volumes may not reach the levels of earlier decades.

The network of rail lines available for freight transportation in the region totals more than 3300 miles of right-of-way. But rail freight service requires something more than the physical presence of rail lines. In the heavily traveled corridors, scheduled service is frequent. On the other hand, outer Long Island is in a rather poor position despite extensive trackage.

Following the 1974 proposals of the Federal Railway Administration, the rail system in the northeastern United States is being "rationalized," with fewer miles of track. Over 750 miles of railroad line in the Hudson Basin region are to be abandoned. This would be 22.6% of the entire rail system in this region. The principal reductions would be in lightly used branch lines.*

Streets and Highways

There are an estimated 76,200 miles of streets and highways in the region. The most heavily used roads are, of course, the state and interstate highways and the toll roads operated by various special public authorities.

The capacity of state, authority, and interstate highways has been immensely expanded in the last 25 years. Whereas they represent only 12% of all the roads in place in the region, they carry about half of the total automobile and truck traffic.

Traffic volume, measured as vehicle-miles of travel (VMT), is greatest in Manhattan. It has 282,600 VMT daily per square mile. The density of VMT drops off rapidly as distance from Manhattan increases. Hudson County, New Jersey, has 95,500 VMT per square mile, while Albany County has an average of 7450 VMT per square mile. The lowest level is 100 VMT per square mile, in Hamilton County.

The amount of vehicular travel per person is quite different. Manhattan and Brooklyn have, respectively, 4.2 and 3.5 VMT per person per day because of the heavy use of public transportation. By contrast, Hamilton County produces 40.0 VMT per person per day. This is the result not only of higher car ownership and longer average trips by residents but also of trips into and through the county by vacationers. The density of vehicle miles of travel, both automobile and truck, occurs in much the same pattern as population density. Since energy consumption and pollution are related to vehicle travel, these same patterns also tend to reflect patterns of air pollution in the region.

The flexibility of the motor truck has been a factor in the dispersion of both population and industrial employment. This dispersion, in turn, has complicated the problems of mass transit, of employment opportunities for inner-city residents, and even of continued efficient operation for the trucking industry itself.

The Tri-State Regional Planning Commission has estimated that half the conventional freight received by establishments in the tristate area originates within that region. About three-quarters of this freight is picked up and

*This information refers to the trackage that was not included in the present Consolidated Rail Corporation (Conrail) system. With few exceptions, the "excessed" lines were not immediately abandoned. Most of them remain in operation under subsidy programs administered by the respective states. If continued operation of a line cannot be justified on either economic or social grounds, the line is abandoned after a transition period in which users are helped to make alternative shipping arrangements. [Ed.]

delivered locally by trucks, which have also gained enormous ground relative to rail for movements into and out of cities.

Truck competition has been a key factor in creating derelict rail freight facilities, but planning for conversion of these old rail facilities to other uses has been conspicuously weak compared with the elaborate planning that has gone into the extension of the highway network.

Mass Transit

Since the demise of interurban trolley lines back in the 1930s, transit usage has been almost exclusively an urban phenomenon—and more than that, a high-density urban phenomenon. Transit use is much more concentrated in the urban centers than automobile travel.

There are about 9720 miles of urban transit routes in the Tri-State portion of the Hudson Basin region, including subways, bus lines, and suburban railroads. There are an estimated 970 route miles of transit lines in the upstate portion of the basin, all in bus systems. Over 90% of bus and subway travel in the region is in the high-density New York–New Jersey metropolitan area, where about 26 million one-way journeys are made each weekday. The major transportation crunch comes not in moving the daily totals of travelers, but rather in moving the rush hour masses. More than two million people work in Manhattan's central business district below 60th Street. About a third of them live in Manhattan, about half in the other boroughs, and the balance—about 400,000 people—in the surrounding suburban counties. Ninety-five percent of the commuters to the Manhattan central business district use mass transit. The extensive congestion during the morning and evening rush hours is produced by the 5% who travel to work by private auto.

The subways and many of the other mass transit systems are facing problems seen across the country—higher costs and declining ridership. While the need for mass transit increases, from both an energy and environmental standpoint, it is becoming more and more difficult to provide it at costs within the reach of city residents.

Airports

Airports are fairly evenly distributed over the region, except in the Catskills and the Adirondacks. However, activity at these airfields varies tremendously—from a few flights per day to the more than 75 arrivals and departures per hour at Kennedy International Airport. The bulk of the air transportation activity is in the New York–New Jersey metropolitan area, which includes Kennedy, LaGuardia, Newark, Islip, White Plains, and Teterboro airports.

Major airports have a substantial impact upon the environment in their vicinities. They occupy large areas of land: 7 square miles in the case of Kennedy Airport. The noise and air pollution produced by aircraft alone are substantial, and added to this is the pollution produced by the automobile and truck traffic required to serve thousands of workers and tens of thousands of daily travelers.

If present trends continue, aviation activity in the New York metropolitan area can be expected to increase, although probably not at the same pace experienced in the 1950s and 1960s.

Pipelines

Three basic types of pipelines serve the Hudson Basin region: (a) natural gas pipelines, (b) liquefied petroleum gas (LPG) pipelines, and (c) pipelines that convey crude oil or refined petroleum products. Within the study area, only the New York metropolitan area and the Utica–Rome area are served by product pipelines. Other areas along the Hudson, Mohawk, and Champlain corridors are served by barges and small tankers, whose loads are then distributed by truck.

Environmental Service Systems

Environmental Service Systems is a collective term for those facilities and activities that support urban settlements by supplying them with water and by removing their wastes. Included are water treatment and delivery, sewage collection and disposal, urban drainage, and solid waste collection and disposal. There are important points of interaction among the four types of systems.

Water Treatment and Delivery

The Hudson Basin has ample precipitation—generally 40 to 50 inches per year. There have been periods of drought, but municipalities generally need only provide collection, treatment, and delivery systems to have enough water for their residents. The larger water-supply systems generally have been satisfactorily regulated by state and local health departments for quality and by the Public Service Commission for setting rates of private operations.

The major problems affecting community water systems in the region relate to the delivery of adequate quantities of water of satisfactory quality to the point of consumption. In the smaller communities, supplies are almost entirely from wells, which may be owned by the public or by private water supply companies. There have been problems in the operation and maintenance of these small systems, which are sometimes neglected and even abandoned by their owners.

Although there are deficiencies in capacity, the facilities for the distribution, storage, and delivery of water to the consumer are generally in good condition throughout the region. Exceptions to this are to be found in many of the region's older communities, which are faced with serious problems in meeting the high costs of renovating obsolete plants and deteriorated distribution lines.

Sewerage

Most of the billions of dollars spent to improve the quality of the environment in the last decade have been used for the construction of new sewage treatment plants and collection systems. These outlays reflect an effort to catch up with unmet sewerage requirements that had been accumulating for decades. Since the mid-1960s, programs at both the federal and state levels have helped localities to build new sewage treatment plants in an effort to make secondary treatment universal.

Construction was spurred also by the federal mandate to industries and municipalities for "zero discharge" of polluting materials into waterways by 1985, a goal that no longer appears feasible, either economically or technologically. The very threat of such stringent controls, however, spurred research and development in several areas of effluent treatment and, importantly, recycling.

Public sewage disposal has traditionally been a municipal responsibility. Outside the metropolitan area, sewer service is usually found only in areas with a density of 500 or more people per square mile, and even such areas are often unsewered. For years, many municipalities did not feel they could afford to build needed facilities. In some cases, the capital costs would have exceeded legal limits on municipal borrowing. These obstacles were largely overcome by new financing mechanisms, including federal aid and state bond issues. Nevertheless, the local share of project costs still represents a burden for many local governments.

Outside of cities and villages, sewage facilities are usually provided on the basis of special improvement districts (SIDs) created by town governments. With suburbanization, SIDs proliferated to meet the needs of expanding town populations, so that several often exist in one town. The resulting patchwork pattern of liquid waste facilities has been a barrier to effective design and operation of sewage systems. This situation persists even in suburban areas that are now densely developed.

With relatively few exceptions, residential construction throughout the area is on a small scale. The typical small builder may construct anywhere from 5 to 35 or 40 residences per year. Since the state health code does not require sewer service for subdivisions with fewer than 50 residential units, most of this construction utilizes septic tanks. Thus, as late as 1970, it was estimated that in Nassau County almost half of the population, or approximately 700,000 people, relied upon septic tanks and cesspools.

Individual septic systems require large lots for adequate drainage fields. In this case, the more scattered the development the better. But septic systems are not without their problems. There can be infiltration of untreated wastes into groundwater, and it is often difficult to ensure proper disposal of siphoned wastes from septic tanks. Nevertheless, properly located and maintained septic tanks offer a usable method of handling wastes in areas of low development density.

There are some perennial operating problems relating to sewage treatment facilities and collection systems, including aesthetics, control of odors, and sludge disposal. The single most pressing problem for the metropolitan area is sludge disposal. Ocean disposal is generally no longer acceptable, and an alternative must be found. Land disposal or incineration of sewage sludge may also have adverse effects. A treatment system providing total oxidation of sludge would cost about 30% more to build and would also be more costly to operate. Controlled spray disposal on tree farms or certain agricultural crops would recycle the nutrients in the sludge, but it is unlikely that enough spray disposal area can be found within an economic distance of the basin's larger cities.

Urban Stormwater Drainage

Widespread urbanization, including the boom in suburban shopping malls with their acres of impermeable surface, has aggravated problems of urban stormwater drainage. This water is rarely treated and often is not even properly collected. In many areas the same system carries both sewage and drainage water. In such combined systems, treatment plant capacity is determined by sewage levels. When the treatment plant is overloaded after a storm, the excess water, now mixed with raw sewage, is dumped into the receiving water body. Older communities that had separate systems now often have de facto combined systems because of the diversion of stormwater into sewer drains. Although rules against such diversions have been poorly enforced in the past, many communities are again beginning to insist on separate systems.

Stormwater is itself a source of pollution to receiving waters. Though not as noxious as sewage water, it nevertheless carries large amounts of debris and dirt, including spilled automobile oil and animal wastes and excess nutrients from fertilizers. The rain itself carries pollutants, since it washes to the ground whatever contaminants are in the ambient air. The pollution caused by stormwater is a problem of such scope that it might be considered the second phase of the current pollution-abatement program rather than an aspect of drainage.

Storm drainage management is also an element in flood control. In the suburban New York area, early construction considered the problem of flooding, but continued development has increased and accelerated runoff and greatly reduced the area of land that previously absorbed precipitation. In Westchester County, for example, flooding frequently closes streets and parkways and poses a health hazard in areas where floodwaters cause overflows of sewage.

Local attempts to correct flooding have usually been too narrow in scope. Improvements in channel depth and stream velocity in one community often aggravate flooding downstream. The agency most involved in dealing with flooding on a basin scale is the U.S. Army Corps of Engineers. Although it has had spectacular success in some large river basins, technical, financial, and institutional obstacles have to be overcome before the flooding problem in small watercourses in and around the metropolitan area can be solved.

Solid Waste

Considered in the light of available technology, solid waste disposal techniques in the region, as in the nation at large, can best be described as backward. They are fragmented, undercapitalized, wasteful of land and materials, and still heavily dependent on hand labor. Solid waste collection and its transport to disposal sites are relatively new services outside of the region's cities and generally inadequate throughout the region: refuse companies and agencies do not collect all that they should and cannot properly handle what they now collect.

The bulk of the solid waste collected in the region, including most of the 24,000 tons produced daily by New York City, is disposed of in landfills. A minor percentage is incinerated, with the noncombustible residue also going to landfills. Although there is some recycling, its impact on the region's total disposal requirements has so far been negligible.

Landfills in the region, typically operated by local government agencies, are much better managed than they were a few years ago. Open burning and open dumping have been virtually eliminated. Nearly all publicly operated landfills in the region now make some attempt at sanitary landfill practice— alternating layers of soil with layers of compacted refuse—but few would meet strict sanitary landfill standards.

Many communities are running out of space at landfills within their own boundaries. Space is sometimes available in neighboring communities, but local officials are rarely willing to accept "other people's garbage."

Unfortunately, sanitary landfill practices use up space more quickly than less sanitary methods. New requirements for controlling water and air pollution have also resulted in increased solid waste. Residue from new air pollution control devices and improved sewage treatment, strict burning regulations, and land disposal of dredge spoil to comply with water quality standards are but a few examples. Pressures on existing landfill space have also been aggravated by regulations that preclude dumping in wetlands, once regarded as ideal sites for landfills. Leachates from existing landfills in wet areas have adversely affected water quality and biological communities.

Incinerators reduce the volume of solid waste that has to be sent to landfills. Nevertheless, many incinerators in the study area have been shut down in recent years and few new ones have been built. The closings were partly due to obsolescence and declining efficiency of older incinerators. The reduction in waste volume by the older facilities was no longer enough to warrant the extra handling and trucking costs involved in incinerator operation. Many incinerators have also been shut down because they could not meet new air quality standards and were too old and/or small to justify the installation of relatively costly emission-control devices.

New high-temperature incinerators, already in use on this continent and in many European cities, can achieve volume reductions of up to 95% and can meet contemporary air quality standards; but cost is a major barrier to the construction of such facilities, as is the difficulty of finding politically acceptable sites. In addition, local officials have sidestepped decisions on new incinerators because of the possibility that some form of recycling may provide a better solution. Nobody wants to build the region's last incinerator. On the other hand, local officials seem equally timid about embracing new technologies of resource recovery.

There has been much interest in facilities that would extract the combustible portion of the refuse, which would then be sold to utility companies for use as a fuel supplement in power plants. New York City expects to have such a facility in operation soon. It is also one of the systems that will be used by Connecticut's new statewide solid waste management authority.

An important barrier to the development of other kinds of recycling facilities is uncertainty over the marketability of recovered products. Theoretically, sales of recycled materials can cover a good part, if not all, of the costs of operating a solid waste disposal facility. However, there may not be an ensured market for all materials in any given area, and most recoverable materials are subject to wide fluctuations in prices.

All of these newer solid waste processing technologies are capital intensive. They are practical only if they are carried out on a very large scale, yet solid waste disposal systems are almost entirely managed at the local level. The principal exceptions are in Connecticut and the New Jersey Meadowlands.

In New York State, Westchester is setting up a countywide solid waste management system. Other efforts at regionalization of solid waste management, i.e., at a county or subcounty scale, are in progress; but it is a tedious and delicate process. There are sharp disagreements over the apportionment of costs, compensation for local facilities to be taken over by regional agencies, and the location of new facilities. Finally, many local officials are reluctant to surrender the autonomy and patronage represented by their control over the town dump.

Although the most critical problems of solid waste management relate to disposal facilities, roughly three-quarters of the total cost of solid waste management is for collecting refuse. Collection costs tend to be highest in areas with low population densities. Labor accounts for most of the collection cost. Some improvements in efficiency could be achieved with more modern collection trucks and properly located transfer stations, but such unglamorous expenditures usually have had low priority on municipal budgets.

A promising technique for solid waste collection in high-density areas is the use of pneumatic pipelines. The "new town" development on Roosevelt Island in New York City is served by such a system.

Energy Systems

Total energy consumption in the Hudson Basin is about 3.5 quadrillion British thermal units (Btu) annually, or about 175 million Btu per person. On a per capita basis, the basin's energy consumption is about three-quarters of the national average.

Because manufacturing comprises a much smaller share of the economy of the region than in the nation as a whole, per capita energy use for industry is only a fifth of the national average. In addition, because the bulk of the basin's population lives in urban areas of relatively high density, there is less travel per capita and much of that travel is by energy-efficient mass transportation modes.

Since incomes in the region are higher than the national average, people tend to use more energy at home. Commercial use is also higher because of the region's heavy concentration of office jobs; but these sectors of higher-than-average energy use are more than offset by the area's much lower use of energy for transportation and manufacturing.

Energy Sources

With the exception of a small amount of hydroelectric power, virtually all of the energy consumed in the Hudson Basin is derived from fuels—oil, coal, natural gas, uranium—imported from other parts of the United States or from abroad. High energy costs in the region, primarily the result of its dependence on those imported fuels, are a significant factor in the region's economic problems.

The present pattern of fuel use in the region has been shaped by its choices in transportation, power generating systems, and building design. Through these choices the region has become over the last 30 years increasingly committed to fuels that are now either scarce or costly or both.

Within the United States, the burden of increasing world oil prices has fallen most heavily on the Northeast, including the Hudson Basin. Because of transportation factors and long-established marketing patterns, domestic oil tends to be consumed in or near the states that produce it. The northeastern states use some domestic oil, but must meet the rest of their requirements with costly foreign imports.

When domestic natural gas was plentiful and exploration was expanding known reserves, pipelines were built to carry the fuel from southern wells to the urban centers of the Hudson Basin. The nation's known reserves of natural gas, however, have been shrinking for the last several years because, producers contend, federally controlled prices for natural gas moving in interstate commerce are too low to justify exploration of new supplies. In the mid-1970s, natural gas was in such short supply that gas utilities in the region had stopped accepting customers and could not supply some existing industrial and commercial users during the winter months.

A generation ago, the region relied mainly on coal for heating buildings and generating electricity. Directly or indirectly, coal also supplied most of the energy for moving people and freight. The massive changeover to oil and natural gas after World War II was prompted by a combination of factors, including price, ease of handling, and the threat of coal strikes. Later on, air quality regulations effectively precluded the use of coal in new electric power plants and large buildings. Subsequent regulations have restricted the burning of high-sulfur oil. These measures have brought about major reductions in air pollution, but have also made the region precariously dependent on low-sulfur oil imports and scarce natural gas.

The United States has very large domestic reserves of coal. Improvements in pollution control technology may make it possible to use more coal, especially for generating electricity, without an unreasonable sacrifice in air quality. The conversion of existing oil-fired installations to burn coal would, however, entail enormous capital costs as well as problems of solid waste disposal.

The present users of bituminous coal in the Hudson Basin region, apart from electric power plants, are generally large industries and institutions. In addition, tens of thousands of older homes and small commercial buildings are still heated by anthracite. Many of these remaining small users have had difficulty in obtaining fuel as local dealers go out of business and distribution networks are cut back.

Nuclear power has lagged far behind the expectations of government and the utility industry, partly because of tighter environmental and safety regulations and partly because of opposition by groups who do not think the regulations are tight enough. At this writing, there are only three nuclear plants in actual operation in the region.

Electric Power

The utility industry in general was not prepared for the environmental "movement" of the late 1960s and for the legislation that followed in its wake. Conventional and nuclear projects have been delayed or abandoned because of environmental regulatory procedures and litigation. Shortages of capital have also contributed to the region's present deficiency in base-load generating capacity. This deficiency has forced utilities to make extensive use of facilities originally intended only for peak-period operation, primarily gas turbine units. Such units can be started up quickly in response to peak demands but are highly inefficient in their use of fuel. Because of heavy reliance on gas turbines and inefficient older generating facilities, the overall system efficiency of electrical utilities in the basin is significantly lower than that of utilities elsewhere in the United States.

The drop in electrical consumption in 1974, in the wake of the Arab oil embargo, reversed a long-term trend in which the use of electricity was doubling roughly every 10 years. The curve has started to rise again, though less steeply than before.

Transportation Uses of Energy

During the fuel crunch of early 1974, there was, not surprisingly, a sharp increase in mass transit ridership. Some of this has persisted particularly on commuter bus lines, but given our existing residential development pattern, it will take many years at best to achieve major savings in energy consumption by shifts to mass transportation. Over the last 20 years, the pattern of development in the region has entailed increasing commitments to the use of private autos. In the extensive areas developed with single-family homes on large lots, population densities are not high enough to support bus routes without massive subsidies. In the foreseeable future, the shift to smaller autos is likely to have a significant impact on fuel consumption and to result in a reduction in pollution from auto emissions. A conspicuous legacy of the 1974 fuel crisis has been the 55 mile per hour speed limit. It is less than zealously enforced, but still has the potential of saving fuel and lives.

Heating

Another large share of the region's energy consumption is used for space heating. The growth in this sector of energy use occurs partly because there is more space to heat—more residential space per capita as people moved from city to suburb and, as office employment rose in the 1960s, more office space per worker. Much of the rise in energy consumption for space heating is due to purely architectural factors: the trends toward office buildings with sealed windows and toward heavy reliance on mechanical heating and cooling. In both commercial and residential construction, builders have favored techniques that minimized initial construction costs—skimpy insulation, omission of individual utility meters and electric switches, electric heaters rather than hydronic or steam heating—without regard to long-term implications for fuel consumption or costs.

Offshore Drilling and Superports

Significant reserves of oil and natural gas are believed to lie beneath the outer continental shelf off the Atlantic coast. These deposits, assuming they live up to geologists' expectations, would mean lower costs and increased dependability of fuel supplies for the Northeast. A federal program to permit oil and gas exploration in this offshore area has, however, so far been opposed by the seaboard states. They want better assurances that offshore drilling will not entail the risk of oil spills or other adverse environmental effects.* There is also concern about the nature and extent of the onshore development—refineries, petrochemical plants, docking facilities, and the like—that would be required or stimulated by exploitation of the offshore deposits. Similar objections have been raised to proposals for construction of an offshore "superport" for deep-draft vessels carrying oil or liquefied natural gas. The region's existing port facilities cannot accommodate the present generation of supertankers, a limitation that adds to the price of the region's fuel imports.

The construction of even one offshore superport would, of course, represent enormous capital investment in a period of acute capital shortage.†

---

*Exploratory drilling in the offshore area was begun in March 1978 under the federal leasing program administered by the Department of the Interior. Many, though not all, of the states' objections have been resolved by certain provisions of the Outer Continental Shelf Land Act Amendments of 1978, which gave the states a greater voice in the program. New York State's own ban on gas exploration in Lake Erie was lifted by the Legislature in 1977. A ban on oil exploration remains in effect, but no significant oil deposits are believed to exist under the lake. Actual exploration for gas in Lake Erie will not begin until the completion of an environmental impact statement on the program, probably in late 1979. [Ed.]

†The deepwater oil terminal proposal is currently dormant. See Volume 2, Chapter 8, Section 8.2. [Ed.]

Moreover, it would imply a long-term commitment to a policy of continued dependence on imported fossil fuels.

Alternative Energy Sources

The energy crisis of 1973–1974 drew attention to various potential "alternative" energy sources. Some of these technologies, such as nuclear fusion or magnetohydrodynamics, are still in the experimental stage. Others, such as geothermal energy, have been used on a commercial scale but are not feasible in this region. The "new" technologies that are most likely to contribute to the basin's energy supply in the mid-range future are the use of combustible solid waste as a fuel in electric power plants and the use of solar collectors for heating and cooling individual buildings.

Refuse-derived fuel, mixed with coal, was burned experimentally at a St. Louis power plant for more than 2 years. The Power Authority of the State of New York plans to use New York City refuse at its proposed Arthur Kill plant on Staten Island.* Some of Connecticut's refuse will also be converted into fuel for power plants. The facility needed to sort out and shred the combustible refuse is relatively simple, making this one of the most cost-effective forms of recycling municipal wastes.

The technology of solar heating is also relatively simple and is rather widely used in other parts of the world, notably in Israel. Solar heating systems are now being offered by a number of manufacturers here. The available solar energy systems can be used for water heating, space heating, and air conditioning. In the latitudes covered by the Hudson Basin region, solar energy cannot entirely supplant conventional fuel sources, but it can cut household fuel consumption by a third or more—enough to pay for the installation cost within a few years.

Potentially large amounts of electricity could be generated by windmills. The primary problems relate to storage—batteries are impractical on a large scale—and to the integration of the power into existing utility networks. For the mid-range future, windmills could be used most effectively in conjunction with pumped storage systems, i.e., to pump water uphill into hydroelectric storage reservoirs for later release to drive electric generators. In the long term (by the end of the century), technology may be available for the storage of wind-generated energy in the form of liquefied hydrogen produced by the electrolysis of ordinary water. The eventual use of the temperature differentials in the ocean currents to generate electrical power could also use liquid hydrogen technology as a means of storage and transfer.

*The Staten Island site is no longer being considered, but another site for the plant is being sought in New York City. [Ed.]

Conservation

Major opportunities to conserve energy exist in the basin although the per capita energy consumption is lower than the national average. As previously suggested, these opportunities are primarily in the areas of heating and transportation.

In the near future, industrial, commercial, and residential users could make a significant contribution by adopting fuel conservation measures through improved insulation, combustion efficiency, and space-use management. In a somewhat longer time frame, significant energy savings should be achieved from improved site planning and structural design.

Owners of single-family homes and private passenger autos may be slower in adopting some conservation practices because of the costs involved as well as prevailing customs. In time, present energy-intensive autos can be replaced with smaller ones having more efficient engines. Energy stringencies may dampen migration from city cores to exurbia, and new population may increasingly be housed in existing settlements. More compact settlement patterns are required to increase the use of public transit significantly. Such a policy will require greater political and economic commitments than have been evidenced so far.

Pricing has different effects on energy consumption practices. In the near future, substantially increased prices for energy may result in particularly severe economic hardship to marginal commercial enterprises, especially those associated with recreation and resort development. Such hardships will also be experienced by low-income workers, mainly those living in rural and exurban areas, who have no alternative to the automobile. For the larger, more affluent share of the population, energy prices may have relatively little effect on energy consumption, although increased expenditures for fuel may curtail other purchases. For example, higher energy prices, combined with difficulties and uncertainty of supply, may discourage purchases of second homes.

Land Use/Natural Resource Management

This policy sector is concerned with the nonurban uses of land that provide man with raw materials—agriculture, forestry, mining—and with land itself as the raw material for urbanization. Nonurban land uses, including vacant land, account for 85% of the region's total area. Although there are wide variations in land use within the region, even a populous county such as Dutchess is nearly 60% woodland, and heavily urbanized Westchester has more woodland than residential land (Fig. 1-3).

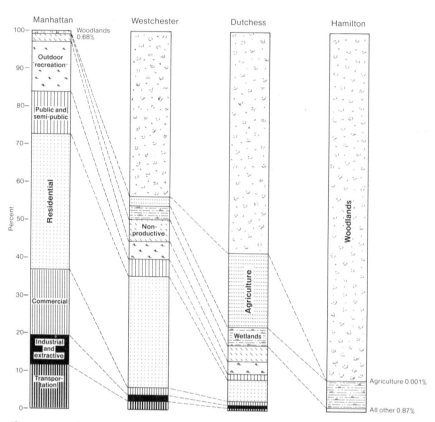

Fig. 1-3. Land cover in selected counties. (*Source:* Land Use and Natural Resources Inventory, New York State Office of Planning Coordination, 1969.)

Agriculture

The amount of land used for farming in the Hudson Basin has been declining for at least 60 years. In recent years about 200,000 acres of New York farmland have been lost each year. Of that amount only 15,000 acres have actually been converted to urban uses. Several times that much is idled by the more indirect effects of urbanization, including land speculation, scatteration, and increases in property taxes and other farm operating costs. Nevertheless, most land being removed from farming today is located in more rural areas. Lands with unfavorable topography and poor drainage cannot compete economically with larger, flatter fields more amenable to mechanized techniques.

During the past three decades, various "pull" factors have helped to speed up the retirement of land from agriculture. Improved roads and mobile industries in search of labor have brought almost all farmers in the Hudson Basin within commuting distance of alternative jobs. Also, urbanization, higher incomes, and expanding leisure time have helped to create a broader market for marginal farms, which are increasingly being transformed into vacation homes and private recreational lands.

In response to the continuing pressures of urbanization and speculation on farmland, New York State amended the Agriculture and Markets Law in 1971 to allow for the creation of "agricultural districts," within which lower tax assessments for land are permitted. Such land is also protected from taxation by special service districts for nonfarm services and from local zoning ordinances that restrict farm operations in favor of residential development. Finally, acquisition of land in agricultural districts for nonagricultural purposes by public agencies is restricted. Another strategy to stem the decline of farmland is Suffolk County's program to acquire control of about 30,000 acres of remaining prime agricultural land, either by outright purchase or by buying development rights.

Forestry

There are many more trees in the Hudson Basin than there were 50 years ago, as land formerly in crops and pasture has reverted to natural growth. But while trees have become more plentiful, the amount of timber harvested in recent decades in New York has either declined or held its own. A major reason is that the quality of the basin's forest resources, for both sawmill and pulpwood uses, has been declining. The average size of harvestable trees has dropped, despite increases in the total volume of timber. Moreover, one out of every four trees in New York's forests is either too rough or rotten to be classified as potentially harvestable.

Another barrier to production is the nature of forestland ownership. The forest industry itself owns only 9% of the "commercial" forestlands in New York State. Farmers own slightly more forestland today than 20 years ago, but 59% of all the potentially harvestable forestland in New York is owned by nonfarm private owners, including rural residents and absentee owners. A survey of the attitudes of forest landowners in the state showed that only 20% were actively interested in selling timber, and a significant number were hostile to the idea of harvesting any trees from their property in any manner.

The sawmill industry in the basin has experienced several periods of decline and resurgence since its zenith in the nineteenth century. Production was high during the 1940s and early 1950s because of wartime demand and the large timber salvage program following the hurricane of 1950. Shortly thereafter, both the numbers of sawmills and total output declined sharply. The industry appears to have stabilized in the last 15 years, meaning that sawmill production has increased moderately while the consolidation of small mills continues.

Within the pulpmill industry of the entire Northeast, a shift to sulfate pulping has paralleled the growing scarcity of suitable softwood species and the increasing dependence on the more abundant hardwoods. The attrition rate among northeastern pulp mills has been high for several decades, partly because of pollution control requirements and because the northeastern mills are smaller and older and cannot compete with more efficient mills in other regions. However, net capacity has increased in the Hudson Basin since the newer mills have tended to be larger. This trend is expected to continue, especially if the increasing demand for paper products places more pressure on the supply of southern softwoods.

Mining

The most significant mining activities in the Hudson Basin are in the sand, gravel, and crushed rock quarries located near the New York and Albany metropolitan areas. Between these two centers are the Portland cement plants, based on limestone outcroppings overlooking the west bank of the Hudson River from Ravena south to Kingston. Other mining activity includes the slate quarries of Granville, dispersed limestone and dolomite quarries, , the largest garnet mine in the world at North Creek, and magnetite and titanium operations at Tahawus, near the headwaters of the Hudson River.

Essentially all the operations use open-pit methods, which often have significant effects on the natural environment. Steeply cliffed quarries are worked and customarily abandoned without any measures to reclaim or restore their sites. This is a particular problem in growing suburban areas, where formerly isolated quarries are subsequently encroached upon by residential development. In addition, there are also threats to important scenic features such as the Palisades, where crushed rock quarries continue to mine the reverse slope. Furthermore, where ore-concentrating processes are used, the huge slag heaps are no less difficult to reclaim than those using the open-pit method. The impact of quarrying on water quality can be severe.

Mining operations in the basin have a long history and are often a major factor in local economies. Much of the mined sand, stone, and gravel is consumed within the region, so that increases in mining costs are reflected in higher construction costs. Effective public action must, therefore, be forward looking as well as strong. Largely preventative programs are often suggested, including the bonding of mining operators to ensure that reclamation programs are carried out. Another alternative is public acquisition of certain mining properties with restrictions on new mining operations to ensure that they meet environmental standards. Strict reclamation requirements, however, may not be economically feasible, even in publicly owned operations. The cost may be far greater than the value of the improved view or water quality. Such judgments, however, must be based on an impartial, case-by-case analysis.

A tempting solution for many to the problems associated with the surface mining of sand and gravel is the mining of these materials from the ocean floor or from Long Island Sound. But again, problems involving both economic feasibility and special kinds of ecological hazard may prove too difficult to overcome. Another possible alternative is the increased recycling of urban rubble.

Urbanization

Most urban expansion begins as a scattering of land uses upon a landscape that is otherwise farmland, open land, or idle. The amount of land used to accommodate urban expansion varies greatly with the existing density of settlement or other factors. In the towns surveyed in a Cornell University study, the conversion of land ranged from 153 to 357 acres per 1000 population increase (Allee et al., 1970). This illustrates that the problem for most urbanizing areas is not one of an overall lack of land for urban expansion. The Hudson Basin has sufficient space to accommodate urban expansion, open space, and a viable agricultural industry, but more attention must be paid to the location of each. The present pattern of urban expansion is only one of the alternatives. Furthermore, the land conversion process and the resulting settlement pattern are already strongly influenced by a variety of public policies. Therefore, the pattern of urban expansion and land use is conceivably amenable to desirable change through the use of public policy.

Land speculation is as ubiquitous on the region's urban frontier as it was on the western frontier. It is a speculation that reaches far out into the countryside to land that is still years away from the potential jump in earning power associated with a shift to urban use.

Speculation is, of course, fueled by the expectation of a windfall when the land is actually desired for a more intensive use. This possibility of selling field or forest for large capital gains hangs like a silverlined cloud over the rural landscape near the growing suburbs. Because of scatteration, however, the "rain" from this cloud may drench one parcel now, but not fall next door for some years to come.

At least as much rural land is idled by the urban conversion process as goes directly into an urban use. But even more rural land is seriously underutilized; expectation of future urban use often precludes profitable use of such land in ways that would be most efficient and desirable over the long term. In total, the area affected by urban pressures is much larger than can reasonably be absorbed by urban uses for many years to come.

It might seem that one advantage of urban scatteration is that it leaves an abundance of open space available to the scattered urban-style residents. But the developed areas are often located such that the undeveloped parcels are not usable open space. They are often invisible, inaccessible, and more of an eyesore than a contribution to the environment. Whatever open-space function this land serves, it is invariably unintentional and undependable in the future.

Water Resources

Water Supply

Although billions of gallons of water per day are used in the study region, hardly any is consumed, i.e., permanently withdrawn from the hydrological cycle. Theoretically, water can be used over and over again, provided withdrawals, discharges, and recharges are properly sequenced, and provided the water is properly treated between uses. In practice, there has been very little reuse of the region's water resources, partly because of inadequate treatment at discharge and partly because it has been relatively easy to obtain additional water from upland reservoirs or groundwater. As pressures on available water resources increase, however, the region will have to make more efficient use of them.

Occasional droughts have stimulated efforts to develop additional water supplies. As a result of the mid-sixties drought, there was a flurry of interest in the desalination of seawater, but the "energy crisis" has dampened the enthusiasm for this technique. Direct reuse of the water supply has also been suggested, but would require sophisticated and thorough treatment of the wastewater through an advanced treatment stage. The costs and/or health risks inherent in direct reuse of water are too high to be justified at this time. Indirect reuse of water, on the other hand, is common in the Hudson Basin. Several communities use Mohawk or Hudson water both for supply and for disposal of treated waste.

Indirect reuse of groundwater is also common. A good deal of groundwater recharge is simply the seepage from septic tank drainage fields and drywells into adjacent soils. Groundwater is also replenished through recharge basins and wells, techniques that have been practiced for years on Long Island. Percolation of water through the soil generally removes pollutants, but this natural purification capacity has its limits. In heavily settled areas of Long Island, sewers have been installed and treated wastewater is discharged into the ocean. Here the groundwater is not recharged, so that the groundwater table has been lowered, permitting some intrusion of salt water in shore areas.

Nassau County is projecting a daily water supply deficiency by 1984. The droughts of the 1950s and 1960s have shown that the New York City system can also run short of water. Its problems during drought periods are aggravated by required releases of water for the Delaware River from the city's reservoir at Cannonsville. In addition, the fact that water service within the city is predominantly unmetered has raised charges of wastefulness resulting in inadequate water releases to the rivers into which the city's Catskill reservoirs drain.

The region's topography has permitted the extensive impoundment of water in upland reservoirs. Some of these impoundments provide hydroelectric power, and both regulate and disrupt streamflow. But most of the region's reservoirs, including those in the vast New York City watershed system, are operated by water supply agencies to whom they provide water of high quality with minimum need for pretreatment.

Access to water supply reservoirs for recreation is generally very limited and is usually confined to carefully regulated fishing. Those concerned with expanding regional recreational opportunities have sought to open the reservoirs for swimming and boating, but water supply agencies contend that broader recreational use would threaten water quality and make costly treatment necessary. However, multiple use of water supply reservoirs has long been practiced in other parts of the United States.

A more immediate threat to the quality of reservoir waters is pollution from development adjacent to watershed lands. This has occurred in the Croton Watershed, which supplies a quarter of the 1200 million gallons per day delivered through the New York City system. New York is considering construction of a water treatment plant within the city. This would eventually require upstate communities that use water from the city's reservoirs and aqueducts to provide their own treatment. The Temporary State Commission on the Water Supply Needs of Southeastern New York has recommended a regional benefit corporation to take over the supply of water to the city and its suburbs.

The most feasible sources of water supply in the Hudson Basin region are the Hudson River itself, surface runoff catchments, groundwater, and indirect reuse. Efficient management at all points of the distribution system is necessary, too, to ensure the efficient use of this vital supply.

Water Quality

The total biological oxygen demand (BOD) in discharges to the upper Hudson River exceeds 250,000 pounds per day, principally from paper mills. The effluents are low in nitrogen and phosphorus, but they contain undesirable toxic elements (e.g., heavy metals) from these industrial sources.

The total BOD discharged to the Mohawk exceeds 120,000 pounds per day. The effluents entering the Mohawk are relatively high in nitrogen and phosphorus because of nearby tanneries and glue factories.

The lower Hudson receives more than 300,000 pounds per day total BOD. Effluents from industries on this stretch of the river are typically low in nitrogen and phosphorus. The section below New York City, however, receives primarily municipal wastewater, resulting in relatively high nitrogen and phosphorus levels.

In terms of dissolved oxygen profiles, the two most critical portions of the Hudson River are the New York City area and the area slightly south of Albany at about mile 125. Counts of coliform bacteria, a standard indicator of the degree of disease hazard in water, are particularly high in these two areas. Coliform counts in excess of 5000 per 100 ml have been found immediately south of Albany and range up to 10,000 per 100 ml, 40 miles south of Albany. Concentrations in the middle portion of the river range from 200 to 5000 per 100 ml, and rise to as much as 50,000 per 100 ml below the New York City line. Unfortunately, there are very few time-series nutrient data and virtually no time-series biological data for the Hudson and Mohawk rivers. Without them, there can be little serious discussion of the physical–chemical–biological relationships relevant to assessing water quality. Additional research is needed to explain the full breadth of these ecological relationships.

In general, water quality in the Hudson from about Tarrytown south is affected by discharges from the New York–New Jersey metropolitan area. This reach, including New York Harbor, now receives over 1600 mgd of waste flows, representing about 1.35 million pounds of biochemical oxygen demand per day. This represents an overall oxygen removal of about 50%. In addition to the organic waste load, large quantities of nitrogen, phosphorus, trace metals, and other organic and inorganic residues are discharged in this region. The trace-metal residual loads originate from a variety of sources, including industrial plant effluents, urban runoff, untreated sewage, and metals in the sludges formerly barged to the New York Bight area.

In addition to its major streams, the Hudson Basin contains several thousand lakes that vary widely in water quality. Some, such as Saratoga Lake, have declined steadily in water quality in recent years. This is reflected in increased biological growth, especially nuisance algae and aquatic weeds. Lake George gets most of its water from precipitation. The lake receives nitrogen and phosphorus from precipitation, runoff, and wastewater effluents. Concentrations have so far been below the critical levels for algal blooms, and recreational use has not been significantly affected by nutrient overload. The lake, however, is rapidly being impacted by phosphorus load-ings, especially at the more populated south end. Sport fishing in the Hudson River is somewhat limited by pollution. This is much less so in the tribu-taries, which include numerous excellent trout streams.

In the past, commercial fishing was a major industry on the Hudson River. Shellfish, striped bass, sturgeon, and shad were abundant. Shellfishing has been stopped because of excessive pollution. Annual commercial catches of striped bass and shad have also declined. However, many factors other than pollution influence commercial catches, including climate, market condi-tions, and level of fishing effort.

Recreational Uses

Considerable recreational use—boating, water skiing, swimming, sport fishing, sightseeing, and camping—is made of the Hudson Basin's water, including the Hudson River estuary, even though poor water quality often limits its extent.

There are about 40 public beaches and waterfront parks on the lower Hudson River. Swimming is not authorized anywhere in the Hudson south of Kingsland Point Park, North Tarrytown, but people nevertheless swim from many private docks and piers along the river despite polluted condi-tions. There are about 98 private marinas and yacht clubs on the Hudson between Ellis Island and Troy. About 125,000 to 150,000 pleasure boats use the Hudson and Mohawk rivers annually.

Recreational fishing for striped bass, flounder, snapper, bluefish, white perch, and croakers is carried out in the lower, brackish waters of the river. In the freshwater portion of the river, and throughout the numerous lakes and other freshwater streams in the basin, species include bullheads, catfish, sunfish, large- and smallmouth bass, various types of lake and brook trout, yellow perch, and carp.

Air Resources

In the Hudson Basin area, most of the air pollution comes from the com-bustion of fossil fuels. There are, however, localized problems of direct emissions such as those from chemical plants and oil refineries in northern New Jersey, from cement plants in the mid-Hudson valley, and from paper mills along the upper Hudson.

Automobiles and electric power plants are the most conspicuous sources of combustion-related pollutants. Another large share of the pollution load, especially during the winter months, is contributed by the heating systems of individual homes and commercial buildings.

The broad geographical variations in air quality within the region are largely a function of population density, but are also affected by development patterns and by the interaction of climate and topography.

From time to time New York City has experienced serious pollution build-ups due to extended atmospheric inversions. Such episodes, however, are infrequent, and the city is well ventilated most of the time. Despite the heavy use of fossil fuels in the city, its air quality is not as bad as one might expect and has, in fact, been getting better. Control measures, especially those on the sulfur content of fuels, have significantly reduced air pollution since the late 1960s.

The suburban counties near New York City in New York State, i.e., Nassau, Suffolk, Rockland, Westchester, Putnam, and Orange, all have much lower population densities than New York City, and have correspondingly lower air pollution levels. Air pollution in these areas would not seem to be a serious issue, but has become one because of the almost absolute dependence of that area on automobiles. It has been proposed that auto use be curtailed to achieve air quality goals. However, it is doubtful whether any mass transit system could provide the mobility required by people living in these low-density areas.

Horizontal air flows in the Hudson Valley portion of the region are restricted by topography. Thus, air pollution generated in New Jersey and New York City can flow northward through the gorge of the Hudson to be confined by the valley and mingle with air pollution generated there. The carrying capacity of the air resources of this valley may be quite limited.

Air quality in the Catskills and the Adirondacks is, of course, very good. There are, however, problems of low-level air pollution and acid rains, resulting from the dispersion of particulates and sulfur oxides from high stacks. These may have ecological effects that cannot be predicted on the basis of present knowledge.

Strategies for the control of air pollution from fossil fuel have included increased diffusion by building tall stacks; reducing the amount of fuel used by lowering speed limits; using less-polluting fuels, such as low-sulfur oil; and reducing emissions by the use of pollution-control devices. All of these strategies involve substantial costs to the consumer—both directly, as in increased car prices and utility bills, and indirectly in higher prices for manufactured products. The air is cleaner. We can see and smell the improvement. But it will be difficult and perhaps impossible to measure the actual effect of these improvements in air quality on human health.

Air Quality Standards

Under the Clean Air Act Amendments of 1970, the Environmental Protection Agency has set primary and secondary air quality standards for six air pollutants—particulate matter, sulfur oxides, carbon monoxide, hydrocarbons, oxides of nitrogen, and photochemical oxidants (see Volume 2, p. 79). The primary standards are intended to protect against adverse human health effects, whereas the secondary standards are intended to safeguard property and plant and animal life.

Primary standards are to be achieved by 1983 with certain extensions possible to 1988.* Secondary standards are to be met within a reasonable time. The Clean Air Act does not prevent lower levels of government from adopting higher standards. New York State's own standards were adopted in 1964 (see Volume 2, p. 81). Those not as stringent as the federal requirements have been either amended or dropped, whereas those that were more stringent, or covered additional parameters, have been retained.

Monitoring

An effective air pollution control program is virtually impossible without a monitoring system to provide measurements of current air quality. Within the Hudson Basin area, separate "regional" monitoring networks are operated by the states of New York and New Jersey. New York City has a third major monitoring network within its own boundaries. Smaller monitoring networks are operated by private utility companies and by the Interstate Sanitation Commission. Nevertheless there is insufficient sampling to give an accurate picture of air quality in the region, even for suspended particulates, which receive the most monitoring. Apart from the gaps in the region's monitoring networks, there is a serious problem of data comparability owing to differences in parameters, sampling techniques, and sampling intervals. This makes it very difficult to correlate data from monitoring stations of different networks.

Sulfur Dioxide

The presence of sulfur oxides is closely associated with respiratory diseases. The oxides are particularly troublesome because of their ability to combine with other combustion products or substances present in the atmosphere to form sulfuric acid or metallic salt compounds.

During the past few years, greater improvement in air quality has resulted from the reduction of sulfur dioxide than any of the other major pollutants. Reductions of over 50% have occurred in New York City since 1970. Most of this reduction can be directly attributed to fuel sulfur restrictions in the

---

*Under the Clean Air Act Amendments of 1970, which authorized the standards, the primary standards were to be achieved by 1975 with extensions possible to 1978. In 1977, further amendments postponed the achievement date to January 1, 1983, with provision for extensions to January 1, 1988, for carbon monoxide and photochemical oxidants (ozone). [Ed.]

New Jersey–New York–Connecticut Air Quality Control Region, where the use of coal has been almost terminated and heavy oil sulfur content has been reduced by over 80%.

Achieving the federal primary air quality standard for sulfur dioxide—an annual mean not to exceed 0.003 parts per million (ppm)—seems well in hand through most of the Hudson Basin region. Exceptions are portions of New York City, Newark, and Albany. This situation could change for the worse if there is a significant return to the use of the high-sulfur fuels because of oil shortages or higher oil costs.

Carbon Monoxide

Carbon monoxide inhibits the blood's ability to carry oxygen. Locally high concentrations of carbon monoxide from automotive emissions dwarf the small amount of carbon monoxide naturally present in the air. For the region as a whole, there has probably been some decline in concentrations of carbon monoxide. It is hard, however, to obtain useful data from the existing monitoring systems. Measurements in urban areas have generally been taken in conjunction with other contaminant measurements at rooftop sites or away from areas of suspected high concentrations. But since carbon monoxide is associated with automobiles and stagnant traffic, the results tend to present a more positive picture than is actually the case.

New York City, which operates three street-level carbon monoxide monitoring stations, reports that carbon monoxide tends to be very high in the box canyons of tall buildings, but drops off quickly with increasing distance from automobile and truck traffic. The national primary standard for 8-hour carbon monoxide concentrations will be difficult to meet in virtually all the downtown portions of the region's cities without the imposition of controls beyond the federal "new vehicle" standards. The federal program was based on assumptions that the new source standards would significantly reduce carbon monoxide concentrations in most areas and that additional control measures would be necessary in only a few instances, such as New York City. Federal motor vehicle standards reducing per-vehicle emissions may have been applied too late to comply with Clean Air Act timetables with respect to carbon monoxide, and extensions granted to the auto industry complicate this problem even further. Additional measures will be necessary to meet the carbon monoxide standards within a reasonable time. Significant reductions in vehicle-miles traveled do not appear to be feasible in the immediate future. The only available alternative is the reduction in per-vehicle emissions. But that alternative would require a massive vehicle retrofitting program that would be virtually impossible to carry out in time.

Escape from this dilemma will require either modification of the Clean Air Act or a determination by the Environmental Protection Agency that 8-hour carbon monoxide values in downtown street-level locations do not constitute a health problem in that people are not actually subjected to these concentrations for an 8-hour period.*

Suspended Particulates

The term "suspended particulates" is a catch-all, as is the common measuring technique that measures total suspended particulates (TSP) in micrograms per cubic meter of air.

The particles that make up contemporary TSP vary a great deal in size and chemical composition. A good deal of TSP also occurs naturally as a result of wind erosion and the airborne dispersion of pollens and organic detritus. Control measures have been most effective with respect to the larger and heavier particles, which are also the most visible. The smaller particles are less easily removed by present pollution control technology, persist longer in the air, and are more likely to penetrate the defenses of the human respiratory system. Not much is known about the relative abundance of toxic substances among these fine particulates, or whether they are actually responsible for a significant amount of illness. Another concern is that toxic trace elements in the air may settle or condense on fine particulates, which then provide a vehicle for carrying these substances into the respiratory system.

As of 1974, much of the Hudson Basin area was meeting the federal primary standard for annual average suspended particulates. Areas in excess of the standard included most of New York City and adjacent New Jersey, and areas around Trenton, Newburgh, Kingston, Catskill, and Albany. But this reflects a major improvement since 1970, when the primary standard was exceeded in most of Nassau County and lower Westchester, as well as virtually all of New York City and large portions of New Jersey.

Hydrocarbons and Photochemical Oxidants

Hydrocarbons, which are unburned components of fuels, are of concern mainly because of what happens to them in the atmosphere. Under the influence of sunlight and other atmospheric conditions, they combine with NO_x to form photochemical oxidants. These substances, often experienced in the form of smog, irritate the eyes. There is evidence that they may increase susceptibility to respiratory diseases, and they are known to impair breathing in people with conditions such as bronchitis and emphysema.

Photochemical oxidant data within the region are rather limited. Indications are that the federal standard is not being achieved throughout much of the region. During 1972, the federal reference method was changed from a potassium iodide method to one employing chemiluminescence, which is specific for ozone. Apart from requiring major alterations in existing

*See the footnote on p. 37. [Ed.]

monitoring systems, this change has been accompanied by a general rise in reported values. This does not, of course, mean that the quantities of these substances in the air have increased, rather that they are being measured more accurately. Air quality should improve as hydrocarbon emissions, the suspected precursors of photochemical oxidants, are reduced within the region.

It should be noted that the federal 1-hour standard of 0.08 ppm, not to be exceeded more than once a year, was based on effects noted using the potassium iodide method. No supportive health studies have been performed using the chemiluminescence method. Also, it has been suggested that photochemical oxidant concentrations (ozone) may be a function of parameters other than urban hydrocarbon emissions, since rural maxima are about as high as those found in urban areas. If studies indicate that reduction of urban hydrocarbon emissions will not significantly reduce ozone measurements, the Environmental Protection Agency will be obliged to reevaluate its standards and control techniques for this contaminant.

Nitrogen Dioxide

Nitrogen dioxide data have been collected at relatively few sites throughout the Hudson Basin. It appears, however, that the portion of the region outside of the New York metropolitan area is well below the national primary standard of 0.05 ppm. Because nitrogen dioxide is not source-specific—concentrations are rather uniformly dispersed in all of the region—the limited data for the urban areas appear to approximate the worst conditions. Outlying areas would show appreciably lower annual averages.

Biological Communities

Man is a natural component of the Hudson Basin ecosystem, but his interactions with other parts of the ecosystem are unique in kind and magnitude. A principal concern of environmental management is that human activity may modify existing ecosystems on such a scale or at such a rate that processes vital to the survival and well-being of the human species may be disrupted.

In seeking to establish relationships between human activity and the state of biological communities in the Hudson Basin, researchers are handicapped by the lack of data to describe and explain the enormous diversity and complexity of the region's ecosystems. These scientists must somehow take into account the effects of cosmic and geophysical processes that are beyond man's power to influence or even, in some cases, to measure.

The long-range forces that shaped the Hudson Basin are still at work. The landscape itself is relatively unstable with respect to the forces of climate and weather, and the present drainage system is still in the process of eroding and redistributing unconsolidated glacial deposits. Climate and habitats continue to change, and species continue to invade, adapt, and compete and, in some cases, become extinct.

For an area of its size, the Hudson Basin exhibits a rather wide spectrum of biologically significant climatic conditions. For example, the basin is divided into four or five plant-hardiness zones, whereas few regions in the country of similar size encompass more than two. Moreover, important differences in climate can be observed with changes in altitude, wind exposure, or proximity to large water bodies. Thus, small areas of tundra still exist in the cold, higher elevations of the Adirondacks, while a species as "southern" as the prickly pear can be found along the lower Hudson as far north as Iona Island. The salt front, more accurately a long mixing zone in which salinity decreases progressively from south to north, shifts seasonally and, of course, with the tides.

Compared to other major river systems of North America, the Hudson is small in terms of both basin area and discharge. The Hudson estuary is relatively long, however, and the total estuary watershed is comparable to that of other Atlantic Ocean basins such as the Delaware, Connecticut, and Potomac. Only about 60% of the total discharge entering the Hudson estuary is through the main stem of the Hudson. This is a direct consequence of the length of the estuary and implies a very gradual transition from freshwater to marine conditions. Within the last two centuries, the vast oyster beds of the lower Hudson estuary have disappeared. Although the effects of pollution, landfill, and overfishing cannot be denied, a long-term decrease in salinity may have been a major contributing factor. However, it is not known whether that decline has been due to long-term climatic changes or to man-made changes that have increased runoff and reduced evapotranspiration.

Although certain species appear to be increasing in number, there are few empirical data to describe the current status of biological communities relative to previous times. Populations of deer, small mammals, and some bird species appear to have increased in recent years because of the increased amounts of edge growth around abondoned farms or where wooded areas have been penetrated by new developments or rights-of-way.

Pollution in the Hudson River and tributary systems has been reduced in the last few years, and this appears to have had a positive effect on fish populations. New environmental regulations have also slowed down encroachment on the region's biologically productive wetlands, which are believed to be crucial to the maintenance of certain fish populations in the Atlantic as well as the Hudson estuary.

Whereas there is reason for guarded optimism about the current status of the region's biological communities, available information is too fragmentary to permit more than tentative judgments on this subject. Most research on the region's biological communities is focused on the relatively narrow range of species that are used by man and subject to human manipulation in the form of hunting, fishing, forestry, and agriculture. Other species are most likely to be studied if they have some bearing on yields of harvestable species.

Although this traditional focus on pragmatic research has been of significant economic value to the region, it has also resulted in a body of knowledge that tends to deal with plants and animals whose populations do not necessarily reflect the health of the ecosystem as a whole. There is a serious lack of information about other organisms, such as plankton and soil microorganisms, that are important to the survival of natural systems and that could be more useful indicators of the biological effects of human intervention.

The management of environmental issues related to the Hudson estuary has been complicated by the estuarine nature of its ecosystem. Its organisms, even those that cannot move under their own power, are constantly being redistributed in three dimensions by the complex interactions of currents, tides, temperature, and salinity as well as seasonal and long-term biological cycles. In addition, as in the case of striped bass, some important questions about biota in the Hudson estuary cannot be answered without considering the role of other estuaries and coastal waters used by the same species. Thus, studies of estuarine biological communities pose difficult problems of methodology as well as enormous costs.

A great deal of biological research is currently being done in the Hudson Basin on the environmental impacts of specific projects. As time goes on, the results of these site-specific studies will shed additional light on the workings of the basin's ecosystems, terrestrial as well as aquatic. The potential usefulness of these studies tends to be limited, however, by the lack of integration and standardization in research procedures so as to produce comparable and combinable data.

Human Health

The United States is so large and its people so diverse and so mobile that it is hard to say whether regional health differences are simply the results of geography or of demographic, economic, or social factors. By northern European standards, physical health in the Hudson Basin is poor. Male life expectancies, in particular, are much lower, while infant mortality rates are higher. Several other health indicators lag behind those of other sophisticated industrialized nations. Of course, compared to developing countries and to many depressed rural areas of our own country, the health of the basin's population is quite good. Yet, given our medical expertise, it could probably be much better. The gross statistics on health in the basin are averages that mask a lot of variation. The upper- and middle-class residents of the basin are among the healthiest people in the world. Its slum dwellers, on the other hand, suffer a wide range of physical maladies and shortened life expectancies. In the basin as in the United States generally, income is a more reliable indicator of health than any other statistical measure except age.

In the urban areas of the Hudson Basin, death rates from cardiovascular and kidney diseases are among the highest in the world. Death rates from cancer, particularly cancer of the lung, respiratory disease, and cirrhosis are also very high. If lung cancer is included among respiratory diseases, they are second only to cardiovascular diseases as a cause of death in the region. There is evidence that poor air quality—both of general ambient air and of the air within buildings and vehicles—is contributing to respiratory problems. However, the exact relationship between air quality and respiratory problems, as with so many causal relationships in the health field, is blurred by social and economic class factors.

Biological Sources of Ill Health

Until the beginning of this century, diseases caused by microorganisms were the leading cause of death throughout the world. They remain the leading cause of death in the developing nations. In the United States and other industrialized nations, diseases caused by microorganisms have been superseded by cardiovascular disease and cancer. Nevertheless, infectious diseases, including influenza and pneumonia, are still the fifth most important cause of death in the United States today. Infectious diseases, particularly acute respiratory and gastrointestinal infections, are also by far the most important causes of acute disability, causing days lost from work and school. Most of the widespread infectious diseases that continue to elude control are caused by viruses.

The microorganisms that have caused the greatest amount of human disease in the past have also been parasitic upon the animals that lived closest to man. They spread because many are adapted to survive and multiply in the insects that prey upon both men and other animals. The eradication of tuberculosis among men has been in part dependent upon its eradication among cattle. Plague, a disease with a natural reservoir among wild rodents, spreads rapidly to the rats that are commensals of men, from rats to men by rat fleas, and from men to men by human fleas. The virus of equine encephalomyelitis has a reservoir in horses, from which it is transmitted by mosquitoes to birds, to other horses, and to man.

In the past 50 years, with the decline in rural population and with improved sanitation on farms, the incidence of disease from domestic animals has been virtually eliminated. In addition, virtually universal access to the washing machine and frequent bathing have virtually eliminated fleas and lice, while the garbage collector and the exterminator have helped in the elimination of rats and mice. As people have separated themselves from the creatures that were their close associates until the very recent past, there has been less and less opportunity to become infected by them, and human health has improved.

With minor exceptions, such as some of the yeasts, plants are not directly infectious to men. However, plant pollens cause many people to have allergic reactions that contribute to such chronic respiratory diseases as bronchitis, rhinitis, and asthma. Fish, and especially shellfish from polluted waters, can also transmit disease. In the early 1960s, there was a serious outbreak of hepatitis in the New York metropolitan area caused by contaminated shellfish from Raritan Bay. Although the contamination of finfish with toxic chemicals has drawn much public attention in recent years, the transmission of infectious diseases by shellfish is probably a more immediate threat to human health.

Pets and wild animals are a potential source of disease. Diseases can be transmitted to man from pet dogs, birds, and turtles, as well as from ground squirrels (plague), rabbits (tularemia), and skunks (rabies), but such cases are relatively rare in the Hudson Basin.

Insects such as mosquitoes, although primarily a nuisance in the Hudson Basin, are also potential carriers of disease. Several years ago, there was an epidemic of mosquito-borne encephalitis in central New Jersey.

Chemical Hazards to Health

In a technologically advanced region such as the Hudson Basin, people are routinely exposed to thousands of different chemical substances that are either artificial or in artificially high concentrations. Some of these are directly handled or ingested, often by children. Other chemicals reach us invisibly through the air and water. Still others are absorbed by plants or animals that may later serve as food.

Excluding occupational exposure, cases of illness or death directly traceable to chemicals in the environment are relatively rare in the Hudson Basin. Poisoning from ingested lead paint has been a notable exception. Of course, such illnesses or deaths are difficult to trace in any event. Nevertheless, there are some good reasons why environmental chemical hazards should be substantially lower in the Hudson Basin than in many other areas of the country. Extractive and primary industries are a relatively small component of the region's economy. Regulation is relatively strict whereas monitoring, formal and informal, is good compared with other regions. Most of the basin's population receives its water from upland reservoirs, rather than from large rivers or lakes that might also receive industrial discharges. Use of reservoirs also minimizes a risk that chlorine used in water treatment might combine with other pollutants to form toxic, carcinogenic, or mutagenic compounds. There have been cases of poisoning traceable to pesticides or to contamination of wells by nitrates in suburban as well as in rural areas. Nevertheless, these are not major hazards and they have been reduced in the last few years by tighter regulation.

If we exclude the hazards of the home medicine cabinet and cleaning closet, the most serious chemical threats to health in the region's environment are probably those that reach us through the air (see the discussion of air quality).

There are enormous problems involved in assessing the potential health hazards of chemicals. First, there is the sheer number of substances to which people are routinely exposed, a number that continually increases as new chemical products are introduced. This multiplicity of substances makes it extremely difficult to isolate and trace potential sources of hazard and paths of exposure. Moreover, science has only begun to understand how pollutants interact with each other to affect health.

Second, unless a substance produces some immediate and dramatic symptom, its effects may not be noticed for weeks, months, or even decades. Finally, even where a causal relationship has been established, it is extremely difficult to say how much exposure can occur before there is a significant effect on human health.

For example, air pollution episodes in New York City have been accompanied by increased numbers of deaths. Investigations have shown, however, that the "excess" deaths were accounted for among people who were already seriously ill or had some preexisting condition that made them susceptible to additional stress. This observation suggests that air pollution precipitates deaths of people who would in any event have died shortly from a more basic cause. There is a much more significant correlation between excess deaths and periods of extremely hot weather. This is not to say that the cumulative effects of air pollution cannot cause serious illness and ultimate death. Nevertheless, it underscores how difficult it is to identify the actual health effect of pollutants in the environment.

Radiation

People in the Hudson River basin are exposed to ionizing radiation from natural sources, from electronic devices such as X-ray machines, and from radioactive substances released to the environment by human activity.

Exposure to ionizing radiation entails the risk of carcinogenic and mutagenic effects. (We are leaving aside, for the purposes of this discussion, the beneficial medical uses of radiation, which are enormous.) Based on present knowledge of radiation effects, it is assumed that the dose–response curve is linear, i.e., there is no threshold below which no risk exists. Also, the risk is independent of dose rate, i.e., it is the same for a given dose whether it is received all at once or a little bit at a time.

All organisms, since the beginning of life on earth, have been exposed to a certain amount of radiation from cosmic rays and from the radioactive minerals that occur in many kinds of rocks. But even very large differences in natural background radiation have not been shown to produce detectable differences in the incidence of cancer or mutations.

After World War II, background radiation from natural sources was augmented by fallout from weapons testing. Most of the fallout radioactivity has subsided, though some of it will persist for centuries. In the United States, the average annual dose from background radiation, including the fallout increment, is roughly equivalent to two chest X rays.

Because nuclear energy was first used in weapons of gruesome effect, its application in nuclear power plants was tightly regulated from the outset. The shipment and use of nuclear materials for medical and industrial purposes are now also closely regulated. Neither the regulations nor their implementation are flawless. Nevertheless, the incidence of injury or potentially hazardous exposure has been very small, even among people who work with radioactive materials.

Detectable amounts of radioactivity are released to the environment by nuclear power plants in normal operation and by nuclear materials in transit to and from such plants. The dose to the general public from these sources is quite small, even in comparison with natural background radiation, and they have had no measurable health effects on the general public. The most significant radiation risk posed by nuclear plants at the present time is that of a major accidential release of radioactivity.

Noise

Sound is a kind of energy, the energy of pressure waves moving through the air or another sound-carrying medium. Much is known about sound as a physical phenomenon. The force exerted by sound waves can be rather precisely measured. There is also a highly developed technology for controlling noise, or unwanted sound.

Relatively little is known about the effects of noise or excessive sound on human health. The effects that we can be most certain of are those on the ears. Hearing loss has long been known as a hazard among people constantly exposed to loud noise, such as that produced by printing presses and heavy construction machinery. Parts of the region's environment have become so noisy in recent years that large numbers of people are exposed to potentially damaging levels of noise at work and even at home.

On a day-to-day basis, the EPA has estimated that permanent hearing loss begins when routine noise exposure averages about 70 dB over the course of the working day, including the trip to and from work. Seventy decibels is the noise level of freeway traffic at 50 feet, but some vacuum cleaners and kitchen blenders often exceed 80 dB. New York subway trains produce 95 dB and passing motorcycles often produce 100. Yet none of these matches those discotheques where people actually pay to hear sound at 115 dB. Noise that would not contribute to hearing loss can still be loud enough to disturb sleep, interrupt conversation, and interfere with work and leisure activity.

Noises of 85 dB and above can produce physiological stress reactions in most people. These include increases in blood pressure and hormonal secretions, dilation of the pupils, and changes in the blood vessels and digestive tract. These reactions are part of the body's normal defense mechanisms. They occur automatically, even when the person is not consciously aware that he is responding to a noise, and usually subside within a few moments. It has been suggested that the repeated triggering of the body's stress responses can contribute to heart disease, gastrointestinal disorders, and some types of mental illness. However, the contribution of stress, and specifically of noise-induced stress, to these conditions is still unclear.

Accidents

Accidents, in the sense of sudden events that cause immediate injury or death, are not often thought of as an environmental problem, but environmental management decisions often affect accident risks. Safety is a major consideration in the planning and management of the man-made environment, notably in transportation, and also in energy, the design of structures, and even in recreation.

Decisions relating to accidents are reasonably well informed. We have excellent systems, coordinated at the federal level, for gathering data on the incidence and causes of accidents and proposing new safety measures.

Nutrition

Diseases directly attributable to malnutrition still occur in the Hudson Basin, and inadequate diet is an important contributing factor to the generally higher rates of illness and birth defects among the poor. The persistence of these health problems is due partly to poverty itself, but perhaps even more to educational and language barriers. Even if one has basic knowledge about nutrition, some sophistication is required to select the proper foods from the bewildering array of packages and produce on supermarket shelves. This is difficult for people who are functionally illiterate, for members of linguistic minorities, or for those whose only source of nutritional information is television advertising.

Environmental management decisions affect nutrition to the extent that they affect the price of food. Decisions affecting transportation costs, for example, are important because the Hudson River basin imports most of its food from other regions, and transportation is a significant component of retail food costs.

Leisure Time and Recreation

An important aspect of environmental management in the Hudson River basin, as in most industrialized regions of the world, is the provision of space and facilities for the satisfying use of leisure time.

Leisure is simply free time not taken up by necessity or obligation. Recreation is one of the things that people can do with their leisure. Recreation is often thought of as the complement of work, replenishing what has been depleted by toil. In addition, there are many people who seek recreation to relieve stresses built up outside of work.

Public Recreational Facilities

In the 1960s, there was a sense of urgency about the acquisition of open land. This was the major thrust of public activity in the recreation area. At the same time, there was a deemphasis of inner-city parks and a decline in their maintenance because of rising labor costs, demographic changes, and the attrition of informal play areas such as vacant lots and unbusy streets.

Today, there is a very striking difference in the quality of public recreational facilities available to people with and without cars. To those with cars, the Hudson Basin offers among the best public recreational facilities in the world. The facilities available to those without cars are frequently crowded and usually poorly maintained. Nevertheless, for day-to-day recreational needs, children and old people in densely populated areas may be better served than in some suburbs because there are schoolyards and small parks within walking distance.

In the 1960s, rapid suburbanization and increased car ownership created a need for more public open space. Toward the end of that decade, federal aid and state bond issues financed a surge of land acquisition by park agencies, who often found themselves in a race with developers for the choicest parcels. Some of the most difficult acquisitions in the Hudson Basin were relatively small parcels in developing areas. These tended to be close to existing roads and sewer lines and were therefore also sought by builders.

Although acquisition of larger and more remote parcels has rarely precluded a planned development, it was often opposed by local officials and real estate interests on the grounds that land was removed from tax rolls and thereby increased burdens on the remaining property owners. It is not clear that park acquisitions have actually had this effect, since property taxes in developing areas have generally gone up faster than in stable areas.

Parkland acquisition in the region has slowed since the beginning of this decade. If acquisition should resume, local opposition is more likely to focus on employment effects rather than on simple removal of land from the tax rolls. Large parkland acquisitions can eliminate or divert jobs, especially in site-specific activities such as lumbering or quarrying. On the other hand, large public recreation areas also create jobs, both inside the public park and in leisure-related businesses in nearby communities.

Employment is sometimes a factor in controversies over the types of facilities to be permitted on public recreational lands. In areas that are economically dependent on tourism, there is usually strong local support for those leisure activities that will draw the most people, make for the longest tourist seasons, and require equipment that is likely to be bought, serviced, or rented by local businessmen. In the Adirondacks, where there is chronic unemployment and a brief summer tourist season, there have been numerous campaigns for more intensive recreational uses on forest preserve land, including additional snowmobile trails and ski areas to attract winter tourist trade.

The Private Sector

Providing large-scale facilities for recreation, especially outdoor recreation, is generally accepted as a responsibility of government. The more passive, audience-oriented leisure pursuits have traditionally been left to the private sector. However, governments in the Hudson Basin have been assuming more responsibility for these pursuits in recent years, especially in the arts.

Governments usually do not become directly involved with leisure activities that can be operated at a profit by the private sector. Exceptions are for some reason other than helping people to have a good time. State lotteries and betting parlors are aimed at raising revenues and thwarting organized crime. Cities build or subsidize professional sport stadiums because big league teams are considered good for local business.

Most leisure activity outside the home takes place in privately operated facilities. Through zoning and licensing powers, governments in the Hudson Basin exert a great deal of control over the availability and location of commercially run leisure facilities. The most regulated private-sector facilities are generally the more urban ones such as movie theatres and bowling alleys, which have rather minor and local effects on the physical environment. There is generally much less control over the more extensive (i.e., space-consuming) leisure uses that occur in rural areas, such as commercial campgrounds, roadside tourist attractions, small resorts, and piecemeal vacation-cottage developments.

The existing regulation of such businesses is directed mainly at limiting nuisance impacts. There is hardly any positive planning to encourage an adequate supply and choice of leisure opportunities in the private sector. A major reason is that information about recreational demand is spotty and fragmented. The "hard" data that are available are often compiled by trade groups that have an interest in promoting specific leisure pursuits.

It is difficult to say how much the demand for specific activities is stimulated by advertising and lobbying of equipment manufacturers. Public provision of facilities for sports that require hardware is, intentionally or not, a boon to equipment manufacturers.

Until a few years ago, rural commercial leisure facilities in the region were rarely controversial. They tended to develop gradually, often as a sideline to farming, and were almost always owned by local people. Such small, locally owned leisure operations have sometimes evolved into major resorts with such facilities as golf courses and ski lifts. However, this kind of self-financed, evolutionary development by local interests is less likely to occur in the future. To be competitive, resorts must now be able to offer facilities that can rarely be financed without outside capital and are rarely feasible except as part of a large-scale complex.

However, it is not unusual for government to step in where private capital fears to tread, providing costly facilities, such as beaches and ski centers, which complement existing commercial ventures and stimulate new ones.

Second-Home Developments*

The private leisure facilities that are most critical from the standpoint of environmental management are second-home developments. The crucial environmental problems from these arise precisely because they are a type of urban development rather than a simple recreational form. Historically, vacation-home developments have tended to evolve into year-round communities, even when the houses were not originally built for year-round occupancy, with all the demands on infrastructure and public services that that implies.

Second-home development in the region has fallen off sharply because of the recession and the mortgage drought that preceded it. In the meantime,

*See also p. 53.

state environmental regulations have been tightened and some local governments have become more aware of the long-term public service costs entailed in such developments. Second-home developments will no doubt continue to be built in the region, but they are likely to be smaller in scale and more carefully located. Also, future demand for second homes may be dampened by uncertainty about the future cost of energy. Developments in remote localities tend to use electricity as the primary form of energy, and the escalating cost of gasoline has also made people think twice about commitments that involve long-distance driving.

1.3   Regional Problem Situations

The Project's objective of developing a better understanding of environmental problems in the study area was approached along two mutually reinforcing lines. The first approach, reflected in the previous section, focused on a given policy area and asked how the conditions and problems observed related to those of the other nine policy areas studied. The second approach focused on selected "problem situations" that illustrate issues, their underlying causes, and interdependencies among the economic, social, and physical environments in the Hudson Basin study area. This section abstracts several of the more instructive of these regional problem situations (RPS) explored by the Project's task groups and other participants.

RPS-1: A Deepwater Oil Terminal off Northern New Jersey

The proposal for a crude oil terminal off the coast of New Jersey is seen from Washington as an element in the physical, economic, and political well-being of the nation. Closer to the local level, the economic attractiveness of the proposal is tempered by fears of degradation of the physical and fiscal environments.

Much of the controversy centers on the possible onshore impacts of the proposed facility. There are insufficient data to support assurances that even a small oil operation would be tolerable, that the probability and costs of emissions are acceptably low, or that an adequate water supply can be ensured. Furthermore, normal patterns of industrial agglomeration suggest that a large operation will be difficult to prevent once a low-level operation is approved.

Alternatives to the northeastern New Jersey terminal include a change in oil consumption, new sources or substitutes for crude oil, and selection of an alternate site or sites. At the federal level, political action would appear to be the only recourse for the affected states, counties, and localities. At the state level, land use legislation could be used to control the location and impact of the proposed facility.

The following issues and questions come to light as the above proposal unfolds:

1. What should be the policy governing the location of growth-producing facilities?
2. Where should energy-related facilities be located in the implementation of that policy?
3. What should constitute an overall energy policy?
4. What should the role of regional planning agencies be in location decisions?
5. What level of economic benefit justifies a given level of environmental degradation?
6. How can adequate information and assessment be developed and brought to bear on the above issues?*

RPS-2: *Boomer v. Atlantic Cement Co.,* A Case Study of the Role of Litigation in Resolving Problems of Air Pollution and Land Use

One of the world's largest cement manufacturing plants was built by Atlantic Cement Co. in the Albany metropolitan area in the early 1960s. It was welcomed as an economic boon to the Town of Coeymans and the Village of Ravena, located about 12 miles south of Albany near the Hudson River. When limestone quarrying and cement production began, however, neighboring property owners protested against the noise and dust. Lawsuits by eight of these neighbors involved the company in a decade of litigation and costly penalties. The courts eventually awarded Atlantic Cement "servitude" or easement rights, allowing pollution of neighboring land in return for compensation to the affected property owners.

A number of state agencies and institutions were involved in decisions leading to the construction of the Atlantic plant. The New York State Department of Commerce assisted in the project's birth, helping to find a suitable location for the plant. Several major banks in the area participated in financing the venture. Once the plant was built and conflict ensued, the New York State Department of Health and later the Department of Environmental Conservation played important roles in measuring air pollution, assessing the environmental damages caused, applying available technology to abate the cement-dust emissions, and enforcing the pollution control law.

---

*For further discussion of the deepwater oil terminal case, see pp. 68–71.

These and other state offices attempted to resolve the issues before the final resort to the courts, but to no avail. The fundamental legal issues involved and the implication of the state government, through several of its agencies, in both the genesis of the problem and its eventual resolution make this a significant, revealing illustration of competing property rights.

This case casts light on the following issues and questions, which are of great importance in the Hudson Basin region:

1. How should the courts, or any of society's institutions, account for economic disparities between competing parties?
2. To what extent should the courts be responsible for the setting of land use and other environmental policy?
3. To what extent may an individual, group, or company impose nuisances on others?
4. To what extent does the public interest in land outweigh its conventional characterization as a commodity?
5. To what extent do economic benefits outweigh degradation of the physical environment?

RPS-3: Second-Home Development

The demand for second homes in the Hudson Basin comes mainly from people living in metropolitan areas. It is a further extension of a type of urban pressure on rural areas that has had a long history. In the most recent wave of second-home development, however, the construction industry has applied its experience in building suburban tracts to the development of large-scale subdivisions of second homes, usually with ancillary recreational facilities.

Concentrations of second homes often help to support the economy of declining rural areas or areas that have traditionally relied on seasonal tourism, as discussed in Section 1.2. In addition, the types of second-home development carried on in the past placed little additional stress on the environment. The present controversy about second homes is essentially over the impact of large recreational developments. These are sometimes carefully designed to blend into the rural landscape, but more often are platted at densities that violate the natural setting and overload local resources and public services. The degree of concern depends upon factors such as the adequacy of the available water supply, the effect of the development on water pollution, and the impact of a concentrated population and settlement on the natural landscape. In addition to these effects on the physical environment, there are, of course, the social effects of increased demand for public services such as highway improvements and police, fire, and medical-emergency protection. If second homes are converted into year-round residences, as is often the case, additional classroom space and school-bus service are needed.

Questions and issues raised by continued construction of large-scale second-home developments include the following:

1. What constitutes a significant impact on the environment?
2. What level of economic benefit justifies a given amount of environmental degradation?
3. Should fiscal and monetary policies encourage or discourage second homes?
4. Do second homes constitute a special class of housing, which should be taxed and controlled differently than primary residences?

RPS-4: The Adirondack Park Agency*

The Adirondack Park, established by the New York State Legislature in 1892, embraces 6 million acres of both public and private land. Under Article XIV of the State Constitution, the state forest preserve land within the Adirondack Park must be kept "forever wild." In addition to its crucial role as a watershed, the park contains many areas of unique or scarce natural quality including mountains, forests, lakes, rivers, and wetlands of recreational and aesthetic value. In recent years, the pressure of private (mostly uncontrolled) development has threatened these special areas.

In 1968, the Temporary State Commission on the Future of the Adirondacks was established to answer some difficult questions. These included the long-range state policy for acquiring additional forestlands, measures to ensure that private land development would be consistent with the long-range well-being of the area, state policy on area recreation, and stronger safeguards for wilderness and flexibility in its management.

On the recommendation of the Temporary Commission, the state legislature established the Adirondack Park Agency (APA) in 1971 and charged it with formulating a land use and development plan for all non-state-owned land in the park, creating a master plan for state-owned lands, and reviewing private land-development proposals in areas not protected by local zoning and subdivision regulations until the adoption of the agency's land use and development plan.

The APA master plan for state lands was adopted as state policy in 1972 and had the objective of striking a ". . . balance in keeping some of the land pure wilderness while protecting recreational opportunities." In 1973, the state legislature adopted the APA Land Use and Development Plan, which

---

*For additional discussion of the Adirondack Park Agency, see Chapter 6, Section 6.4.

imposed strict government regulation on the use of private land, again balancing private development with the park's natural resources and character.

Support for the APA came from individuals and groups throughout the state. Opposition to the agency centered in those affected by the restrictions and/or living in the area. The strongest and most powerful opposition came from land developers who had bought large tracts of highly scenic land with the intention of subdividing it for second homes.

Questions and issues raised by this problem situation include the following:

1. What can or should the role of local government be vis-à-vis other levels of government in the management of environmental problems of interjurisdictional concern?

2. How can information acquisition and use, program assessment, coordination, and restructuring be undertaken to improve environmental management?

3. How can regional, state, and multistate interests and the needs and values of local residents be balanced when dealing with environmental resources having unique characteristics?

RPS-5: Okwari Park

Montgomery County, in the Mohawk Valley 35 miles west of Albany, proposed the construction of a 3700-acre outdoor recreational facility for regional use. Funds were to be provided by the county government, with federal participation. The park plan called for three lakes, a ski area, a golf course, a camping area, a hunting preserve, riding trails, and a conference center, among other facilities.

The park was purportedly to provide recreational facilities for all people regardless of sex, race, religion, national origin, or place of residence. It was claimed that the park would maintain—even enhance—the unique ecological resources of the site and would provide "optimum potential revenue sources to the county for maintenance and operation, as well as stimulate economic development in all parts of Montgomery County." It later appeared, however, that the park was also intended to serve as the focus for a second-home development of up to 2000 units. Proponents argued that the park would thereby stimulate the county's economic growth, but the park was opposed by many county residents. Water supply, sewage disposal, and water pollution were among the matters involved in the controversy. New York State's Department of Environmental Conservation (DEC) responded by holding a public hearing on the park and permitting a public referendum to be held on the issue. In both cases the verdict went against the park.

Because of informed activism and persistence, the opponents were able to focus the attention of both the public and the state regulators on the weaknesses of the county's park plan. After a prolonged battle, requests for permits to build the dams for the park's three lakes were denied by the Commissioner of Environmental Conservation.

The DEC held that, given the nature of the proposed project, the "piecemeal" approach used by the applicants did not represent the sound, comprehensive environmental planning required. The applicants were unable to counter the department's finding that the park would have a substantial detrimental impact on the environment of the state. The DEC also found the applicant unable to show sufficient "need" by the residents of the county for a project of such size and diversity; hence the requested dams were neither reasonable nor necessary. The applicant failed to demonstrate that a sufficient potable water supply was available, or that acceptable sewage facilities would be provided. In addition, incomplete cost analyses for key elements of the project made projections of alternatives impossible.

Questions and issues raised by the Okwari Park dispute include the following:

1.   How can plans for such facilities best be developed and presented?
2.   What kind of information base and assessments of economic, social, and political consequences are needed for public agreement on such proposals?
3.   What limits should apply to counties in developing recreational facilities that are clearly of multicounty impact?
4.   How can the need for outdoor recreational facilities be met, while controlling the development-inducing effects of such facilities?

RPS-6: Location of a Fourth Major Jetport in Lower New York State

The proposed expansion of Stewart Airport, a former military airbase near Newburgh, New York, 65 miles from New York City, exemplifies the high cost of a single-purpose land use decision made without adequate prior assessment of either the public transportation need or the impact on the existing natural and man-made resources of the region.

Stewart Air Force Base was established in 1942. In October 1970, the federal government transferred 1552 acres, most of the base property, to the Metropolitan Transportation Authority (MTA), an agency of the State of New York.

In August 1971, the MTA, without local consultation, condemned an additional 8650 acres extending west from the existing airport boundary. The stated purpose of the acquisition was to provide land for future airport development and to provide a buffer between the airport and its neighbors. Before a plan for the ultimate development of the airport was completed, the MTA announced it would immediately extend the existing 8000-foot runway by 4000 feet. The airport would then be available for intensive commercial use and, indeed, could provide facilities more massive than those of John F. Kennedy International Airport.

It was generally anticipated that such large-scale and intensive public land use would bring about major changes in the physical and economic environment of the surrounding area. Indicative of changes to come was the almost immediate skyrocketing of land values in the vicinity of the airport.

There had been no evaluation of the impact of the proposed airport expansion at the time it was announced. There was also a conspicuous lack of coordination and cooperation with either local or federal agencies with responsibilities in the area. MTA took the position that, since no federal funds were being used for the proposed runway extension, no environmental impact statement under the National Environmental Policy Act of 1969 was required. The FAA intervened and ruled that an environmental impact statement was, in fact, necessary and that they would prepare it. The FAA review, however, looked simply at the runway extension rather than at the more critical question of its relationship to the larger facility envisioned by the MTA master plan, which was by then under development.

The Tri-State Regional Planning Commission, which has formal responsibility for fostering coordinated planning in the New York metropolitan region, remained silent concerning the need for a fourth jetport, the suitability of the Stewart location, and the impact of such a facility on the surrounding region. The Regional Plan Association and Mid-Hudson Pattern, Inc., which are private, nonprofit regional planning organizations, questioned the need for a fourth jetport. They advocated a smaller facility with limits to be set in advance on airport operations to protect surrounding communities from noise impact and to provide a buffer from community encroachment on airport activities.

The advent of the Arab oil embargo, the recession, and a new administration at MTA resulted in the abandonment, at least temporarily, of plans for a fourth jetport and the adoption of the size limitation and land use control approaches recommended.

This regional problem situation raises the following questions and issues:

1. What institutional arrangements are required to ensure that agreed-upon regional needs, goals, and policies, rather than the more narrowly defined missions and ambitions of the sponsoring agencies, are given primary consideration in making decisions on major regional facilities?

2. How can limits best be set on the use and size of a major facility before it is built so that surrounding communities can know what effects they must accommodate?
3. How should the community facilities needed to serve the airport and the consequent peripheral development be financed?
4. Should there be a system for sharing new tax ratables generated by the airport?
5. How can land taken from private citizens, and possibly no longer needed for a jetport, be conveyed to other public and private uses in an equitable manner?

RPS-7: Freight Transportation in the New York–New Jersey Metropolitan Area

The New York metropolitan area requires massive inbound shipments of food and raw materials. Much of the required tonnage is shipped overland for long distances. Historically, such long-distance shipments were by rail to vast freight yards on the New Jersey shore, from which entire rail cars were barged to destinations on the east side of the Hudson River.

In recent years, trucks have gained enormous ground relative to rail, not only for local distribution but also for long-distance movements into and out of the metropolitan area. The growth of trucking at the expense of rail has created new terminal problems. In addition, given the secondary impacts, trucking may increase the real cost of long-distance shipments out of all proportion to the door-to-door convenience that trucks provide.

Jersey City, in particular, is burdened with many acres of abandoned or unprofitable rail terminals. Ironically, it is still one of the best geographical locations in the United States for this purpose, and has numerous rail facilities which potentially add to the value of this location. However, these facilities in their present condition are a liability to Jersey City and the entire metropolitan area.

Unless rail-using activities can be encouraged to locate around the existing rail terminals, there is likely to be a further deterioration in rail freight service to the metropolitan area, accompanied by increases in consumer prices for goods.

Questions and issues raised by the problem of freight transportation include the following:

1. What is the quantitative impact of the shift to truck transportation on the cost of the food and consumer goods needed by the New York metropolitan area?

2. How can the metropolitan area make the best use of the flexibility of truck transportation, while minimizing its adverse impacts?
3. What measures can be taken to draw rail-using activities to the existing rail facilities in northern New Jersey?

RPS-8: The Hudson River Striped Bass Fishery*

A large proportion of the striped bass in northeastern coastal waters, perhaps as much as 80%, are spawned in the Hudson River. The fish eggs and larvae are subject to entrainment in the cooling systems of power plants, whereas the somewhat larger juvenile fish may be trapped by the current at the plant intakes and killed by impingement on the intake screens. The magnitude of impingement and entrainment losses depends on the location of the intakes and the amounts of water withdrawn during the critical spawning and nursery seasons.

Many state and federal agencies affect, directly or indirectly, striped bass populations supported by the Hudson River. Traditionally, it is state governments that directly manage fishery resources. New York has the usual array of limits on nets, seasons, and sizes, largely aimed at preventing overfishing of the young before they have had a chance to spawn. But this has not been integrated with any policy to limit entrainment and impingement.

Connecticut and New Jersey laws affect the management of the fishery, since Hudson-spawned fish are taken in those states, but neither has as much control over the striped bass life-cycle as New York.

Of the federal agencies, those that act in the context of licensing projects, such as the Federal Power Commission and Army Corps of Engineers, have the most impact on the Hudson's striped bass. The major actors in these licensing procedures tend to be the applicants—utility companies in the case of power plants—and nongovernmental intervenors such as conservation groups. The federal agencies that have the most expertise and responsibility regarding fisheries—the Bureau of Sports Fisheries and Wildlife in Interior and the National Marine Fisheries Service in Commerce—have tended to remain in the background in federal licensing proceedings. There has been no coherent federal position on the fishery and little effective guidance to the licensing agencies.

The Environmental Protection Agency is likely to have a considerable effect on the Hudson striped bass as a result of the Federal Water Pollution Control Act Amendments of 1972. The amendments require the best practical or best available technology to reduce discharges to navigable waters. In

---

*Abstracted from the original Biological Communities Task Group Report.

the case of power-plant thermal discharges, the requirement can be waived if it can be shown that a discharge has no significant adverse impact on aquatic biota. In the absence of such a showing, any new plants on the Hudson will almost certainly be required to have recycling cooling systems. The massive size of the cooling towers required and their highly visible vapor plumes pose a serious threat to the scenic beauty of the Hudson River Gorge.

It is unclear how much weight EPA will give to entrainment effects. There is the possibility that EPA's determinations may not be subject to impact assessment by any other federal agency, but this remains to be seen.

Since only 1100 acres of shoals remain in the major Hudson nursery grounds, almost any project requiring fill in the river is significant to the striped bass fishery. Permits for fill projects are issued by the Army Corps of Engineers, which lacks a coherent policy on such activities. Thus, the incremental effect of a number of small fill projects may do major damage to the striped bass nursery grounds. The state Tidal Wetlands Act may work to control filling intrusions, but it remains to be seen how the law will be implemented by DEC.

The lack of a coherent governmental policy on the Hudson striped bass fishery might be excused by a lack of biological data, but more is probably known about the striped bass in the Hudson than most other fish populations as a result of extensive studies done for governmental agencies and the utilities over the last 10 years.

Data are still needed on the contribution of the Hudson to the overall coastal fishery, and whether there are compensating phenomena that prevent losses of eggs, larvae, and juveniles from being reflected in adult populations. The latter problem is an extremely difficult one on which to do research. It is questionable whether existing research techniques can provide better answers than the available historical and circumstantial evidence.

The problem of relative contributions, though more easily approached by methods such as tagging studies, raises the question of why appropriate studies were not done before the enormous commitments of resources represented by the utility projects. One reason is the low level of public awareness of such matters prior to the passage of the National Environmental Policy Act. Another is the virtual inaction of the state and federal agencies that are supposed to know about fish, largely because they lack the manpower and research budget necessary to answer the questions raised by large-scale projects.

Questions and issues raised by the Hudson's striped bass fishery include the following:

1. What should be the federal–state policy toward the Hudson striped bass fishery?
2. How can private parties seeking to use public resources be made accountable for the adverse environmental effects of their actions?
3. How can the specialized agencies concerned with fisheries be equipped to take a more effective role in licensing proceedings affecting fisheries?

RPS-9: Allocation of Hudson Basin Water Resources among Competing Uses in Southeastern New York

For centuries, water resources in southeastern New York have been sufficient to satisfy virtually all demands upon them. In recent decades, however, population and economic growth have resulted in competition and conflicts among a variety of users of water resources. Such uses of the Hudson River include transportation, drinking water supply, industrial water supply, recreation, energy production, and assimilation of sewage effluent and other wastes. The river provides a cheap and energy-efficient form of transportation of bulk commodities which are important to the region's economy. This use can, however, conflict with or preclude recreational uses.

New York City and other communities make heavy demands on the Hudson River and its tributaries for water supply. This moves the estuary's salt front upstream, which in turn affects the location and quality of the remaining freshwater supply. These demands, in turn, decrease the flows of upstream tributaries, thereby affecting recreational enjoyment and the stability of the biological systems in these water courses.

The Hudson is also used, and in some cases overused, as an assimilator of point sources of pollution such as sewage effluent and waste heat. This function is in direct competition with domestic and industrial water supply. Current power-generation technology entrains organisms that are part of the food chain of fish and that are important to vast commercial and recreational fishing interests. Evaporation loss of water in power-plant cooling towers will place increasing demands on available water supply.

Land-related activities are also placing stress on the quality of the region's water resources. Examples include agricultural runoff—a pervasive polluter of Hudson tributaries—and urban storm drainage, carrying sediment and silt to waterways. In older urban areas, combined sewage systems overload treatment plants during storms, allowing untreated effluent to overflow directly into receiving water bodies. The lack of adequate institutional mechanisms for the rational allocation of water resources among the various competing and conflicting uses poses serious environmental management problems. In some cases, lack of protection of the quality of the Hudson's waters reflects performance deficiencies on the part of existing institutions in the region. Although the 1970s have seen significant improvements in enforcement by agencies such as DEC, EPA, and the Army Corps of Engineers, citizens' groups concerned with pollution abatement have felt the need to conduct their own "river watch" on the Hudson, and to call those responsible to account when they have been slow to move. The fragmentary nature of regulatory efforts reflects the lack of water resource allocation policies.

The problem of allocating Hudson River and other water resources in the basin raises the following issues and questions:

1. What institutional arrangements are needed to achieve equitable allocation?
2. Where should the authority to allocate resources rest?
3. What trade-offs of other water uses might be required to ensure adequate water quality and quantity for the long-term future?
4. What means should be used to abate some of the more pervasive nonpoint sources of pollution such as urban and agricultural runoff?

RPS-10: Declining Agricultural Lands*

During the past 60 years, about 12 million acres, more than one-half of the farmland of New York State, have gone out of agricultural use. Some lands in the Hudson Basin have been pushed out of farming by technological obsolescence alone. The process has been speeded, however, by "pull factors" such as improved roads, the private car, and alternative employment opportunities for farmers. In addition, general trends toward increasing urbanization, higher incomes, and expanding leisure time have helped to create a new, growing market for marginal farmlands. Increasingly, they are being transformed into homesites and recreational lands. This transformation, in turn, increases the value of remaining farmlands and increases tax pressures.

The following issues and questions arise with respect to declining agricultural lands:

1. At what levels of government must public action be taken to help ensure reliable sources of foodstuffs for the United States and to discourage the escalation of costs associated with providing housing?

*Also see above, the discussion of agriculture in Section 1.2.

2. Is New York's Agricultural District Act strong enough to protect remaining farmlands from urban pressures?
3. How should agricultural areas be treated in a general strategy of land use management?

RPS-11: Local Land Use Control—Ramapo

Since World War II, people and industries have moved in large numbers to the suburbs, where the lack of adequate planning and land use controls has contributed to wasteful urban sprawl, destruction of natural landscapes, soaring tax rates, and inadequate public services. Communities in the Hudson Basin and elsewhere have often been unable or unwilling to develop the facilities, including water-supply and sewage systems, needed to catch up with uncontrolled development. Some suburban communities have enacted zoning restrictions designed to exclude housing for low-income and minority families. In addition, some localities have resorted to moratoriums on any new construction that would overtax their existing capacity to provide services.

As an alternative to such stopgap procedures, the Town of Ramapo, in Rockland County, New York, undertook to control growth in accordance with an adopted plan that specified land uses and with a capital improvement budget that spelled out the timing of required facilities and services. Proposed projects are evaluated on the basis of a point system which credits the present and programmed availability of such services. Permits are denied for projects on sites lacking the required number of points. The plan was challenged in court, leading to a decision that is one of the most important in the field of zoning law in recent years.

The 1972 decision by the New York State Court of Appeals in *Golden* v. *Town of Ramapo* upholds the right of a community to restrict its own development through careful exercise of its planning, zoning, and capital budgeting powers, without having to compensate property owners for losses in current property values occasioned by forced postponement of their development rights. If a community commits itself to a long-range capital investment program that is not a mere guise for halting growth or excluding people, it may limit development to areas served by public facilities and thereby regulate growth in accordance with such a program. Moreover, as in the case of Ramapo, a community may regulate its development in accordance with a master plan that identifies areas to be maintained in their natural state, with concurrent provisions, such as average density, cluster zoning, and development easements to preserve open space and to provide related public amenities.

The following issues and questions arise:

1. If each community decides to control the amount and rate of regional growth that it will accept, will the needs of the region as a whole be met?
2. What kinds of mechanisms are needed to ensure that the allocation of growth among units of local government represents a "fair share" from the standpoint of both regional needs and local capabilities?

RPS-12: Impact of Fiscal Structure on Land Use Decisions

Fiscal impact is probably the single most powerful incentive in shaping land use decisions by local communities in the Hudson Basin region. In fact, assessed valuation often appears to be the major criterion for granting or denying zoning changes. Zoning ordinances are typically devised to maximize nonresidential uses, which are seen as net producers of revenue, in the hope of attracting tax ratables with low municipal service costs. This policy has the effect of encouraging low-density, large-lot residential development without adequate concern for natural resource allocation or accurate assessment of fiscal or social impact. At the same time, communities are often unwilling to accept needed but tax-exempt facilities.

In the decade from 1962 to 1972, local governments in New York became increasingly dependent on state and federal revenues. In 1962, total property tax collections came to $2.37 billion and total revenues were $5.2 billion, including education. By 1972, real property taxes had more than doubled to $5.4 billion, but total revenues had more than tripled to $17.1 billion. State aid went from $1.3 billion to $5.1 billion, whereas federal aid rose even more sharply, from $253 million to $2.62 billion. In the New York portion of the Hudson Basin, these increases have been accompanied by a declining relative dependence on the property tax. This is less true for Connecticut, which does not levy a personal income tax. Nevertheless, property taxes have gone up steadily in most areas, and are still a critical influence on local government decisions affecting land use.

The largest user of the property tax is the school district. New Jersey has adopted an income tax as a direct result of a court order to change the basis for funding education in that state. In New York and Connecticut, the seeds of change have been planted. The arguments being heard in the courts note the wide differences in expenditures per child and their relationship to the tax base per child, even under state-aid formulas that are supposed to correct such inequities. The equal protection clause of the Constitution is cited in arguments against the use of the property tax as the basic revenue source for public education. The trend of litigation of this issue could lead to changes that would remove much of the motivation for "tax zoning" by suburban communities.

Clearly the property owner has an obligation to pay his fair share of taxes. Traditionally, the criteria for a fair share of the tax burden have been based upon a mix of ability to pay and service rendered.

The real property tax does not measure up well under any of these criteria. If actual market prices are used to set tax valuations—and the trend is to do this more strictly—then the market's bias to value more land than is needed for intensive uses puts substantial pressure on those who would prefer to retain their land for extensive purposes (e.g., agriculture, forestry, open space). At the same time, the capital gains on land sales are taxed at the preferential rate. This tax advantage inflates land values. Frequently, tax districts that provide public services, such as sewer and water, charge on an average-cost basis for operating costs and on an assessed-valuation basis for capital facilities. This system may not charge enough for hard-to-service outlying properties; on the other hand, it may excessively charge the developed land to the benefit of the undeveloped land. For extensive land uses that do not need such services, this system of user charges represents a heavy cost burden that tends to force land into more intensive uses.

Other questions and issues are the following:

1. How can fiscal policies be adjusted to remove disincentives that thwart the pursuit of a community's development and resource-use objectives?
2. How can the necessity for "fiscal zoning" by local communities be reduced?
3. What would be the impact of shifting a greater share of local school and welfare costs to higher levels of government?
4. How can the inequities created when local communities host non-taxpaying regional facilities be reduced?
5. How can the fiscal disparities created by unequal distribution of industrial and commercial development among communities be reduced?
6. What would be the impact of reducing fiscal disparities among communities by intermunicipal sharing of tax revenue from major industrial and commercial development?

1.4 Governmental Capabilities for Environmental Management

The Hudson Basin region is made up of portions of New York, New Jersey, and Connecticut—three states that have quite different governmental structures. New Jersey, for instance, has little effective power at the state level and tenuous funding capacity. New York, by contrast, has one of the strongest state governments in the nation.

The charter county governments in New York are relatively strong. New Jersey counties, where executive and legislative functions are not separated, often lack strong professional policy and program direction. In both states, county legislatures and agencies play important decision-making roles. In Connecticut, on the other hand, county governments have been eliminated.

Governmental bodies whose decisions affect the area's environment are numbered in the thousands. There are 567 subcounty, general-purpose governments in New Jersey, 1550 in New York, and 169 in Connecticut. But the complexity of the region's institutional structures goes far beyond county and general-purpose municipal governments. Daily impacts are made by the judiciary and U.S. Congress and by various federal departments and agencies. In addition, there are interstate and intrastate regional bodies such as the Tri-State Regional Planning Commission, the Interstate Sanitation Commission, the Metropolitan Transportation Authority, the Capital District Regional Planning Commission, and the Adirondack Park Agency.

There is a host of local boards, commissions, and special districts that affect the environment: municipal planning boards, zoning boards of appeal, recreation commissions, environmental management commissions, sewer districts, water districts, mosquito control districts, and many more.

Strains at the Local Level

The most serious problems of institutional incapacity to manage the environment are at the local level. Most small local jurisdictions are run by part-time officials who have little or no access to professional expertise. The majority of local governments rely on part-time legal assistance to unravel the welter of laws, rules, and regulations that govern their operations. Often public officials are not aware of the nature or extent of their powers. In New York State alone there are 13 volumes of statutes, totaling 6000 pages, that deal directly with the structure and power of local government. Much more legislation on local operations affecting the environment is contained in statutes pertaining to matters such as education, highways, housing, public health, and condemnation.

Rapid population growth has placed tremendous stress on local governments. For years, they have strained their administrative and fiscal resources to build facilities such as schools, roads, sewers, and public water-supply systems and to hire the teachers, policemen, and firemen needed by their urbanizing communities. The sudden tapering off of economic growth in the early 1970s has left jurisdictions burdened with heavy debt service, whereas demands for public services must be met largely with revenues from a relatively static property tax base. In the region's major cities the leveling off of growth has been accompanied by a major shift in the social and economic composition of their populations, requiring greatly increased expenditures for public services such as welfare, education, and police.

The American system of sharing responsibility among local, state, and federal governments is largely rooted in the Constitution. Our history has been characterized by a continual search for an effective balance between the efficiency of centralized government, on the one hand, and the responsibility and accountability of local automony on the other. But if contemporary problems are too broad in scope to be dealt with by local governments acting individually, and if this inability is eroding confidence in government, then the present balance may need reassessing.

Dissatisfaction

There is an increasing dissatisfaction with the level and quality of public services. Much of that dissatisfaction is an inevitable result of the pressures of rapid growth. Traditional revenue sources and aid formulas do not have the flexibility to respond to such rapid change.

But there are other things that contribute to public dissatisfaction and frustration with government. One problem is that jurisdictional responsibilities do not correspond with logical service areas. Another is that people's expectations of government have risen. New public services have been introduced in recent years in response to changes in technology, scarcity of resources, increased awareness of environmental hazards, and the growth of social concern for and by the poor and the ethnic minorities.

Project participants have also noted an increasing tendency to question the status and role of public bodies charged with regulation. Such agencies were designed to protect sensitive areas of public interest and it was generally assumed that they would do so. But this assumption can no longer be taken for granted. From the federal level to the local boards of zoning appeal, regulatory agencies have developed vested interests in their areas of jurisdiction, as well as constituencies to which they respond. A local zoning board dominated by business and land development interests is likely to give high priority to increasing land values and fostering development. Similarly, one should not be surprised to find that the former Atomic Energy Commission's devotion to the development of nuclear power may, at times, have led to insufficient weight being given to the environmental (including social and economic) consequences of their actions.

Managing Interdependencies

One of the major concerns of this Project has been to explore the inter-dependencies between various components of the environment. The institutional deficiencies that made dealing with these interrelationships difficult, if not impossible, are well illustrated by the fact that transportation and land use, though highly interdependent, are administered at opposite ends of the governmental scale. Transportation, which affects land use, is for the most part governed by single-purpose federal and state institutions; control of land use, which determines the demand for transportation facilities, is the almost exclusive province of local government. Thus, decisions in land use and transportation are generally made quite interdependently of each other.

The institutions regulating zoning and the creation of subdivisions—and therefore land use patterns—are mainly local ones. The profusion of water and sewer services, the infrastructure supporting urban and suburban land use, is provided by both municipal and county institutions. In contrast, as the hierarchy of road types is ascended from local access roads to expressways, the controlling institutions shift to the state and federal levels. To the extent that transportation influences land use, the strongest influence is exerted by the higher levels of government, though that influence is often quite inadvertent.

It is noteworthy that transportation decisions are rarely consciously directed to shape the environment. The higher the level of government that is building a highway (and thus, ironically, the larger the facility and its impact), the less the project has been used to implement or reinforce any population distribution policy. This fact relates, of course, to the lack of an explicit population distribution policy at the federal or state level, even though so many federal and state programs directly and powerfully affect where industries locate and where people live.

Similarly, suburban residential development patterns are very much influenced by federal mortgage insurance programs. In fact, urban sprawl has been blamed in large part on the Federal Housing Administration, whose policies have historically provided strong incentives for construction of housing in outlying areas, thereby sapping the vitality of cities.

Compounding the problem is the incapacity of federal and state bodies even to monitor the multitude of lower-level decisions affecting land use. The capacity may exist in theory but it is limited in fact by the size and organization of agency staffs.

The case of the deepwater oil terminal (see pp. 25 and 52, Volume 2, Chapter 8, Section 8.2) illustrates another aspect of institutional deficiency in managing interdependencies. As shown by Fig. 1-4, the principal agency

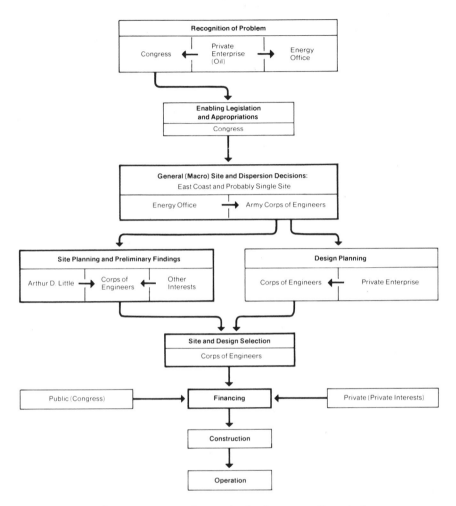

Fig. 1-4. Decision diagram for the deepwater oil terminal.

involved in the planning and decision-making for the terminal is the Army Corps of Engineers. The opportunities for input by other institutions are essentially in the site-planning stage and, to a lesser extent, in the subsequent financing stage.

In the financing stage, the Corps must rely either on Congress, which may be influenced by feedback during the planning and decision stages, or on private sources of funds. In the latter case, the emergence of a voluntary code of environmental ethics by private institutions may serve as a check on the Corps' decisions. However, once decision-making has progressed to this stage, there is likely to be little recourse other than to the courts.

In the site-planning stage, on the other hand, there is opportunity for intervention by other institutions (Fig. 1-5). The purpose of such involvement may be not so much to resolve the issue as to focus adequate attention on all aspects of it so that the best informed decisions can ultimately be made. This potential has hardly been realized in practice.

The issues are so complex and interrelated that many supposedly con-

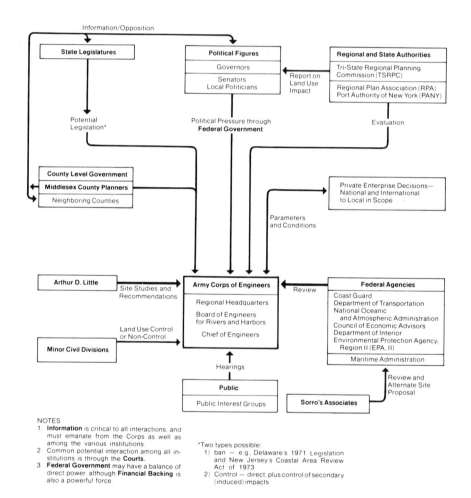

Fig. 1-5. Opportunities for intervention in planning the deepwater oil terminal.

cerned parties either decline to take a stand or simplify the issues so much that they are led to a less than well-informed decision. A firm stand by the institutions with power to make the principal decisions (the Corps of Engineers, in this case) can easily lead other potential intervenors (for example, the governors and legislators) to accept, or at least not seriously challenge, their decisions.

There are several reasons for this lack of effective power: (a) a perceived weakness of any opposition stance because of a lack of data and information upon which to base that stance; (b) the threat of embarrassment if the opposition is overridden or otherwise ineffective; (c) inability to form a sufficiently powerful bloc on account of the diversity of interests and lack of individual commitments; and (d) inability to force the Corps to consider the opposition or issues raised.

This last point is especially true for offshore activities that can stimulate subsequent onshore activities. Perhaps little can be done by concerned institutions until onshore activities are actually begun, at which time they could take the issue to court. By that point, however, the burden of proof of negative impacts would rest on the intervening parties, rather than on the Corps, to show that no such negative impacts exist. In addition, committed expenditures for matters such as site acquisition, engineering studies, and design often make it difficult to abandon a project.

The Environmental Protection Agency represents a potentially powerful influence on the Corp's decision. Interested parties could bring pressure upon the EPA to become actively involved in project planning and review, forcing consideration of important environmental interactions that may otherwise be ignored. One of the main roadblocks to this form of intervention, however, is the lack of data and information upon which to base both challenge and answers.

The Need for Criteria

One pervasive problem illustrated by the case of the deepwater oil terminal is the lack of clearly defined criteria for assessing projects that may affect the environment. Governmental and public criteria tend to be vague and often reflect conflicting objectives.

Clear objectives, and criteria for operationalizing those objectives, are essential. Without them environmental planning will lack direction and will be continually thwarted by "contingencies" and mitigating circumstances. Lack of criteria to guide governmental action is not the only problem. The environmental criteria used by private enterprise are also usually inadequate and misdirected. There are, however, some indications that a greater sense of environmental responsibility—reinforced by fear of governmental regulation and consumer reprisal—has become a factor in business decisions, and may help alleviate part of this problem.

Establishing Causal Relationships

Related to the clarification of objectives and criteria is the problem of establishing causal relationships between environmental conditions such as ambient air quality and pollution discharges.

Present regulatory controls are largely directed toward emission reduction, coupled with ambient air quality monitoring to assess the performance of the control. Such an approach often fails to address issues related to locational factors, both on the "micro" scale and on the regional scale. Further technical research is required to relate emissions and ambient air quality adequately. Such research should ultimately take into account (a) the regional focus of air pollution impact and control; (b) provision for future impacts in an area, e.g., as a result of induced growth near the oil pipeline terminus; and (c) the efficient use of our air, including its carrying capacity and the provision for catastrophic occurrences and episodes.

Ambient air quality data are useful because they relate to air pollution effects and they are relatively easy to collect, but they do not relate to regulation. Emission data, on the other hand, are less useful because of the elusive link to effects and because there are really too many data for any regulatory agency to collect. On the other hand, it is easy to relate emissions to regulatory efforts.

The Major Institutional Deficiency

States and many of their constituent units of local government have assigned most of their functions to single-purpose agencies and departments. The fundamental weakness of the single-purpose unit is the limited scope of its mandate, mission, authority, expertise, and funding, which result in the *inability to manage the consequences of its actions.*

Most environmental management problems in the region are caused, or at least complicated, by the traditional practice of treating problems in isolation, when they are in fact parts of an interdependent whole. The degree of interagency coordination possible with existing institutional arrangements is simply inadequate to the problems we face. More functional integration of related programs is urgently needed.*

*For additional discussion of single-purpose agencies see Chapter 6, Section 6.4.

Coordination and Integration Efforts

In the last decade or so, the limitations of single-purpose agencies have been increasingly recognized by legislative bodies at the federal, state, and municipal levels. Their efforts toward functional integration have taken several forms. In the late 1960s, for example, there was a movement toward the consolidation of functions in *superagencies.*

As a part of the Hudson Basin Project, a study was made of four environmental superagencies: the New York State Department of Environmental Conservation, the New Jersey Department of Environmental Protection, the New York City Environmental Protection Administration, and Region II of the United States Environmental Protection Agency (Enk, 1975).* The study showed wide variations in the capability of the four agencies. In most cases the formerly separate single-purpose departments seem to have retained their functional autonomy within the new umbrella agencies, although the federal EPA provides a few exceptions to this pattern. Overall operational and long-range objectives and policies still seem to be lacking in some cases. The day-to-day crises of the operating branches, such as the Sanitation Department in New York City, still occur. There is also a void in monitoring criteria to measure agency performance. Shortage of funding and personnel have particularly plagued the New York City EPA and the New Jersey DEP.

The federal revenue-sharing program, under which money is allocated to local governments for broad purposes, might encourage a shift away from the single-purpose approach. Yet it is at the local level that policy formulation and analytical techniques for assessment of impacts are the weakest, and where needed intergovernmental coordination mechanisms for meeting regional needs are in short supply.

A significant recent development in environmental management is the potential formation of *coastal zone commissions* in each of the three states. The creation of such commissions is encouraged by the federal Coastal Zone Management Act, which aids states in establishing programs for the effective management, beneficial use, protection, and development of coastal lands and waters.

As eventually defined by each state, the geographical jurisdiction of coastal zone commissions may reach inland only 1000 yards, but may include the shores of rivers, estuaries, and swamps wherever there is an admixture of saline and fresh water. The zone extends seaward to the 3-mile limit and can incorporate the regulation of the traffic on the surface, as well as the regulation of the use of the bottom and resources below.

*The New York City Environmental Protection Agency has since been dismantled. [Ed.]

The recognition of the coastal zone as a resource problem area and the establishment of a federal program to encourage its management are important and necessary steps. Coastal planning, however, like conventional land use planning, is a derivative of state powers. It has been customary for states to delegate land control to local governments. Now the states are being asked by the federal government to draw back selectively this delegation of authority so that coastal resources of state and national significance will not be dissipated by decisions based on local and short-range objectives. This is a difficult step and requires that the coastal states proceed with respect for existing prerogatives. If local governments become unduly alarmed at the shift in planning power, they can cripple or kill a coastal program.

Small watersheds have also been units of multiple-purpose resource management. Despite numerous studies, only a few small watersheds in the region are today formal organizations with projects. This can be explained partly by lack of local support and the sometimes related question that a technical basis for a favorable federal project evaluation could not be demonstrated. But perhaps the basis exists for something of a revival of the small watershed as a resource management unit.

The small watershed movement was an outgrowth of the small watershed protection program of the U.S. Soil Conservation Service (SCS). Its emphasis was on structural flood protection for farmland. Projects that involved other benefits, such as recreation and urban flood risks, were at a disadvantage until 1974, when a new Water Resources Development Act authorized at least 80% cost-sharing for flood-risk reduction measures such as flood proofing, relocation of buildings and activities, and purchase of wetlands and development easements. It remains to be seen whether the bias against urban flood risks will continue in the SCS program.

More to the point is the opportunity for the counties to use the small watershed as a unit of public management. Any government has problems providing a different intensity of management and control of resource use in one part of its jurisdiction than another. Counties in the New York portion of the region have few such opportunities, but the small watershed protection district is one of these. The enabling legislation puts emphasis on flood risk management and other water quantity questions. Water quality questions should also be considered, not the least of which would be nonpoint sources of pollution.

Another approach to improving institutional performance has been the "A-95" *review process,* through which requests for federal grants by local governments are reviewed by regional planning agencies. The Tri-State Regional Planning Commission, for instance, is the review agency for grant applications from the tristate metropolitan region. This process has had only limited success in achieving functional integration or true coordination, but has helped to foster intergovernmental cooperation.

New York has a rich history of experimentation with the *state central planning and coordination* function. The fiscal crises of 1970 and 1975 saw the neutralization and eventual abandonment of the function, but it taught several valuable lessons. New York's experience suggests that the task of organizing and coordinating the central planning and budgeting functions is an exercise in the delicate balancing of the tensions between needs and capacities; between the powers to plan and the powers to control the expenditure of public funds; between the legislative and executive branches; and between the needs for regional perspectives and the desire for local control. The experience also indicates that the strong support of planning by the chief executive can only go so far. Of critical importance is the need for public perception of environmental interdependencies and public recognition of the need for institutional capacities to deal with them. The environmental management councils and commissions recently created in New York State, although focused primarily on the physical environment, are one means of fostering such perception and recognition.

Within the existing context of public ignorance and suspicion, and the lack of explicit policies, government officials frequently deal with environmental management issues in terms of relatively narrow political objectives—supporting a program or agency when immediate interests are served and dismantling it when their constituents no longer preceive its value.

Theoretically, these complex and interrelated forces can be brought together to provide for planned environmental impact. The actual process, however, is frequently of an adversary nature. Thus the balance among interests impinging upon the environment is often arrived at by a contest of power (be it financial or legal or rational) rather than by comprehensive, cooperative analysis and planning. The *Boomer* v. *Atlantic Cement* case (see p. 52) illustrates the power and potential breadth of this adversary process.

Much can be gained in environmental management from enriching the professional mix that is brought to bear on problems. Political and court decisions will undoubtedly negate and frustrate the efforts of both the proposing staff and reviewers, who together could be the possessors of the best body of expertise available to make the internal recommendation in the first instance. Of course, the technical experts may not have the best qualifications for making public value judgments. Both types of expertise are needed to arrive at the "best" decisions.

Resort to the courts is often the worst way to deal with matters that should be treated in a dynamic decision-making framework. No doubt justice in one form or the other will tend to be done, but formalized adversary proceedings are doubtful forums in which to implement any kind of comprehensive planning, even by default.

To avoid "solutions" through litigation, there must be more interagency cooperation and more access for various points of view at the early stages of planning and decision-making—before positions have hardened, and before "sunk costs" have made it expedient to throw good money after bad.

Among the devices that might help to avoid such conditions are the following:

1. *Early notice.* A proposing agency should be required by law or regulations to give all other parties in interest early notice of its intentions, so that those other agencies could determine how the proposal might affect their areas of competence or responsibility.

2. *Accountability.* Elected and appointed officials should be made aware of their responsibilities, with sanctions and penalties for capricious, irresponsible, and uninformed action.

3. *In-house advocacy.* In-house advocates of different viewpoints within agencies, perhaps on temporary loan from other agencies but charged with doing productive work, might act as constructive critics of the programs and projects of their sister agencies.

4. *Centers of competence.* There should be more consideration of designation of "centers of competence" both within the government and within the learned bodies at the universities and professional societies. They would have review power and automatic standing, including the right of review, the right of notice and so forth, to encourage them to respond on specific matters that they are qualified to examine.

5. *Multiagency task teams.* Teams of various professionals, preferably ad hoc, assigned to specific subject areas should be fostered in governments. Competent professionals and administrators brought together for specific purposes, within a limited time frame and with a limited mandate, can achieve a productive working relationship, free of the apparent necessity of protecting their long-term positions or prerogatives.

6. *Incentive programs.* The clear recognition of effort is a great incentive. Professional merit and protection of the less well-represented public interests should not go unappreciated. One is tempted to suggest some American equivalent of the British honors system, ceremonialized in the traditional Queen's Birthday Lists. Carrying titles of merit behind one's name is not unknown in this country, as with academic degrees, and there is no reason why this could not be expanded into the public service in a meaningful and serious way.

7. *Terms of reference.* There is little doubt that some of the difficulties

between agencies stem from disagreement on terms of reference, terminologies, semantics, and other areas of potential misunderstandings. This should be remedied by systematic attempts to establish clearer common vocabularies and other common points of understanding from which to proceed.

8. *Performance monitoring.* The legislative and administrative branches of government should share responsibility to monitor agency performance in discharging assigned environmental management reponsibilities and achieving interagency cooperation.

With the exception of item 8, all of these devices make up one possible spectrum of cooperative administrative actions which could be directly fostered and effectuated by the agencies themselves, provided the will exists to bring them about. None alone will mean much; taken together they could do much to decrease reliance on the formal adversary process.

1.5 Environmental Management Needs

Although much of the region's environment is still of high quality, the increase in serious, persistent, and widespread problems noted by Hudson Basin Project participants reflects the basic deficiencies in the region's existing environmental management capability.

The following list of ten environmental management needs that require priority action is drawn from the work of the Hudson Basin Project's participants. A comprehensive listing would, of course, be much longer; these ten were selected because they have the highest component of "unfinished business." This is not to say, for example, that the need to expand opportunities for leisure time and recreation is not of great importance; instead, many problems not listed are well recognized and substantial resources have already been allocated to them. Society is relatively further along in meeting needs of this kind. The New York State Legislature has recently taken a significant step in environmental management by expanding the Scenic and Wild Rivers Act. Comparable progress has not been made on stubborn problems such as housing or land use planning.

In a general way, the items in the following list are ranked according to the magnitude of their unfinished business. Thus, the list constitutes an initial cast at setting priorities for some of the more important goals of environmental management in the Hudson Basin region:

1. Rehabilitate inner city environment and control urban sprawl.
2. Reduce health hazards in the work and home environment.
3. Improve institutional capacity for regional water management.
4. Fill gaps in land use planning and regulation.

5. Moderate solid waste generation and improve disposal techniques.
6. Protect ecologically significant land and water resources.
7. Integrate the planning of transportation modes and land use.
8. Moderate energy demand and augment supply.
9. Strengthen interstate arrangements for air quality management.
10. Optimize public and private investment policies affecting the environment.

Note that each of the above needs is either regionwide or exists in local areas throughout much of the basin. Each has a demonstrable and direct relationship to the physical, social, and economic welfare of the vast majority of the basin's people. This is a significant consideration, because the effectiveness of these and other initiatives will inevitably be judged by their constituents in terms of each citizen's very personal cost–benefit analysis.

Four of the ten listed needs have been selected to illustrate interdependencies among the area's problems and needs and to indicate some of the secondary and tertiary consequences of efforts to meet needs on a single-purpose basis.

Rehabilitate the Inner-City Environment and Control Sprawl

A basic conclusion of the Hudson Basin Project is that "the urban problem" is one of the most important components of the overall problem of environmental management. It is in the basin's urban areas that most of its people live and spend most of their time. The way the area's cities are built and used affects the quality of life in both the urban and rural environments in fundamental ways. In the area of environmental health, for example, the two most serious problems of the region are its deteriorated and degrading housing stock and its dangerous and depressing places of work.

The urban problem requires coordinated action in two interrelated areas: rebuilding and replacing the decaying and obsolescent physical plant of the urban core while controlling the expansion at the periphery. The Hudson Basin is using about twice the amount of land necessary to handle its growth. The resulting pattern of urban sprawl not only is expensive to provide with public services, but also squanders basic natural environmental resources. For example, in the process of constantly expanding our cities, we are filling our swamps, polluting our subterranean water tables, and wasting energy on the extensive transportation systems required for this spread-out pattern of development. In the process, we are polluting the air with the by-products of internal combustion engines needed to move about in such a decentralized environment. Perhaps the single most important environmental management objective that the Hudson Basin might pursue would be to improve the processes by which its cities are expanded and rebuilt.

The prospect of rebuilding the region's cities while controlling urban sprawl raises a broad array of interdependent physical, social, and economic issues. There are a number of basic preconditions for meeting this need. Among the more important ones are

A viable economy that ensures all citizens' access to adequate personal income.

A stable society with the institutional capability for providing the health, safety, and educational resources necessary to permit the individual to develop to his or her full potential. This, in turn, requires sufficient financial resources for the public and private sectors to provide needed services and facilities.

An agreed-upon human settlement policy for the region which sets forth basic goals, objectives, and implementing actions for land use and population distribution.

In large measure, a viable regional economy is determined by national, and even international, factors that also strongly influence the region's institutional capability to provide health, safety, education, and other services, and to control land use and population distribution. Despite this qualification, there remain many opportunities for initiatives to improve the general quality of life within the study area. However, as the work of the Task Group on Land Use and Human Settlement points out, there is an overriding principle that has been largely ignored to date, and which has hobbled past efforts to establish more rational patterns of human settlement in the Hudson Basin study area.

This principle, sometimes referred to as "carrying capacity," can be stated as follows:

There is an upper limit to the amount of activity that the resources of a given environment can support over a sustained period of time without depleting these resources and/or adversely affecting the welfare of its occupants.

To illustrate, there is an upper limit to the number of people with a given income, culture, and value set that can be safely, healthily, and happily accommodated in a given land area with a given kind and condition of housing, and a given level and quality of support services and facilities. A tour through the deteriorating sections of New York City and other older urban areas in the basin suggests that such upper limits, or carrying capacities, have already been exceeded for millions of people.

It can be argued, however, that a change in any of the "givens" such as housing, support services, or public facilities alters the carrying capacity of the environment. Indeed, some of the region's worst slums have lower population densities than some high-income areas where occupants are housed in structures of similar age and type. Raise incomes, improve the quality of housing and community services, ensure public health and safety, and deal with personal and social disorganization, and what might otherwise be an "overloaded" environment becomes livable. Thus, such "givens," which are social and economic as well as physical, are in fact the "resources" referred to in the preceding definition of carrying capacity, and must be regarded as integral components of the environment. The same principle applies to the natural as well as the man-made environment. Similarly, there is an upper limit to the noise that airports can generate without adversely affecting the psychological and physiological well-being of the people who live in the surrounding areas. In the case of Kennedy International Airport, it has been estimated that this upper limit has already been exceeded for more than 750,000 people (NAS/NAE, 1971).

There is also an upper limit to the amount of groundwater that can be withdrawn from a given aquifer without depleting it. In the absence of alternative water supplies, limits are thereby imposed on the number of people that can live or work in the area. There is evidence that this limit is rapidly being approached, or possibly has been already exceeded, on Long Island, where saltwater intrusion is also contaminating groundwater supplies.

There also is an upper limit on the environmental stress which commercial and industrial development, transportation, and housing can place on the resources of any natural environment without impairing or destroying basic ecological functions, possibly in irreversible ways. This upper limit may have already been exceeded in portions of the New Jersey meadows or the lower bay of the Hudson River estuary. Similarly, there is an upper limit on the amount of pollutants which the region's water resources can receive, whether they be chemicals from industrial and agricultural activities, organic wastes from domestic sewage, or surplus heat from electric power plants.

Although it can be argued that such "upper limits" can, and in some cases should, be raised by technology (i.e., higher-density housing, quieter aircraft, artificial groundwater recharge, reducing pollution emissions, sewage treatment), it must be noted that there are also both scientific and economic limits to what technology can do, as well as aesthetic and value-based limits to what it *should* do.

Viewed in these terms, the questions of where to build, how to build and where not to build become critical. It becomes clear that settlement patterns are constrained by land suitability, technological and managerial capability, and economic capacity as well as by simple consumer preference and economic advantage.

Public interest groups such as the Regional Plan Association and Mid-Hudson Pattern, Inc., and a number of the region's state and county planning agencies, as well as Hudson Basin Project participants, have urged that planning policy encourage the clustering of future growth in and around existing centers, principally near the region's cities (RPA, 1968; RPA and Mid-Hudson Pattern for Progress, 1973). One advantage of a policy of containment and concentration is that it reserves major land areas for future needs that are impossible to foresee at this time. Such a policy would also have the effect of conserving the region's natural resources by protecting the open countryside from sprawl, reducing the costs of public services by concentrating them in specific high-density areas, and conserving energy and reducing pollution by fostering more effective mass transit and cutting down on travel distances.

Of course, there is a wide variety of alternative scenarios for applying such a concept in the Hudson Basin region. Moreover, the political consensus and the institutional capacity required to adopt and implement such a policy have yet to be created. Nevertheless, the idea does represent an emerging consensus on the direction of future efforts to understand and manage the environment of the Hudson Basin.

Improve Institutional Capacity for Regional Water Management

Although the Hudson Basin region still contains rural areas that are not supplied with adequate water, the principal and more difficult water problems are associated with the millions of people concentrated in the vast areas of urban sprawl that have developed during the past several decades. Nassau and Suffolk counties and the counties north of New York metropolitan area exemplify such problem areas.*

Three options are available for supplying water to suburban development: connection to an existing public water system; use of a separate water system which may be owned and operated by the developer or, eventually, by a governmental entity; or use of individual home water systems (normally wells, which draw on groundwater). Concurrently, the developer may elect to provide a community sewage collection and treatment system, hook up to public sewers, or use individual septic tanks or cesspools.

During the past two decades, tens of thousands of individual water and sewerage systems have been built to serve homes in new suburban developments. Because as much as an acre or more of land is needed to ensure

*See Chapter 4.

disposal of the waste effluent and separation of the septic system from the well, the American dream of the single-family home has created a demand for huge amounts of land. A common problem has been the inability of some types of soils to absorb the discharge from individual home systems. In dense developments, groundwater contamination has become a serious health or nuisance problem. Other problems include high maintenance and replacement costs, dependence on a continuous supply of electric power for water pumps, and the frequent need to treat well water to remove excess amounts of naturally occurring chemicals such as iron, sulfides, and carbonates. At some point, such problems provoke demands for community water and sewer facilities. Expansion of community systems leads to the search for new water supplies from limited groundwater reserves or from surface sources requiring new reservoirs or to the use of lakes or rivers which, because of pollution, often require treatment systems.

These pressures, in turn, have secondary effects on other components of the environment. The water demands of the City of New York and the surrounding counties, for example, have already resulted in the preemption of large upstate areas in the Hudson and Delaware river basins for reservoirs. Proposed new reservoirs threaten the scenic gorges and valleys of the Adirondacks, while New York City's proposed withdrawals from the Hudson River might move the river's "salt front" upstream to contaminate the water supply of Poughkeepsie. Excessive freshwater withdrawals in eastern Long Island have already depleted the groundwater, resulting in saltwater intrusion.

Paradoxically, new and expanded sewer systems pose their own hazard to human health, recreation, and biological communities by polluting land or water with the sludge left by the treatment process. Research at centers such as Rutgers University Water Resources Institute has identified the water pollution problems created by stormwater runoff, particularly from urban land. Such problems are additional examples of the strong interdependence existing between water and land resources.

Water, then, is a critical factor in determining the location and timing of community growth. When water supply is coordinated with other services such as sewerage, transportation. and energy, it becomes a potent tool for managing human settlement. Water quantity and quality also have a direct bearing on ecological communities (e.g., aquatic life, forests, wildlife). Space does not permit a full discussion of all the interactions of water resources management with the other policy areas studied by Hudson Basin Project participants. However, a quick overview can be gained from the Interaction Matrix (Fig. 1-6) developed by the Water Resources Task Group.

In the Hudson Basin region, pollution resulting from urban development, industrial growth, and agriculture and rural erosion has degraded water

WATER RESOURCES (sub areas)	Land use/ settlement	Transportation	Environmental systems	Energy systems	Land use/ natural resources	Air resources	Biological communities	Health	Leisure
POLICY AREAS									
Municipal water supply	R		A					R	A
Industrial water supply	R	A	A	A					
Waste disposal	R		R	R	P	A	R	A	A
Power	P		R	R		A	A	A	
Irrigation	A				A		A	A	A
Transportation		R			P		A		R
Recreation	R	R	P	P	A	A	R	P	R
Biological systems	P	P	P	P	R		R	A	R
Aesthetics	R	P			A		R	P	R
Flood control	R	A	A	A	R		A	A	A

Legend (arrow symbols):

↗ (A) Indicates Water Resources Sub Area significantly affects Policy Area.

↵ (P) Indicates Policy Area significantly affects Water Resources Sub Area.

⤾ (R) Indicates reciprocal relationship.

Fig. 1-6. Interaction matrix.

quality in the lower Hudson River and downstream from the Albany–Troy area. Pollution-control programs initiated by the City of New York and other cities with state and federal financial support should alleviate these conditions in a few years.

Second-home and recreation developments have caused concern over the deterioration of water resources and the effect on the natural environment of the Adirondacks, Catskills, and similar scenic areas.

The New York City water supply, involving the interbasin transfer of water into the Hudson Basin from the Delaware River system, has created conflict with adjoining states. In light of these problems, the establishment of well-organized and effective institutions for management became a high-priority need in the Hudson Basin region. Because of their strategic influence on other policy areas, proposals to develop new water-management mechanisms are often frustrated by conflict and controversy.

With few exceptions, responsibilities for water supply and wastewater treatment and disposal have been delegated to local governments by the state. Cooperation among communities within counties has been fostered by state policy for well over a decade, with state funds provided to the counties as incentives to develop regional water-supply and sewer agencies, but action has been slow. Regional water pollution control institutions, too, have been promoted by the state with little success to date. Now, under federal guidelines and funds, the regional control of water pollution is again being attempted but the outlook is not promising.

Since the early 1950s, New York City has experienced two major droughts. In one case, only a 25-day supply of water was stored in its upstate reservoirs. In search of a regional solution to a problem affecting millions of people, the state legislature established the Temporary Commission to Study the Water Supply Needs of Southeastern New York. Earlier, the federal government had sponsored a Northeastern United States Water Supply Study to respond to the needs of cities and industries for an ensured supply of water. The proposals developed by both the Southeastern New York Study Commission and the larger federal study have become the casualties of conflict over where the water will come from and how it will be allocated; the proper way to organize for intergovernmental cooperation; who is to pay for new developments; and where the responsibility will rest for the management of proposed programs.

The Hudson Basin is the only major drainage basin in the northeastern United States which lacks an arrangement for coordinating water-resources development with the related subjects outlined in the interaction matrix. Both the Delaware and Susquehanna river basins have river basin commissions. New England water resources are coordinated by the federal–state partnership in the New England River Basin Commission. Although it might not necessarily be desirable for the Hudson Basin to establish such a commission, some kind of mechanism is needed to translate water needs into water-management programs that are sensitive to changing conditions, that respond to a variety of public values, and that do not significantly impair the environmental quality of the region.

Moderate Solid Waste Generation and Improve Disposal Techniques

Solid waste problems in the Hudson Basin area are growing. Pressure on limited disposal facilities has increased not only with increased population but also, more importantly, with increased per capita consumption and higher standards for pollution control. For example, the residues produced by new air pollution control devices and sewage treatment plants, stricter burning regulations, and on-land disposal of dredge spoil in compliance with water-quality standards have all contributed to the increased volume of solid waste. The increased variety and quantity of packaging materials used in consumer products have also made an impact. On the other hand, where kitchen grinders are used extensively, the burden of disposing of organic solid waste has been shifted to sewerage systems.

Although sheer quantity is probably the most critical solid waste problem, leading directly to health and aesthetic problems, the "quality," or composition, of waste is also cause for concern. Heavy metals dumped into the many improperly designed and operated landfills in the region have polluted both soils and water supplies, affecting drinking water, recreation, and biological communities. The cumulative impact on groundwater is not yet fully known.

Sewage sludges, dumped off Brooklyn in the New York Bight, have been loudly indicted for fouling the beaches. Runoff containing wastes, fertilizer, and soil from agricultural lands poses serious pollution problems in the region that are difficult and expensive to solve.

One measure of the scale of modern solid waste production is New York City's output, which is estimated at 30,000 tons a day—more than Paris, London, and Tokyo combined—and increasing by 3 or 4% per year (Elish, 1973). On a per capita basis, these rates are 200 to 300% greater than those of Western European countries (Weast, 1972). EPA projections suggest that in the next decade per capita rates in the United States will increase by over 20% (EPA, 1971c).

New York City is not the only community in the study area faced with an immediate problem of where and how to dispose of solid waste. Responsibility for solid waste management is split between the private and public sectors and among various levels of government. The federally funded "New Jersey Solid Waste Management Plan" (Planners Associates, 1970) describes a situation similar to the one in New York State:

> The problem of solid waste management most apparent to New Jersey's citizens is the rapid increase in the price they must pay for collection and disposal services. The citizens of the State are also becoming more aware of the aesthetics of the existing disposal facilities, particularly those which they must pass with any regularity. To the communities of the state, the problem of solid waste management manifests itself in the increasing difficulty of finding disposal facilities when current sites are exhausted, and also in the rising costs of providing collection service to their citizenry.

The report's analysis of current practice revealed that

1. There are basically 567 independent waste management systems now operating in the state, far too many to function effectively according to most authorities.
2. The collection and disposal system is too fragmented to invest in new technology or to sponsor research and development.
3. The data, which were adequate for estimating current waste generation, were found to be too imprecise to be of use in projecting future levels.

Both states are encouraging counties to play a larger role in solid waste management and to promote the development of technologies for recycling, improved incineration, and the production of valuable heat and electricity as energy by-products of waste disposal. Such technologies have been invented but are just now being tested in large scale applications. Many areas have been reluctant to commit huge investments in unproven systems. Furthermore, many do not feel they can afford increases in disposal costs—even though disposal represents only 20% of the solid waste dollar, the rest going toward collection. The higher disposal costs may in many cases be offset or even exceeded by the returns from the recovered energy and materials.

The handling of solid waste in Dutchess County, New York, is typical of many suburban areas in the New York and New Jersey portion of the Hudson Basin. Most domestic solid waste is collected by private companies, although there is public collection in some of the more urban areas and no collection at all in some more rural areas. Costs of collection for the individual household, which are approximately $5.00 per month, have risen by as much as 50% over the past 4 years.

Solid waste disposal, on the other hand, is mainly handled by publicly owned and operated sanitary landfills. Each of the 30 communities in the county has its own site, with the exception of five contiguous communities, constituting the most densely populated area in the county, which have joined together in one landfill operation. This cooperative venture was undertaken because four of the towns ran out of individual landfill space acceptable to their residents, while the fifth, Poughkeepsie, was forced to abandon its incinerator by new state air pollution laws.

Two things became clear in the process of locating a joint site: residents were unwilling to tolerate a landfill operating within sight or hearing—or smell; and the five communities by themselves could not afford a technology other than landfill. After considerable controversy, it was decided to lease from the county a landfill site next to the Dutchess County Airport, which two of the five communities were already using. The site had the virtue of being (a) already off the tax rolls, (b) already in use, (c) out of sight of existing residences, and (d) near sources for soil cover. In the absence of any specific county plan for the siting of disposal facilities, the county agreed to lease the site, which is still in use.

Several consequences, which in retrospect appear obvious, were unanticipated. The sloping site lies between the airport and Wappingers Creek, just upstream from the county's Airport Park, with its swimming beach and brick bathhouse. Stormwater runoff from upland areas quickly drained into the landfill, leaching pollutants into the adjacent creek. Only months after the jointly operated landfill was opened, the county was forced to close its swimming facilities. Meanwhile, the amount and potential effect of toxic heavy metals disposed of at the site are unknown.

Solid waste management entails consideration of a wide range of contributory causes and side effects. Settlement patterns, socioeconomic demands, and the use of energy and other resources affect the quantity and composition of solid waste. Collection and disposal have to comply with human health standards and avoid degradation of land, water, and air resources. Transportation is an integral part of collection and disposal.

The tax burden, even when collection is privately paid for, is substantial; municipal and county governments in New York State were expected to spend more than $500 million for waste management during 1975.

Project participants have noted that the solid waste crisis is exacerbated because the public generally sees only part of the problem. The individual citizen is most directly interested in whether his garbage is collected on time and in the cost of the service. What happens after refuse containers are emptied usually is not a matter of concern, unless the resident lives or works near a disposal facility. Given this partial perception of the situation, it is not surprising that the public is seldom motivated to support needed public actions in managing solid waste.

Public officials and environmental leaders, on the other hand, have a more holistic view of the problem. When interviewed in seven northern New Jersey counties and 20 upstate New York counties, the leaders named solid waste as one of the three most important environmental issues

(Capener *et al.*, 1974; Holcomb *et al.*, 1974). No significant technological breakthroughs are needed to moderate solid waste generation and to improve disposal techniques. However, the achievement of significantly improved solid waste management depends on the modification of some of the fundamental conditions under which our society operates—its economy, its resource consumption preferences and practices, and the functions and organization of government.

One major precondition for change is certainly the dissemination of more adequate information to engender clearer public perception and strengthened will to take the required actions.

Integrate the Planning of Transportation Modes and Land Use

The achievement of better integration of various transportation modes, as well as between transportation and land use, is a major regional environmental management need. Better integration is required not only to achieve the efficient movement of people and goods but also to save land, energy, air quality, and dollars for public services. The accompanying map (Fig. 1-7) tells a dramatic story: growth in the New York metropolitan area tends to follow the access provided by rail, mass transit, and, in modern times, highways. To say that the results have been something less than optimal is an understatement.

As pointed out in the earlier discussion of the need to rehabilitate the inner city environment and control sprawl, the region has used about twice the amount of land actually needed for urban expansion, resulting in damage and depletion of the natural resources of air, land, water, biological communities, and excessive costs for public services and transportation. Efforts to conserve energy and control air pollution by reducing dependence on the private automobile are frustrated because for huge numbers of people throughout the Hudson Basin, alternative transportation does not exist and cannot be provided at today's costs. With the exception of the denser portions of the region's cities, the population is in general simply too dispersed to be served economically by available mass-transit technology.

The region's present pattern of growth did not "just happen." It is the result of forces which can be predicted and managed if we wish to acquire the understanding, will, and institutional capacity. With better regional development patterns in the future, however, the private automobile and mass transportation could complement one another rather than compete, as is presently the case. The same observation is true of air, intercity rail, and water transportation modes; each has a logical role to play in an integrated transportation system for the region. As it is, however, public investment in air and highway transportation has resulted in the decline of the region's rail

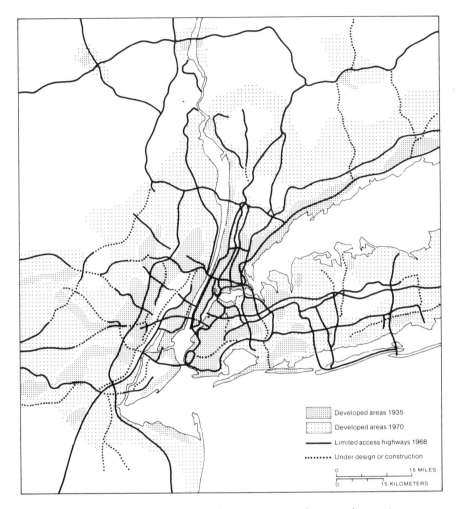

Fig. 1-7. Highways and urban development—New York metropolitan region.

and water facilities, which are two of the most efficient forms of transportation available in terms of criteria such as energy, land use, and air pollution.

The interacting relationship between land use and transportation is illustrated in conceptual terms in Fig. 1-8. A local community decides to control land use (1), or perhaps decides not to control it; in either case, the resulting pattern of human activity results in trips (2) which are, in turn, expressed in transportation needs (3). Transportation facilities (4), such as highways, are built in response to these needs. This is a classic phenomenon; highways are generally built to "serve" land use.

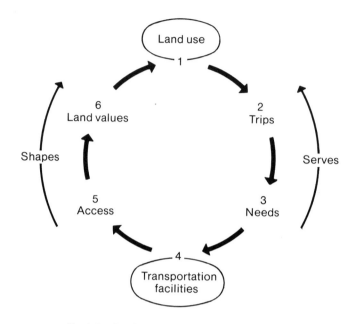

Fig. 1-8.   Land use–transportation facilities cycle.

Something else also happens, however. The availability of transportation facilities affects access to land (5), and access affects land values (6). The cycle is completed as land values tend to determine land use. Thus, highways and other transportation facilities not only serve existing land use but also tend to shape future land use. A similar cycle can also be used to describe the interacting relationship of land use and other functions such as sewers, water, and energy.

The Interstate 84 case (Glick and McCormick, 1975) provides an example of how some of the principles and phenomena just discussed are actually playing out in the region. A segment of I-84 passes through Orange, Dutchess, and Putnam counties in New York State that, together with Fairfield County in Connecticut, constitute the northern zone of the New York metropolitan area.

I-84 was completed as part of the national Interstate and Defense Highway System. Its funding, location, and design were under the control of the federal government. Its principal purpose was to supply a route from New England to the west and south, avoiding the New York metropolitan area and providing for the more efficient and speedier movement of people and goods. The highway also serves as the major east–west link for the growing suburban communities.

The highway promotes both intra- and interregional access and mobility. Increased accessibility, however, has increased the demand for existing vacant land. The magnitude of this effect has depended on the market and on the character of the land and the access provided. The area through which this part of I-84 passes is within easy reach of a substantial latent demand and much of it is highly suitable for development, consisting of gently rolling fields and woodlands. In an economic sense, I-84 increased the price of land for development by lowering overall transportation expense to and from the land. Market reaction to this phenomenon was typically swift. Land in key areas was snapped up, in some cases years before the road was actually built.

Areas adjacent to interchanges are often the first targets of land developers. Because of misconceptions by the highway planners about the outlook for growth in the area, or for reasons of economy, or both, most of the I-84 interchanges were designed in a "diamond" configuration, suitable only for stable, rural areas. This interchange design uses the minimum amount of land and affords the least protection from land development around the interchange. Developments such as shopping centers, apartments, and industry are drawn to the interchanges and generate high volumes of automobile traffic. As a result, the interchange of I-84 and Union Avenue in Newburgh had to be rebuilt to a higher standard within 10 years of its original construction. There are several other places where rebuilding will be necessary in the future.

The impact of I-84 on land use extended beyond the interchanges. Cheaper and easier journeys to work, shopping, recreation, and markets stimulated the demand for land for housing, commercial, industrial, and institutional developments. These in turn generated a new round of demands on local governments for services such as local roads, sewers, water, schools, police and fire protection, and refuse disposal. The highway also opened up the region to second-home developments for those living outside the region who could take advantage of increased access to the open countryside.

The most important negative effect of I-84 has been the dimming of the area's identity as it becomes indistinguishable from the national image of suburbia. How soon southern Dutchess County will come to look like northern New Jersey is a matter of increasing concern to the area's residents.

The impact of the four-lane highway on outdoor amenities is twofold. Existing outdoor amenities can be diminished in attractiveness by the encroachment of development. Equally important, increased land costs complicate the problem of protecting open space. The strain is felt especially strongly by local governments whose financial resources are already stretched by demands for other services such as schools, roads, sewers, and water, which must receive higher priority during early stages of community development.

But the impact of a major highway improvement such as I-84 reverberates for miles. In competition with newly accessible outlying areas, the older areas of the region's cities decline. Gradually, the focus of economic activity—especially retail trade and manufacturing, but also service industry—shifts from established centers to the areas near the interchanges and strip developments along main arteries. Because the area's poorer and older populations are concentrated in the urban centers, they suffer diminished opportunities for jobs and other activities and services close to their residences.

Another effect of major highway improvements such as I-84 is to promote greater use of the automobile and a corresponding decline in the public transportation on which the poor rely. Thus, the poor are isolated from the new sources of employment and services even as their accustomed resources are disappearing.

This scenario, which is drawn from the early experience of I-84 and other similar highway projects in the region, reflects the fact that the New York metropolitan area has yet to adopt a coherent and workable set of regional development goals and policies which integrate land use with transportation. Although there are policies for each transportation mode and for land development in specific subareas of the region, these policies often tend to conflict and compete. They do not add up to a coherent whole.

Conclusion

Studies by the broad array of planning agencies serving the basin demonstrate that the area does not, in general, lack the technical capacity to address the myriad environmental management needs confronting it. What is lacking, in many cases, is the public understanding necessary to generate the political motivation and will to address such needs, and the institutional capacity to implement the required plans and programs.

1.6   Directions for Response

The weakness of environmental decision-making lies in the limited capacity of institutions to identify, assess, and manage the consequences of such decisions. The following steps are recommended to correct present deficiencies:

1. Improve information management.
2. Broaden assessment processes.

3. Increase and strengthen arenas for conflict resolution.
4. Improve the substance and explicitness of policy.
5. Strengthen institutional capacity to formulate and execute policy.

Proposals relating to the last two initiatives in this list—improving environmental policy and strengthening institutional capacity to carry it out—have been the focus of a large number of reports and studies, including those of prestigious groups such as New York's Joint Legislative Committee on Metropolitan and Regional Areas, New York's Temporary Commission to Study the Powers of Local Government (the Wagner Commission), New Jersey's County and Municipal Study Commission, and the Federal Advisory Commission on Intergovernmental Relations (ACIR). But few of these well-considered recommendations for policy and institutional change have been implemented. The underlying cause of this inaction, this Project concluded, is that the *preconditions* necessary for effective policy formulation and implementation are often lacking. Those preconditions include public understanding of the implications of existing environmental trends and of the secondary and tertiary effects of past and proposed actions, and better procedures for involving the affected public interests in the resolution of environmental conflicts.

Thus, the preconditions for improved policy formation and institutional performance (steps 4 and 5) would be assisted by improved information management, broadened assessment techniques, and stronger conflict resolution arenas (steps 1, 2, and 3). These five steps are fairly well recognized, although their interdependent nature is not as clearly perceived. Taken together, they constitute the elements of a strategy which, if pursued over time by all affected interests, would respond to the primary need to improve institutional capacity for environmental decision-making. The remainder of this chapter attempts to articulate such a strategy and suggests some initial actions for its implementation.

Step 1: Improve Information Management

In evaluating the basin's existing information base for environmental decision-making, one of the Project's summer conference work groups concluded that "Sound information is the most fundamental requirement. There is a wealth of information on the basin in the files of public and private agencies, but much of it is not readily accessible either to the public or to public decision-makers, especially at the local level, and there is no facility for centralizing and correlating that information." (Hudson Basin Project, unpublished report, 1974).

There are also serious gaps in the knowledge that would be required to assess the environmental impacts of various types of proposed projects or activities in the basin. The reliability of much of the information hitherto compiled, and of conclusions drawn from it, is often questioned because the work has been done by or for proponents of various kinds of development.

To strengthen environmental decision-making, information must (a) provide a valid basis for decision, (b) be organized in usable formats, (c) be available to the prospective user, and (d) be accurate and credible with respect to the objectivity of those who produce it.

Failure to meet one or more of the above specifications is one of the major causes of the substantial differences in the way environmental problems are perceived by affected interest groups. The prescription for improved information management emerged as a response to this failure. Simply defined, information management treats the acquisition of information, its organization for use, and its communication to affected interests as elements of a continuous and coordinating process. "Management" suggests that such efforts are most effective when they have defined goals and priorities. This, in turn, calls for a degree of consensus among information producers and users on what information is needed, what formats are appropriate for its expression, and what media are to be employed to ensure its timely injection into the decision-making process.* Significant progress could be made if research in the Hudson Basin region were organized and pursued under four levels of information required for environmental management:

1. Basic inventories (What do we have?)
2. Systems dynamics (How does it work, and how is it changing?)
3. Prediction (How might it change in the future?)
4. Prescription (What do we want to do about it?)

Each of these information levels provides input for the next. Together they provide a framework within which researchers and funding institutions and users can develop an agenda of needed environmental research for the region. In conclusion, the Project did not find any general need in the basin for more data per se. Rather, the critical need is for better organization, analysis, and communication of existing data. There will, of course, be a continuing need for new data for specific purposes. Inevitably, too, there will be a gap between the information relevant to a decision and the information actually available. The test of whether there is "enough" information is whether additional information (i.e., new data or existing data organized differently) would alter the decision.

---

*See Appendix C for a summary of Project findings on information needs.

Step 2: Broaden Assessment Processes

Assessment, as used here, is defined as a process to determine the primary and indirect consequences of actions that significantly impact the environment. Thus, assessment can be used to clarify the relationships, dependencies, and interactions among objectives, policies, and programs. To be useful in identifying the multiple and subtle effects of seemingly single-purpose actions, assessment requires a definition of the environment sufficiently broad to permit the resultant actions to be fully tested. Such a definition includes not only natural and man-made components (e.g., land, water, air, biological communities, housing, and transportation) but also the nonphysical dimensions of the environment (e.g., psychological, social, economic, and institutional) which affect man's welfare.

Assessment already is well established in some decision-making processes. Since 1969, the National Environmental Policy Act has required "environmental impact statements" for federal decisions having major effects on the environment, including nonfederal projects involving federal funds or permits.

Title I of NEPA states that it is federal policy to ". . . foster and promote the general welfare, to create and maintain conditions under which man and nature can exist to productive harmony, and fulfill the *social, economic, and other requirements* of present and future generations."* NEPA also requires that agencies of the federal government "utilize a systematic, interdisciplinary approach which will insure the integrated use of the natural and social sciences and the environmental design arts in planning and decision-making which may have an impact on man's environment."

In the face of this broad charge, the administration of NEPA may be too narrow. For example, NEPA assessments of major construction projects rarely address the programs and policies that engender such projects. In addition, consideration of policy alternatives to a given project (such as reducing demand rather than increasing supply) is sometimes precluded because the assessment assumes existing policies as "givens."

Hudson Basin Project participants also noted that NEPA, as currently administered, does not require sufficient analysis of nonphysical impacts of proposed projects. The scope of NEPA environmental impact statements should be expanded to include more consideration of physiological, social, economic, and institutional effects.

Greater attention should be paid to measuring costs and benefits of policies and projects to affected individuals, groups, and society as a whole. More work is needed on the problem of quantifying "second order" bene-

*Emphasis added.

fits and costs, such as the effects of a given environmental proposal on income distribution. Assessment should also be concerned with effects on various groups within society of matters such as fairness and equity, health, opportunities for participation in public affairs, and the achievement of satisfactory levels of goods and services.

In addition to serving as an early warning system for identifying and dealing with future conditions, assessment can also be retrospective. Evaluation of past actions provides useful feedback for current and future decisions.

Some assessment processes have been established within the Hudson Basin, although their scope is not as broad as is advocated in this report. Connecticut law provides for assessment of state-financed projects, but concern about its ambiguity has resulted in a moratorium on its enforcement. Connecticut, like New York and New Jersey, may, at its discretion, require impact statements for power plants; however, no assessment of other private projects is apparently required by Connecticut law.

New Jersey's requirement for the assessment of state-funded projects is apparently limited to certain areas defined in its Wetlands and Major Coastal Zone Facilities Review acts (which also require such assessments for private projects).

New York, like New Jersey, requires various kinds of assessment for certain private projects requiring state permits. Also, New York's "little NEPA" law, the State Environmental Quality Review Act (SEQR), requires state review of publicly funded "actions" having significant effects on the natural environment. *

So far, there has been relatively little experience with the broad scope of assessment recommended here. One obstacle to more inclusive assessment is the inadequacy of existing processes for information acquisition, organization, and transfer. Lyle and Von Wodtke, who developed an information system for environmental planning under a Ford Foundation grant, have observed that one of the major limitations in applying their system is the problem of achieving "integration of information systems dealing with the physical environment with those used in dealing with social and economic factors" (Lyle and Van Wodtke, 1974).

The problem of unnecessary time delays in decision-making is being addressed in current efforts to improve assessment procedures. Opponents of proposals frequently use the review and permit process to force consideration of what they believe to be more desirable alternatives. Unfortunately, they sometimes also use such processes not to solve a problem but to forestall its solution.

---

*SEQR has now been extended to cover nearly all state and locally funded or permitted actions that would have significant environmental impacts. [Ed.]

To avoid needless delay, assessment should play a part in the earliest stages of the planning process. A valid criticism of NEPA is that required reviews come so late in the process that alternatives are often posed simply as "straw men" by proponents to demonstrate compliance with NEPA's requirements, and by opponents as a pretext for delay. If provisions were made for assessment early in the process, questions could be raised and dealt with, and legitimate alternatives could be considered, in a timely sequence. The resulting process would be more responsive, less subject to misuse and, overall, permit more prompt decisions than is currently the case.

The establishment of wide-ranging assessment need not stagnate the decision-making process in mountains of paperwork. Indeed, better techniques and management might actually result in a reduction of the time and effort required to review a given proposal. For example, it is widely recognized that significant portions of NEPA impact statements are redundant and that large sums of money have been spent to gather identical information for different proposals. Previously acquired information and analysis could be gathered and made available under a standard format for all subsequent assessment of similar proposals.

New analyses need only be done for significantly different aspects of proposed actions. Indeed, reform along this line is already under way at the federal level (Anonymous, 1975). In addition, if assessment is expanded to policies and programs, assessment of specific projects would be facilitated. Such efforts could go a long way toward streamlining the assessment process.

Hudson Basin Project participants also expressed concern about who performs the initial assessment. NEPA has been criticized because a project's sponsors are usually the initial authors of the impact statement. There was considerable support among Project participants for independent and neutral entities to prepare environmental impact statements on proposals that affect the environment in significant ways.

Developing more appropriate and practical assessment procedures is in itself a major research need. It is a goal that will not be easily achieved.

Step 3: Increase and Strengthen Arenas for Conflict Resolution

Hudson Basin Project studies clearly show the need to increase and strengthen available opportunities to define and represent conflicting interests in the variety of processes involved in environmental decision-making. One Hudson Basin Project participant noted, "It is necessary to hunt for potential complementarity (among competing interests) and to learn how to enhance it. Competing relationships need to be identified and analyzed in terms of tradeoffs rather than absolutes."* Another participant noted the need to create arenas where people could view and compare their values in the context of other values. Others suggested the need to strengthen the mechanisms for the creation and support of public consensus at the community level.

The subjects of environmental conflict are numerous and varied. They include matters such as problem definition; the identification of goals, policies, and plans; the issuance of approvals and permits for specific projects; and the regulation of rates and prices for services and commodities.

A variety of arenas at the local, regional, state, and national levels have been created by the public and private sectors to aid in the resolution of environmental conflicts. Public hearings before legislative, administrative, and judicial bodies at all these levels on varied matters such as zoning and land use, highway development, power plant siting, and water resource management are familiar examples of governmentally created arenas. Citizens advisory groups, appointed by government action, are increasingly used to extend interest group participation in environmental decision-making. Also, self-constituted public interest organizations play important roles in conducting research, convening and informing various affected parties, and developing positions and recommendations which also provide input to such decisions.

Such efforts are increasingly visible and plentiful in urban areas. This is due in part to the requirements and incentives for public participation in planning and decision-making provided by federal legislation of the 1960s. At this local level, issues are usually more readily perceived and engender more direct conflict and concern. Although citizens have the easiest physical access to arenas for the resolution of local conflicts, their intellectual access is often limited by a bewildering array of officials, boards, commissions, policies, and procedures. Moreover, it is at this level that the citizens' motivation to argue their interest in decisions affecting their environment is often frustrated by lack of authoritative information about the effect of a given decision and the relative desirability of alternative courses of action.

In contrast, at the regional level, where the multijurisdictional governmental setting further complicates environmental issues, there are relatively few formal mechanisms for environmental conflict resolution. The lack of such resources is particularly evident in the New York metropolitan area, where existing regional governmental agencies have made little effort to create them. Privately supported public interest groups, such as the Regional Plan Association, Mid-Hudson Pattern, Inc., and the Middlesex–Somerset–Mercer Regional Study Council, have helped fill the vacuum by

---

*Ruth P. Mack (Institute of Public Administration), 6 August 1974, letter to Chadbourne Gilpatric.

assembling relevant information and bringing affected interests into open discussion of regional issues. However, such regional efforts by both the public and private sectors need to be expanded and strengthened throughout the Hudson Basin.

State and federal legislatures, through their advisory committees, hearings, and debates, provide arenas for the resolution of conflicts on a scale ranging from local to national. Such deliberations, however, are often inaccessible to individual and local interests. This is also true of administrative hearings of public agencies.

The judiciary has also played an increasing role in environmental conflict resolution. As previously discussed, however, there is growing concern that too much reliance is being placed on the courts for this purpose. The courts can and have clarified and strengthened the application of existing laws such as NEPA. But courts cannot initiate; they can only react. Even then, their decisions are necessarily limited by the issues brought to them and by the quantity and quality of the evidence developed in the adversary process. The courts are hampered in situations where basic information does not exist or is not brought to bear. Also, the adversary process is not designed to serve unidentified or unrepresented interests. Finally, court calendars are overcrowded with a backlog of cases and this often precludes a timely decision.

The courtroom works best as an arena of last resort. This places both practical and theoretical limits on its ability to correct the deficiencies of the legislative and administrative branches of government. Therefore, society must continue to expand efforts to improve environmental management in ways which are not dependent on the courts.

Arenas for environmental conflict resolution in the Hudson Basin could be strengthened in three ways. First, their number and coverage could be expanded, particularly at the regional level. Second, their accessibility could be improved by reducing the complexity and increasing the legibility of their processes, providing technical assistance to those who lack the resources to provide their own, and improving geographic access. Finally, the availability of information and analysis concerning alternative actions and their effects on affected interests could be increased.

By such means, not only can existing interests be served, but also previously undetected interests can be identified. Given the incomplete knowledge and imperfect processes with which groups define and defend their interests, it is not surprising that individuals often have a dim or erroneous perception of where their interests lie, or the actions that should be taken to advance them.

These reforms would encourage clarification of values and more meaningful debate and bargaining among competing interest groups. It is quite likely that in such a give-and-take situation any superficial consensus or conflict might evaporate. In due course, this kind of well-informed public haggling might be expected to produce decisions grounded in a deeper awareness of the real interdependence of competing interest groups within society.

In summary, the environmental decision-making process must be sufficiently legible so that those affected by it can gain access to it and will, indeed, feel encouraged to do so. Good information management and assessment procedures are the essential preconditions for purposeful public participation. The achievement of these first three recommended measures will provide the indispensable foundation for the last two, which involve the substance of policy and the institutional capacity for its formulation and implementation.

Step 4: Improve the Substance and Explicitness of Policy

Substantive policy may be defined as "a settled course of action toward a stated objective." Current controversies over the shape and direction of federal energy policy, the problem of integrating the planning of regional transportation modes and land development, New York City's fiscal crisis, and frequent voter rejections of local school budgets and bond issues are familiar illustrations of some of the consequences of existing deficiencies in the substance of policies which shape and enhance all dimensions of the region's environment.

Although it was not within the scope of Hudson Basin Project primary objectives, a number of Project participants included in their reports policy proposals that address the substance of regional environmental management.

For instance, the Land Use/Human Settlement Task Group proposed a policy of "reciprocal limits," which would discourage growth in environmentally significant (fragile) areas by providing disincentives to suburban sprawl and incentives to new development within urban areas.

Several participants advocated more effective control of the timing and location of community facilities such as transportation, sewers, water supply, and energy as a means of indirectly influencing the location and timing of land development at local and regional levels.

Restructuring of taxation policies was strongly advocated to improve the fiscal capabilities of communities in the region and to redress revenue disparities which inspire "have" and "have not" communities to environmentally destructive competition. The Land Use/Natural Resource Management Task Group recommended a steeply graduated capital gains tax on land transfer profits, based on duration of ownership and amount of "unearned increment," as a curb on land speculation.

Project participants have pointed out that policy also operates in tacit form, and that such implicit policy can have profound effects on environmental management. There is, for instance, no explicit policy to prompt scatteration of development in the region or to weaken urban centers, to impose heavy costs on both city and suburban dwellers, and to deplete natural resources needlessly. Nevertheless, the aggregate of a variety of federal, state, and local actions does, in fact, produce these results.

Unfortunately, in current assessment procedures implicit policies are not usually recognized as such. Thus, there is little opportunity for affected interests to come together to resolve the issues they raise. It is important to make implicit policies explicit, so that those which are unacceptable can be rejected and those which promise good results can be formally adopted and translated into effective programs. Because it is not in the nature of the public sector to view policy in implicit terms, a special challenge is posed to public interest groups to recognize and question this potent aspect of policy.

Step 5: Strengthen Institutional Capacity to Formulate and Execute Policy

As noted previously, a number of private and public groups have published well-considered reports and recommendations for institutional strengthening which have relevance to the Hudson Basin. It was not this Project's purpose to duplicate this work. Rather, this Project addressed underlying causes for what appears to be a widening gap between what the region's policymaking institutions are being called upon to do and what in fact they are doing. As the pace of change continues to accelerate and as issues become more complex, finding solutions to this problem is a matter of increasing urgency.

Each of the four types of initiatives discussed so far (improvements in information, assessment, conflict resolution, and policies) contribute to this Project's central recommendation to improve environmental decision-making. Such efforts, however, will not be effective unless they are accompanied by corresponding improvements in institutional capacity to formulate, adopt, and execute the policies and programs that will flow from these efforts. Project participants felt that three complementary but nevertheless distinct approaches should be simultaneously pursued to achieve this kind of improved institutional capacity.

The first approach is to *strengthen the fiscal and administrative capability of governmental agencies to utilize existing power and discharge existing responsibilities.* Planning and zoning, subdivision control, building codes, capital improvement budgets, and environmental protection laws are examples of existing growth management tools which are not being fully utilized by local governments in the region. The Town of Ramapo in Rockland County, New York, has received national recognition for its example of what can be accomplished when local government decides to take its growth management responsibilities seriously and applies available powers with skill and precision.* Improved manpower training for public officials, model codes, ordinances, administrative procedures, and technical assistance are examples of important ways to strengthen the existing policy and program capacities of the public sector.

The second approach is to *restructure existing institutions to discharge new duties and responsibilities.* In some cases, capacity for policy formulation and execution could be improved by a transfer of responsibility from one governmental level to another. For example, Project participants concurred with the Wagner Commission and other study groups that it would be desirable to transfer to the county level certain responsibilities that are now handled at the municipal level (TSCPLG, 1973). These include the review and veto of land use decisions that significantly affect the interests of several jurisdictions or the county as a whole. A bill that would permit New York State to reclaim from local governments similar land use decision-making power for matters of "critical environmental concern" to the state as a whole was considered by its legislature. Although the measure failed to pass, it is likely that such proposals will be reconsidered in the future.

The third approach is to *create new institutions to discharge responsibilities that cannot be handled effectively by existing institutions.* Examples advocated by some participants include the creation of multi-county districts for environmental planning and management in accordance with state guidelines and in cooperation with localities. The Adirondack Park Agency is an example of one such intercounty agency. One task group proposed the formation at the state level of an Institute for Technical Assessment and Research to prepare independent impact reports on major environmental actions.

Recommendations under all three approaches tend to focus on a specific institutional need cited by many participants—that of increasing the effectiveness of federal, state, regional, and local land use decisions. Stronger federal and state policies are required as a framework for local decision-making. Since land use decisions directly affect nearly all other aspects of the environment, they must receive special and continuing attention. It is a Project conclusion that, despite the spotty performance to date, comprehensive planning is still one of the best tools available for developing effective policy, and that future planning efforts will be substantially enhanced by the five types of initiatives discussed in this chapter.

As an instrument for comprehensive planning, the "development guide" is finding increasing application in the Hudson Basin. Unlike the traditional master plan, which focuses on a desired "end state," the development guide

*See p. 63 and Volume 2, Chapter 2, Section 7.2.

is more flexible and emphasizes the process of guiding growth and change within a general framework of adopted policy.

Appendix H includes an extract from the "Twin Cities (Minneapolis–St. Paul) Metropolitan Development Guide," which reveals the scope of one such effort in a region that has gained national recognition for its success in establishing a continuing process of regional development coordination as an integral part of governmental decision-making.

In brief, the guide consists of a compilation of policy statements, goals, standards, programs, and maps prescribing the physical, social, and economic development (public and private) of the municipality, county, region, or state to which it applies. The guide can function as a manual for the use of policymakers and administrators in preparing and evaluating specific proposals affecting the environment. It can also provide a checklist of factors to be considered in project planning and development efforts, and spell out the standards and criteria against which decision-making bodies can judge the acceptability of such efforts. The need for such an instrument is particularly acute at the regional level, where problems of achieving consensus and coordination for development policies and programs are complicated by multiple jurisdictions.

The work of the Nassau–Suffolk Regional Planning Board, the Tri-State Regional Planning Commission, the former New York State Office of Planning Coordination, the Regional Plan Association, and Mid-Hudson Pattern, Inc., provides examples of this approach by public and private planning groups in the region.

Conclusion

The five types of initiatives discussed in this section are intended to indicate directions that could be pursued, in the region and elsewhere, in designing policies and programs for improved environmental management. These initiatives are also intended as a general framework for possible future collaborative efforts to develop a regional research and action agenda for the guidance of researchers, policy makers, and funding institutions concerned with strengthening environmental management in the Hudson Basin.

1.7   Some Next Steps

A wide variety of persons skilled in science and public policy have participated in the Hudson Basin Project (See Appendix B). There is a risk that if they all go their separate ways at the end of the Project, the energy generated by their coming together will be dissipated, efforts to pursue the Project's conclusions and recommendations will soon become diffused, and everybody's business could end up being nobody's business. The alternative is to communicate the Project's results to a broader audience and to enlist interested individuals and institutions in a renewed collaboration to test and pursue the recommended directions for action.

Implementing Process

A suggested general process for implementing the Hudson Basin Project's recommendations is outlined in Fig. 1-9. Column A restates the idea that there is no single environmental issue in the region that transcends all others, unless it is the question of how to strengthen the ability of the region's decision-makers to account for the environmental consequences of their actions, and to meet the kind of environmental management needs identified by this Project (column B).

Taken together, the previously discussed initiatives listed in column C comprise a strategy to improve decision-making and to provide a general framework for developing and considering specific implementation programs and projects. Column D suggests implementation action at two levels:

1.   Design and execute projects and programs that lead to more effective decisions to solve specific environmental problems in the region.
2.   In the context of specific problem-solving efforts, develop, refine, and test the concepts and techniques underlying the five response strategy initiatives and, at the same time, promote their understanding and broader application by affected interests and institutions.

Finally, paragraph E states that the cumulative effect of such efforts would be to foster needed public consensus concerning the policies, programs, and institutions required for making improved decisions about environmental management in the basin, thus moving toward the prime objective identified in column A.

This proposed process does not suggest that the diversity and competition of ideas that characterize environmental decision-making in the Hudson Basin can or should be eliminated. Rather, it suggests that the vitality of this kind of pluralism will be expressed more creatively and productively if there is a general underlying agreement on basic facts and conditions, goals, and priorities.

Prime Objectives

The prime objectives of a post-Hudson Basin Project effort would be to increase the capacity of the region's institutions to make the decisions re-

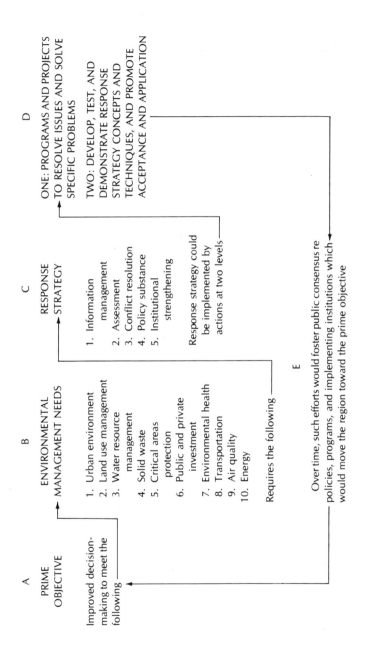

Fig. 1-9. Outline of a process to strengthen decision-making for environmental management in the Hudson Basin region.

quired for managing the kinds of environmental problems and needs identified by this Project.

A first-phase effort would have three objectives:

1. Communicate the Project's results.
2. Engage the region's institutions concerned with environmental management in devising an agenda for research and action, using as an initial input materials from the Hudson Basin Project.
3. Initiate implementing programs and projects.

Such a first-phase effort to implement the Hudson Basin Project's conclusions could lead to a broader consensus regarding the need to pursue a continuing collaborative endeavor among users, funders, and producers of research required for environmental management.

Premises

Post-Hudson Basin Project implementation efforts should be guided and constrained by a number of premises. Three of the most important are

1. The Hudson Basin Project was initiated as an experiment, and the implementation phase must by definition be considered a continuation of a developmental process. Future tactical decisions will depend on how the process unfolds.
2. The need to improve environmental decision-making in a regional context exists throughout the nation. No demonstration of practical approaches to this task has been effective. The Hudson Basin Project has established the preconditions for such a demonstration in this region.
3. Such a demonstration can be undertaken only with the active support of many public and private agencies within and outside the region, and the direct participation of many skilled persons from such agencies. There is already in existence a substantial body of information and ideas that could contribute to a successful demonstration program.

Scope

Although this Project had no preconceptions concerning follow-up activities, participants were concerned throughout with the question, What then? The process for strengthening decision-making for environmental management, illustrated by Fig. 1-9, was developed in response to this concern. It reflects this Project's effort to explore a very wide variety of environmental matters and the broadened view of the environment that has emerged.

Given this somewhat ambitious definition of a desired process, it is important that post-Hudson Basin Project implementation efforts be carefully circumscribed to respect the practical limitations of resources and the voluntary basis on which participants would work. Accordingly, such efforts should not attempt to address all environmental matters affecting the region, but rather concentrate on those which, on the basis of priorities to be consensually established, would be of maximum assistance to public and private decision-makers.

Proposed First-Phase Program

The Hudson Basin Project has identified environmental problems and their underlying causes sufficiently to support its principal conclusion concerning the need to strengthen environmental decision-making. However, improving environmental decision-making cannot be accomplished in the abstract. What is needed are investigations aimed at developing solutions to real-world problems.

Primary Task

Although the Project's task group reports and other research contain recommendations on a number of the subjects examined by them, prescribing solutions or approaches to specific problems was considered to be the proper focus of whatever follow-up activities might result. Therefore, the *primary task* is to develop and execute projects and programs that lead to more effective decisions about specific environmental problems in the basin. Over time, under a general research design, such efforts could produce a body of knowledge concerning practical ways to improve the decision-making process by the more effective employment of the five initiatives listed in the proposed response strategy (Fig. 1-9, columns C and D). Illustrations of problems to be given first consideration in the pursuit of this task, derived from the Project's task group reports, include

1. Policy and program conflicts between and among land use management, air quality control, energy production and consumption, and transportation
2. Conflicts resulting from locally controlled developments entailing regional costs and benefits, as well as regionally initiated developments which impose local costs and benefits (e.g., energy facilities, water supply projects, and waste disposal)
3. Achievement of equitable water allocation among competing uses

Policy studies have been made on environmental problems in various locations at different times. The task envisioned in this program would concentrate such efforts within a field laboratory having a defined geographic scale. Such an approach produces a number of significant benefits. It affords an opportunity over time to address a basic cause of past environmental management deficiencies and failures, namely, the lack of in-depth understanding of the linkages and interdependencies between and among components of the environment, producing decisions that result in unanticipated secondary and tertiary consequences. Also, the resources and capabilities of environmental management institutions can best be analyzed and strengthened in a regional context under a variety of circumstances on a continuing basis. Furthermore, the opportunity is afforded to derive general principles from a series of specific and interwoven case studies.

Environmental research efforts made outside an overall strategy for the improvement of decision-making processes will continue to have a limited impact on the quality of life in the basin. Lacking such a strategy framework, such research, like many planning efforts, ends up on the shelf, isolated from the political processes which determine what will be done about the area's problems.

Given the limited financial resources available, continued interest in funding environmental research that is unrelated to a means for injecting the results into decisions affecting the environment is highly questionable.

Concurrent Tasks

The pursuit of the primary task would be supported by concurrent efforts in three areas.

(1) Information Transfer   The results of the Hudson Basin Project—its basic findings and recommendations as well as the details contained in its body of reports—should be brought to the attention of public and private leaders for their information and comment. Meetings with the general public and a series of small, informal sessions are proposed to be held with regional leaders to foster understanding of the Hudson Basin Project's purpose and to transfer its findings and recommendations. Several such meetings have been held in this and other regions. The insights and feedback to be gained through such discussions provide important guidance to the other tasks in this proposed first-phase program.

(2) Regional Research Agenda   There is a need for the region's principal information users, producers, and funders to develop collaboratively a statement of research and action priorities for their guidance. Because funds for research are limited, and timely and effective action is required in meeting the region's environmental management needs, a continuing general consensus concerning priorities and a division of labor should be achieved, and as soon as possible.

Although this Project has acquired a substantial body of information on regional environmental problems, needed research, and action, as previously noted, it was not possible to obtain consensus on a regional research agenda. Under the aegis of the proposed organization, an operationally useful agenda could be formulated and continually revised to reflect changing requirements.

(3) Basic Research Basic research is needed on the five response–strategy initiatives. As noted earlier, the applied problem-solving efforts involved in the primary task will provide some opportunity to develop, test, and validate the five response strategy initiatives. It is likely, however, that research directed primarily at development of the concepts and techniques underlying these initiatives will also be required. Therefore, basic research, although fed by applied research on specific problems, should be a distinct task in the collaborative program.

The first three initiatives in the response strategy, *information management, assessment,* and *conflict resolution,* are seen as a means of advancing the understanding and use of the remaining two, which focus on *improving the substance of environmental policy* and *strengthening institutional capacity* to implement policy. Considerable attention has been given to basic research on the last two initiatives. Therefore, the bulk of the proposed basic research would focus on the first three, where the need for additional knowledge is relatively greater.

Progress to Date

Initial organizational support for the establishment of the proposed collaborative has been provided by Mid-Hudson Pattern, Inc., through a grant from the Harriman Foundation. A small group of individuals involved in the Hudson Basin Project, representing a variety of disciplines, has been convened to assist in the design of the organization and the development of its initial program.*

This action will provide the basis for a subsequent effort to broaden participation in the proposed collaboration by involving information producers, users, and funders in the pursuit of the general program outlined in this section.

Concluding Overview

The picture that emerges from this Project's study of environmental problems in the Hudson Basin is one of disparities: between resources and

---

*As a result of this activity, The Center for Environmental Management has been formed within Mid-Hudson Pattern, Inc. [Ed.]

demands, between the complexity of problems and the public's comprehension of them, and between the urgency and difficulty of the issues to be faced and the capacity of institutions to deal with them. It is a Project conclusion that significant opportunities exist to experiment productively within the basin to reduce such disparities.

The Hudson Basin study region is a particularly appropriate laboratory for a continuing experiment in improving public perceptions and strengthening institutional processes affecting environmental management. The area contains a wide variety of human settlement patterns, ranging from intensely urban to rural. It displays a broad range of human conditions as well as large geographic areas in a relatively natural state. It includes an international center of trade and communication. The Hudson Basin is, however, part of a larger and relatively mature region when viewed from a demographic, economic, and resource-development standpoint; indeed, signs of decline and deterioration are highly evident. The people of the basin, in their efforts to deal with pressing economic and social challenges, must learn to adapt to resource scarcity while at the same time minimizing the stresses being placed on their environment.

The processes, initiatives, and implementation efforts discussed in this report could, over time, lead to significant improvements in environmental management in the Hudson Basin.

Chapter 2

LAND USE/HUMAN SETTLEMENT

2.1 Human Settlement Patterns and Environmental Quality Relationships

The Relevant Questions

Although it is beyond the limited purview of this task group to define and determine the demographic or environmental parameters for the basin, it is relevant to pose the basic questions that must be understood and answered if a rational settlement pattern is to be devised. They are

1. How many people should be in the region?
2. What are the environmental loads resulting from each use and activity?
3. What are the constraints?
4. What are the consequences of exceeding the constraints?

The first question need not imply an absolute or finite number. Yet for each quantity and distribution of population there is an implied impact on the environment. Therefore, it is important to be able to estimate and project the results of human activities on the natural system. This leads to the second

Members of the Land Use/Human Settlement Task Group: Lee E. Koppelman, Dorn C. McGrath, Vincent J. Moore, and William K. Reilly.

question. Sufficient knowledge and experience are available to respond to these issues. The third question can only be partially answered at the present time. The scientific base required has to be greatly expanded. However, broad issues of water and air pollution and, to a more limited extent, thermal pollution can be examined. The deficiency is not solely in basic science. There is a need to translate scientific findings into management language. This leads directly to the fourth question.

Environmental Loading Concept

Much environmental stress can be viewed as a result of our traditional patterns of human settlement. In some cases, excessive density has put strains on our natural systems (air, water, etc.), but perhaps the most destructive settlement pattern has been "sprawl" or rapid suburbanization. The assumption has too often been that some natural system (such as the ambient air, a waterway, or the earth itself) will dispose of wastes that the economy rejects. It has become all too apparent, however, that the natural systems that comprise the region's physical environment (including airsheds, watersheds, wetlands, beaches, rivers, and streams) have limits that society has failed to respect. "Environmental overload" symptoms are present in many parts of the region. It is encouraging that the traditional vague sense of public confidence in the inexhaustibility of the region's resources is giving way to a growing concern that neither the resource base nor compensating technology may be sufficient to guarantee acceptable environmental conditions in the future.

Environmental Limits

Attempts have been made in recent years to advance the concept of land "carrying capacity" or suitability for development. The concept relates the amount and location of development to characteristics of the land slope, soil permeability, soil compactibility, vegetation, depth of the water table, and other features. Ideally, determinations are made of how much of a given kind of development can be sited without adverse impact on the landscape. Several experiments testing the feasibility of this concept are under way at Lake Tahoe, in Vermont, on the South Fork of Long Island, and in several other areas.

The concept of carrying capacity is perhaps most useful in dealing with critical environmental areas—shorelands, wetlands, recharge areas, scenic areas—where the ecosystems are so fragile that any intrusion of unnatural development can wreak havoc. The concept has less utility in those areas where it is costly or difficult, but technologically possible to build. As a land use planning tool, carrying capacity is least useful where the land can support any number of alternative development schemes. The decision-making perspective no longer can be just scientific; it has become economic, legal, social, and political. We are probably further along in devising the methods to make development sensitive to the land from a scientific perspective than we are from these other points of view.

2.2   Public Policy and Regional Settlement Patterns

Existing Conditions—Overall Patterns

As the demographic analyses in this chapter indicate, land use and human settlement patterns in the Hudson Basin reflect the dominance of a highly mobile, affluent urban society, in which the primary locational constraint has been economic, rather than ecological or environmental. Public policy affecting land use and settlement patterns has, in the past, been fragmented and localized, permitting the evolution of regional settlement patterns that threaten large-scale environmental deterioration beyond the control of any single level of government or functional agency.

Within the basin, however, there are major variations in land use and settlement patterns to be considered in setting an overall public policy for guiding future growth. The various physiographic zones of the Hudson Basin shown in Fig. 2-1 can be described in terms of three general types of land use/human settlement patterns. The following is a general description of those patterns, along with analyses of population trends for the separate physiographic zones defined by this task group.*

Metropolitan Land Use and Human Settlement

The Hudson Basin contains three major metropolitan complexes. The largest is the New York Metropolitan Zone, which covers, in addition to the New York Standard Metropolitan Statistical Area (SMSA), smaller SMSAs in Connecticut, New Jersey, and the lower Hudson Valley (Poughkeepsie). The second metropolitan complex, the Upper Hudson Metropolitan Zone, is focused on the urban centers of Albany, Schenectady, and Troy at the confluence of the Hudson and Mohawk rivers. The third metropolitan complex, the Upper Mohawk Metropolitan Zone, is focused on the cities of Utica and Rome at the headwaters of the Mohawk River.

As illustrated in Fig. 2-2, the three metropolitan zones have similar overall population growth trends—relatively stable or declining core populations,

---

*Note that the physiographic zones described in this section differ from the subregions used for the statistical data given in Appendix E.

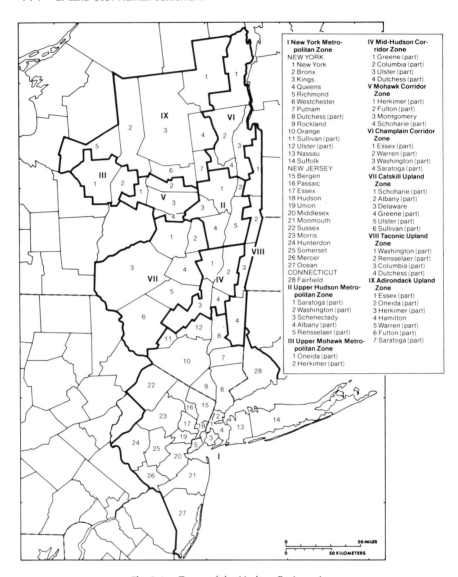

Fig. 2-1. Zones of the Hudson Basin region.

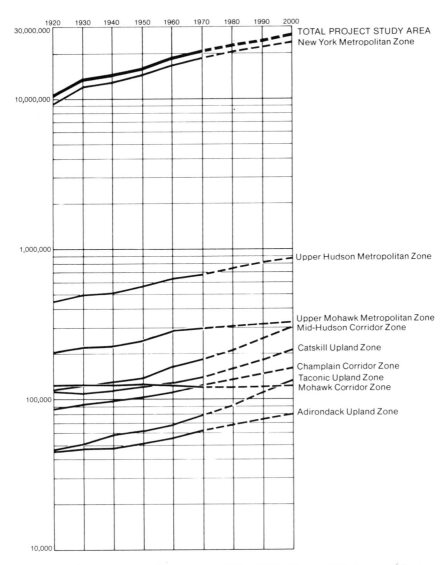

Fig. 2-2. Settlement trends and projections, 1920 to 2000. (*Source:* U.S. Bureau of Census, 1970, and New York State Office of Planning Services, 1972.)

more rapidly growing suburban sectors, and exurban areas where growth rates are as rapid or more rapid than the suburban sectors. Thus, the metropolitan zones of the basin show a common pattern of decentralization and dispersion from their high-density core areas to the surrounding countryside for many miles out.

The general metropolitan land use pattern can be constructed from these trends. The cores are beset by problems of deteriorating residential, commercial, and industrial land areas, although the more viable portions of the cores have come under renewal and redevelopment over the last decade. Whether these efforts are sufficient to stem the powerful forces of decentralization and core decline remains to be seen, but some promising beginnings have been made in each of the zones. In each case, the cores have extensive vacant land resources, particularly in riverfront locations, which provide a potential for large-scale infill developments.

From the cores out, urban density, generally responding to high-speed highway transportation improvements, quickly drops. Much of the suburban sector in each zone can be written off as developed, although generous open spaces are interspersed throughout the suburban sectors. Low-density residential development (on the order of 4000 persons per square mile) occupies much of the suburbanizing areas, but it is largely in the form of sprawl and only occasionally concentrated in outlying, higher density, traditional communities.

Open space still dominates most of the exurban sector beyond suburbia. Because of the initial location of urban centers in the middle of productive agricultural areas, much of the open space is active or potential agricultural land. Although there is some tract development, a considerable amount of new growth is clustered about traditional small communities, and much of the tract development is of a very low density. There is considerable variety, as well as similarity, in the settlement patterns of the Hudson Basin's metropolitan zones.

In the New York Metropolitan Zone, scale is the most obvious variation. In 1970 this zone, with about a third of the basin's total land area, contained almost 91% of the total basin population of 20.3 million. Growth forces in this zone emanate largely from a single high-density core, pushing outward into the coastal corridor toward Trenton and Philadelphia, the Lower Hudson Valley Corridor to the north, the Connecticut Coastal Corridor, and Long Island to the east. Historically, the coastal corridors and Long Island have absorbed the greater portion of the growth of the New York Metropolitan Zone, but more recently the Lower Hudson Valley Corridor has begun to accommodate a larger share of the zone's overall growth.

In the Upper Hudson Metropolitan Zone, a unique arrangement of traditional center cities encased the primary suburban expansion in the center of the zone, defined by the triangular road network connecting the three cities. Naturally, but mistakenly, the decision was made to locate the zone's major commercial air transport facility in the center as well. This in turn affected major expressway planning, amplifying the locational potential of this interior suburban area and stimulating the development of new commercial, office, and industrial uses.

The result is a conflict of expansion requirements for each of these uses, and a potential environmental wallow of major proportions. The metropolitan expressway network, of relatively recent vintage compared to some areas of the state, is slowly nearing completion. Major segments, however, have been delayed by financing problems and by public opposition to the destruction of both urban communities and remaining open space in built-up areas. This lack of transportation access to the interior of the traditional core has diverted even more growth into the few exurban corridors where expressways have been easier to locate.

In contrast to the other two zones, the Upper Mohawk Metropolitan Zone has a linear core influenced by historic transportation elements—the river, the canal, the railroad, and the Thruway. Each of these has reinforced the locational impact of its predecessor. The expansion of a linear system such as this, if facilitated by a greater peripheral capacity, may explain the comparatively larger and more rapid expansion of the Upper Mohawk Zone's suburban sector as opposed to its exurban sector. Aligned along the river, the zone has a central open-space spine of floodplain, flanked by commercial/industrial corridors. Behind these are the gently sloping valley walls, which offer exciting potentials for residential and institutional locations. Suburban development in this zone has been primarily on the south side of the river, but recent trends indicate growing developer interest on the north side as urban land has been used up. Principal commercial and employment centers are in three locations: Utica in the center; Rome to the west; and the complex of the villages of Mohawk, Ilion, and Herkimer to the east. Despite the attractive topography and good location on a major east–west transportation route, this zone does not have a primary north–south corridor like the metropolitan complexes to the east and west. The economic transition from its early water-powered textile and manufacturing base to a hard-goods or service-industry base has been slow and painful, and was sustained until recently only by government intervention (e.g., Griffiss Air Force Base and Defense Procurement Center, General Electric defense contracts, the SUNY Upper Division College).

Corridor Land Use and Human Settlement

The Hudson Basin also contains three major corridor zones, following its principal lowland river corridors and connecting the metropolitan zones.

The first of these is the Mid-Hudson Valley Corridor between the New York Metropolitan Zone and the Upper Hudson Metropolitan Zone. The second is the Champlain Corridor extending north from the Upper Hudson Metropolitan Zone and generally following Interstate 87 (the "Northway") along the eastern shore of Lake Champlain toward the Canadian border and Montreal. The third is the Mohawk Valley Corridor connecting the Upper Hudson and Upper Mohawk Metropolitan Zones. These three zones, unlike the metropolitan zones, do not share similar growth trends. However, their current patterns of land use and human settlement, dominated by traditional river-oriented communities, are quite similar. Population is mainly in these communities, most of which owe their location to a historic river landing or to a feeder stream that afforded water power for an early mill. Between these communities lies valuable agricultural land with many small hamlets at the junctions of important transportation arteries. The river towns often have obsolete and deteriorating waterfronts; their main streets have buildings of historic charm and significance, but usually with vacant upper stories. Despite economic problems, the residential quality of these communities can be quite high, and the general life style is an attractive alternative to the tension and pace of the dense urban centers.

The Mid-Hudson Corridor Zone is the fastest growing zone of the three. Growth is most rapid in the southern reaches oriented toward New York City. On the western shore, the major centers are Kingston, Saugerties, and Catskill, all linked by the New York Thruway. A section of this zone extends southwest between the Shawangunk Mountain range and the Catskills, where new development proposals are threatening some of the basin's most accessible, yet most scenic, natural landscapes. On the eastern shore, the principal communities are centered around Rhinecliff and Hudson, connected by the Penn Central Railroad main line. The zone is flanked on the east by the Taconics and the Taconic Parkway. Two major bridges link the two sides of the zone, connecting Catskill with Hudson and Kingston with Rhinecliff. Land use issues in the Mid-Hudson Corridor are a mix representing the conflicts of economic development and urban expansion versus the conservation of agricultural, natural, and scenic resources.

Conditions in the Champlain Corridor are similar to those in the Mid-Hudson Corridor, with settlement characterizing the southern portion around Glens Falls. Industrial pollution of the river in this area, primarily from pulp and paper manufacturing, has long been a major problem. A few years ago, the Niagara Mohawk Power Corporation removed a dam across the river just north of Fort Edward, releasing years of accumulated silt and debris. It promptly spread for several hundred yards downstream, turning the once peaceful and beautiful river into an environmental sink which cost an estimated $5 million to restore. Above Glens Falls, Interstate 87 has generated pressure for seasonal home development—a trend happily accepted by most natives of the area, but viewed with some concern by environmentalists and proponents of the "forever wild" policy for the Adirondack Park.

The Mohawk Valley Corridor Zone is the only one of the Hudson Basin's physiographic regions showing a population decline. The only county sector showing positive growth consists of the three towns in Schoharie County traversed by U.S. 20, which was a major east–west transportation route prior to the construction of the Thruway. The principal urban centers of the Mohawk Corridor are Amsterdam, Gloversville, Johnstown, and Little Falls. There are several small village complexes along the Mohawk, including Fonda, Fultonville, Canajoharie, Fort Plain, and St. Johnsville. Most of these communities owe their location to the Erie Canal and/or the water power resources of feeder streams. An exception is the upland village of Sharon Springs, in the southwest corner of the zone, a former spa that still attracts a number of summer residents.

Several years ago, economic development of the corridor was a popular issue with its residents. Lately, however, the idea of added growth and development in the zone has not stirred much enthusiasm. A bitter battle was waged to defeat a proposal by the Montgomery County Board of Supervisors to construct a 3700-acre regional recreation facility, Okwari Park, in Southern Montgomery County. Many of the area's newer residents are exurbanites, and only a small portion of the total population is actively engaged in agricultural activity. These people enjoy the low-density rural way of life, including comparatively low tax rates, and are anxious to prevent any change. The conservative stance of the population does not provide much support for planning except as a means to discourage development.

Upland Land Use and Human Settlement

The basin also contains three upland zones of hilly to mountainous terrain that include the headwaters of the Hudson watershed. Although these zones are sparsely populated (1.4% of the basin population on 40.3% of the basin land area), recent growth rates are equal to or higher than the growth rates of the other zones in the basin.

The Catskill Upland Zone contains the historic Catskill Mountains and Forest Preserve. These are wholly within the Hudson Basin Project area, but not completely within the Hudson watershed, since they include drainage areas belonging to the Delaware and Susquehanna systems as well. Most of the population is in a series of small urban centers lying in a crescent along the southern and western edges of the zone in Sullivan, Delaware, and Schoharie counties. These communities are mainly along the Susquehanna, Schenevus, and Schoharie rivers.

Although most of the Ulster County porton of this zone is included in the Catskill Forest Preserve, the population growth rate in this area over the last 20 years has been most dramatic, particularly in the Woodstock area. The four "hill towns" in southern Albany County are also showing dramatic increases. In both cases, these are exurban phenomena. Schoharie, Delaware, and Greene counties have growth rates reflecting more normal migration factors.

The State of New York has created a temporary commission (Temporary State Commission to Study the Catskills) to investigate growth trends in the Catskill Forest Preserve area. The commission has already pinpointed areas where soaring land values indicate increasing use of the area and the advent of substantial land speculation activity.

The Taconic Upland Zone is also experiencing rapid growth in the southern section covered by Dutchess County. Again, these increases are exurban in nature. They are generating substantial pressure on the natural resource base, which includes some excellent agricultural land. This portion of the zone also lies outside the Hudson River watershed.

The Adirondack Upland, the largest of the upstate zones, is almost wholly within the Adirondack Park. Yet this zone also evidences accelerating population growth, particularly along the periphery of the Park, as indicated by the trends of population growth in Oneida, Herkimer, Fulton, Saratoga, and Warren counties. Even remote Hamilton County is growing (by about 7.5% between 1970 and 1973). Only the High Peak section of Essex County shows a declining permanent population, but this area has seasonal populations that, if counted in terms of human settlement impacts, may be greater than those in the other sectors of the zone. Major land use changes are evident in this zone, particularly in the development of large-scale seasonal communities and extensive tourist-oriented commercial establishments.

"Environmental Wallows"

Historically, development in the Hudson Basin region has tended to follow and intensify early patterns of settlement. The ports, beaches, river valleys, and low-lying lands along rivers and streams have borne the brunt of increasingly intensive human settlement and economic exploitation. Public policy, preoccupied with the viability of local rather than regional resources, has fostered the continuous intensification of development and dependence on original settlement sites.

Technology has provided the means to make use of originally troublesome sites, such as those with steep slopes, unstable soils, difficult access, or vulnerability to flooding, for at least temporarily acceptable economic purposes. Thus the traditional appeal of dramatic open spaces filled with activity sustains the continuing intensification of development along the Hudson Palisades, the Connecticut and Long Island shores, and even on Welfare (Roosevelt) Island.

It is now a characteristic of the Hudson Basin region that dramatic and functionally defective urban concentration persists, with increasing environmental costs, even as the hinterlands suffer economic decline and natural resource neglect. Within the overall pattern of urban settlement in the Hudson Basin region, the centralizing economic forces have combined with natural geographic factors to produce acutely defective subsectors of environmental stress for their human populations. Such areas, or "environmental wallows," are the product of a convergence of adverse environmental factors, usually accumulated over substantial periods. Once established, however inadvertently, these environmental wallows may be intensified by both official public policy and the pressure of attitudes.

Regional folklore easily acknowledges the Hackensack Meadows, much of the Raritan River basin, East Harlem, and the immediate environs of Kennedy International Airport, and Jamaica Bay as examples of areas caught in long-term trends of environmental overload and neglect. In the perspective of regional settlement patterns, such areas are environmental liabilities. It is questionable whether public policy should permit further intensification of settlement, particularly by poor people, before measures can be taken to reverse the deterioration of these areas.

Jamaica Bay and the onshore environs of Kennedy Airport illustrate the problems of such environmental wallows where large numbers of people are concerned. Adverse environmental factors present include water pollution in the bay from overflow domestic sewage and oil spills; air pollution from aircraft operations and high-volume traffic arteries bordering and crossing the bay; solid waste disposal and miscellaneous landfill operations; and, overall, the pervasive effect of aircraft noise at levels substantially above the maximum permitted even for federal mortgage insurance. One of the consequences of this concentration of adverse environmental factors (none of which seems susceptible to early alleviation by either technical or political means) has been the intensification of public housing projects and, perforce, racial minority groups, around the margins of Jamaica Bay during the past 15 years. Since 1959, more than 30,000 public or publicly assisted dwelling units, housing an estimated 120,000 to 150,000 people, have been built in the environs of Kennedy Airport alone. Nearly all are within zones of noise exposure that would require rejection of housing and related land uses under well-established federal environmental policy. Such a concentration of subsidized housing is questionable on functional and social grounds. This type of housing, once in place, is nearly impossible to modify. Unfortunately, too, each successive proposal for such housing tends to be rationalized on the specious grounds that similar housing is already in place in the area. The rigor of environmental impact assessment for such projects is absent.

Such "wallows" should be recognized as areas of critical environmental concern and should be given priority for public policy attention in planning for the future distribution of population within the region. The private market has relegated such "wallows" to marginal status, particularly for human occupancy. Public policy should not aggravate the process of environmental degradation by fostering marginal usage of such areas when more healthful locations cry out for new investment.

2.3   Future Need for Regional Perspectives

Reciprocal Limits

This task group has concluded that a significant departure from past practices is needed to cope with environmental quality as a function of human settlement realistically. Accordingly, the concept of reciprocal limits is advanced as the basis for a regional strategy to gain more effective control of random growth factors, to realize greater benefits from existing commitments to both public and private investment in regional development, and to achieve necessary objectives of environmental salvage and future quality control.

The growth policy implied by the reciprocal limits concept is essentially a policy of strong constraint and challenge to routine practices with respect to all increments of further urbanization at the fringes of metropolitan areas in the Hudson Basin region and in certain subareas of critical environmental concern.

It is easiest to understand the application of this policy in the latter case, which is typified by the open land areas and relatively low-density neighborhoods in the environs of Kennedy, Newark, and LaGuardia airports. There are probably at least 10,000 acres of land, either open or in marginally productive use, in the environs of these three airports. Because such land is within easy range of the utility systems and other infrastructure elements of the metropolitan area, it is under substantial pressure for additional development or redevelopment. Unfortunately, it is also within well-documented invisible zones of adverse noise exposure around the three airports, and most of this acreage would be rejected by HUD or the Veterans Administration if proposed for mortgage insurance. Expedient compromises with environmental quality criteria have resulted in intensive residential development in these noise-exposed areas. Upwards of 150,000 people, almost all disadvantaged minority group members, have been installed in publicly sponsored housing in these defective settings.

Such public actions have been rationalized on the grounds that no other land for subsidized housing was available at the time, and that housing in a noise-blighted environment is probably better than the traditional slum. This rationalization has been reinforced by the equally specious and casual observation that there is no way to control the expansion of the zones of noise exposure around the airport if air travel continues to increase.

As a result of this interplay of misinformation and short-sighted public policy, the population in the airport environs is intensifying each year. Airport officials, viewing unrestrained encroachment of housing on well-known noise zones, feel no obligation to impose restraints of their own on air traffic.

Clearly, there is a need for both airport operators and the proponents of mass housing to recognize the finite limits of the land resource essential to meeting their respective needs. Thus, both must exercise simultaneous restraints on their respective contributions to the urban environment—oppressive noise (on the one hand) and people in permanent housing (on the other). All that is really sought is a restraint on any further development of housing in noise-blighted areas and a concurrent restraint on air traffic volume and operational factors to stabilize the current degree of conflict until engine technology provides a way to reduce the zones of noise exposure.

Thus, in exchange for withholding, or at least deferring, housing development in noisy areas, airport authorities can be encouraged to concentrate on measures that would stem the spread of adverse environmental impact. This action would benefit the metropolitan community in terms of lessened litigation against the aviation industry and improved environmental quality for large numbers of center-city people. An additional benefit would be derived from preventing the intensification of already extreme concentrations of low-income minority group people in manifestly marginal quarters of the cities involved.

Away from the relatively small areas of critical environmental concern, such as airport noise-exposure zones, the "reciprocal limits" policy would be based on the need to subject all development proposals at the urbanizing fringe of metropolitan areas to a rigorous determination of social, economic, and environmental costs and benefits.

Accordingly, any proposal for development that would expand the present pattern of urbanization beyond the present limits of utility service systems would be subject to rigorous challenge and, at least, to whatever delay might be required to determine that the purposes of the development (housing, commercial facilities, public facilities) could not be fulfilled by development elsewhere on infill area. Infill areas are those lying within the general periphery of urbanized areas of cities, counties, and metropolitan areas of the Hudson Basin region and also within the service limits of their existing utility systems. It is hoped a regional approach to requiring a rigorous justification for all centrifugal expansion would create substantial incentives for infill intensification of marginally developed land within the areas already generally urbanized.

Challenging the validity of proposed urban expansion beyond the present limits served by utility systems might be accomplished by a variety of means, including sewer moratoriums, large-lot zoning, outright public acquisition on key parcels or tracts of land, ramifications of the Ramapo growth-control model, or transferable development-rights systems. In any event, the approach would have to be rigorous to be effective. Obviously arguments arise against any such approach on the grounds that any suggested limitation on fringe growth (a euphemism for sprawl) would have a discriminatory effect, particularly against center-city and other low-income people who aspire to suburban life styles and amenities.

Concomitant to application of rigorous criteria for determining affordable limits to peripheral growth would be the provision of incentives for the regeneration of older cities throughout the region. Thus, some of the discouragingly slow tendencies of older areas to become newly fashionable and desirable might be accelerated by public policy—and on a scale that might bring benefits to people of all income levels.

Infilling

Adopting the concept of reciprocal limits as a basis for regional growth strategy does not imply a policy of "no growth." The Regional Plan Association has estimated that perhaps 40% of the acreage in the New York metropolitan region is vacant. Most of this acreage has far easier access to major utility systems, including transportation, than the typical suburban fringe development dependent on attenuated service systems and financing. Much of this vacant land (now seen, in an economic and policy context of complete laissez-faire, as simply bypassed by the market) would regain investment appeal and development potential in the context of consistent challenge to conventional proposals for expanding the suburban fringe. It is the hypothesis of this task group that there is more than enough infill acreage in the Hudson Basin to rehouse and upgrade both quality of life and access to opportunity for populations segregated by economic and racial factors in traditional slums, ghettos, etc. It is important to recognize infill development opportunities for relatively small-scale builders and developers. This potential is discussed in a later section.

In addition to this advocacy of a concept of reciprocal limits, this task group recognizes an alarming trend of neglect in public policy at every level with respect to the central cities of the Hudson Basin region. Sheer disenchantment with the monotony, expense, and social stratification characteristic of suburban living is not sufficient to precipitate reinvestment and redemption of prior investment in the central cities. Positive public policies favoring the creation of new environments and economic opportunities in the central cities are needed to enable these strategic sites to resume earlier roles as centers of activity and functional importance within the Hudson Basin region. Although encouraging steps have been taken in Albany and several smaller cities to reestablish the vitality of traditional urban centers, far stronger efforts are needed to prevent obsolescence and physical decay from negating the economic potential of the region's older cities. One complementary effect of the policy of reciprocal limits would be the regeneration of demand for both services and capital investment in the older strategic centers.

2.4   Illustrative Cases

The Nassau–Suffolk Region

Nassau and Suffolk counties occupy one-sixth of the land area of the New York region. They have been two of the fastest growing counties in the United States since the end of World War II. In 1960, the combined population of two million persons represented one-eighth of the total regional population of 16 million. It is projected that 25% of the additional six million persons that will inhabit the region by 1985 will be living in the two counties. In a sense, Long Island is part of, and a microcosm of, the entire Hudson Basin. Therefore, its planning experiences and approaches are germane to planning for the basin.

One of the major aspects of the plan developed for the two counties is the concept of growth limitation related to available water supply. A second is the model of corridors, clusters, and centers. This is a direct reflection of the linear shape of the island. Since the Hudson Basin is also a corridor, it might be susceptible to similar treatment. The following are excerpts from the text of the Nassau–Suffolk Regional Plan.*

Corridors, Clusters, and Centers

Three concepts—corridors, clusters, and centers—are the essence of the plan. These concepts are the guideposts against which individual projects should be judged. In deciding on the merits of a specific proposal, each

*Preparation of the Nassau–Suffolk Regional Plan was aided by a grant from the U.S. Department of Housing and Urban Development under Section 701 of the Federal Housing Act of 1954.

community should be guided by the goals, the three concepts, and the locational criteria derived from them.

Not every new development will conform fully to the corridors, clusters, and centers concepts. If these concepts were rigorously and absolutely followed immediately, they would not substantially change the appearance of the western third of the Island over the next 15 years, except in the heart of some of the larger centers. Nassau County and the westernmost portion of Suffolk are already almost fully developed. About half of the housing in Nassau will be single-family homes on scattered lots. This infilling will merely accentuate the present development pattern. But, over time, the concepts of this plan, if followed, will accommodate necessary growth while respecting the needs of the people and their environment, and will encourage the use of mass transit by placing greater densities of housing, jobs, and shopping within walking distance of mass transit facilities.

Corridors   Consider the geography of Nassau and Suffolk counties—long, narrow, attached at one end to one of the world's major cities, surrounded everywhere else by water. Clearly, the most valuable recreation land is at the waterfront; the best location for housing is adjacent to the recreation areas. Equally clearly, the most logical location for industry and other employment is along the center spine of the Island, close to the major transportation facilities. In this location, equidistant from both the north and south shores, jobs will be most accessible to residents, yet the inevitable harmful effects of industry—noise, traffic—will be minimized.

The Island has two broad residential corridors: one along the north shore and one along the south shore. These bands, each fairly well served by its own highways and rail, are within easy reach of both the central employment–transportation spine and of the parks and seashore. Residential densities are lowered along the shore, increasing toward the central employment–transportation corridor, where existing limited-access highways, together with rapid and efficient rail service coordinated with a network of feeder bus lines, can provide rapid transportation to work, shopping, and other activities.

Clusters   New development should be clustered wherever possible. The concept of clustering is simple: for example, suppose that instead of placing 50 homes on 15,000-square foot lots, they were placed on 10,000-square foot lots—at a saving of 5000 square feet per parcel. The 250,000 square feet thus saved throughout the development could then be used for playgrounds, greenways, and other community open space. Both the original house purchase price and the annual taxes might be less, yet the value of the house might be greater because of the enhanced quality of its environment. Of course, if the original lot were 1 acre or larger, clustering to a quarter acre would save a greater amount of open space without increasing the overall density.

Clustering also allows for the combining of town houses and apartments with single-family detached houses while maintaining the overall original permitted density. This is important because apartments will help to ease the critical housing shortage in the two counties and to slow the rapid rise in the cost of housing. Single-family homes in established neighborhoods may become more readily available where nearby apartments provide for the changed needs of the present occupants of these homes. Apartments relieve the mounting cost of public services, because the cost of public utilities, fire and police protection, and roads is lower per unit for apartments than for single-family dwellings. In addition, new apartments on Long Island are a tax asset to schools because they generally pay more than three times as much in taxes as the cost of educating the children from these units.

The proper use of clustering techniques is one of the most effective tools for open space preservation at no acquisition cost to the community. Through clustering of adjoining developments and the dedication of contiguous acreage, alert communities can acquire extensive open space systems. Linear parks, which can be created by judicious planning of adjoining cluster developments, can be valuable for watershed protection, hiking, horseback riding, cycling, passive recreation, preservation of spots of particular scenic beauty or ecological significance, and the articulation and delineation of communities. The Smithtown–Islip greenbelt is an example of such a linear park.

Centers   The centers concept is an extension of the concept of clustering. Centers are accessible concentrations of activity. These centers are generally of two types: the single-use center, exemplified by an educational institution such as Stony Brook, a government center as at Hauppauge, or a grouping of industrial establishments such as that along the Long Island Expressway in Plainview; and the multiuse center containing a variety of land uses and activities, such as those proposed for Mitchell Field and for the revitalized downtowns along the major east–west transportation routes. These multiuse centers can be large or small (those proposed range from a regional center at Mitchell Field to a local center in Southold), but in every instance they include housing and shopping, and in the case of all but the local centers, they also include other activities and facilities—employment, education, transportation, special services, and recreation—all placed in an accessible location.

Activity centers can be formed through the revitalization and expansion of an existing nucleus such as an older central business district or a small business district, or through the creation of an entirely new center as the focus of a planned new community. Every effort should be made to transform those older central business districts situated near the major transportation routes into activity centers. Many of these business districts have deteriorated because of their inability to compete with the new outlying shopping and office centers. Ease of access and ample parking space have lured customers from the older traffic-clogged downtowns to new convenient shopping centers along the major roads. Lower-income residents have moved into the aging and decaying housing bordering the business districts. The tremendous existing investment in railroads and public utilities is underutilized even while roads, water mains, sewers, and power lines are extended to serve new commercial and residential growth in other areas.

Better access to the downtown areas and improved parking, together with a substantial increase in permitted densities, will stimulate private renewal, provide needed housing, and promote economic and social integration. New activity centers should be planned only in the portions of the Island that are presently undeveloped and where it is not possible to expand existing small concentrations of nonresidential uses. For example, three entirely new activity centers are proposed for eastern Brookhaven, at Middle Island, Yaphank, and Manorville.

The central corridor of the Island should contain the major employment centers and other traffic generators. To serve this traffic, transportation centers are planned for Mineola, Hicksville, East Farmingdale, Ronkonkoma, Yaphank, and Calverton, at the points where the main line of the railroad crosses major north–south highway routes. The North and South Shore corridors should contain as little industry as possible, and the commercial and office centers within the outer corridors should be smaller than those projected for the central spine.

Activity centers will encourage the use of public mass transportation by providing concentrations of commercial activity, employment, and housing. The central line of the railroad would be improved to provide high-speed transportation. Provision of such a system would encourage greater density of uses near the railroad stations that would, in turn, reinforce the economic justification of the original creation of the high-speed line. The concentration of a large proportion of the projected population increase in centers would permit the retention of the open character of the remainder of the Island.

The Adirondack Park Agency

Another area of the Hudson Basin that illustrates the evolution of public policy directed at regional settlement patterns is the Adirondacks. Although located at the northern reaches of the basin, settlement and land use issues in the Adirondacks are in some ways as critical as those of the Nassau–Suffolk area.

After more than a century of exploitation of its natural resources, the Adirondack Park was established by the New York State Legislature in 1892 after a storm of public protest over the ruthless destruction of this unique area. Shortly after its demarcation by the now famous "Blue Line," the Park was designated a State Forest Preserve. All state lands within the Preserve were placed under the protection of the New York State Constitution's Article XIV, declaring the lands to be "forever wild."

The constitutional status prevents management of the state forestland in the counties either wholly or partially within the boundaries of the Blue Line. Of the Park's 5.9 million acres, approximately 3.7 million acres are still under private ownership and, until recently, were subject to the whims and fancies of their owners. For many years, the relative inaccessibility of the Adirondacks protected them from extensive commercial exploitation. Many large tracts were held by wealthy people. There were few resorts or recreational facilities available to the average citizen, and little demand for such development. Those existing were clustered along the major railroad running from Utica to Lake Placid.

The advent of the automobile as a means of common transportation in the 1920s increased the use of the Adirondacks. The beauty of the area was more widely promoted. The Great Depression and World War II slowed the use of the Park, but during the 1950s and 1960s, pressures on the Park soared.

The construction of the Northway (Interstate 87) in the mid-1960s opened the relatively undeveloped eastern sector of the Park, including its famous High Peak region. In the past few years, the popularity of mountain climbing, back-packing, canoeing, skiing, and snowmobiling have caused the use of the Park to skyrocket. Thousands of acres of land, mostly around the Park's many small lakes, have been subdivided and developed for seasonal homes. The top of Mount Marcy, the state's highest peak, on any good summer afternoon resembles Grand Central Terminal—the trail to its summit bears the marks of thousands of boots. A few years ago, the Adirondack Mountain Club members collected and carried out almost 3 tons of rubbish left behind by thoughtless "nature lovers."

In 1968, the state government established a temporary state commission to analyze the impact of the extensive use and development of the Park. After the completion of the report, which called for a state master plan and land use control, the Adirondack Park Agency (APA) was formed in 1971. By 1973, the APA had prepared a master plan for the Park. This plan set major policies for the use of state lands, which were zoned according to their uniqueness, suitability for various uses, and susceptibility to environmental degradation. Private lands were zoned according to broad land use and development density criteria. After considerable public controversy, the Legislature adopted the plan. Under its provisions, the Adirondack Park Agency must approve any project of regional significance, whereas local governments have jurisdiction over projects of lesser importance. Local governments can enact their own land use plans and development controls. They must, however, work within the broad land use and development density criteria established by the APA. A special state program has been formulated to provide technical and financial assistance to local government planning programs.

Thus, a good portion of the Hudson Basin is now subject to a state-promulgated regional growth policy and settlement plan. Although local opposition to the APA remains strong and vocal, the benefits of the plan already are visible in the quality of recent land developments. The new requirements have not reduced development interest in the area by major developers, who can afford the quality-controlling demands that mandate consideration of intrinsic environmental capacities of the land.

The Adirondacks, because of their size, uniqueness, and fame, have a ready constituency of environmental defenders. But is not the entire Hudson a resource of equal, if not greater, value to all the citizens of the state? Certainly the state's intervention to protect the future of the Adirondacks demonstrates our capacity to build the institutions necessary to plan and implement public policy for land use and human settlement on a regional basis.

2.5   Conflicting Modes of Development

Large-Scale Development

In the United States, development has been historically a partnership between the public and private sectors. Government builds the framework— the utilities, roads, schools—and the private sector builds the other pieces— homes, offices, churches, and stores. Other nations rely on government to furnish the homes, shopping centers, and industries, as well as the utilities and roads. Their traditions favor direct government involvement more than do ours. And if we learned nothing else from our experience with the urban programs of the 1960s, it is that in this country, without a drastic expansion of powers and responsibilities, government cannot bear complete responsibility.

The great sums spent by private enterprise in building parts of the communities in which we live represent an opportunity to strive for quality. But with few exceptions public policies to attain a quality environment via private-sector spending have relied on the minimum standards of zoning, building codes, and the like. Their failure has been conspicuous.

Private builders are motivated by profit, and few would argue against a fair return on an investment. We need, then, to peg the financial return on quality; that is, we need to devise incentives to make clear that the highest return depends on the quality.

The development decisions of local governments are coming under increasing question. Angered by rising tax rates, congested roads, polluted air, overcrowded schools, and other signs of haphazard and piecemeal urban growth, citizens have begun to protest rezonings and land development schemes of all kinds—large and small, good and bad. Their concerns are more than just economic—that is, how much the proposed development will cost their community. The Rockefeller Task Force on Land Use and Urban Growth (Reilly, 1973) called this phenomenon a new mood in America.

The protests are symptomatic of a search for an elusive quality of life, the dreams of which once drew families out from the city to the suburbs and smaller communities across America. Protests span the continent—New York, California, Colorado, Michigan, Florida, Massachusetts, Illinois, and so on. In large cities, small communities, suburbs, exurbs, on statewide and local levels, the issues of land use planning and urban growth have roused the citizens' wrath. Citizens have become suspicious of decision-making bodies that too frequently rezone land or grant variances to development schemes. They view with suspicion the developer's promise of more jobs and more taxes. And they have grown savvy to the potential conflicts of interest among appointed and elected officials.

The report of the Rockefeller Task Force on Land Use and Urban Growth (Reilly, 1973) documented in depth the situation in four selected areas of the nation. The task force members concluded that the new mood represented a significant force in land use management, a force challenging long held assumptions that a community's growth is desirable or even inevitable.

Not all the opposition to growth, however, is really motivated by environmental concerns. Some use the environmental banner as a justification for closing the door behind them to keep out ethnic or minority groups who have just reached an income level that allows them to pursue a dream of their own home and plot of land.

Despite this element of negativism, the task force observed that the opportunity was at hand to harness this new mood in behalf of quality development.

The Need for Development

What many of the "new-mooders" fail to recognize is that although we have reached a fertility rate that makes achievement of zero population growth feasible, we will not stop growing for some time. A high household formation rate over the next several decades means we will need more homes, more shopping facilities, and more public works. These are needed to take care of people already born or who will be born and will be forming their own households. The issue at hand is not development vs. no development, but rather where should development go and of what quality should it be.

National debate often focuses on a growth-center strategy which would channel population growth into selected economically depressed areas of the country. The Agricultural Act of 1970 went so far as to direct that in all federal programs the highest priority be given to the revitalization of rural areas. A number of thoughtful commentaries have indicated, however, that some governmental programs have minimal impacts on patterns of economic development. A report prepared for the Economic Development Administration, for example, came to the conclusion that out of 200 federal assistance programs only a handful had a significant effect on altering patterns of population growth or economic development.

The conclusion to be drawn from this and other analyses is that, barring a substantial increase in responsibilities and powers exercised by the federal government, population growth would continue to have its heaviest impact in existing metropolitan areas, particularly on the fringes.

Within the New York region, the issue becomes one of accommodating this development in a manner that results in higher quality neighborhoods and communities. Proponents of large-scale development have been convinced that the opportunity to realize this objective through large-scale development is at hand. Several policy research groups, most notably the National Policy Task Force of the American Institute of Architects (AIA) (Leone et al., 1973) and the Rockefeller Task Force on Land Use and Urban Growth (Reilly, 1973), have recommended this strategy. Though not without problems, large-scale development appears to couple the opportunity to attain quality with the incentives to strive for it.

The AIA Task Force has recommended channeling development into what it calls "growth units." The report explained, "America's growth and renewal should be designed and executed not as individual buildings and projects, but as human communities with the full range of physical facilities and human services that ensure an urban life of quality." Growth units are not fixed in size but are generally from 500 to 3000 residential units, a size large enough to support a community center, elementary school, convenience shopping, open space, and recreational opportunities. The report's authors concluded that this scale would be sufficient to stimulate innovations in building construction and maintenance, health care systems, waste collection and disposal, and other areas. Finally, the scale should be large enough to realize the benefits of unified planning, land acquisition, site preparation, and design of public facilities.

The Rockefeller report has recommended that government should use all acceptable means to channel development into new communities or, to the extent that is unachievable, into the AIA's proposed growth units.

In Support of Large-Scale Development

Proponents of large-scale development argue that it provides strong opportunities and incentives to create quality environments. Because the return on an investment comes slowly over the years, a developer has a stake in ensuring that the product is of sufficient quality to attract and retain people. Consumers are more likely to evaluate an entire plan favorably than they are a piecemeal development process. In short, achievement of quality becomes a necessary part of financial success.

Large scale also can mean an increased return as well as quality. It is common practice among developers of large regional shopping centers, for example, to acquire more land than is needed for the center itself. If planned well, the shopping center causes real estate values to rise, and the developer can realize a substantial return on the unused portion of the site. The developers of Columbia, Maryland—one of the better known planned new communities—also note that property values have risen at a faster rate than they had anticipated. Comprehensive planning, amenities, and other benefits have proved to be sound economic investments. Large-scale development also allows a sufficient monetary cushion to engage adequate planning skills from the beginning. The developer is in a position to explore alternative concepts, to involve social scientists (as in the planning of Columbia, Maryland), to prepare environmental impact analyses, and to incorporate the findings into the project planning.

At the largest scale of development—that of new communities—financial planning can be applied more realistically to meeting community service and facility needs. A long-range perspective ensures that these needs can be met and economically supported as part of the community's overall development program. The costs of capital improvements, for example, can be spread over time and borne by all the residents, not just the newcomers.

The opportunity to provide a full range of services is also present in larger developments. At a small scale, developers cannot economically justify provision of many facilities and services. This task is left to local governments. But localities are not always in a fiscal position to do so. Thus, they discourage development altogether or exact mandatory improvements and dedications, the costs of which are passed on to consumers.

Large regional shopping centers are an illustration of these benefits. The most successful ones contain a range of urban design amenities within the enclosed mall. A more attractive setting draws more shoppers. Over time, the added income more than compensates for the original investment.

Large-scale development offers the opportunity to plan and develop from the start with the entire site or property in mind. Conventional practices result in development on a parcel-by-parcel basis—separate owners in pursuit of maximum profits, separate design schemes, separate developments. In a large-scale development, a single developer (or a number of smaller developers acting in accord with an overall plan) can consider and effectively control the interrelationships among the various land uses, the circulation network, and the urban design elements of buildings and structures.

At the same time, local governments can apply more sophisticated reviews and regulations. Instead of viewing proposed developments on a parcel-by-parcel basis (which cannot take into account the cumulative impact of these projects and which often ignores the overall community context), localities can evaluate a proposal in its entirety. Most importantly, localities can ensure in their reviews that alternatives have been explored.

Large-scale developments also offer the opportunity to accommodate a wider range of life styles, economic classes, and racial and ethnic groups. Builders of new communities, for example, have noted that there appears to be less resistance to such mixing than is usually the case if homeowners know from the start, according to an overall plan, what kind of housing will go where, how much will be for different income groups, and so forth.

Energy conservation can also be promoted by large-scale planning and development. The opportunity exists, for example, to tie land use planning to transportation and circulation systems. Dependency on the automobile, prevalent in so many suburban and even urban communities, can be offset by locating day-to-day activities, services, and convenience goods in close proximity—even walking distance—to residential areas. Development can be located or placed to support elements of public transportation, such as a feeder bus system connecting residential neighborhoods with town centers and rapid transit stations.

Against Large-Scale Development

Large-scale development is not without its opponents. Some base their reasoning on past experience, and others on intuition. Some have argued that incentives and regulations favoring large-scale development would drive out small developers. Most homebuilders, for example, build only a few units each year. They could not afford to prepare environmental impact statements or to negotiate lengthy review processes. They may not have access to large sums of necessary planning money, nor could they afford to wait long periods for a return on their investment. Moreover, in many areas of the country, the markets for large-scale development or new communities do not exist.

Large scale is no guarantee of quality or environmental sensitivity. Some of the most attractive urban settings have resulted from piecemeal, small-scale development. Many urban renewal projects offer an example of large scale development having disastrous social and environmental effects. In addition, few developers have the expertise to do an adequate job on large projects, especially in planning new communities. The management, urban planning, financial, and related processes are so complex that lack of skills may defeat even the best of intentions.

Large-scale development also means high visibility. The general mood in many communities is decidedly against large developers. Public policy encouraging large-scale development may simply be politically unrealistic at this time.

Land assembly can be a formidable problem. Moreover, the marketability of small parcels of land may suffer. Countless small property owners would undoubtedly be opposed to a large-scale development philosophy. In contrast, the price of large parcels would be inflated. Housing and other facility costs would increase.

Review procedures for large-scale development would be complex and time-consuming. Yet once a developer purchases land the money is tied up and alternative investments are ruled out. As a rule, profitability of large-scale development would have to be great enough to interest investors. This means either higher consumer costs or public subsidies (special tax treatment, for example). If alternative markets exist, consumers may be unwilling to pay higher costs.

The imposition of higher standards for quality would inevitably widen the housing gap between middle-income households and the poor. The public costs of correcting this deficiency would increase.

Among the more serious charges leveled at the movement toward large-scale development is that it would drive the small-scale operator out of business. The residential building industry is fragmented. Its 30,000 firms are mostly small companies operating in single local markets. A 1969 study for the National Association of Home Builders (Sumichrast and Frankel, 1969) indicates that over half of the single- and multi-family homebuilding firms produce fewer than 25 units per year. Just over 10% build more than 100 units.

In the single-family housing market, the trend over the previous decade is toward smaller and smaller operators. Thirteen percent of the builders produced more than 100 units in 1959, compared to only 6% a decade later. And yet the largest firms are dramatically increasing their share of the total housing market. The top 2% in terms of output captured 28% of the housing market in 1972 compared to 18% 3 years before. Nearly three-fourths of their production was in multifamily housing (up from 66% in 1971); and there has been a significant increase in low-, middle-, and high-rise apartment buildings that accounted for almost half of the major builders' output in 1972. These figures point to a changing industry: a growing tendency toward smaller firms, but with production concentrated more and more in the hands of a few large ones.

Superficially, channeling construction into large-scale developments would seem to serve poorly all but the largest homebuilders. Few homebuilding firms have the resources to undertake large-scale complexes—they would be unable to assemble the land, secure the financing, draw up the extensive plans, provide adequate environmental safeguards, and construct and promote the units. Furthermore, without changes in lending policies, front-end planning money would be difficult to secure when the financial return is several years away.

But large-scale development and small-scale operations are not as incompatible as they might first seem. A distinction can be made between the land-development responsibility and the building responsibility. A land developer prepares the overall neighborhood or community plan, assembles the land, and pulls together the many pieces. The builder, on the other hand, constructs individual pieces within the overall framework established by the land developer.

An instructive example of this division of labor is found in the new town of Columbia, Maryland. From the start, the land developers recognized that a quality community would demand large-scale comprehensive planning. They were convinced that the cumulative impact of independent decisions by small-scale developers would not result in a project that would meet their standards of quality. Instead of a conventional development strategy, they chose to establish the framework and at the same time encourage others— smaller development firms included—to fill in the pieces.

Separating the land development and homebuilding functions allows homebuilders to concentrate on what they know best—homebuilding. Finished lots are available; all the permits have been secured; the utilities have been furnished; and the schools and recreation areas and other facilities have been provided. The price of a finished lot is higher than a developer might otherwise pay for raw land, but the hassles and headaches are gone. Homebuilders can keep their advertising campaigns to a minimum since Columbia's developers maintain a full-time promotional drive to attract residents. Everyone shares in the benefits in much the same way stores collectively profit from being near each other in a large shopping center.

Thirty homebuilders are now operating in Columbia. Some build only one or two custom homes a year; others build 10 to 15 units or more. For their part, the developers of Columbia rely heavily on small-scale operators and find no justification for taking advantage of all the potential business opportunities that building a new community offers. Others, more specialized in the necessary knowledge and skills, can do the job better. Supervising and coordinating development of a new community are full-time jobs. Small operators are important, too, for creating diversity and variety in a community. Columbia's neighborhoods do not look as if they had been stamped using a cookie cutter, partly because there was a conscious decision to employ different builders for different parts of the whole.

There have been some casualties under this system of split functions, particularly among those firms that derive a large measure of their profit from land development as opposed to building. Columbia spokesmen are quick to point out that the successes under their system of operation are far more plentiful. And the results are hard to fault.

There is ample room, in other words, for small building firms to operate in the context of large-scale development. Indeed, we have seen there may be advantages in that the small operator is relieved of many of the burdens normally associated with the development game—land assemblage, preparation of environmental impact statements, provision of infrastructure, and other public facilities. Large-scale development will not force small builders out of the market business. It will, however, change the way in which they do business.

Another charge—that large-scale development does not ensure quality development—is also made frequently. The point to be made in favor of large-scale development, however, is that it enlarges the opportunity and even the incentives to strive for quality.

Many of the popular neighborhoods that have resulted from piecemeal, small-scale development evolved at a time when technology was more limited—3 or 4 stories were the limit as opposed to 30 to 40; circulation was by foot or streetcar as opposed to automobiles and high-speed elevators. Accelerated depreciation in the U.S. tax code, often cited as a spur to speculative development, was first introduced in the mid-1950s. In-city land prices and housing costs have soared, leaving only the wealthier households to enjoy these neighborhoods.

In other words, the ground rules for urban development have changed to the point where even popular sections of the city stand in danger of losing their sources of popularity to speculative development. The day when ad hoc decisions could yield lively, interesting neighborhoods may be over. As an alternative, we might look to large-scale development with planned diversity, that is, a mixture resulting from different builders doing individual pieces within an overall scheme.

The market for large-scale projects indeed may not exist in many sections of the country. That is not the problem, however, in the New York metropolitan region. The visibility of large-scale developers is high, but not more so than, for example, that of the Urban Development Corporation. Some communities will undoubtedly be receptive; others may be hesitant or suspicious. In all instances public education is necessary for winning public support. Unless a community fully understands the need and opportunity, the project is likely to run into trouble.

Land assemblage, lending policies for front-end planning money, management expertise, time delays for reviews, and the provisions of low- and moderate-income housing are obstacles to implementing successfully a large-scale development strategy. But if we are willing to accept public intervention to encourage large-scale development, they are surmountable.

The Need for Public Intervention

Despite the arguments against large-scale development, both the AIA Task Force (Leone et al., 1973) and the Rockefeller Task Force on Land Use and Urban Growth (Reilly, 1973) recommended that it be encouraged. Both recognized, however, that the market system and governmental policies and practices often work against development at a larger scale. The reports of these groups pointed to the need for public intervention in support of large-scale planning and development.

Land assembly is, of course, of great concern to developers. The developers of Columbia, Maryland, for example, have observed that it would be far more difficult today, if not impossible, to repeat their discreet assembly of the thousands of acres included in the Columbia development plan. Beyond the problems of negotiating with the plethora of individuals and fragmented land ownership patterns, many landowners have high, perhaps inflated, expectations of what their land is worth. Once the site of a large-scale development is made known (the preparation and review of environmental impact statements virtually guarantee that the site location would be made a matter of public record), land values may soar to a point where the economic feasibility of the entire project is threatened.

If channeling developments into large-scale projects is the objective, then developers may need governmental assistance. Acquisition by public agencies and resale of land to private developers (with write-downs if necessary) or public use of eminent domain to help private developers, who have assembled some specified percentage of the land they will require, might be considered.

Public assistance for large-scale development must be considered for other aspects as well. The length of time before a financial return can be expected will be great. Public guarantees of bonds issued by private developers for land acquisition and installation of utilities and other infrastructure elements, then, may be needed if developers are to obtain investment capital. Direct grants may be in order, as may be special priority status for such related items as home mortgage insurance.

As overloaded treatment plants, insufficient fuel resources, and antigrowth campaigns make moratoriums on utility hookups or installations more commonplace, developers will probably need governmental assistance to service large-scale projects. Financial aids or overrides on local decisions by higher levels of government, perhaps by the state, may be necessary.

Transportation policies, as well as utility policies, need to be supportive of large-scale development. Direct grants and loans are one obvious form of assistance. Priority status for location of access highways and improvements of bus service are other possibilities.

Transportation Policy

The second major mode for the establishment of a more desirable, environmentally sound pattern of land use and human settlement is through integrated transportation policy planning and development.

Assuming the implementation of the reciprocal limits concept—with attendant mechanisms for the use and density classification and timed release of lands for development, and the capacity to undertake large-scale community development within an overall plan for urban renewal and expansion—it is apparent that transportation policies must be formulated and implemented in accordance with a basin-wide growth policy.

Several principles should guide such an effort. First, a working transportation policy cannot be achieved fully without prior legal adoption of land use and development density controls and the subsequent elimination of speculative activities that can generate excess demand on existing or programmed transportation networks. Transportation planning must be integrated with a regional land use and development density control system so that transportation facilities can stimulate and support desired land use patterns.

The alternative to this policy is acceptance of the traditional closed loop of congestion—relieved by improved access, leading to increased use and development density, leading to more congestion. The process also works in reverse. The current state of passenger rail service in the basin is a classic example. Thus, the attempt to maximize choice at every geographical location can eventually reduce the number of available options from which to choose.

Intercity, high-speed transportation facilities, which would support the intensification of major urban centers within desired urban growth corridors, should become the key facility component of the basin's transportation policy and plan. To date there has been no systematic analysis of existing demand or potential impact of an integrated intercity public transit system to serve the major urban centers of the Hudson–Mohawk Corridor. Individual analyses have been made of high-speed rail, air, and bus services, but these have not been integrated, nor have they been prepared in concert with a basin-wide growth policy. Yet the technology is available to place centers as remote as Albany within reasonable daily commuting distance of midtown Manhattan. If this potential were realized, the enormous development pressures presently exerted on the metropolitan New York suburban and exurban zones could be reduced substantially. There could be more balanced distribution of population, and critical land areas without natural capacity to support urban growth could be saved for needed open space.

Within metropolitan areas, priority consideration should be given to those transportation facilities that support the redevelopment and/or infill of the traditional core areas. Since the advent of the automobile as a generally used means of personal travel, urban centers have been shaped increasingly by the needs of cars rather than of people. Billions have been spent to bring the automobile into the urban centers more quickly, only to clog city streets because there is no room to park them. Public funds might be better spent to subsidize efficient mass transit systems, or at least to balance the provision of urban parking facilities and urban expressways. If this were the case, it is probable that the economics of land utilization would quickly establish automobile density limits in city centers.

Transportation facilities serving ecologically sensitive areas of natural resource value, such as important agricultural areas and the Catskill, Adirondack, and Taconic uplands, should be provided in a way that imposes time-cost penalties for access. The relative ease of access to the basin's ecologically significant areas has encouraged the overuse or development of these areas. Although access is important for a variety of reasons, it is also important to protect the environmental benefits they provide to the basin's population, such as watersheds, food and timber production, wildlife habitat, and recreational resources. Prior to the development of the Adirondack Northway, development within the Adirondack Park was limited by the transportation facilities then serving the region. Efforts to relieve the congestion of these facilities opened the area to use levels now threatening to deteriorate the environment. The same phenomenon has occurred on Long Island, where development has preempted major land areas that once served valuable agricultural and natural functions.

Land acquisition for sites or rights-of-way for major regional transportation facilities should include the public acquisition of development rights to adjacent land areas, achieving value increments from improved transportation access.

Currently, private landowners and developers realize major profits from the development of lands with increased values because of the improvement or new construction of regional transport facilities. In many cases, development of these areas takes place far in advance of service capabilities, and often in an unplanned and uncoordinated fashion that later generates an environmental wallow. Several regional airports in the basin have generated extensive surrounding development to the point where the future expansion and utilization of the facility are jeopardized, or where the residents of these areas are subjected to excessive environmental hazards. In addition, areas are opened to development before coordinated plans to service such areas can be prepared.

Finally, potential alternatives to personal travel, such as telecommunications, should be evaluated as an element of any basinwide transportation policy. Since this study deals with the long-term development of the basin, plus the planning and institutional capacities necessary to achieve a balanced overall growth pattern, any transportation policy planning must deal with the impact of potential alternatives to personal travel. Over the next 25 to 30 years, we are certain to witness advances in telecommunication technology that may eliminate the necessity for much personal travel. These projected advances need to be evaluated in view of the probable competition for public financial resources.

2.6   Implementation

Social Implications

Pursuit of the basic concept of reciprocal limits, together with the complementary policies of infill development and reinvestment in central cities and towns, poses difficult questions of social policy which must be addressed. In the Hudson Basin region, as in other areas of the United States, there is a de facto pattern of racial and economic segregation. This represents a serious challenge to any effort that would elevate environmental quality issues for the more affluent to a higher plane of public policy concern.

Accordingly, it is important to examine the specific implications of any system of public policies that might adversely affect the interests of people seeking equity in all aspects of human settlement.

This task group sought the assistance of the Suburban Action Institute in evaluating the social implications of the proposed concept of reciprocal limits. Ostensibly, this concept might seem to limit opportunities for improved access to housing, jobs, education, and amenities for racial minorities and other disadvantaged groups, and to counteract the effects of important gains made in lawsuits to overcome discriminatory practices in development regulation. The entire response of the Suburban Action Institute is included in Appendix G because of the difficulty of abstracting its findings without compromising the context and substance it reflects.

Transportation Implications

The implementation of the reciprocal limits concept as a land use/human settlement pattern guidance system should mean more efficient transportation systems. Infilling would generate heavier utilization of existing transportation infrastructures in areas released for urban development. This suggests substantial potential for congestion unless public transit systems are improved to enrich the modal balance between personal and public transportation.

The resultant land use and development density patterns would, however, work in favor of improved intercity and intracity transit potential. Such patterns also imply support of goods movement by rail and, with improved technology, by water transport in the navigable sections of the Hudson and Mohawk rivers. High-speed rail service between the major metropolitan and selected corridor urban centers would become more practical. Such use would reduce demand for air transport between the metropolitan centers in the basin.

For short-range travel in the urban centers, safe bikeways and walkways could provide an additional alternative to automobile use. In addition, the social implications of improved public transportation in the basin are broadly beneficial. It is largely the poorer sectors of the population who suffer from the American penchant for "wheels."

These changes would have corollary impacts on the quality of the natural environment. With the establishment of an appropriate balance between travel modes and more reasonable time–distance relationships between home, workplace, shopping, and other community facilities, there would be a decline in vehicle-miles per capita of automobile travel. This, in turn, would lead to reductions in air pollution from exhaust emissions, and a general abatement of traffic noise and vibration. Per capita energy use would decline, but shifts in transport fuel sources from fossil to nuclear and coal-powered electrical generating facilities could cause localized air and thermal pollution problems in the basin.

Conversely, attempts to infill and intensify the density of urban places without a program of improved public transit could easily lead to major problems of congestion, air pollution, and the entire range of adverse impacts caused by the automobile.

Recreational travel from the metropolitan and corridor zones by public transit might increase, but the automobile is likely to remain a preferred vehicle for such purposes. Greater dispersion of the basin population can be expected to strain the capacities of roads extending to such areas. Congestion might become an important factor, since transportation expenditures by the state and federal governments would be directed at priority needs in the metropolitan and corridor zones—particularly in the event that publicly sponsored, large-scale development activities are part of the future.

In summary, it is difficult to see how any system that reduces reliance on the private automobile would not represent a major step forward in the improvement of transportation services and, subsequently, the natural environment.

The Hudson Basin's particular potential to provide a wide range of transportation options and environmental quality has been eroded largely by the automobile. The vast public sums that have been expended in bringing about this lamentable condition might have been better used to strengthen the enviable array of choices provided by the basin's physiography and historic transportation corridors.

As indicated previously, the key to flexible and efficient transportation policy is land use and development density planning on a regional basis. The primary implication of a reciprocal limits policy for transportation would be more rational and more effective planning.

Institutional and Legal Requirements

There are indications that substantial legal and institutional devices, many tantamount to basic reform, are emerging in good time to be employed in the implementation of the key concept of reciprocal limits and its complementary policies. Powerful precedents have emerged in the Ramapo plan for timed release of developable land, in the Nassau–Suffolk Development Plan and supporting programs of open-space acquisition and development-rights management, and in the Coastal Zone Management legislation. Additional support may be found in the wave of change in land use regulation represented by the American Law Institute Proposed Code. These examples offer much potential for refinement and application to the Hudson

Basin region, particularly with respect to constraining growth at the "fringe" and to inducing large-scale development.

Local governments have always seemed to be the logical entity to exercise control over piecemeal development. But this role is limited by insufficient resources for planning and capital improvements, by insufficient authority to influence development decisions, especially on the fringe, by legitimate but competing demands from different interest groups, by uncertainty, and sometimes by a narrow perspective. Localities do not always live up to their potential. Communities cannot exist without a full range of support facilities—utilities, water and sewer lines, circulation networks. These are the tools for shaping urban growth at the disposal of public bodies. More often than not, however, land use planning has been ad hoc and the public opportunities have been all but thrown away.

Private landowners and public officials expect that decisions on what, where, and when to develop are to be made in the marketplace. Public policies, the sentiment goes, should be supportive of these privately made decisions: roads, sewer and water lines, and other public works should be made available in response to private initiatives. This strategy for land use planning derives from a fundamental tradition of sacred property rights: that is, the right of a landowner to develop is somehow inherent in the land itself.

The legitimacy of public regulation of private land use in this country was confirmed by the U.S. Supreme Court in *Euclid* v. *Ambler*, a 1926 landmark decision upholding a zoning ordinance in Euclid, Ohio. The ruling based the public's right to regulate development on private land on a state's police power to protect the health, safety, and general welfare of the people. Yet in the succeeding decades public policies on land development have taken no more stringent a course than control of building setbacks, building heights, lot coverage, and the like. The central decisions of what and when and how to build were left to the marketplace. These zoning restrictions may have been the extent to which public opinion, backed by the courts, was willing to accept government regulation of private lands.

But now, as more and more communities begin to assail the growth ethic, the ground rules are changing. No longer are more and bigger developments so sought after. No longer is population growth the ultimate measure of community prosperity. Changing attitudes toward development in part reflect a growing awareness that such development does not always pay its way. Externalities such as traffic congestion, deterioration of air and water quality, and overcrowded schools are not always recorded in the balance sheets.

Planners have always been aware of the crucial link between infrastructure planning and community development. Once a trunk line has been put in place, it becomes difficult for community officials, even if they were so inclined, to argue successfully that one development proposal is well served by public facilities whereas another, only slightly farther down the road, is not. Little by little, the pressures mount to extend the branch lines, then the trunk line. Planners point to this as orderly growth and development.

Community residents questioning the growth ethic are becoming more sophisticated. They are learning that the availability of the infrastructure is among the most important factors in determining whether a specific development proposal is feasible. The decisions to extend sewer lines or local roads, often made in anticipation of or in response to development schemes, can be as important as the zoning change, site-plan review, or the final sign-off.

In response to the pressures of urban growth, several communities have adopted plans to phase growth over an extended period of time. Among the most widely publicized is the development plan of the Town of Ramapo in Rockland County, New York.* Land in unincorporated portions of Ramapo becomes available for development according to a schedule that awards points for the availability of public services or facilities (e.g., sewers, roads, firehouses, and recreational facilities). An essential element of this plan is an 18-year capital improvement program that will provide these services and facilities to all areas in the community, eventually making all the land available for development. In some areas of the community, development would have to be deferred for the full 18-year period while in others it could begin immediately. New York's highest court upheld the development plan in a 1972 decision. The impact of this phased scheme has been reflected by a drop in the average number of dwelling units constructed annually from approximately 1000 to 350. Unfortunately, the Ramapo plan stops at the town's boundaries. Developers who may be unhappy with a strict timing schedule can take their plans to a neighboring jurisdiction.

From this experience we learn that for a growth strategy to be successful—and the objective of channeling growth into large-scale developments is indeed one element of a growth strategy—a regional perspective is essential. Unless all the holes are plugged, the option of ignoring the incentives for large-scale development will remain open. If they can go next door to build, small operators will continue building at a small scale instead of within a larger framework; and a large-scale builder can threaten to move a project to a neighboring community. Because of the development's proximity, all the problems could spill over into the first community anyway, yet the revenues would go to another jurisdiction. The pressures on decision-makers to abandon their demands or to exact a lesser quality development can then become very real.

*See Volume 2, Chapter 7, Section 7.5.

Nonetheless, the link between infrastructure and community development has been underscored by the Ramapo plan. In simplified terms, it is an attempt to redefine the concept of orderly growth by injecting another measure of public objectives into development decision making. Infrastructure planning, considered from a regional perspective, supports community development objectives. No major innovations are needed to use it. We have the capability now.

Road building illustrates how infrastructure planning has been used to support community development objectives. Before the automobile, housing was located near places of work or near streetcar lines. Development densities were high compared to today's standards. The automobile made possible lower density development that was easily accessible to jobs, shopping, and schools spread throughout an urban region. With the American family's preferences for lower density development—a preference stemming as much from the desire for a home and a piece of land, a yard to play, and more privacy, as from the desire to escape the poverty and ills of the city—the automobile has assumed its preeminent position in our society. But the automobile could never have become the mainstay of suburban development if not for the roads and highways that were put in place at public cost and located by public policy, a policy responding to private development initiatives.

Chapter 3

TRANSPORTATION

3.1 Introduction

The Transportation Task Group is dealing, in effect, with two major systems, both of which have the multiple, interdependent interactions that characterize "ecosystems." The two systems are

1. The "man–structure–vehicle" (MSV) system, by which is meant man and the sum total of all his buildings, fixed transportation facilities, moving vehicles, and machines that collectively support—and strongly influence—society. In the MSV system, man is the principal *biotic* element, whereas his buildings and vehicles may be considered the principal *abiotic* elements.

2. The "MSV–natural environment" system is the system in which man, his fixed structures, and his moving vehicles interact with the natural environment—drawing upon its soils for food, its rivers and lakes for water, and its mines for materials, and using the environment as the "sink" into which to pour his wastes.

These two systems could, of course, be considered as one total system for the Hudson Basin region. However, separating the two is helpful because

Members of the Transportation Task Group: Roger L. Creighton, James Hughes, Richard S. Miller, James R. Nelson, and Louis Pignataro.

the *internal* relationships and organization of the MSV system are extremely important in the way that the system relates to the natural environment. The MSV system in an industrialized region is dominant; it initiates change. It is perhaps through understanding how the MSV system works and through modifying that system that man can best control his impact on the environment, rather than through direct devices such as emission controls on vehicles, although they are important, too.

All of this is reminiscent of Toynbee's examination of societies. The purpose of the Hudson Basin Project is to respond, in advance, to a threat to society: that society might, by its own blindness, permit environmental degradation that would go beyond the absorbing capacity of either the natural system or the man–structure–vehicle system. For example, was the Mayan civilization of Yucatan destroyed by an external climate change or by a social failure that permitted the jungle to resume its former place? Do similar, critical risks face us today? This is the kind of challenge that the study is facing, and it is a challenge that is rendered all the more difficult to grasp by the confusions of an enormously complex and powerful technology.

The Transportation Task Group prepared a highly simplified diagram of certain key relationships within and between the two systems just described. This diagram is shown in Fig. 3-1.

The top set of boxes in Fig. 3-1 suggests certain relationships within the MSV system. People, in their residences and other activities, create travel demands. (Travel demands include requirements for the movement of both people and goods.) These travel demands are channeled through different transportation systems, and create flows of vehicles carrying people and goods. Traffic flows create congestion, which modifies both demand for travel and the locations of human activities. At the same time, transportation facilities, by providing faster (or slower) transportation, change the accessibility levels of different parts of a region, and so modify the locations of housing, workplaces, and other human activities.

It is quite clear that these relationships are continuously self-modifying. A loss of gasoline energy, for example, might reduce mobility and cause settlement to become more dense.

The lower set of boxes illustrates how the MSV system affects the natural environment. In part this is through the taking of land for transportation facilities, and in part through the consumption of energy, which produces most of the noise, water pollution, and air pollution that impacts biological communities.

Figure 3-1 is, of course, a stylized and very limited view of the interactions that are actually taking place. The limitation is necessary because, for a region as large as the Hudson Basin, this task group is breaking into uncharted territory. At the urban level, by contrast, one would be working with

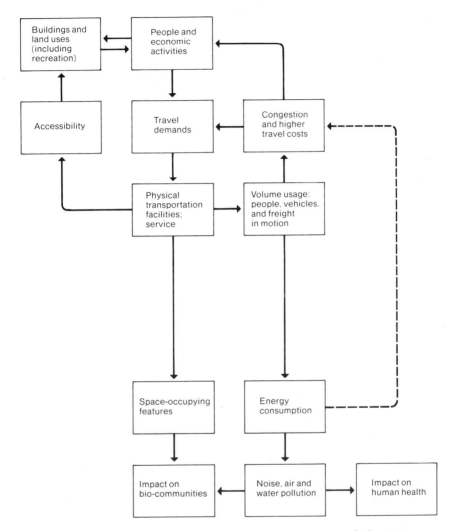

Fig. 3-1. Direction of selected relationships within the man–structure–vehicle (MSV) system and between the MSV system and the natural environment.

tools built up over more than two decades, where detailed traffic and transit interactions can be simulated by computer with highly credible results (Chicago Area Transportation Study, 1962). But at the regional level, explorations are still being made, and many ideas are borrowed and have not been tested over such a large field. Various studies of the "state of the art" of statewide transportation planning, which is comparable in many ways to regional transportation planning, have come to the same conclusion (NCHRP, 1972).

It would have been impossible for the Transportation Task Group, acting in the short time available, to have considered all of these relationships, even in preliminary fashion. What was therefore done was to select certain relationships for study, and to use these studies as examples. In some cases it was possible to assemble data for the entire region, but in other cases a nongeographic approach was taken. The various studies have been organized into five sections, to make the report compatible with the work of other task groups. The five sections are physical factors (3.2), linkages (3.3), issues and alternatives (3.4), institutional capacities (3.5), and recommended strategies for research (3.6).

3.2 Physical Factors

In this section, selected measurements of the man–structure–vehicle system are presented for the Hudson Basin region. These include population, physical transportation facilities, and some measures of usage of the physical facilities. (Usage is reported in person-miles of travel, vehicle-miles of travel, and ton-miles of rail freight shipment.) From these measurements, various deductions are made about impacts upon the environment. The deductions are very general. Further work on linkages is reported in Section 3.3.

Population

The 20,247,000 persons who lived in the Hudson Basin in 1970 were distributed by county as shown in Fig. 3-2. Figure 3-2 is a perspective of the region, drawn looking from the southeast, as it might be seen from a satellite. The drawing was made by computer. The height of the bars is proportional to the population, with the highest bar representing Kings County (Brooklyn), New York, which had a 1970 population of 2,602,000. By contrast, the lowest population is in Hamilton County, in the center of the northern tier of counties shown at the top of the perspective.

To put measures of population, physical transportation facilities, and travel on a comparable basis, the remaining computer displays in this report are *density* displays. Quantities have been divided by the area in each county to give quantities per square mile.

Figure 3-3 shows 1970 population per square mile. As might be expected, the highest density is in Manhattan, where there is an average of 67,000 persons per square mile. By contrast, Hamilton County in the Adirondacks has a population density of only three persons per square mile. The tent-like

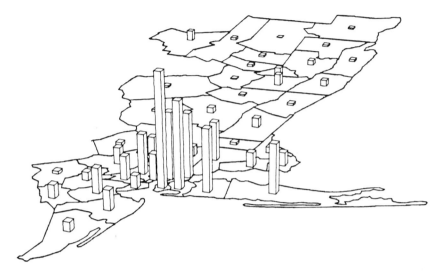

Fig. 3-2.   Hudson Basin region 1970 population distribution by county.

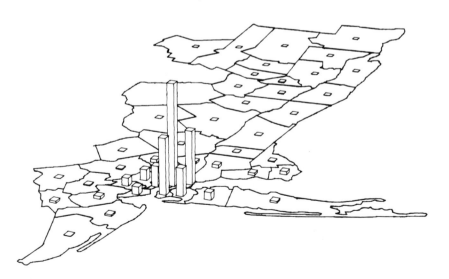

Fig. 3-3.   Hudson Basin region 1970 population density by county.

effect, with very high population densities at the core of a major metropolitan area, dropping off very rapidly to a very low "background" density, is typical of regions with major metropolises at their centers.

Had it been possible to show population density at a township (instead of county) level of detail, a different pattern would have emerged. One would then be able to discern the cores of the minor metropolitan areas, such as Utica, Rome, Amsterdam, Poughkeepsie, and many others.

In the following discussion, it will be seen how this pattern of population density is reflected in the distribution of transportation systems and services. And it does not take much imagination to see how and where environmental problems will result.

Transit Systems

The Present System

In the tristate portion of the Hudson Basin region (basically, the New York–New Jersey metropolitan area) there are about 9720 miles of urban transit routes. They include 8750 miles of bus systems, 240 miles of subway–elevated systems, and 730 miles of suburban railroads. There are an additional 990 miles of bus systems in the upstate portion of the basin, making a total for the basin of approximately 10,710 route miles. (In many cases, bus routes overlap along a single street, and hence route-miles of bus service are greater than the miles of streets on which bus service is available.)

Data on route-miles of bus service in upstate New York and in the four New Jersey counties of the Hudson Basin region that are not included in the tristate region can only be approximated. It is estimated for the purposes of this project that there are about 990 miles of such bus routes, making the grand total of 10,710 transit route-miles in the Hudson Basin region.

Usage of the System

Comparative usage of transit and automobiles as a means of person transportation is always of interest. Figure 3-4, which is taken from the 1973 Master Plan for Transportation of New York State (New York State Department of Transportation, 1973), gives a clearer reading than most graphs of the relative importance of transit. In this case, the unit of measure is the person-trip. The "downstate central business district" is defined as Manhattan south of 60th Street. The "downstate non-CBD" is the New York urban portion of the tristate region. The only "upstate CBD" in the Hudson Basin region would be the CBDs of Albany, Schenectady, and Troy. Note that these data are for the peak hours only; on a 24-hour basis the percentage usage of transit would be significantly lower.

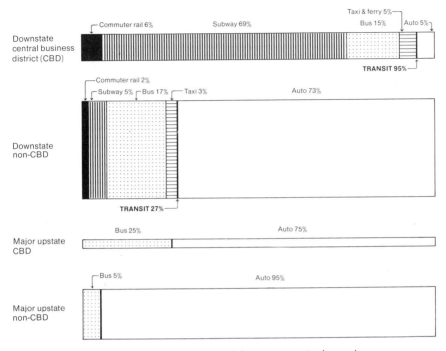

Fig. 3-4. Urban weekday peak-hour person-trips by mode.

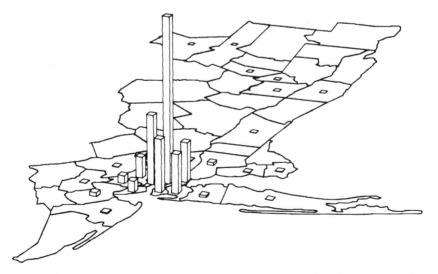

Fig. 3-5. Hudson Basin region 1970 daily bus person-miles of travel per square mile.

The distribution of urban transit usage within the Hudson Basin region is shown in Fig. 3-5. Here the person-miles of travel *by bus only* are shown for most of the counties of the region. Where there is no bar in a county, no data were available. Since most of these counties have no known commuter bus lines, the overall picture is reasonably accurate.

It can be seen that transit usage is almost exclusively an urban phenomenon—and more than that, a high-density urban phenomenon. Transit use is *much* more highly peaked toward the urban center than automobile travel.

Streets and Highways

There are an estimated 76,200 miles of streets and highways in the Hudson Basin region—seven times as many as there are route-miles of transit systems. By jurisdiction, these miles are distributed as follows:

State and authority	9,053 miles	(12%)
County	16,818 miles	(22%)
Town	28,535 miles	(37%)
City and village	21,805 miles	(29%)
Total	76,211 miles	(100%)

Substantial jurisdictional differences exist between the states. Connecticut, for example, has no county roads, and some roads that in other states would be classified as city and village streets are town roads.

In general, however, state and authority highways carry most of the higher speed, heavier volume, and longer distance traffic. Probably half of the daily vehicle-miles of travel (VMT) are carried on state and authority roads, which comprise only 12% of the system. County roads tend to be mainly "rural secondary" highways. Average volumes are quite low in rural areas (in Montgomery County, for example, the average weekday traffic volume on county roads is at the level of 250 vehicles). Town roads (except in urban regions such as southwestern Connecticut) are mainly rural land-access roads with extremely light volumes. City and village streets are primarily urban land-access roads, although in some cases heavy-volume urban arterials are included in this category.

Suffolk County has the greatest mileage—6042 miles of streets and highways; Dutchess County has 2127 miles. The mileage of roadways in a given county is generally (but not always) a function of population and land area.

The density of all streets and highways is shown in Fig. 3-6. As expected, Manhattan has the highest density—22.1 miles of highways per square mile of land. The lowest density is in Hamilton County in the Adirondacks, with 0.3 miles per square mile. If roads in each county were laid out in a uniform

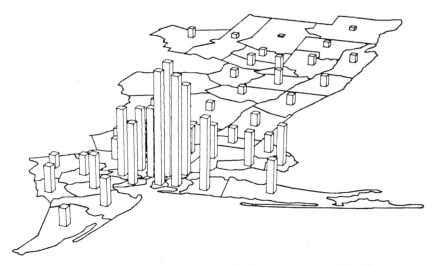

Fig. 3-6.   Hudson Basin region miles of highway per square mile of land.

grid (which is, of course, not true), Manhattan would have roads spaced 0.1 miles apart, whereas in Hamilton County roads would be spaced 6.7 miles apart. Dutchess County would have its roads spaced 0.8 miles apart.

This spacing of roads is, naturally, of tremendous importance to the environment. (This is the "space-occupying feature" identified in Fig. 3-1.) In dense urban areas, when roads are spaced one-tenth of a mile apart, and when most of them are four lanes (40–48 feet) in paved width, then a significant part of the land area is paved. But in the rural counties, roads are widely spaced, are narrower, have much less traffic, and hence have much less impact upon the environment.

Vehicle-Miles of Travel

The use that is made of the region's roadway system is measured in "vehicle-miles of travel" (VMT). Ten thousand vehicles passing over a mile of road is 10,000 VMT. All figures given here are in daily terms. The distribution of vehicle-miles of travel per square mile is shown in Fig. 3-7.

As might be expected, the density of vehicle-miles of travel is greatest in Manhattan—282,600 VMT daily *per square mile*. At these densities, the production of noise and air pollution reaches levels that are claimed to be injurious to health; certainly the emissions are unpleasant and a nuisance. As distance increases from Manhattan, the density of vehicle-miles of travel drops off rapidly. Hudson County, New Jersey, has 95,500 VMT per square mile, whereas Kings, Queens, and the Bronx counties all exceed 125,000 VMT per square mile. Albany County has an average of 7450 VMT per

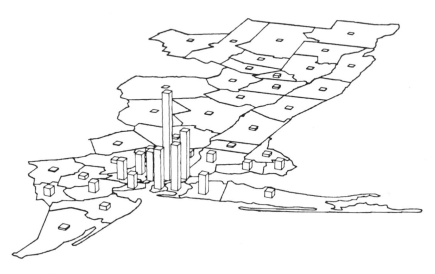

Fig. 3-7.   Hudson Basin region 1970 vehicle-miles of travel per square mile.

square mile. The lowest level is 100 VMT per square mile, in Hamilton County.

The amount of vehicular travel in relation to population is quite different. Manhattan and Brooklyn have, respectively, 4.2 and 3.5 VMT per person per day. This low level occurs because of the heavy use of buses, subways, and suburban railroads in these counties. By contrast, Hamilton County produces 40 VMT per person per day; this high production is the result of not only higher car ownership and longer average trips but also trips, such as vacation trips, driven into and through the county by nonresidents.

Since vehicle-miles of travel requires energy consumption, and the burning of fuels creates air pollution, the density of vehicle-miles of travel shown in Fig. 3-7 can also be read, almost directly, as a figure showing gallons of gasoline and diesel fuel consumed per square mile or as a figure showing tons of pollutants discharged into the atmosphere.

Waterways and Canals

The Present System

The primary inland water transportation system in the Hudson Basin is, of course, the Hudson River. It is navigable to ocean-going vessels (water depth, 32 feet) as far north as Albany. Water depths of 12 feet are maintained between Albany and Hudson Falls.

From the upper Hudson, the Mohawk River penetrates 130 miles through the region, eventually connecting with both Lake Ontario and Lake Erie via the New York State Barge Canal. It has a depth of 14 feet through the region. The waterway is closed to all traffic during the winter.

North of Albany, the Champlain Canal is open except in winter months, following the route Waterford–Fort Edward–Whitehall, from whence it uses Lake Champlain northward, eventually connecting by the Richelieu River to the St. Lawrence.

The "back door" of the Hudson Basin region is accessible via the Delaware River, which is navigable as far as Trenton, New Jersey.

Usage of Waterways and Canals

Usage of the inland waterways is probably best described as stabilized. In recent years, records of tonnages shipped on the New York State Barge Canal past Amsterdam show some declines.

Even recreational use of inland waterways has stabilized. Lock records show declining usage by recreational craft since 1966, but this may be due in part to adverse weather and the impact of the Holding Tank Law of 1970.

In the future, the most reasonable forecast is for continued stability in usage of inland waterways by commercial interests. Recreational travel (subject to energy restrictions) may grow, although recent records cast doubt that longer trips on canals will increase much. Recreational use of the waterways will continue to be a seasonal activity.

Environmental Impact of Inland Waterway Usage

Any form of transportation requires power, inland waterways not excepted. (Sailing is not a major activity on canals and rivers in the Hudson Basin, although there are a few sailing clubs on the lower Hudson River.) Power boats and barges burn diesel fuel and gasoline, and produce both exhaust fumes and oil traces in the waters through which they pass. Larger craft and speed boats produce both noise and waves.

How these transportation impacts affect fish, birds, and other wildlife is a matter for experts to determine. The situation is, however, a mature one, and the balance between man and nature, from the viewpoint of water transportation, has probably not changed much in the past 50 years. Given stability in usage of these waterways, the balance does not appear to be threatened.

Intercity Rail Freight System

The network of rail lines providing freight transportation in the Hudson Basin region is shown in Fig. 3-8. This is an extensive system of 3340 miles of railroad right-of-way (not miles of track).

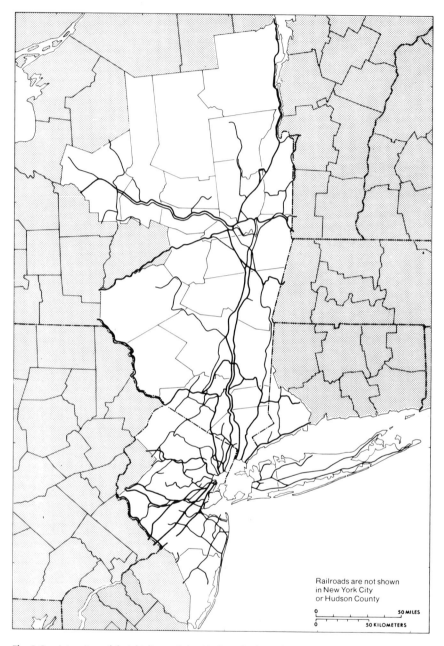

Railroads are not shown
in New York City
or Hudson County

Fig. 3-8. Intercity rail freight lines of the Hudson Basin region. (*Source:* U.S. Department of Transportation, 1974.)

Rail freight *service* has to be distinguished from the physical presence of rail lines. Rail service is influenced by directness of routing, frequency of scheduling, reliability, and, of course, cost. In the heavily traveled corridors, scheduled service is frequent. Elsewhere, it is less good. Thus outer Long Island, although it has extensive trackage, is in a fairly poor position because access to it is very circuitous: Penn Central freight cars, for example, must cross the Hudson near Albany, travel south to Beacon, and then into Connecticut to reach the Hell Gate Bridge before proceeding eastward to Nassau and Suffolk counties. Lehigh Valley freight cars must be lightered across New York Harbor.

Usage of the Rail Freight System

Traffic density on the freight lines in the Hudson Basin region is portrayed in Fig. 3-9. In examining this figure, the reader should understand that traffic densities flowing to the New York metropolitan area from the southwest, and traffic flowing along the Mohawk to Albany (Selkirk yards) and into New England, are *not* to scale. These densities exceed 40 million ton-miles annually, but the amount of the excess is not obtainable from the source used.

Environmental Impact

The environmental impact of the rail systems in the Hudson Basin region should be studied by experts. In such an examination, however, the following points should be considered:

1. The rail system in the Northeast is a very mature system; many of its routes were laid out over 125 years ago.
2. Traffic usage of the system has stabilized, except for passenger traffic, which is sharply down from the levels of 1930–1945. Even with increased Amtrak service, passenger volumes are not likely to reach earlier levels.
3. Rail service is, for moving freight over land, more efficient from the viewpoint of energy consumption and air pollution than its major competitor, truck transportation.

Although there may be points on the rail system, such as in northern New Jersey or the Selkirk yards near Albany, which are sterile or adverse to biological communities, the system as a whole is not adverse to the region. No major changes threaten with increased impacts.

Pipelines

Figure 3-10 illustrates the three basic types of pipelines serving the Hudson Basin Region: (a) natural gas pipelines, (b) liquefied petroleum gas (LPG)

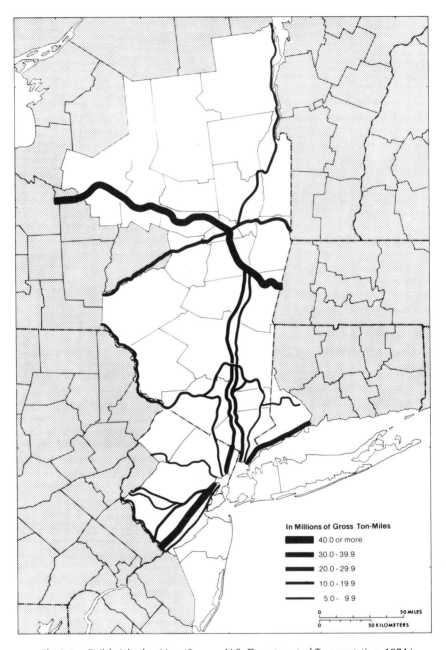

Fig. 3-9.   Rail freight densities. (*Source:* U.S. Department of Transportation, 1974.)

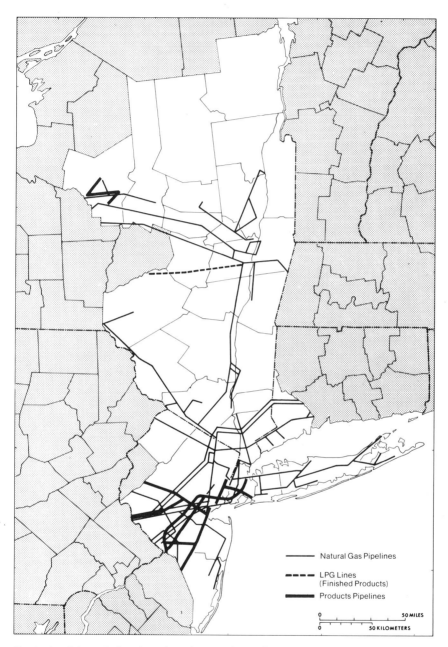

Fig. 3-10. Schematic location of pipelines in the Hudson Basin region. (*Source:* American Petroleum Institute, 1973.)

pipelines, and (c) products pipelines that convey crude oil or refined products. Note that products pipelines serve the New York metropolitan area and the Utica–Rome area in the northwestern part of the region, but nowhere else. This is because the cities along the Hudson are served by barges and small tankers, whose loads are then distributed by truck.

Pipelines are probably as harmless to the environment as any form of transportation. The principal harm would come during construction.

Airports

The airports of the Hudson Basin region are fairly evenly distributed as shown in Fig. 3-11, except in the Catskills and the Adirondacks, where terrain and low population density combine to reduce needs.

Activity at these airfields varies tremendously, of course, ranging from a few flights per day to the more than 75 arrivals and departures per hour of commercial and general aviation aircraft at Kennedy International Airport (NAS and NAE, 1971).

The primary air transportation center of the Hudson Basin region is metropolitan New York. Located there are Kennedy, LaGuardia, Newark, Islip, White Plains, and Teterboro airports.

Major airports have a substantial impact upon the environment in their vicinities (NAS and NAE, 1971). They occupy large areas of land—Kennedy Airport, for example, covers 7 square miles. The noise and air pollution from aircraft alone are substantial, and added to this is the pollution produced by the automobile and truck traffic required to serve thousands of workers and tens of thousands of daily travelers.

If present trends continue, aviation activity in the New York metropolitan area can be expected to increase, although probably not at the same pace experienced in the 1950s and 1960s. In any continued study of the environment, pollution from aviation will have to be monitored carefully.

Conclusion

More than 90% of transit usage occurs in the high-density New York–northern New Jersey metropolitan area. The density of vehicle-miles of travel, both automobile and truck, occurs in very much the same pattern as population density. To the extent that energy requirements and pollution go along with vehicle and personal travel, these same patterns can be read as the patterns of air pollution of the environment.

The long-distance transportation routes—rail, water, and even highway—appear not to be threatening to the environment. Rail and water transport are mature systems, and are unlikely to expand in usage. Rural highway

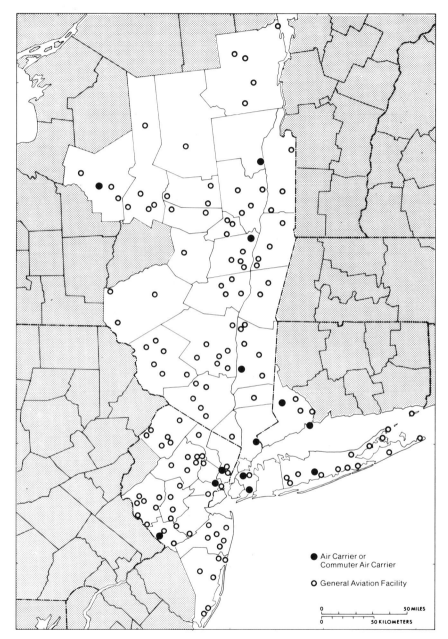

Fig. 3-11. Air transportation facilities in the Hudson Basin region (*Sources:* Connecticut Department of Transportation, 1972; New Jersey Department of Transportation, 1972; New York State Department of Transportation, 1972.)

travel is so dispersed that it probably is not a significant threat as seen from a regional viewpoint. Air travel, however, is harder to assess: Major airports are major polluters, and it is not known what continued impact air travel will have upon the upper atmosphere.

3.3   Some Key Linkages

Transportation and Energy Consumption

In 1970, transportation in the United States consumed 24% of the nation's energy and this proportion is expected to continue (U.S. Department of the Interior, 1971). This section discusses passenger traffic and its energy efficiencies, and comments upon future trends of energy consumption in transportation. "Energy efficiency" is defined as passenger miles per British thermal unit for passenger transport.

Owing to increased levels of traffic, shifts to less energy-efficient modes, and decreases in energy efficiency for individual modes, the energy requirements for transportation increased by 52% between 1960 and 1970. The automobile is the primary vehicle of passenger traffic between cities; airplanes, buses, and railroads play lesser roles. Table 3-1 shows that, according to mid-1960s efficiencies, the automobile averaged 32 passenger-miles per gallon of petroleum. (In intercity traffic, the average number of persons per car is 2.0). Although buses can average 125 passenger-miles per gallon, they are the least popular mode of travel. Also, even though buses are 11% more efficient than air travel, airplanes are growing more popular because of speed, comfort, and convenience.

Table 3-2 shows that, in the past 20 years, the automobile has remained

TABLE 3-1.   Energy Efficiency for Intercity Passenger Transport[a]

Mode	Passenger-miles per gallon	British thermal units[b] per passenger-mile	Ten joules per passenger-kilometer
Bus	125	1100	710
Railroad	80	1700	1100
Automobile	32	4250	2800
Airplane	14	9700	6400

[a] From Hirst (1973), reproduced by permission.
[b] Assuming 136,000 Btu/gal (37.9 billion joules/m^3).

TABLE 3-2. Intercity Passenger Traffic and Energy Consumption[a,b]

Year	Total passenger-miles, ($\times 10^9$)	Passenger-miles, as a percentage of total				Total energy (10^{12} Btu's)[c]	Inverse efficiency (Btu's per passenger mile)
		Automobile	Airplane	Bus	Railroad		
Past							
1950	510	86.8	2.0	5.2	6.4	2,040	—
1955	720	89.5	3.2	3.6	4.0	3,000	4,210
1960	780	90.1	4.3	2.5	2.8	3,390	4,340
1965	920	88.8	6.3	2.6	1.9	4,100	4,470
1970	1,180	87.0	9.7	2.1	0.9	5,510	4,690
Future I—continuation of current trends							
1980	1,710	85	13	1.5	0.5	8,370	4,890
1990	2,240	84	15	1.0	—	11,280	5,040
2000	2,770	83	17	—	—	14,340	5,180
Future II—shift to greater energy efficiency							
1980	1,710	86	7	4	3	7,570	4,430
1990	2,240	85	3	6	6	9,120	4,070
2000	2,770	84	2	7	7	10,970	3,960

[a] From Hirst (1973), reproduced by permission.
[b] Conversion factors are from passenger-miles to passenger-kilometers (1.609); from British thermal units to joules (1055); from British thermal units/passenger-kilometer (656).
[c] Total energy consumption computed using energy efficiencies given in Table 3-3.

constant in transporting approximately 88% of the total passenger population. Buses and railroads, although more efficient means, have decreased. They carry 2.1 and 0.9% of the population, respectively. If current trends continue to the year 2000, there will be a 10% decline in passenger energy efficiency. If, however, a steady, but not revolutionary, shift toward more energy-efficient transport modes is made (excluding possible technological changes that might affect energy consumption), an 18% increase in energy efficiency for intercity passenger transport is possible by 2000. The automobile will still be responsible for 84% of the total passenger mileage.

Urban passenger traffic is also carried primarily by automobiles. In the city, autos average only 17 passenger-miles per gallon (1.5 persons per car), as opposed to 37 passenger-miles per gallon using mass transit. Bicycling is 40 times as energy efficient as the auto (see Table 3-3).

Table 3-4 shows that, in the past 20 years, the car has increased steadily from carrying 84.8% of the passenger-mile total to 97.2%, while mass transit declined to 2.8% of the total. Energy efficiency decreased 7% between 1950 and 1970, while total passenger-miles increased by 13%.

TABLE 3-3.   Energy Efficiency for Urban Passenger Transport[a,b]

Mode	Passenger-miles per gallon	British thermal units[c] per passenger-mile	10^3 joules per passenger-kilometer
Bicycle[d]	—	200	130
Walking	—	300	200
Mass transit	37	3700	2400
Automobile[d]	17	7900	5200

[a] From Hirst (1973), reproduced by permission.

[b] Data from the Federal Highway Administration, (Connecticut Interregional Planning Program, 1968), the Automobile Manufacturers Association (Connecticut Department of Transportation, 1972), the American Transit Association (Hindawi, 1970), and the U.S. Federal Highway Administration.

[c] Assuming 136,000 Btu per gallon (37.9 joules/m^3).

[d] Efficiencies for bicycling and walking are computed as follows: An excess of 890 Btu/hr (225 cal/hr) is required for moderate walking or bicycling. Assuming 5 mph (8 km/hr) by bicycle and 3 mph (5 km/hr) by foot yields the values given.

Effects of Automotive Air Pollution on Vegetation

Automobile exhaust has many chemical components: unburned hydrocarbons, carbon monoxide, oxides of nitrogen, and often lead. The components with which this section is most concerned are the hydrocarbons and the oxides of nitrogen. In the presence of sunlight, these two compounds combine, split up, and recombine with the oxygen in the air to form two classes of phytotoxic compounds: peroxyacyl nitrates (commonly referred to as PAN) and ozone. These are the main components of photochemical smog. Smog is somewhat of a misnomer, since technically it refers to a mixture of smoke and fog, which reached its most disastrous concentrations in London in the early 1950s. The term was applied to air pollution in the Los Angeles Basin before the actual chemical makeup of the pollution was discovered, and it is still used. In some areas, PAN and ozone form a large part of the air pollution load; in others their concentration is not so large. This all depends, of course, on the density of automobile traffic and the meteorological conditions of an area.

It has been known since the 1950s that oxidants from automobile exhaust can injure plants. Suspicions to this effect were aroused in the mid-1940s when growers in the Los Angeles Basin began to notice new kinds of leaf injury on their crops. These symptoms were later reproduced in controlled experiments where plants were fumigated with chemicals from car exhaust.

PAN attacks the mesophyll cells of the leaf, where it breaks down the chloroplasts. It also affects the permeability of the guard cells around the stomata so that they become engorged with water and often burst. This

TABLE 3-4. Urban Passenger Traffic and Energy Consumption[a,b]

| Year | Total passenger-miles, (× 10⁹) | Passenger-miles, as a percentage of total | | | Total energy[b] (10^{12} Btu's) | Inverse efficiency (Btu's per passenger-mile) |
		Automobile	Mass transit	Bicycle, walking		
Past						
1950	302	84.8	15.2	—	2,190	7,250
1955	345	91.0	9.0	—	2,590	7,520
1960	424	94.1	5.9	—	3,250	7,650
1965	551	96.0	4.0	—	4,260	7,730
1970	713	97.2	2.8	—	5,550	7,780
Future I—continuation of current trends						
1980	1,010	97.5	2.5	—	7,880	7,800
1990	1,310	98.0	2.0	—	10,240	7,820
2000	1,610	98.5	1.5	—	12,620	7,840
Future II—shift to greater energy efficiency						
1980	1,010	93	4	3	7,570	7,500
1990	1,310	90	7	3	9,660	7,370
2000	1,610	87	10	3	11,680	7,250

[a] From Hirst (1973), reproduced by permission.

[b] Data from Bureau of the Census (Landsberg and Schurr, 1968) and American Transit Association of America (Chicago Area Transportation Study, 1962). Conversion factors are from passenger-miles to passenger-kilometers (1.609); from British thermal units to joules (1055); from British thermal units/passenger-mile to joules/passenger-kilometers (656).

[c] Total energy consumption computed using energy efficiencies given in Table 3-3.

causes the stomata to close, so that no more carbon dioxide is taken into the plant and more water vapor is transpired out. This completely disrupts the physiology of the plant. External symptoms may vary, from a glazing of the underside of the leaf, to a water-soaked appearance followed by brown and black splotches of dead tissue. Ozone also breaks down the chloroplasts, although in a different way. The affected cells appear as lesions on the upper surface—at first white, and then brown or red as the cells die. Photosynthesis is, of course, slowed by the lack of chlorophyll, and, at the same time, carbohydrate metabolism is increased so that the plant depletes its starch reserves. Plants in this condition either die or are unmarketable.

There is considerable evidence that PAN and ozone reduce plant growth even at concentrations too low to produce visible symptoms. Reduced growth is hard to document in the field, but much work has been performed growing plants in filtered and unfiltered air, or filtered and fumigated air, and the plants exposed to the pollution have invariably been smaller. Reduced reproductive capacity is another possible result of exposure to pollutants. Citrus yields have been reduced from exposure to smog in southern California, and reduced pollen germination has been shown in tobacco and corn following exposure to ozone. Carnations and geraniums exposed to ozone have produced fewer flowers and initiated buds later in the season than usual.

Although air pollution damage to plants has been most extensively studied in southern California, where there exists a unique combination of high levels of air pollution and intensive agriculture, this is not to say that the problem is unique to that area. New Jersey farmers have suffered extensive losses, and the Connecticut Valley tobacco crop was seriously affected by a disease which was at the time referred to as "weather fleck." Splotches on the leaves which rendered them useless as cigar wrappers were found to be caused by exposure to ozone.

How much exposure to PAN and ozone can plants tolerate? This is a hard question to answer, because the degree of injury depends on many factors. Some species, or some varieties within a species, are very susceptible to pollution damage, whereas others are very resistant. Susceptibility is influenced by the age and the condition of the plant, and young leaves are usually more sensitive than old ones. Season and time of day of exposure both make a difference, as do the length and concentration of exposure. PAN and ozone both enter the plants through the stomata, so that any factor that influences stomatal activity will influence the degree of injury. This means that if the plant has moist, fertile soil and bright sunlight, it will be even more severely injured. Farmers wanting to protect their plants from external injury—insects, bacteria, or fungi—know that one way to do this is to keep their plants healthy. In the case of air pollution damage, however,

TABLE 3-5. Threshold Values of Air Pollutants Affecting Different Plants and Observed Ambient Pollution Levels

Compound	Plant	Concentration (pphm)	Length of exposure (hr)	Reference	Ambient air levels
PAN	"Sensitive plants"	0.5–1.5	8	Treshow (1970)	One to 2 pphm in Los Angeles and Utah on normal days; up to 5 pphm on smoggy days
		2	2–4	Treshow (1970)	
	Tobacco, petunia	10	5	Treshow (1970)	
	Pinto beans	1	6	Hindawi (1970)	
Ozone	Beans	5	Prolonged	Treshow (1970)	One to 2 pphm in Asheville, N.C. (very rural) and in the desert. Five to 38 pphm in Los Angeles. Peaks of 50 pphm in San Francisco. Twenty-two in Salt Lake City. Sixteen pphm in Washington, D.C.
	Broccoli, tomatoes	25	2	Treshow (1970)	
	Carnations	7	10 days	Treshow (1970)	
	Apples	1.8	3 days	Treshow (1970)	
	Eastern white pine	3	Several hours	Linzon et al. (1975)	

the factors contributing to plant health are those that also make the plants most susceptible. The most vigorously growing plants are the most seriously damaged.

Despite all these difficulties, very rough threshold values have been established for certain species. Most of these values have been set in the laboratory, rather than in the field, partly because of the difficulty in the field of separating the effects of one compound from the effects of another. Table 3-5 presents the results of some of the work that has been done.

It is evident both from these figures and from empirical observation that the concentration of automotive pollutants in and around major cities is certainly high enough to cause plant damage. It is known that these pollutants do not travel far and that they are unstable compounds, so that they do not remain in the air long after they are emitted. One could assume, therefore, that plant damage would be relatively localized, but the extent of injury in the Connecticut Valley shows that serious effects can be felt over a region and not just in the immediate vicinity of a highway or a city.

3.4   Issues and Alternatives

Freight Transportation Issues

A casual reader of the New York press would assume that the only transportation problems of New York City were those of maintaining a given level of subway fares, or of convincing the Port Authority of New York and New Jersey (and holders of its bonds) that they should assume additional responsibilities for financing commuter transportation in the New York–New Jersey area. The truth is, however, that New York City could not have *become* the commercial metropolis of the United States without having efficiently exploited its geographical advantages with respect to the international movements of passengers and, especially, freight. Also, New York City could not remain a metropolis of any kind without both adequate terminal facilities and efficient linkages with other parts of the United States and the world at large.

Our prime emphasis is not on how New York City became what it is now but, rather, how it may expect to retain its position. The rise of New York to the first rank among American cities was the product of a combination of an unusually innovative approach to commercial organization, an unusually bold approach to state investment in public works (in the form of investment in the Erie Canal), and unusually favorable geography—the water level route. The port of New York no longer plays the role in the life of the city that was assigned to it as recently as the 1920s. Passenger ships are disappearing, bulk cargoes are shifting to specialized terminals generally well removed from Manhattan, and general cargo has deserted the finger piers of the North river estuary of the Hudson and the East River for container facilities at Port Newark, Port Elizabeth, and elsewhere in New Jersey. In the process of containerization, dockside employment has greatly declined—which was, in fact, much of the point to the containerization.

This tendency to reduce port employment per ton of general cargo moved across the docks is especially important because general cargo never has been and is not now of primary importance relative to other freight movements into and out of the metropolitan area, if importance is measured in terms of sheer tonnage.

For example, in 1972 the region covered by the Tri-State Regional Planning Commission received 210 million tons of freight from all external sources, domestic and foreign, by land, sea, and air; it shipped out 99 million tons of freight; 321 million tons of freight moved within the area, about three quarters of it by truck (TSRPC, 1974).

Of this total of approximately 309 million tons moving into or out of the tristate area, 61 million were accounted for as foreign trade. Of the 61 million tons that entered or left the port of New York in 1972 as imports or exports, the dominant mass was in the form of inbound bulk cargo. This accounted for 44.8 million tons, as against fewer than 1 million tons in outbound bulk cargo, 10 million tons in inbound general cargo, and 4.8 million tons in outbound general cargo. Thus general cargo, in tonnage terms, accounted for just under 25% of all foreign trade through the port of New York. General cargo was relatively even less significant in coastwise trades. It accounted for only 5.5 million of a total of about 68 million tons in 1972, or well under 10% (Port Authority of New York and New Jersey, 1973).

The importance of general cargo has stemmed, in the past, both from its relatively high value per ton, and from its resistance to the cheap "pump-or-dump" techniques that can be employed for petroleum and its products or for many solid bulk commodities. The unit value characteristic serves to provide employment for a range of insurance and brokerage firms. As already noted, the need for special handling in the past has provided the basis for the employment of stevedores, longshoremen, and other dock workers. But despite containerization, foreign trade in general cargo through the port of New York shows no consistent growth trend. Total tonnage in 1972 was below that of the 1920s or 1940, or any year from 1966 through 1970 (Port Authority of New York and New Jersey, 1973). Imports through the port of New York have grown, but exports have declined.

Containerization has helped to restore the position of the port of New York in coastwise trades. Total general cargo of 5.5 million tons moving in these trades in 1972 was at least twice the average for the 1950s, but still below even the depression year of 1938. The impact of containerization shows more clearly in the data for the unloading of export rail cars, which has dropped from an average of 232,000 in 1951 and 1952 almost without interruption to under 29,000 in 1972. But by far the most dynamic aspect of the tonnage data for New York's foreign trade is contained in the statistics for airborne trade. This amounted to only 5609 tons in 1950, but grew to 32,376 tons in 1960, to 308,991 tons in 1970, and to 421,271 tons in 1972 (Port Authority of New York and New Jersey, 1973). This indicates the quantitative importance of airborne trade in the future of long-distance freight transportation involving the New York metropolitan area.

Geography is gaining ground on employment. Petroleum is the leading bulk commodity—and petroleum raises geographical issues, with particular reference to those relating to the environment, at all stages of its production, transportation, refining, and use. At the other end of the freight transport spectrum, the optimum time for many air freight movements is at night. From the standpoint of residents near airports, this is normally the worst time. Even containerization introduces a geographical dimension, because container terminals substitute acreage for manpower. In terms of the New York area, the net effect is to release waterfront space, especially in Manhattan and Brooklyn, and to mortgage additional space inland from specialized terminals at or near airports.

The importance of the New York metropolitan area as a final consumer is gaining ground relative to its importance as an intermediary or transit point. Air freight may provide an exception to this generalization.

Trucks have gained enormous ground relative to rail, not only for local distribution but also for movements into and out of the metropolitan area. The importance of this increase in truck transport is at least fivefold:

1. The problems of congestion and pollution created by trucking are both more serious and more pervasive than those created by rail or water transportation, because trucks consume far more fuel per ton moved, and are able to move into practically every cranny of a metropolitan area.
2. Trucking creates "new" geographical and environmental problems, as opposed to the "old" problems, long since created by railroads.
3. Truck competition has been a most important factor in creating derelict rail facilities, but planning for conversion of these facilities to other uses has been almost nonexistent in comparison with the elaborate planning that has gone into extension of the highway network.
4. The flexibility of the motor truck has been a factor in the spread of

population and industrial employment in the New York metropolitan area. This, in turn, has complicated problems of mass transit, of expanding employment opportunities for inner city residents, and even of continuing efficient operation for the trucking industry itself—for the sprawling response of industrial location to the flexibility offered by the truck has threatened to hoist the trucking industry by its own petard.

5. The New York metropolitan area not only is the largest and densest *individual* concentration of population in the country, but also occupies a central position amid the largest and densest *general* concentration of population in the country. This entire northeastern area requires masses of inbound food and raw materials even to survive. Much of the required tonnage is shipped overland, and shipped for long distances. The growth of trucking at the expense of rail has substituted an industry that creates new terminal problems, and offers less in the way of reducing the cost of long-distance transportation.

The issues discussed below are based on the preceding statements.

Since the "old" rail terminal facilities are concentrated on or near the New Jersey shore of the North river estuary of the Hudson, and the "new" air freight facilities are concentrated at Kennedy International Airport, is there any way to offset the disadvantages of decrepitude and exuberant growth? The obvious first step would seem to be to explore the advantages of Newark Airport, and its surrounding area, as a site for completing the concentration of freight transportation advantages which already exist—these being Port Newark, the New Jersey Turnpike, with its uncongested access to practically the entire United States lying west and south of New York, and the extensive rail piggyback facilities. At one stage of aviation development, Kennedy was the obvious terminal for combined passenger and freight planes, but movement of freight to and from this airport by truck merely serves to contribute to what has been called the world's longest parking lot. Meanwhile, why not use northern New Jersey?

Manhattan and Brooklyn were historically the centers for waterborne commerce, and especially for waterborne foreign trade, whereas northern New Jersey contained most of the heavy industrial development that served the metropolitan area directly, as well as most of the heavy-duty overland freight terminals and related facilities. Containerization has already produced a shift of waterborne trade toward New Jersey, which also has outstanding advantages as a site for truck and even air terminals.

The obverse of these possibilities is presented by Jersey City, and by Hudson County in general. Jersey City has unwillingly found itself to be the home of abandoned or unprofitable rail terminals. It has one of the best geographical locations in the United States, and it has rail facilities that could add to the value of its location. But the existence of these facilities in their present condition is doubtless a negative influence on Jersey City. How then, can an actual liability be converted into the asset that it potentially is?

Ranging farther afield, even if New York had no port and no foreign trade, its citizens would rely on the railroad systems of the northeastern states for most of their food and many of their industrial raw materials. These systems are now in a state ranging from decay to collapse. An increase in subway fare is an obvious event, but what about threatened increases in transportation costs for most of the essentials of life?

There is also a problem of relating freight to passengers. The Hudson Basin contains a number of freight/passenger interrelationships of particular importance.

Since the early days of the Erie Canal, freight access by New York City to the countryside west of the Hudson Valley has been increasingly divorced from passenger access. The early canal boats carried passengers westbound, and subsequent canal boats carried their produce eastbound. Since the canal era, however, the ties binding New York City to the Hudson and Mohawk valleys have not been considered systematically in terms of their relationships to both passengers and freight, and in terms of the interrelationship between the two. The Twentieth Century Limited was not intended to connect the river towns of the Hudson Valley to Manhattan Island, nor are present airline schedules designed to give them easy access to LaGuardia or Kennedy airports.

Thus many of the Hudson Valley towns have suffered a geographical application of the Law of the Excluded Middle—they are too far out to be suburban, but too close to be independent transportation nodes in their own right. This fate may be, in part, inevitable, but it has been hastened and made more severe by the financial weaknesses and the divided interests of railroads passing along the Hudson Corridor on their way to New York. The traditionally first-class rail line on the east bank of the Hudson supports only limited passenger traffic. The West Shore line is being allotted a more important role in freight transportation without the maintenance expenditures that would be required to support such a role. Meanwhile, for many excellent reasons, the dominant express highways close to the east bank of the Hudson are reserved at one stage or another for passenger vehicles. The net upshot is that the geographical advantages of the Hudson Valley towns are not being put to maximum use. What is needed is an approach to the problems of moving passengers *and* freight, by highway *and* rail.

Closer to New York City, northern New Jersey is the center of both present controversy and future possibilities. A reluctant Port Authority is being nudged ever closer to the assumption of deficits in connection with New Jersey commuter passengers. Meanwhile, no agency is entrusted with the ownership, or even the planning, of *integrated* passenger and freight facilities in northern New Jersey or anywhere else in the metropolitan area. Many of the North Jersey commuter lines have little, if any freight traffic; some of the more important Jersey freight lines have no passenger traffic. But they are intertwined, take up valuable land areas, and have the extra advantage of providing corridors into and out of heavily populated centers.

Obviously, the question of the Port Authority's role in New Jersey commuter transportation involves legal issues with respect to the Authority's commitments to present bondholders. It involves issues as well of the proper functional role of the Authority. Whatever the decision with respect to the Port Authority's role in commuter transportation, however, this decision should not be reached independently of its role in providing the entire freight infrastructure for the metropolitan New York area. In particular, to slice off North Jersey rail commuter lines and present them to the Port Authority without reference to the rail freight facilities that are so prominent a feature of the geography of North Jersey would be to reverse the entire purpose for which the Authority was first established.

In terms of the relationship between automotive transportation and the existence of congestion and pollution in the New York metropolitan area, it would be unwise to pay too much attention to the passenger vehicle at the expense of the truck. Commuters to Manhattan, unlike commuters anywhere else in the United States, already overwhelmingly rely on public transport. This simplifies future transportation planning, even if it remains unusually difficult to lure commuters out of their automobiles and into public transportation.

Economic activity in the older portions of the New York metropolitan area depends less, per capita, on sheer tonnage of freight than in practically any other part of the United States. But, partly because of the density of residential and working populations, a heavy volume of freight must move to provide livelihoods and essentials of life to the inhabitants of the area. Careful location of facilities, both for transit and for terminal operations, is therefore more important in terms of the numbers of people affected than any possible plan for the future of commuter railroads serving New York's commercial areas.

On Manhattan Island, places of employment have been located only after careful attention to existing and projected public transit facilities. This has not been true elsewhere in the metropolitan area. If job problems for central city residents are ever to be solved, the solution must involve heeding the requirements of outbound commutation. And these requirements cannot be met satisfactorily if the only criterion for suburban industrial location is the area of vacant land available for parking lots near an express highway.

3.5   Institutional Capacities

Introduction

Institutional capacities to deal with transportation, land use, and environmental matters within the Hudson Basin region are subject to a host of complexities. Many of these are common to all regions; other complexities arise that are unique to this region.

The region under study comprises portions of three states; the governmental and institutional structures of each are quite different. New Jersey, for instance, had little state power and a multiplicity of local municipalities highly dependent on the property tax to finance local public and educational services.* The state has no internal focus; its largest city, Newark, is but a subcenter within the New York metropolitan area. New Jersey's Department of Transportation is burdened by a lack of state resources.

New York, in contrast, has exerted a larger degree of state control on the basis of much greater financial resources. Its statewide income tax emphasizes the differences among the tax structures of the three states.

Other unique complexities emerge from the political geography of the region. For example, most of the heavy industry in the New York metropolitan region lies across the Hudson River in New Jersey. Hence much of Manhattan's air pollution problem lies outside the jurisdiction of New York City. A multiplicity of similar problems adds further complexity to the following difficulties of evaluating institutional capacities.

Transportation within the Hudson Basin region is the province of various institutions directly concerned with transportation and institutions focusing on other types of activities, the most significant being the control of the use of land. Patterns of land use not only determine the requirements (or demand) for specific types of transportation but also adjust themselves to new transportation systems (supply). For example, the rapid development of freeways, the proliferation of automobiles, and the abundance of cheap gasoline permitted an unprecedented degree of regional dispersion in the post-World War II era. The decentralized land use pattern that resulted is one which is least amenable to being served by public transportation, and

*New Jersey now has a state income tax to support public education. [Ed.]

one whose travel demand movements can most efficiently be carried out by highway systems.

Thus, land use and transportation must be understood as two interdependent, interrelated phenomena. When, however, the governmental hierarchy of institutions controlling these two activities is examined, it is found that the major capacities for control are at opposite ends of the hierarchy. Transportation, for the most part, is governed by federal and state institutions, whereas control of land use is almost the exclusive province of local governments and their constituencies. Although land use and transportation are functionally highly independent entities, decision-making on each is undertaken quite independently from the other; i.e., federal and state institutions have little direct effect on the land use control powers of local government, but the latter may determine the demand and utility for the transportation system formulated at the higher levels. Somehow, these decisions must be made interdependent, reflecting the functional relationships of the two elements.

The full complexity of these institutional relationships is sketched out in Table 3-6, where the various types of power that influence land use, transportation facilities, and environmental matters are related to the different levels of government, local through federal. The institutions controlling zoning and subdivision regulations—and therefore land use patterns—are mainly local ones. The provision of water and sewer services, the infrastructure supporting urban and suburban land use, is provided by both local and county institutions. In contrast, the capacity for affecting broader suburban residential development is underlain by federal housing insurance policies. For example, the Federal Housing Administration has historically pursued a policy of promoting the construction of nearly all housing in suburban areas, thereby aiding a dispersed land use pattern.

As the hierarchy of road types is ascended—from land access roads to expressways—the controlling institutions shift to the federal and state levels. Thus, to the extent that transportation influences land use, the strongest influence is exerted by the higher levels of government. The same is true of environmental controls. (In the succeeding analyses, reference should be made to this table to clarify the relationship between control powers and governmental levels.)

The complexities thus illustrated suggest that the only way to secure an effective linkage is to decentralize transportation planning to the regional level, and to recentralize land use planning powers to this same governmental level. Effective overall transportation planning in the Hudson Basin region probably depends on ensuring that the decision-making in the three areas (including environmental controls) is undertaken in a formally interdependent and coordinated fashion.

TABLE 3-6.   Land Use, Transportation, and Environmental-Control Power by Level of Government

Type of power or control	Local (municipal or town)	County	Authority	State	Federal
Direct police power control over land use (zoning)	Yes	No	No	No	No
Subdivision regulations	Yes	No	No	No	No
Provision of sewers, water	Yes	Yes	No	No	No
Housing insurance policies	No	No	No	No	Yes
Provision of land access roads	Subdivider or developer	No	No	No	No
Provision of arterials	No	Yes	No	Yes	Yes[a]
Provision of expressways	No	No	Yes	Yes	Yes[a]
Public transportation	No (generally)	Rarely	Yes	Yes[a]	Yes[a]
Environmental controls	No[b]	No	No	Yes	Yes[c]

[a] Mainly through financing.
[b] Except in New York City (other municipalities to a limited extent).
[c] Primarily federal emission controls.

This section of the report will be a discussion of the capacities of land use control and transportation institutions as they basically exist at the different levels of government. In this evaluation, the focus is mostly on what can realistically be achieved according to existing arrangements and situations. The question of what could be done if we could start from scratch is given much less concern. Thus a pragmatic approach is favored over one defined in utopian or idealistic terms.

There are really two dimensions of institutional capacity. The first is legislative or authorized capacity—what the institution could possibly do. The second is the actual operative capacity—how the institution actually functions and its ability to carry out designated responsibilities. Although precise delineation of these two elements at all governmental levels is clearly not possible, the distinction must at least be recognized. The following evaluations begin at the local level and proceed up through the governmental hierarchy to the federal government.

Local Governments

Roads

Local government transportation efforts tend to have only minor influence on regional structure.* Local municipal road systems can affect access to local land areas, but state and federal highways (as well as those of public authorities, e.g., the New Jersey Turnpike Authority) are the principal determinants for the demand for that access. In large urban centers, a somewhat stronger influence can be wielded on intraurban vehicular movements. Consequently, the ability to foster a "trends" future versus a "noded" future is very limited indeed. But since local governments can control their own land use, they can, within market forces, control the land use consequences of their local road-building efforts.

Mass Transit

Municipal systems may be effective in the largest urban centers, i.e., New York City's financial subsidy to its subway system (and formerly direct operation). But intraurban or intrametropolitan transit conceptually should be tied to a functional region. (In effect, mass transit is already largely regional. However, new systems—for example, dial-a-bus—may be local functions.) Urban localities may have the capacity to shift courses of events if actions are in concert with federal and state aid and policy. Again, the primary influence is intrametropolitan or intraurban, and not interurban or corridor movement patterns. In a "trends" future, local mass transit efforts may almost be termed ineffectual, that is, dispersion will continue, and not be altered simply by local public transit. But in terms of the "infilling" and "noded" alternatives, metropolitan capacities for undertaking transit operations, particularly busing, are important prerequisites to these land use patterns and may be necessary to support them (and vice versa).

Land Use Control

At present, land use planning and control functions are largely the province of local municipalities. Although states differ widely in the amount of power they grant to local communities in this respect, far too often local governments have almost complete power to protect their own "general welfare" and fiscal standing through land use control. Because of this fragmentation of zoning power, policies that benefit individual communities

---

*The weakness of local government with respect to transportation derives from two sources: (a) limited financial resources, and (b) the jurisdiction of local governments mainly over "local" or "land-service" roads, which follow, rather than precede, development.

often result in land use controls that are inimical to regional needs. The operative reality of their power is that it is fully wielded, but to ends dictated by local constituencies.

The relation of land use patterns to regional transportation needs is rarely the concern of local municipalities. Such bodies, making decisions independently, have generated the region's current decentralized distribution of economic and human activities. This pattern determines the limited demand for public transportation.

An underlying cause for the unsatisfactory performance of local zoning has been the states' fiscal structures, which rely heavily upon local governments to finance services via the property tax. In fact, the pressures of local financing may ensure that land use patterns will be environmentally deleterious and socially inequitable. The clamor for industrial ratables by suburban municipalities reinforces broader decentralization trends. The decentralization of industry, in turn, results in journey-to-work patterns amenable only to the private automobile. Moreover, the overall fiscal system as such rewards municipalities for restricting low- and even moderate-income, deficit-producing housing; the result may be an increase in the hardships of minority and moderate-income groups who are thereby forced to reside at unreasonable distances from emerging employment opportunities. Thus, a significant role is played by the property-tax-dependent fiscal system in determining local zoning patterns, and therefore the spatial patterns of metropolitan economic activities.

If the region's goals are to foster public transportation, higher-density residence patterns and centralized workplaces must probably be fostered (noded and infill alternatives). But as long as the power to regulate this element is dispersed—i.e., defined by autonomous local zoning power— jobs and residences will be located according to local criteria, regardless of the implications to public transportation systems. Investments in new systems will have less than optimal returns unless land use patterns are formulated with these investments in mind.* It appears that only by moving land use control decisions to higher levels of government can the origin– destination patterns required for feasible transit operations be implemented.

But to make such a move equitably, the fiscal pressures on local municipalities must be changed. A change in the level of government controlling land use decisions must be underlain by a change in the responsibility of financing local services. (In any succeeding recommendation of regionalizing land use control powers, such institutional changes in financing local services must be taken as a prerequisite.) Whether such a course of

---

*Or as long as current FHA insurance policies make it easy to build low-density structures on vacant land.

action is feasible is intimately related to the goals and beliefs of the region's citizens. Do they desire the high-density living patterns associated with land use patterns designed for public transportation, or are they willing to bear the costs necessary to support a low-density residential environment? Local autonomy also has a strong effect on the patterns of interurban movements and the possibilities of fostering or not fostering large urban centers necessary for strong corridor movements.

County Governments

Roads

County road-building efforts must still be ranked as having minor influence on regional structure. Most county roads are in place, built during the Depression, and current efforts mainly involve widening and updating. Thus the capacity to effect change is strictly limited, since county governments can influence access to local areas and tracts of land while not really determining the demand for that land. Their most probable capacity is to reinforce the "trends" future of dispersion.

Mass Transit

Counties form a much more logical area within which to control certain mass transportation facilities, since they probably encompass most of the longer desire lines of movement. Workers, for example, rarely live in the same community where their workplace is located. Thus, municipality-based mass transit efforts, particularly in suburban areas, have little utility in regard to the routes that most of their residents must travel. Many New Jersey counties have or are instituting countywide bus systems Thus a capacity appears to exist to assume a powerful interurban transit role. Yet actions may still be dependent on state and federal programs. Although countywide transportation authorities may not be a principal lever of change, they may provide necessary, but not sufficient, thresholds of transportation capacity required to effectuate a "noded" or "infill" land use pattern.

Land Use

If public policy is to reduce automobile trips or their length, then two basic alternatives present themselves. The first is to create centralized employment nodes amenable to public transit systems. By concentrating new industries and offices in a few major nodes in each of the region's subareas—perhaps linked existing urban centers or regional shopping facilities—clustered destination points can be created for workers and shoppers using public transportation. Second is a better match of residential zoning capacities to jobs, enabling residences to be located closer to the workplace. Both of these solutions may require the establishment of county authorities to control land use and to establish formulas for sharing property tax revenues (unless the states provide a new way of funding local services). It is at this level, as well as the regional, that alterations are feasible in the mechanisms that foster the competition between local communities for property taxes and, hence, the dispersal of facilities. Yet any designated county land use control capacity is dependent on statewide legislation, and most likely this capacity would have to be responsive to various political influences—home rule forces, environmentalists, real estate groups, and other political forces.

State Governments

Roads

To the extent that transportation influences land use, state departments of transportation (DOTs) have the strongest influence on the distribution of population and economic activities throughout the Hudson Basin region. Major freeways affect regional structure. Thus state DOTs may act as significant levers of change, especially if they act in concert with the federal government. One example is the change in speed limits, federally enacted and carried out by the state, an action which in the long term could have important effects on the locational decisions of many human activities.

Generally, DOTs have little capacity to deal with the localized land use consequences of their road-building efforts. Change in regional structure is certainly a consequence of state actions, but they cannot directly control these changes. However, the requirement to consider environmental limitations may be a constraint to alter or inhibit local and regional growth patterns through adherence to federal standards.

Mass Transit

State DOTs have significant capacities to deal with mass transportation operations, given a viable federal funding mechanism. The capacity of the state DOTs within the Hudson Basin region mainly is to build, operate, and maintain highways, and not urban transit systems. Their mass transit authority is focused on giving aid to the institutions actually operating such systems. By virtue of this authorized funding lever, states do exert a modicum of control over the operating public transit systems. Moreover, subsidized fare structures present an opportunity for altering the demand for public transit.

Land Use

The ability of DOTs to deal with the general land use consequences of their investments in both highways and mass transit is strictly limited. Such powers are the province of local municipalities. This situation, as we have suggested earlier, is critical in regard to the undesirable consequences of freeway-building efforts (sprawl, decentralization, urban decline, and the like), and in regard to the noded land use patterns (centralized high-density workplaces at a minimum), necessary to give some level of viability to new public mass transportation endeavors.

Moreover, the current capacities to deal simply with the monitoring of lower level decisions regarding land use are strictly limited, either by state DOTs or by planning agencies. Theoretically, the capacity may exist but the operative realities are currently quite limited in regard to staff overlays.

Federal Government

Roads

By virtue of spending power, the federal government can exert wide influence in the direction it wants. From 1957 through 1970, the federal government expended $44.7 billion through the Highway Trust Fund. The results of this spending are the massive freeway systems in the Hudson Basin region, as well as elsewhere, and the emergence of "donut" cities, with burgeoning suburbs and decaying core areas.

Mass Transit

The federal capacity for the control of mass transportation location and establishment is chiefly through the allocation of resources. Capital grants, for example, through the Urban Mass Transit Act of 1970, have a critical effect on mass transit supply. In contrast, operating subsidies, yet to be established definitively, have the potential to affect demand through influencing the pricing structure and service standards. Federal policies on fuel pricing have a similar potential to modify demand for mass transit.

Land Use

The land use consequences of the federal government's massive investments in roads clearly were not anticipated nor were they controllable under current institutional capacities. Increasing federal concern with critical-area regulation, environmental impact regulation, and wetlands and shorelands regulation still does not hit the heart of the land use–transportation interface. The federal government is probably too far removed from the local scene to regulate land use patterns efficiently.

Special Authorities

Special authorities are more specialized institutions and are creatures of state and national policies. A number exist within the Hudson Basin region that have the capacity both to plan and operate mass transit facilities. Generally these are tied to functional metropolitan areas, i.e., the Capital District Transportation Authority and the Metropolitan Transportation Authority. They do not have taxing power or elected officials, thereby limiting their capacity as strong regional agencies. They control through funding by the federal government the supply of facilities, and through their pricing structures they can affect demand. These are the most likely institutions with which to provide the transportation capacity associated with the "noded" or "infill" alternative futures. Again, they have little control over the land use consequences of their transportation decisions.

Whereas the above two agencies attempt to fulfill their capacities, the same cannot be said of the Port Authority of New York and New Jersey, which has authority in two states to develop terminal and transportation facilities within a 25-mile radius from the Statue of Liberty. Although the theoretical capacity to deal with mass transit supply and demand is enormous by virtue of its financial strength, the structure of this body makes it difficult to increase its public transit role. It remains to be seen what changes a new administration can initiate.

One final type of transportation-related institution is the Tri-State Regional Planning Commission, which has been designated by the federal government as the planning agency for the tristate metropolitan region. Its capacity as a lever of change is centered on research and monitoring capabilities, its power of review, and its coordinating activities. It has also delegated to county or subregional agencies responsibility for evaluating the effects of federal aid projects on county and regional plans. Whether these activities really affect local land use control decisions is open to serious question.

Regionalization

Much of the county-level discussion is relevant to the following discussion.

It appears that transportation decisions undertaken at state and federal levels are far removed from the local context of land use control decisions. As we have suggested earlier, a movement toward the regional level appears to be, at least conceptually, a way of linking land use control and transportation decision-making. The reasons for transportation regionalization are (a) greater knowledge about the immediate concerns of people and local governments, (b) the opportunity for creating a forum in which local concerns can be voiced, (c) forcing decisions on statewide transportation down to the lowest possible level at which they can be readily handled, and (d) by obtaining local decisions, to obtain legitimacy for plans.

By moving transportation planning down to the scale of Hudson Basin region and/or its subregion, we may find a greater capacity to ensure that local land use decisions are undertaken with a greater awareness of broader transportation considerations. At the same time, were land use control capacities shifted up beyond the local level to that where transportation planning has been suggested, then a more formal integration of land use and transportation decision-making can be made. It may be possible, then, to take into account adequately the local consequences of regional transportation actions or proposals.

Although these shifts may maximize the potential to move toward any of the aforementioned alternative futures, they actually represent the necessary, but not sufficient, thresholds for change in regional land use patterns. The capacity to influence change, however, is bounded by the goals of the region's citizens—how they desire to live, and how they desire not to live. These often are expressed in pressures on the institutions affecting their way of life, the patterns of local zoning being one example of this phenomenon. Institutional capacities will continue to be restrained and responsive to these greater political forces.

3.6   Recommended Strategies for Research

This section responds to the question, "What direction should future research take?" The Transportation Task Group reviewed the current status of data, knowledge, and techniques (Table 3-7) and selected the areas that it felt were of highest priority; these areas are summarized at the end of this section.

Strategies

The elements of the preceding report involve transportation and its linkages with other policy areas and the general environment. The tools for gaining, communicating, and utilizing knowledge in all of the areas discussed vary greatly in their quality, availability, and the extent to which they are used. In the following pages, the elements of this study as they relate to transportation are evaluated for current status and usefulness, leading to the priority listing of suggested areas of required data, methods of analysis, or basic research.

Referring to Fig. 3-1, one can distinguish two major categories of areas for consideration, the man–structure–vehicle (MSV) "system" or interaction area, and the interaction between the "system" and the external world, or the natural environment (Fig. 3-12). As will be seen, most of the areas noted as requiring additional research that pertains to the Hudson Basin are within

TABLE 3-7.   Status of Current Knowledge and Techniques and Areas for Future Research

Elements affected by transportation	Status of information	Status of knowledge and techniques	Potentially fruitful areas for further research

Population
  Density, age sex, economic, other demographic stratifications
    Car ownership
    Employment
	Good	Good	Relationships of transportation to special population
			
			groups
			Relation of transportation to employment

Travel demand	Current: good Future (forecasting) (long-term and regional): poor	Good Poor	Demand by mode Attitudinal (opinion) surveys Methods for forecasting attitudes Methods for shaping demand (marketing)

Land use and travel
  Topography: availability of material and water resources
  Quality of resources (water)
  Accessibility
	To be gathered	Generally measurable	Complete geological mapping of Hudson Basin required
			Methodology at good level

Land requirements			Relationships between land requirements and transportation mode
Land use	Generally good	Good to poor	Relationships between land use and transportation mode (both passenger and frieght) Attitudinal measures Methods for introducing new energy sources
Mode choice	Current: good Future: poor	Good Poor	new power sources new population-density patterns Methods for shaping mode choice (marketing)
Freight generation	Current and future: poorly fragmented among private operators	Poor to good on theoretical basis; not practical	Data pooling and banking Methodology improvements Integration of data and methods into standard transportation planning methods
Freight and mode choice	Related almost entirely to economics	Related to economics	Develop methods of control over mode choice

TABLE 3-7   (*Continued*)

Elements affected by transportation	Status of information	Status of knowledge and techniques	Potentially fruitful areas for further research
Engineering and planning			
Regional planning	Good		
Urban planning	Good	Some more advanced than	
Route selection	Good but limited	others	Central data banks
Modal choice	Poor		
Design	Good	Some (transportation	Inclusion of social and
Construction	Good	planning) more numeri-	ecological environmental
Operation	Good	cally oriented than others	considerations
Maintenance	Poor		
Land use	Good		Improving linkages between
Zoning	Good	Some (most) not geared to	methodologies
Subdivision	Good	inclusion of:	
Energy use	Good	Environmental impact	
Noise, safety	Good	Public opinion	
Accessibility, etc.	Good		
Transportation and energy consumption			
Fuel requirements: auto, bus, truck	Excellent	Good	Development of knowledge concerning effects of future changes in power sources, fuels
Energy requirements of urban rail transit	Good	Good but indirect, therefore more obscure	Measurement of all energy considerations whether direct or indirect
Rail freight	Good to poor	Poor	Extraction from purely economic considerations
Pipeline	Poor	Good, but in private sphere generally	Central data banks Incorporation into transportation planning considerations
Waterway transportation	Good	Poor	Central data banks Inclusion in overall regional planning, modal split
Energy use to build and operate facility	Can be calculated	All have developed methodologies	Refinement of calculation methods Development of relationship between energy lost and energy installed; also energy saved by installation
Energy use in terms of resources	Can be calculated	All have developed methodologies	Improvement and refinement of methods
Energy destroyed in natural ecosystems	Can be calculated	All have developed methodologies	Improvement and refinement of methods

(*Continued*)

TABLE 3-7   (*Continued*)

Elements affected by transportation	Status of information	Status of knowledge and techniques	Potentially fruitful areas for further research
Energy and pollution			
Energy type and consumption by mode	Poor to good	Good	Refinement
Mode and pollution	Good	Good	Refinement
Pollution and health by energy type	Poor: better for long range	Basically primitive	Immediate effects
Mode vs. safety	Good to poor	Basically primitive	Long-range effects by degree
	Good	Poor to good	Standardize methods of reporting, assessing, measuring, counting
Effects of removal of portions of ecosystems	Poor to good	Poor	Threshold of critical levels of destruction
Effects of elements of pollution on ecosystems	Poor	Good, but onerous, time-consuming	Thresholds of specific pollutants
Air composition, density, visibility, rainfall, light, winds dispersion	Poor to good	Methods available	Effects on lower order plants and animals
Chemical quality of water, soil	Poor	Methods available	Refinement of methods
Effects on plants, animals, man (physically)	Poor	Limited	Data banks
Effects on man-made structures, materials, devices	Good	Good	Additional research into effects
Transportation and society			
Socioeconomic factors:			
Housing			
Employment			
Business			
Services and utilities			
Institutions	All data available in varying degrees	All measurable	Data banks
Amenities			
Land use			
Property values			
Accessibility			
Leisure time			
Sociopsychological factors:			
Community cohesion			
Community integrity	Very poor	Measurable but no agreed-upon method	Intensive research needed in all areas
Community pride			
Family life			
Individual life styles, etc.			Model building

TABLE 3-7 (*Continued*)

Elements affected by transportation	Status of information	Status of knowledge and techniques	Potentially fruitful areas for further research
Transportation and society (*continued*)			
Recreation: Density, distribution, character, location	Poor to good	Poor to good	Development of clear-cut relationships to types, densities, clientele
Transportation and economics			
Cost of Planning Building Operations Maintaining	Costs more easily measured than benefits	Generally middling	Improve methods, include social and ecological costs
User costs Accident costs Environmental impact costs (physical, social, psychological)	Physical more easily measured than social	Fair	Improve methods, include social and ecological costs
Benefits Employment Recreation Accessiblity	Poor to good	Poor	Improve data base and methods
Location of economic activity groups	Good	Good	Relation of transportation mode to economic activities
Location of freight terminals; facilities	Mediocre	Poor	Development of data bases, techniques separate from private sector control
Institutional capacities			
How to meet or modify transportation demand	Poor	Poor	Improve knowledge of "demand" Introduce environmental element
How to institute changes in transportation policy (state, county, authority)	Poor to good	Marketing techniques rudimentary Political techniques inefficient	Improve public "sell" Improve nonpartisan aspects
How to guide changes in land use	Poor	Poor	Institution of controls Agreement on implementation of master plans
Specific legal methods: Land use Negligence Annoyance Personal damage Zoning	Poor data bases	Methods available	Review of legislation at federal, state, and local levels

(*Continued*)

TABLE 3-7   *(Continued)*

Elements affected by transportation	Status of information	Status of knowledge and techniques	Potentially fruitful areas for further research
Specific legal methods *(continued)*:			
Aesthetics			Review of court cases as they apply
Pollution effects			
Emmission controls			
Goals			
Natural environment	Limited	Poor to good	Develop policies related to elements and stages of natural environments
Economy	Excellent	Excellent	Develop means for relating intangibles to purely economic assessment methods
Alternative futures:			
Land use	Good/poor	Good	Ideal combination of modes for each land use
Density	Good/poor	Good	Thresholds for mode vs. density
Location	Good/poor	Good	Relate to ecology
Environmental effects	Poor	Poor	Improved assessment methods
Consequences of alternatives			
Capital cost—new building	Good	Good	Effects of inflation
Capital cost—new transportation facility	Good	Good	Effects of inflation
Energy consumed/transportation	Good to poor	Good	Improve
Air quality	Good	Good	Improve diffusion knowledge
Extent of arable land	Good/poor	Good/poor	Improve objectivity
Quality of natural resources	Good/poor	Good/poor	Improve objectivity
Impacts on the economy	Good/poor	Good	Improve objectivity
Impacts on social structure and organization	Poor	Poor	Improve objectivity

the man–structure–vehicle interface area, since they relate to methods and means (and basic data) for the proper planning and design of such systems. But the remaining major area is the relationship of transportation as a system to *its* environment, particularly its physical and social milieus, and the effects of transportation systems locally and regionally, short-term and long-term, temporary and permanent.

Based on a review by the task group members of potentially fruitful areas

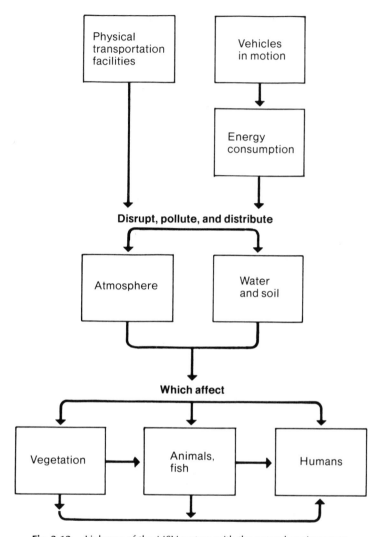

Fig. 3-12. Linkages of the MSV system with the natural environment.

for further research and a ballot rating the relative importance of the ten most needed areas, the following discussion of each of the selected research areas was prepared.

Land Use and Transportation

There are a number of subjects under this topic that, for the Hudson Basin especially and for planning generally, are unclear or unresearched.

Land Need

The current and future land requirements of the Hudson Basin region for specific uses have not been documented or projected in a uniform manner. New York State has its Land Use and Natural Resources (LUNR) system and a "plan" or projection by land use type; Connecticut has had the Connecticut Interregional Planning Program (CIPP), which is relatively advanced and deals with alternative futures (New York State Office of Planning Coordination, 1969; Connecticut Interregional Planning Program, 1968).

Since land is generally dealt with by private speculators and developers, there is little in the way of centralized knowledge of land availability, directions for expansion, and future needs. Clear definitions in this realm lead to a much clearer capacity for projecting transportation needs.

Land Use

Concomitantly, there is a need for information acquisition and storage concerning land use and its generative capacities for movement, whether of people or goods. Traditionally, land use planners plan for interrelationships between land uses and connect them with an appropriate transportation link. Traditionally, transportation planners also evaluate "demand" and "accessibility" needs and relate them to land uses as best possible. *There is no real basic knowledge of the interaction levels, needs, capabilities, or capacity for change inherent in land use–transportation relationships.* In the Hudson Basin this general lack in the professional field manifests itself in a great deal of extant knowledge available in the lower basin (New York metropolitan area) and scant knowledge in the upper basin beyond such studies as the Capital District study. For example, there has been no updating of material collected under the Federal Aid Highway Act of 1962.

Mode/Land Use Relationships

A related area of need for future research is in relating transportation *mode* to specific land use and density. A relationship can be developed in terms of general cargo or passenger movement versus level of commercial, industrial, or residential activity, but no methodical approach exists for then deciding upon an *ideal* mode or combination of modes to fit the situation. This is again a failing in or absence of general methodology.

Ecological Impact of Transportation

Impact Thresholds

There is little available knowledge of precise, or even general, levels at which specific effects can be predicted in considering the various gaseous, liquid, and solid emissions emanating from transportation facilities. The well-known "thresholds" are those at which toxicity is obvious: coughing, illness, death to laboratory animals. But the long-range, low-concentration effects are unresearched. Other impacts, such as those caused by the physical presence of a facility in obliterating all or part of specific ecosystems, are even less well documented.

Danger Warning

Another aspect of this area of research need involves the capacity of government at various levels to accept, ingest, and utilize the knowledge and judgment of researchers and other specialists when their warnings of impending crisis are made known. Warnings of fuel shortages, temperature inversions, and the effects of the SST on the stratosphere went unheeded until some elements of physical or economic crisis had already taken place. Improved mechanisms for long-range planning or forecasting and for acting upon such planning or forecasting are required.

Air Pollution

Greater research is most especially needed on the constitution, dissemination, and specific effects of air pollution. Not only the obvious transportation sources such as the internal combustion engine must be considered, but also the energy sources for public transportation—power plants and substations—must be evaluated in greater detail.

Data and Methodology

Data Banks

Basic information on the Hudson Basin is widely scattered or nonexistent. The lower basin is well covered by agencies that collect relevant data, but overlapping jurisdictions cause a lack of centralization. Usable data are available from the Tri-State Planning Commission, the Port Authority of New York and New Jersey, the New York City Planning Commission, and other city planning agencies such as the Regional Plan Association. There are also studies of the upstate metropolitan regions; New York State and county organizations have needed information, but it is certainly not as detailed as that for the lower basin.

What is required for the Hudson Basin region is a centralized data bank containing basic information on standardized geographical components, transportation, land use, population, utilities, and environmental qualities. The *format* of data collection must be standardized as must be the geographical area. Definitions must be standard among all reporting agencies.

Methodology

Standardization of study approach is a related necessity. Agreement on planning approaches must be obtained among all participants in planning activities in the Hudson Basin.

Planning Scope

This latter consideration leads to a requirement to embrace, within the scope of standard planning practices, the ecological requirements of the Hudson Basin region, and consequent ecological impacts of planning decisions. Such inclusion must be on a systematic basis for ease of application of ecological principles.

Transportation for Special Groups

Current transportation planning methods are directed toward the large middle group of the population, economically, physically, and even mentally. Although designing for an "average" permits greater ease and standardization of method, many groups within the general population can find new mobility or increased mobility if consideration is given them specifically in planning and designing new facilities. These groups include the aged, the handicapped, the young, and the poor. In relation to this last entry there is evidence to indicate that improvements in public transportation can have a direct effect on employment rates. The specialized needs of all the above groups as they pertain specifically to the Hudson Basin require intensive study.

Planning Controls and Marketing

An area of prime importance to the development of the Hudson Basin lies in developing means for controlling or shaping transportation demand and modal choice.

Demand

Transportation "demand" is an elusive quantity and methods for gauging the depth of such demand, rather than simply forecasting by extending traffic volume trends, must be developed and refined. Especially elusive is the concept of "latent demand." For instance, although much has been written about latent demand among the elderly, little increase in mobility of the elderly has been demonstrated through increased availability of transport. The control of demand lies to a great extent in the control of land use characteristics and in the density or concentration of activity types.

Modal Choice

If demand is measurable and expected, then the choice of transportation *mode* must be to a great extent shaped or directed in the planning process. Recent years have shown the folly of designing facilities on the basis of satisfying a "demand" for one mode at the expense of others. Modal choice by consumers must be available, but it must be made among logical alternatives related to current problems and overall needs.

Marketing

Beyond the influences over demand and modal choice that should be inherent in the planning process, there are market-psychology methods for bending public taste and interest toward public transportation. Marketing techniques especially designed for selling transportation modes are in their infancy. Comprehension of such techniques and their applicability is not complete. For the Hudson Basin they must be honed, particularized, and updated.

Population Density

There remain relationships between population *density* and transportation mode that are largely undeveloped. The general view is that higher concentrations of population are required to justify mass transportation, but the levels—threshold levels again to be sure—remain to be discovered. The relationship may indeed include many of the psychological marketing principles mentioned above.

Governmental Self-control

A question basic to American life and to the ideal development plan for the Hudson Basin is, How do pluralistic governments exercise self-control for long-term gains?

How do governments steeped in the tradition of free enterprise, permitting land to be bartered freely with minimal regulation as to its ultimate use, find a means to regulate the locations and densities of specific uses, and thereby the means, modes, and intensities of travel among those land uses? The question includes, but goes beyond, the failings of zoning. Zoning as the implementing arm of the planner has shown itself too amenable to petty localized interests to implement the balance of general plans.

But beyond this, how can the new requirements of environmental impact be integrated? This is the basic question of "institutional capacities" to confront modern-day problems with out-of-date views and tools. The implementation of master plans, if agreed upon by majorities, must be carried out on the master plan scale, and not piecemeal at the zoning variance level.

Rail Freight

The question of rail freight (and to a lesser degree freight movement by other modes) has become one almost entirely of economic considerations. The movement of freight by the rail mode affects (as does the movement of anything by any mode) the physical and social environment, and has significance and impingements far beyond the limited view of tariffs and rates. The planning of balanced transportation systems cannot go forward as long as carrier economics is the sole criterion for rail planning. The need for an artificially induced "competition" among failing rail lines serving the same general area can be questioned.

Pipelines

Pipelines should be brought into the planning sphere, especially the transportation planning sphere, to a much greater degree than at present, which is almost nil. Again, a balance by mode must be the sought-after goal, and pipelines can carry a larger share of such a balanced entity.

Chapter 4

ENVIRONMENTAL SERVICE SYSTEMS

4.1 The Technologies of Environmental Services

Technology in the Hudson Basin Region

The use of machines is an inextricable part of modern life; indeed, machines have in large measure defined what is modern. They are our technology. In a more abstract sense, our technology can be said to be all concerted efforts that organize resources and energy to accomplish a task. The means may be mechanical, or electronic, or even bureaucratic.

The Hudson Basin Project task groups are all intimately involved in technology because they are intimately involved in the modern life-style of the people in the basin. One can quickly separate, on a coarse scale, those task groups whose technological concerns are social from those that are mechanical. Of course, in the Hudson Basin Project's environmental study, everyone is concerned to some degree with the life and earth sciences.

In this vein, then, environmental services are dependent on mechanical technologies. This is also true of the closely related areas of water resources and energy systems. Generally, the adequacy of available technology dictates the adequacy of services received by a community. The economics of

Members of the Environmental Service Systems Task Group: Robert M. Bellandi, William G. Borghard, William R. Ginsburg, Joseph M. Heikoff, Robert D. Hennigan, and David A. Johnson.

delivering the service may preclude the application of some techniques, but technology often influences economics as well.

Without sophisticated treatment and construction techniques, the Hudson River, which is polluted for more than half its length, would not be as clean as it is. Cities as small as Glens Falls would not be as healthy, and the teeming metropolis that is New York City would never have been built. The urbanite requires that fresh water be brought to him and that his wastes be removed.

The term *urbanite* characterizes most of the population of the Hudson Basin area. In the region's New York portion alone, 18 of 30 counties are themselves metropolitan or parts of metropolitan areas. Ninety-five percent of the 1970 population in the Hudson Basin Project study area is metropolitan. In light of these figures, it is evident that there is a vast, underlying reliance on the techniques of environmental service systems because they are indispensable in maintaining the present character of the Hudson Basin.

The Hudson Basin is blessed with adequate precipitation—approximately 40 to 50 inches (102 to 127 cm) per year. Municipalities need only provide collection, treatment, and delivery systems, and sufficient water is available to basin residents. (Of course, this is easier said than paid for.) Occasional droughts occur, such as that of the mid-1960s, and these complicate considerably the efforts local governments must exert to provide water. In such periods safe yield estimates are lowered and additional supplies must be found.

One of the greatest advances in urban health came with sewerage systems. Removal of wastes is relatively simple. One must, however, insure that they are not simply removed from one area to become a problem in another area. With increasingly intense and competitive use of land, treatment will provide this insurance.

As urbanization increases, land is paved or otherwise made impermeable. The moisture that naturally falls on these lands cannot percolate into the ground as before but collects and drains into low-lying areas. As this happens, the urban surface is washed and the water is thus polluted. Many communities have sewerage systems into which both sewage and stormwater drain. These are called *combined systems*. During dry periods, this water is generally treated before being returned to a water source. During large storms, however, the water flowing into the treatment facilities exceeds their capacity. If storage is unavailable, as is often the case, the excess incoming polluted water is dumped into a water source without treatment. This is a growing problem and methods to alleviate it must be implemented.

Another serious environmental service problem—one that is not only growing but also literally mounting—is solid waste. In the United States, per capita collections of solid wastes grew from 2.8 pounds (1.3 kg) per day in

1920 to 4.5 pounds (2.0 kg) per day in 1965. Solid waste production continues to grow, apparently with affluence. Unfortunately, solid waste disposal has been given less scientific attention than any of the other concerns of pollution control.

Water Supply

Residents of the Hudson Basin area generally rely on collected surface runoff for their water supplies. Some areas in New Jersey and the New York counties of Queens, Nassau, and Suffolk on Long Island rely on groundwater. The use of catchments for runoff and wells for groundwater supply is not new. Technological advances in water supply include better design and construction techniques in the distribution systems as well as better treatment of source water. To be sure, increased pollution levels have mandated more reliable analyses of water sources. More efficient supervision of the water system is being instituted on the management level.

A few rather exotic modes of supply have been advanced, including desalination of seawater. Various means of removing dissolved salts have been proposed: physical (flash distillation, freezing, and reverse osmosis), electrical (electrodialysis), and chemical (the hydrate process). These processes vary in cost, but are usually more expensive than providing more water through the collection of additional runoff. Several of the desalination techniques raise serious objections because of attendant thermal pollution and energy requirements; in addition, disposal of the brine raises the problem of increased temperature, salinity, and content of heavy metals in the adjacent waters. Desalination could provide an emergency system but the economics of this move are suspect. Were a desalination plant built in conjunction with equipment that could separate the dissolved heavy metals and chlorides, perhaps sale of the salts, copper, arsenic, lead, and mercury would improve the economics of the process. Competition in the sale of these products from other sources would determine the practicability of this move.

To augment water supply, some have proposed weather modification to produce more rain. Silver iodide crystals are scattered into clouds, causing condensation. This form of weather modification is less than 30 years old. Unfortunately, the artificial production of precipitation is not reliable. In addition, water rights and the problem of equity are raised with cloud seeding. If New York were to seed the clouds over Westchester County for the New York City water supply, Connecticut *might* not receive the amount of rain it otherwise would. Of course, Connecticut might get enough rain but the outcome cannot be predicted within reasonable bounds. No body of law has yet evolved that deals with cloud seeding. This fact, together with the intrinsic uncertainties of rainmaking, eliminate it as a practicable method of water supply.

Direct reuse of the water supply has also been suggested. However, treatment of the wastewater must be sophisticated and complete through the tertiary stage. Only one place in the world is now known to reuse its water supply—an arid part of South Africa. The reused water there is only domestic (not industrial) wastewater; it is stored for 30 to 40 days, diluted with fresh water, and used only part of the year. Generally, the health risks inherent in reuse of water are too high to be justified. The U.S. Environmental Protection Agency has issued a statement discouraging the direct reuse of water while encouraging additional study and research on the subject.

Indirect reuse of water, on the other hand, is a common practice. Several communities use the waters of the Mohawk and Hudson rivers both for supply and for disposal of treated waste. Indirect reuse of groundwater is also common. Much groundwater recharge takes place when water seeps from cesspools into adjacent soils. For other water, recharge is through recharge basins and wells. Such techniques have been practiced for years on Long Island, where there are 2000 recharge basins and 2500 recharge wells. Water used for cooling purposes is recharged, mitigating the harmful impacts of heated water on the ecology of an area.

Percolation of water through the soil generally removes pollutants, but not when the pollution level is high. In heavily settled areas of Long Island, sewers have been installed. The collected wastewater is treated and discharged into the ocean. Here the groundwater is not recharged and the groundwater table is lowered.

An area's water supply can be augmented by building new reservoirs or finding new sources, or an existing water supply can be better managed to reduce use and waste. Techniques available include metering, price changes, and elimination of leaks. Altogether, the most feasible methods of providing water supply are implementation of catchments for surface runoff and groundwater use, along with indirect reuse. Efficient management at all points in the distribution system is necessary to ensure the adequacy of this vital supply.

High water quality for municipal water delivery systems can be maintained adequately. Plants are available with extensive automation and control systems that check treatment factors. Raw-water turbidity, coagulant and dosages of aids for coagulation, flow rate, backwashing, and final effluent turbidity are easily monitored. Proper levels of chlorination and fluoridation, if desired, can be maintained.

A serious water supply concern, especially in the older communities of the Northeast, is the high costs that must be faced in the near future. Not only must obsolete plants be renovated or replaced, but large metropolitan population increases must also be absorbed. Here again, efficient management is an essential facet of water supply.

Sewerage

Since indirect reuse is growing, the concern upstream communities have for the quality of the water they discharge will have a direct relation to the water supply available to downstream users.

Sewerage systems suffer many of the same maladies (such as obsolete plants) as water systems. Since the mid-1960s, there have been federal and state aid programs to help localities build new treatment facilities in an effort to make secondary treatment universal. In New York State, thought is now turning to increased state assistance for the operation and maintenance of treatment plants.

Behind the flurry of construction activity is the federal mandate to industries and municipalities for "zero discharge" into waterways by 1985—if such a condition is economically feasible. This mandate is based on the philosophy that no one has the right to pollute. Industry has said that treatment processes needed to effect zero discharge are astronomical in cost and unrealistic.

Regardless of whether or not zero discharge will be achieved, the idea has spurred research and development in several areas of effluent treatment and, importantly, recycling. Biological and chemical treatment of wastewater is adequate to meet today's effluent standards. With effluents increasing at a greater rate than the population increase, current methods may be obsolete. New methods are being advanced. A wealth of literature exists about both primary and advanced treatment of industrial and municipal waste. The many compounds used by industry complicate the treatment of wastewater considerably. When one excludes such industrial waste, municipal waste is simple by comparison.

Let us mention a few waste treatment methods. Granular media filtration is, as the name implies, a process whereby the waste with solids suspended in liquid is allowed to seep through a filter of one or more layers of coal, sand, garnet, or other media. Filter-bed design is flexible to the point that nearly any effluent quality can be achieved. Usually there is automatic monitoring of the system to maintain the quality within certain predetermined parameters. With additives in the filter, certain chemicals such as phosphorus can be precipitated from the polluted liquid. Such filters are also able to remove oil.

Dissolved air flotation is a process used to remove particles suspended in water that have a specific gravity close to 1.0 (e.g., oil). Air is dissolved in a pressurized liquid stream. The air is released from the solution as micron-sized bubbles that become attached to the suspended materials in the wastewater. The bubble and particle will rise if and when the specific gravity is less than that of water. This process is more effective than the common gravity thickening for concentrating metal hydroxides and biological sludges.

An effective way to treat already precipitated inorganic solids and to remove suspended solids is solids-contact chemical treatment. With this method, a suspended particle in the raw wastewater becomes coated with the added chemical (a coagulant such as lime) and then aggregates other particles to it. Thus, the solid particles grow and settle to the bottom of the tank and are easily removed. The lime may be recycled. This method is effective for removal of suspended solids, heavy metals, and phosphorus.

Organic materials can generally be removed by adsorption on activated carbon in a manner similar to granular media filtration. Certain organics, however, pose difficult problems and cannot be handled by this method. Often, in these cases, the process is repeated, with the spent carbon processed and reused (Price et al., 1972).

Depending on the pollutants, these processes and others may be used singly or in combination. Advanced treatment of wastewater is designed to remove pollutants that are not removed by common secondary treatment techniques such as those mentioned above. A secondary treatment plant has effluent consisting of soluble organic and inorganic compounds, particulate solid material, and pathogenic organisms.

The level of treatment of wastewater should be dictated by the water's potential for a particular type of reuse. To meet the zero-discharge guideline, some industries anticipate totally closed water systems. The water would then be taken in, used, treated with problem wastes removed, and recirculated. Municipalities cannot, as mentioned, rely on direct reuse yet. Infectious hepatitis, for instance, has been confirmed to be a water-borne viral disease with the virus capable of surviving 10 weeks in clean water (Culp and Culp, 1971).

Treatment of wastewater and sewerage generally is as much a management problem as a scientific and technological one. Recently enacted federal legislation has spurred activity on both of these fronts, and creative problem-solving methods are evolving.

Urban Drainage

Because urbanization disturbs a landscape, the normal interactions between physical processes are disrupted. For example, rain cannot percolate into the soil if the surface is paved. With widespread urbanization, this problem is aggravated. The runoff from streets has to be managed, and artificial drainage systems have to be built to handle it. The boom in suburban shopping malls has added to the problem. Their huge parking lots and roofs create acres of impermeable surface.

The runoff from these paved and sealed areas flushes the urban landscape, carrying with it debris and dirt, spilled automobile oil, and animal wastes. Thus, this water is a source of pollution. In fact, the rain itself carries pollutants from the atmosphere—whatever pollutants exist in the ambient air—and washes them to the ground. This water is rarely treated and often is not even properly collected. The wastewater that results from urban drainage is different in several respects from sewage wastewater. Generally, the drainage water is not as rich in nutrients, and its pollutants and their concentrations are not as noxious as those of sewage water.

☞ Nevertheless, the improper collection of drainage water causes several problems. In many areas a combined system carries both sewage and drainage water. Of course, the capacity of the treatment plant at the terminus of the system is determined by sewage levels. When a storm adds water to the treatment plant in excess of its capacity, the excess, which now includes raw sewage, is dumped into the water source. Older communities that had separate systems now often have combined systems through misuse. For example, a homeowner who has had a problem in managing the drainage from his roof may collect the water in a rain gutter and divert the downspout into a drain in his basement. Such connections are almost universally prohibited by building codes. Other ordinances—of health departments and operating departments—also require separate sanitary and stormwater collection systems. The failure to enforce these rules has now created acceptance of the situation. Many communities are again beginning to require separate systems.

Drainage-water management is a basic concern of urban planning and an essential part of the urban infrastructure. It is an initial tool in flood control. Treatment of stormwater is rarely considered because the pollution level is slight. Literature on urban drainage is not plentiful, but it is becoming more available. A notable work is a comprehensive study of engineering criteria, written by a Denver engineering firm in 1969 for the Denver Regional Council of Governments (Wright-McLaughlin Engineers, 1969).

Solid Waste

The long-term solution to easing the tremendous solid waste disposal problem is to manufacture products whose components can be easily recycled. Presently, urban and industrial wastes are mounting. In the United

States, 80% of all waste is dumped in open landfills; about 10% is incinerated. The following table shows the typical composition of residential solid
waste (Price et al., 1972).

Composition of Residential Solid Wastes[a]

Paper products	43.8%
Food wastes	18.2%
Metals	9.1%
Glass and ceramics	9.0%
Garden wastes	7.9%
Plastics, rubber, and leather	3.0%
Textiles	2.7%
Wood	2.5%
Rock, ash, etc.	3.7%

[a] From Price et al. (1972), reproduced by permission.

Not only is waste being generated at an increasing rate—a rate that apparently mirrors the gross national product—but spaces in which to put the
waste are decreasing. Urban growth and spread preempt large tracts of land
from becoming landfill sites, thus increasing transportation distance and
hauling costs. Environmental considerations such as potential groundwater
pollution, decomposition fumes from landfills, and air pollution from incineration further limit disposal sites. That landfills are aesthetically displeasing
further limits the areas where such sites are acceptable.

Since collection accounts for a large part of refuse disposal costs, different
modes of transport influence total cost. It is known that the movement of
goods via pipelines is generally the cheapest method. Certain wastes could
be shredded and mixed with water; this slurry could be transported through
a community's existing sewerage system or through a specially constructed
system.

Where suitable land cannot be found for the disposal of waste, mixed-
mode transport systems have been suggested. The waste would initially be
accumulated in scattered locations throughout the urbanized area. Some
means of local compaction will undoubtedly be used. Large apartment developments, medical centers, college campuses, and similar complexes
would be required to provide for the collection of wastes generated by
residents. These wastes would then be collected, possibly by truck, and
brought to rail cars or ships for long-distance transport to sparsely settled
areas or to ocean depths. It has been suggested that the New York City
subway system use special cars in off-peak hours to carry solid wastes to
such shipping points.

For urban areas where land is within economic distance of the centers of waste generation, other means of disposal could be utilized. Storage ponds for area streams could be dug. If the area's geology is suitable, these could be sand and gravel pits, with sand or gravel being sold to defray operating expenses. Solid waste would be disposed of near the pits, and some of the extracted material could be used to cover the waste cells. These ponds would help control drainage and also provide limited recreation opportunities. For existing pits in surface-mined areas, solid waste could be used as fill and lead to eventual reclamation. Some communities are purposely mounting their covered waste cells into hills for eventual use as recreation sites.*

Incineration is a common disposal method. Only one-fourth of the 300 municipal incinerators meet air codes (Price et al., 1972). Industrial incinerators generally are more likely to meet air standards. The most attractive aspect of incineration is its volume reduction: 95% reduction is common and 98% is possible under some conditions. An attractive by-product of incineration is the energy produced either in the form of heat or of burnable gases.

Montreal has an incinerator that burns 1200 tons (1091 metric tons) per day and generates 100,000 pounds of steam per hour. The city estimated incineration costs of $7.00 per ton, with costs reduced to $3.50 per ton once markets are found for the steam. These figures include amortization of the incinerator, which cost $15 million.

Compaction and baling of waste reduce volume for items that may or may not be suitable for incineration, but these methods are generally most useful on wastes that do not decompose, such as old appliances and automobile bodies. Shredding is a useful method for reducing volume, especially for problem wastes such as rubber tires.

For organic wastes—those that have some nutrient values—composting is a disposal technique that allows the nutrients to be reused. Of all urban wastes, about half can be degraded biochemically into a sanitary humuslike material. The product is fertilizer or soil conditioner. The process costs about eight dollars per ton before sale of the product. Unfortunately, the potential supply is much larger than demand. A firm called Ecology, Inc., in Brooklyn, is packaging and selling compost rich in artificially added nitrogen for fertilizer.

Using liquid waste and the sludge residue of sewage treatment plants as fertilizer has been suggested. Odor and transportation of the waste are no longer problems, since they can easily be managed. However, large acreages are necessary for processing the waste, and these are usually unavailable in metropolitan areas. Such a disposal technique would not be feasible, for example, on Long Island. Sludge was generally dumped in the ocean or other large bodies of water. But other disposal techniques are now available. Dried sludge can be incinerated. Methods of reducing sludge moisture content and volume are in use. The sterile cakes that are the products of these new methods are suitable for composting or landfill.

The disposal technique that many solid waste experts think is the most promising is pyrolysis. Wastes are baked in an air-free chamber at temperatures as high as 3000°F (1650°C). Pyrolytic techniques reduce volume more effectively than incineration, and air pollution is not a problem. Operating costs for a 1000-ton-per-day pilot plant in New York City are estimated to be two-thirds that of pollution-free incinerators.

The greatest advantage of pyrolysis is its reuse of the materials in solid waste. Some wastes, such as plastic, lend themselves to direct reuse after pyrolysis; hard and soft waxes, adhesives, tars, and greases could all come from pyrolized plastic. Metals melt to the bottom of the solid waste mass during pyrolysis and can be removed. Several U.S. and European engineering firms and the U.S. Bureau of Mines are investigating pyrolysis. This method is expected to cause a revolution in metropolitan waste disposal.

A revolution is needed. But the revolution required in the discovery and application of techniques will be secondary to the revolution in solid waste management. The problem of solid waste must be seen in relation to resource management, because the mounting refuse of U.S. cities and industries is directly related to the problem of natural resource depletion. Today's wastes should be transformed into marketable products and the recovery of used materials should be facilitated. The technology exists to recycle refuse, but economic incentives do not. For example, the copper in today's automobiles is irretrievable from an economic viewpoint. The concept of resource recovery should be made an integral part of manufacturing and consumption. Only then will the solid waste problem be solved.

4.2   Problems in Selected Counties of the Upper Hudson Region*

Problems with environmental service systems are not grave in the upper Hudson region. Water resources are plentiful, populations are sparse (and

*To present the existing state of environmental service systems, the task group organized itself to examine representative areas of the Project's study area. To represent the region fairly, five areas were chosen for descriptive examples: the upper Hudson–Adirondack area, Mid-Hudson West, Westchester County, the Albany–Schenectady–Troy metropolitan area, and New York City. These areas reflect rural, urbanizing, suburban, and medium to large-sized urban concentrations of people.

not likely to increase greatly), and land for disposal of wastes seems abundant. However, environmental service system problems do exist in the upper Hudson area, even if they are relatively less severe than in the regions to the south. Moreover, the upper Hudson area is an important part of the whole basin. The upper Hudson River, much of which is within the Adirondack Park "Blue Line," is the source of some of the water used in the urbanized portions of the basin further south, and it is the potential source of future supply. Moreover, it is an area of extraordinary natural beauty and a prime recreation resource for the more than 40 million people who live within a day's drive of it.

The area is of interest to this task group for two additional reasons: it typifies the problems of nonurbanized counties throughout the Hudson Basin and, as shown in Fig. 4-1, a large part of it is now under the review control of the Adirondack Park Agency. The experiences of the APA in controlling development in open regions will certainly provide useful lessons for similar areas elsewhere in the Hudson Basin Project study area.

All or parts of Essex, Warren, Washington, and Herkimer counties are within APA jurisdiction. As the map indicates, parts of Essex, Warren, and Washington counties discharge wastes into the upper Hudson Basin and also into the Lake Champlain Basin. Herkimer discharges into both the Mohawk and St. Lawrence basins.

As shown below, population growth in the four counties has been modest. It is not expected to accelerate greatly in the next several decades. On the

County Populations (thousands)

Counties	Census		Projected	
	1960	1970	1980	2000
Essex	35.3	34.6	37	40
Herkimer	66.4	67.6	74	84
Warren	44.0	49.4	55	67
Washington	48.5	52.7	50	60

basis of several consultants' studies prepared for these counties, the broad pattern of environmental system problems and possible technical and administrative solutions are analyzed. Water supply, sewerage systems, and solid waste disposal proposals will be considered in turn. The problem of handling urban runoff, although not altogether inconsequential, is not major and is therefore not considered here.

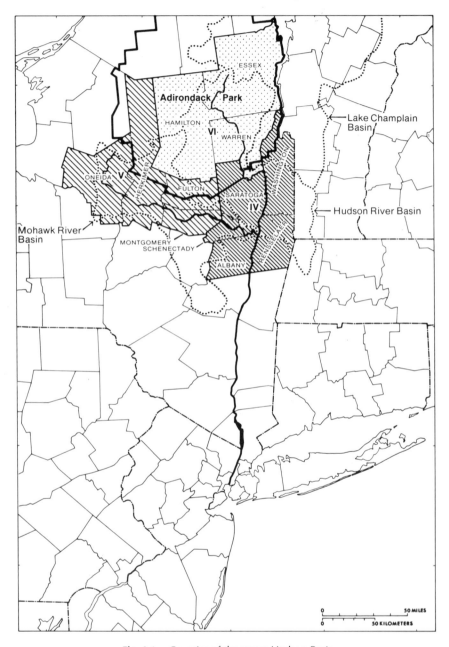

Fig. 4-1. Counties of the upper Hudson Basin.

Water Supply

As one might expect, good water is plentiful in the Adirondack area, both in surface lakes and streams, and below ground. Water is supplied in the area either through individual wells or through one of the many municipal or private systems in the area, most of which are relatively small.

Plans for improvement of public water supply systems in the area emphasize new or expanded local systems. Countywide systems are not feasible because of the scattered nature of development. In Warren County, for example, plans call for eight separate new systems and expansion of most existing systems. Although countywide water districts do not appear feasible, consultants favor the establishment of county water agencies to assist in the planning and regulation of water supplies by towns.

User costs for central-system water supply are not high, ranging from $70 to $100 per household. Where settlement is scattered, the costs of supplying water from a central system are considerably higher. If economies of scale prevail, settlement should be concentrated around existing centers.

In Essex County there are 39 public and private water supply systems, of which 14 serve fewer than 200 persons each. Only five are classified as moderately large. Twenty-three of the 39 systems utilize surface waters, the remainder relying on groundwater. The consultants' plan for Essex County calls for new or enlarged systems at 24 separate points (Rist–Frost Associates, 1971).

Herkimer County contains several cities and towns with populations over 10,000. Herkimer, Little Falls, and Ilion are all located on the Mohawk River some distance from the Adirondack region. Consultants call for several projects for these municipalities, but no expansions of systems in the northern half of the county, which lies in the Adirondacks. The plan does, however, urge construction of 11.3 billion gallons of storage on branches of the West Canada Creek to permit increased withdrawals from Hinckley Reservoir, the water source for the city of Utica, which lies in the northern half of Herkimer County (Malcolm Pirnie Engineers Inc., 1969). The Temporary State Commission on Water Supply Needs of Southeastern New York has also looked on Hinckley Reservoir as a water source for urbanizing areas on the mid-and lower Hudson Basin. The commission urged that the existing dam be raised 50 feet, increasing capacity by 90 billion gallons and also flooding some 10,000 acres of forest and agricultural land (TSCWS, 1973). A possible alternative suggested by the commission is increased reliance on the Sacandaga Reservoir in Fulton and Saratoga counties. Both of these proposals would have local environmental effects that would have to be weighed carefully. Neither alternative would have a significant relationship to local water supply problems in the Adirondack region, since reservoirs and connectors are, or would be, located at the southern edge of the region.

Sewage Treatment Facilities

Water availability is not often a constraint in open-area development since a satisfactory well can usually be dug. Sewage disposal is another matter. Generally, public sewage treatment per household costs six times what it costs to supply public water. Similarly, septic systems are many times more expensive to construct and maintain than wells. Consequently, the most serious and most neglected environmental service system problem in the upper Hudson Basin is that of sewerage.

New York State now requires that no effluent be discharged into state waters unless 75% of both BOD and suspended solids are removed. In effect, this mandates at least secondary-level treatment. Requirements are even more stringent in the Lake Champlain Basin, where no effluent may be discharged, thus requiring percolation beds or other tertiary treatment.

Many new treatment facilities will be required to meet state standards. In Warren County, for example, consultants have called for the construction of 15 new treatment plants and expansion of three existing plants. Annual costs for such facilities would be substantial, up to $600 per household.

Economies of scale in sewage treatment are even more pronounced than in the provision of water. A 100,000-gallon-per-day (gpd) plant costs not half what a 200,000-gpd plant costs, but two-thirds as much. Yet the scattered development characteristic of the area often precludes large plants or con-solidated sewage treatment districts. Because of the expense involved, it is imperative that new development be concentrated around existing settle-ments and not be of such low density to preclude economic construction of connectors.

Individual septic systems, on the other hand, require large lots for adequate drainage fields. In this case, the more scattered the development, the better. Septic systems are not without their problems. Rarely are such systems properly maintained over long periods. Often there is infiltration of untreated wastes into nearby water tables. Also, proper disposal of siphoned wastes from septic tanks is not ensured (Goldstein et al., 1972; Patterson et al., 1971). County health departments are charged with ensuring proper design and maintenance of septic systems, but such regulation is often per-functory, and the septic system itself is at best a marginal solution to a difficult problem.

Solid Waste Management

Solid waste management in open or sparsely settled counties presents problems not found in more densely populated areas. The availability of land is an invitation to local dumping by households or firms, and to the establishment or perpetuation of substandard town or village dumps. A widely dispersed population militates against large-scale organization and technology to cope with solid waste disposal properly. Economies of scale are difficult to realize, and hauling costs are prohibitive. The small population and economic base in villages and towns may not accommodate necessary expenditures to provide facilities. Some compromises are thus inevitable.

Rist–Frost Associates, consultant engineers to Warren and Washington counties, recognizing the need to make a trade-off, have recommended an immediate action plan for solid waste disposal (Fig. 4-2).

Each county would assume overall responsibility for solid waste disposal within its boundaries. A new county department of solid waste disposal would be established or responsibility would be given to an expanded county highway department. The latter is the preferred approach because of the functional relationship between highway maintenance activities and waste haulage and disposal.

Each county would be divided into zones (three in Warren and five in Washington) comprising several towns that together can support and justify a sanitary landfill operation. Each zone would be served by a properly managed sanitary landfill ranging from 25 to 240 acres in size. To serve residents in outlying areas, eight containerization stations would be established at convenient points in the two counties to which residents could bring their refuse for collection and haulage to the zone landfill.

Nineteen of the existing 27 substandard dumps will be closed to comply with New York State law. The remaining eight facilities can be improved and managed according to acceptable landfill standards. Burning is prohibited and daily compaction and covering with 6-inch layers of soil are required for conformity with accepted landfill practices (EPA, 1971a,b). *

Costs could be covered in one of three ways: county real property taxation; an annual proportional service charge paid by each city and town; or an assessment of charges at the disposal site on a flat-rate, volume basis. Rist–Frost recommended the annual service fee method, because it is more equitable in balancing benefits and costs, is easily administered, and helps eliminate unauthorized dumping at disposal sites (Albert et al., 1974). Estimated annual costs for the program are modest—about $35 per household, including collection, haulage, and disposal.

Other methods were considered: at one extreme, individual municipal landfill systems, and at the other, county and two-county consolidated disposal at one site. These were rejected, the former because of high unit costs,

---

*As of late 1978, some of the towns had begun cooperating on joint solid waste management programs, but the overall bicounty plan has not yet been implemented. [Ed.]

(A)

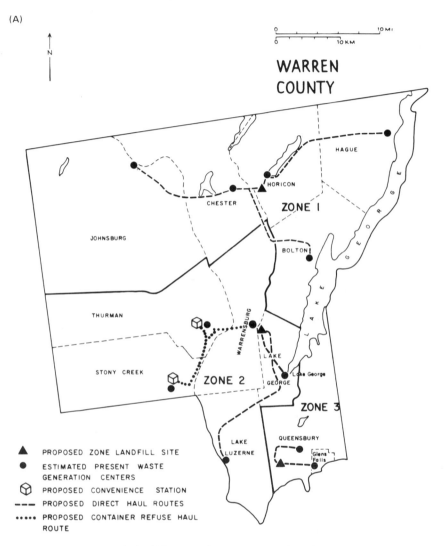

Fig. 4-2. County multiple landfill systems for Warren (A) and Washington (B) counties. (From Rist-Frost Associates, 1971, reproduced by permission.)

and the latter because of high haulage costs. Incineration was found to involve plant costs too high to be justified by population size, whereas land is available for a landfill system. Recycling techniques were not ruled out, but were regarded as not sufficiently developed to be immediately applicable to current needs.

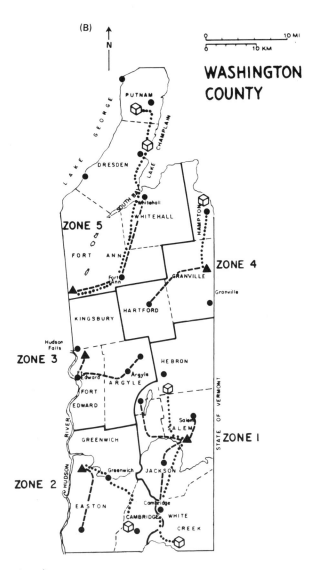

Fig. 4-2. (Continued).

The following main themes emerge from this review of reports on environmental service systems in the Adirondack counties.

Because of a dispersed settlement pattern, water and sewer system improvements and new systems must be developed on a localized basis. Countywide systems are not feasible. Solid waste disposal districts may consist of several adjacent towns but, as with water and sewage, cannot be efficiently handled on a centralized, county-system basis.

Counties, however, do have coordinating, planning, and financing roles to play in the development of environmental service systems.

Service systems for new settlement will be most efficient and least expensive where settlement can be concentrated around existing population centers.

Service system improvements must be coordinated and should reflect conscious growth strategies originating in local and regional planning bodies. Most consultants' plans simply reflect an implicit assumption that each community will and must grow. By providing for environmental service systems, such forecasts then become self-fulfilling prophecies. Desirable growth patterns should be considered and environmental services should be provided to support the chosen patterns.

Environmental Service Systems and the Adirondack Park Plan

The Adirondack Park Agency Plan, officially adopted by the state on July 20, 1972, classifies both state-owned and private land on various levels. The most restrictive category is "resource management." It permits, on average, no more than one building on each 42 acres. About 53% of private land is in this classification. In the "rural" category, which makes up 27% of private land, no more than one building per 8.5 acres is permitted. On another 10% of private land, one building per 3 acres is permitted. Existing hamlets and industrial areas are exempt from the APA density guidelines.

The typical pattern of zoning is a "gravity" pattern, in which the most intensive uses are permitted closest to existing hamlets. This will not only help to preserve the general character of the region but also tend to channel development within the Park into patterns better suited for the provision of water, sewers, and waste management. However, localized compact development patterns will not necessarily occur under the provisions of the Park plan. Despite the laudable efforts to control densities provided for in the legislation establishing the APA, the undeveloped zones in and around the various hamlets will allow considerable new development. In fact, the controls may stimulate scatteration, for isolated construction may be deemed less intrusive than construction of large multiunit projects. An accretion of many small-scale development decisions, each acceptable in itself, may yield a less desirable outcome than a single, equivalent, multiunit project.

Environmental service system problems within the APA boundaries, therefore, remain similar to problems found in like patterns of settlement outside the boundary, except that large developments may be excluded altogether or controlled for impact through the "regional project" review process. Here is a summary of these problems:

1. Channeling development to areas where water and sewer infrastructure capacity exists or may be efficiently expanded
2. Ensuring that development is at sufficiently high densities to permit economically feasible system development but, at the same time, at densities and concentrations that protect the natural and scenic quality of the environment
3. Guaranteeing that development in nonurban, restricted areas conforms to minimum standards for on-site water supply and for sewerage (septic field) drainage
4. Ensuring that most new development is sufficiently compact to permit economically efficient solid waste collection
5. Prohibiting on-site disposal in low-density areas to guarantee that approved sanitary-landfill disposal practices are followed

A number of fiscal, policy, and administrative obstacles impede the achievement of solutions to these problems. First, zoning patterns (both APA and local) now permit or require development in hamlet vicinities at densities too low to justify water and sewer infrastructure development. A greater differentiation in permitted densities between intensive (urban) and extensive (open or rural) areas would be beneficial in and around hamlets.

Planning for, and control of, development to ensure that new construction and new water and sewer facilities are coordinated is weak or nonexistent in many areas. Zoning alone cannot guarantee such coordination. Positive inducements and development controls are necessary, though few localities have the expertise or personnel to undertake such programs. County, regional, or APA monitoring and coordination may offer a solution. In particular, water systems should be extended concurrently with sewer systems; water service should generally not be provided unless connections to sewage treatment facilities are available.

Many towns and villages do not have the fiscal capability to expand water supply and sewage treatment facilities. Assistance from the state and federal governments will be necessary if future needs and standards are to be met. Such assistance should be predicated, however, on local control of densities to ensure efficient service.

4.3 Mid-Hudson West

On the west bank of the Hudson, at the geographic center of the Hudson Basin Project study area, are six counties sandwiched between the suburbs of metropolitan New York on the south and the Capital District on the north. These counties are Orange, Sullivan, Ulster, Delaware, Schoharie, and Greene. They comprise a useful study area that, for purposes of this discussion, we will call Mid-Hudson West. Although this area is suburban and rural in character, substantial population density has developed along the Hudson, particularly around Kingston, New Paltz, and Newburgh.

The region is varied in its geography, governmental structure, and economic base. It also presents a wide range of issues with respect to the organization and delivery of environmental services. Its elevations range from sea level to 4204 feet. It is bordered by the Hudson River on the east. The Hudson Highlands and the Ramapo Mountains cross the southern portion of Orange County and, to the north, the landscape is dominated by the Shawangunks and Catskills.

Mid-Hudson West is an area of contrasts. On a county basis, population density ranges from 267 per square mile in Orange County to 30.4 per square mile in Delaware County. Delaware, Greene, Schoharie, and Sullivan counties are largely agricultural and rural, whereas Orange and Ulster have been rapidly suburbanizing. Table 4-1 illustrates this demographic variety.

In some towns in the western Catskills, there are fewer than 10 people per square mile. Along the Hudson, however, Kingston has a density of 3452 per square mile and a 1970 population of 25,544. Newburgh has a density of 7086 and a 1970 population of 26,219. As shown in Table 4-2, Mid-Hudson West reflects the governmental fragmentation as well as the demographic contrasts typical of New York State as a whole (New York State Comptroller, 1971).

Two major factors influence the nature, quality, and cost of environmental service systems in the Mid-Hudson West area: institutional structure and population density. In rural areas, where density is low, institutional structure is of less importance because the need and demand for services are low. There is little or no industry or commercial activity. Most residents rely on

TABLE 4-1. Population Density by County in the Mid-Hudson West Area

County	Population, 1960	Population, 1970	1970 as a percentage of 1960	Population density, 1970
Delaware	43,540	44,718	102.7	30.4
Greene	31,372	33,136	105.7	51.0
Orange	182,734	221,657	120.7	267.0
Schoharie	22,616	24,750	109.5	40.0
Sullivan	45,272	52,580	116.2	53.0
Ulster	118,804	141,241	118.9	123.6

TABLE 4-2.   Local Government Jurisdictions in the Mid-Hudson West Area

County	Number of villages	Number of towns	Number of cities	Number of environmental service districts (water, sewage, refuse)
Delaware	10	19	—	6 (water)
Greene	5	14	—	9 (water)
Orange	16	20	3	42 (sewer), 31 (water), 4 (garbage and refuse)
Schoharie	6	16	—	1 (water)
Sullivan	6	15	—	17 (sewer), 13 (water) 1 (garbage and refuse)
Ulster	5	20	1	3 (sewer), 15 (water)
Totals	47	104	4	142

private wells for water supply, septic tanks for liquid waste disposal, and the town dump or a ravine behind the barn to accommodate solid waste. This is not to imply that problems do not exist in such rural areas, but the problems are scattered and, in a broad context, relatively minor.

In the major urbanized areas in the southern and western portions of the region, environmental services of varying quality, cost, and scope are provided by public and private agencies. Institutional fragmentation contributes to these wide variations. There is a third pattern of development in addition to the urban–suburban and rural areas. This "middle ground" includes relatively high-density villages and town centers surrounded by relatively low-density rural type areas. These scattered high-density clusters have urban–suburban environmental service problems without the financial base, geographic size, or institutional structures necessary to address them effectively. A brief review of the present organization, quality, and delivery of environmental services in Mid-Hudson West will aid in framing the issues.

Solid Waste

Solid waste may be collected by a public sanitation department, private carters operating under municipal contracts, private carters dealing with individual households, and sometimes by the householders individually hauling wastes to the dump. The waste may be disposed of in private landfills, public landfills, or public or private incinerators.* There are various collection and disposal methods. Thus, some communities may use private collection and a public landfill site for disposal; others may have public

*Public incinerators are now rare. The last one in Orange County was closed down in October 1975. [Ed.]

collection and a combination of public and private landfill sites for disposal. The cost of collection and disposal of solid waste varies considerably, depending on frequency of collection, population density per square mile, distance to the disposal point, and the nature of the disposal operation. Private landfill operators generally charge more than public landfill facilities. Recent studies of the cost of solid waste collection and disposal indicate that monthly collection costs in the area range from somewhat over two dollars to more than five dollars per household. The cost of collection appears to be between 60 and 75% of the total cost of collection and disposal. This is due, in some measure, to the usually inadequate and often illegal handling of solid waste disposal. Although different methods of disposal (including separation for recycling and use of combustible wastes for energy production) would result in substantially increased costs, even a doubling of present disposal costs would increase overall costs of waste collection and disposal by only 25%.*

Both collection and disposal are now handled almost entirely on the town, village, and city levels, as in the rest of New York State. The literature on the subject indicates a consensus that, although improvements are necessary, the *collection function* can be handled adequately at the local level.

It is equally clear that the responsibility for solid waste *disposal* must be shifted in the immediate future at least to the county level. Local landfill sites are being rapidly filled and in many instances are, by their nature, too small to be operated in compliance with state health standards. New sites are unavailable or undesirable for environmental or political reasons. Almost no recycling takes place and, as of this date, no appreciable amount of waste within the area is being utilized for fuel. The situation has been summarized as follows:

> There is an increasing volume of solid waste, increasing difficulty in locating sites for disposal, and increasing awareness of the environmental, health and aesthetic issues involved.... Efficient waste disposal must be the responsibility of a jurisdiction which covers a relatively large geographic area. (Price *et al.*, 1972)

There is an increasing awareness on the part of town, village, and city governments that time is running out. There are few politically acceptable answers. Solid waste disposal is a function that may well move up the governmental ladder in the near future, as local governments recognize it as a function they can no longer perform, yet for which they will be held accountable by their constituents.

---

*County solid waste studies have been done under DEC auspices. They include information on costs and problems of collection and disposal. For examples of such studies refer to Bowe, Walsh and Associates, Engineers, and William R. Trautman Associates, Engineers.

Liquid Waste

Most of the six-county Mid-Hudson West area is unsewered. Sewer service is found only in areas with 500 or more people per square mile, and even such areas are often unsewered. Treatment plants are usually designed for secondary treatment. As in the field of solid waste, there are large variations in the per capita gallonage of liquid waste created, and in the costs and nature of the treatment. Private as well as municipal sewage treatment plants are utilized. With the exception of major population centers such as Newburgh, Kingston, New Paltz, and Middletown, overall density is low. Density has, however, risen in many locations, particularly in villages, to a point where sewer systems are definitely required.

Many of these jurisdictions lack the fiscal base necessary to finance the required facilities. With relatively few exceptions, residential construction throughout the area is on a small scale. The average builder may construct anywhere from 5 to 34 or 40 units per year. Since the state health code does not require sewer service for subdivisions with fewer than 50 residential units, most of this construction utilizes septic tanks. Because the major population growth has tended to cluster in a few townships, the cumulative effect of residences served only by septic tanks has been rather substantial.

The institutional mechanism most frequently used to provide for construction of sewers and treatment plants in unincorporated areas is the special improvement district (SID), sometimes referred to as a special benefit district. Such districts have been created in areas of towns in which the population density has risen to the point where sewage collection and treatment are necessary. They are financing mechanisms, operated by town government and designed to allocate costs directly to the geographic areas benefited. This has been politically necessary since less densely populated sections of towns are seldom willing to help finance facilities from which they will receive no direct benefit. Special improvement districts often proliferate rapidly to meet the needs of expanding town populations. Several SIDs might exist in one town. The resulting patchwork pattern of liquid waste facilities has been the very antithesis of effective design and operation. Even in densely developed suburban areas, a conglomerate situation prevails. Thus, as late as 1970, it was estimated that almost half of the population of Nassau County, or approximately 700,000 people, relied upon septic tanks and cesspools (Knight et al., 1972).

Various institutional arrangements have been suggested to rationalize the financing and construction of liquid waste collection and treatment facilities. It would appear that some changes in institutional arrangements must be effected in order to implement national policy as set forth in the Federal Water Pollution Control Act Amendments of 1972 and related state legislation. It is also apparent that any institutional changes in this area should be directly related to land use control mechanisms. Unless and until the extent, nature, and location of new residential and commercial construction can be regulated to coordinate with the location of existing and planned liquid waste collection and treatment facilities, such facilities will be built largely on an ad hoc basis, chasing development around the countryside. Ideally, the overall framework of such land use controls and sewage collection and treatment planning should be established on a state or regional level, but it would appear that the county is the only existing unit of government large enough to make any meaningful improvement in the current situation, while small enough to be sensitive to local needs. As with the solid waste field, localities can still be responsible for the collection aspect by financing and installing local sewers. Questions with respect to the location and construction of treatment plants and major interceptor lines should, however, be resolved on a higher level.

Increased county responsibility need not and should not be synonymous with large, central treatment plants. There are many sites in Mid-Hudson West where sewerage and sewage treatment are necessary but where location and topography indicate a relatively small collection area. An example is the Town of Woodstock, on the Saw Kill in Ulster County. Natural water courses flow away from Woodstock, so that the area is not affected by liquid wastes from any upstream community. The situation in Woodstock clearly can, however, affect the water quality of streams flowing into other towns. Woodstock has grown substantially since 1950, when its population was 2271. By 1960 it was 3836 and by 1970, 5714—an increase of approximately 150% over this 20-year period. These figures include only permanent population as shown by the U.S. census and do not reflect second homes, which are a significant factor in the area.

The density resulting from this growth must be analyzed. The town has an area of 69.9 square miles, giving it a 1970 density of 82 persons per square mile. Since over 9 square miles is in the Forest Preserve, the net area available for settlement is approximately 60 square miles, giving a 1970 density of 94.1 per square mile. Even this figure is quite misleading. Since colonial times, the population in Woodstock has centered about the junction of New York State Routes 212 and 375 and along Tannery Brook. This central area of the town, occupying about 2 or 3 square miles, contains roughly half of the total population. The population density of "downtown" Woodstock is about 1000 persons per square mile. This area contains the town's retail stores, as well as cultural facilities such as the Woodstock Theatre and the Tinker Street Movie House. There is no sewage collection or treatment, and a lot of liquid waste finds its way into Tannery Brook.

Particularly in the summer, when Woodstock is a crowded center of arts and tourist activities, there is an unpleasant odor from the brook, and studies have indicated that it is highly polluted. The town has discussed the question of sewage and sewage treatment for many years. Engineering studies have been done, but no action has been taken. It is clear that that portion of the town's population which lives outside of the central area, and which feels no particular need for sewers or sewage treatment, will vote against sewers if they are going to have to bear any meaningful portion of the cost. In addition, the cost of the system would be quite high if it were extended out to these relatively rural portions of the town. Thus, it will make more sense to create a sewer district within the town so that the costs are borne by those directly benefited. Such a sewer district, however, would place the entire cost of the improvement on an area of approximately 2 or 3 square miles containing 2000 to 3000 inhabitants. Such a cost could not be accepted politically or economically on that tax base.

A proposal discussed as a compromise would create four classes of property owners with different rates for each class. One class, with the lowest rate, would consist of all property owners in the town. An additional amount would be charged those who would eventually be connected to the system. The third classification, paying a higher rate, would be those serviced by the initial system. Nonresidential (that is, commercial and industrial) properties would constitute the fourth and highest category. *

Water Supply

There are two distinct aspects of water supply in the Mid-Hudson West region. One is the huge water supply system, based largely in the Catskills, which is under the jurisdiction of the New York City Board of Water Supply and which furnishes water to the city and certain jurisdictions north of the city. There are also numerous local water supply systems, both private and public, as there are in other areas of the state. It should be stressed that the relationship between land use planning and the construction and operation of water supply facilities is directly analogous to the relationship between liquid waste disposal systems and land use planning already discussed. Until fundamental issues concerning the nature, density, and location of human settlement are resolved, it is difficult, if not impossible, to plan and build liquid waste disposal facilities except on an after-the-fact basis. Moreover, particularly in the Catskills, where the surface water system for New York City is based, the nature of land development and the operation of the water supply system are directly related to scenic and recreational factors that form the basis of the Catskills' economy.

---

*Since this chapter was written, the "compromise" proposal and a subsequent scaled-down proposal have both been rejected by Woodstock voters. [Ed.]

From a structural–legal point of view, New York City's extraterritorial powers in the Mid-Hudson West area are unique. Pursuant to state law, the city has adopted rules and regulations to protect its water supply from contamination. These prohibit the discharge of manufacturing wastes (unless treated in a manner satisfactory to the New York City Department of Water Resources) and restrict the disposal of sewage and household waters. In theory, these powers, together with those of the state pursuant to the Public Health Law, could go a long way toward controlling sources of pollution in the watershed area. In practice, however, these existing mechanisms have been totally inadequate.

Under Section 1116 of the Public Health Law, plans for real estate subdivisions must show adequate water supply and sewage facilities and must be approved by the State Department of Health. Where county health departments exist, the state has delegated this approval power to them. Implementation of these powers has been less than satisfactory, as indicated by the Deerfield Acres example (see the section on interrelationships). This section of the Public Health Law, as applied in the Catskill area, has been declared unconstitutional by the decision in *Herrick* v. *Ingraham* (Supreme Court, Delaware County, 1972).

The court held that those sections of the Public Health Law requiring the subdivider of property to file plans and to obtain approval for water supply and sewage facilities have no application to "recreational acreage" or "recreational lands." The court found these sections of the Public Health Law unconstitutional as applied. For purposes of the statute, a subdivision is any tract of land divided into five or more parcels for sale as residential lots or residential building plots. The court pointed out that, in theory, the statute could apply to the sale of five 2000-acre parcels from a 10,000-acre tract. Putting aside for the moment the question of whether a 2000-acre parcel is a "residential lot" or "building plot," the hypothetical construct appears to be inapplicable to the case under consideration, which involved parcels ranging from under 2 acres to more than 10 acres. In *Herrick,* the court compounded the definitional problem by determining that the Public Health Law sections in question are not applicable to recreational land, but did not define "recreational land."

This decision is now being appealed. If it stands, it will effectively prevent the state from exercising any control over the impact of residential subdivisions on water quality in those areas of the state which are most in need of such regulation.*

*The decision was upheld on appeal (46 A.D. 2d 546, 363 N.Y.S. 2d 665). In 1977, however, the Legislature amended the Public Health Law to include precise language-making "recreational" subdivisions subject to the provisions of Section 1116. [Ed.]

It should be noted that local governments in Mid-Hudson West have been less than enthusiastic in exercising their own land use control powers. According to the interim report of the Temporary State Commission to Study the Catskills (TSCSC, 1974), of the 19 towns in Delaware County, only one had subdivision regulations and none had a zoning ordinance. No town in Greene County had a zoning ordinance, although 4 of the 14 have subdivision regulations. The situation is different in the more populous counties. Of the 15 towns in Sullivan, 8 had subdivision regulations and 7 had zoning ordinances, while in Ulster 17 out of the 20 towns had subdivision regulations and 16 had zoning ordinances.* These local ordinances and regulations are not, of course, any substitute for a well-enforced health code. Most of them require only the filing of a basic plot plan with minimum lot sizes and road-construction specifications.

Interrelationships

Environmental service systems are necessary because of population density and land use factors. Human settlement, in turn, is influenced by governmental decisions in areas such as transportation. Decisions with respect to environmental service systems may themselves determine development patterns and recreational opportunities through their impact on water quality, scenery, and other environmental considerations. These interrelationships can readily be illustrated in Mid-Hudson West.

Because of the mountainous topography, few major east–west transportation arteries cross the Catskill region. The three most important are Route 17, which joins the New York State Thruway at the Harriman Interchange in Orange County and runs west through Sullivan and Delaware; Route 28, which joins the New York State Thruway at the Kingston Interchange in Ulster County and runs west into Delaware and Otsego; and Route 23, which joins the New York State Thruway at the Catskill Interchange in Greene County and runs west into Delaware and Otsego. The only east–west rail line in the Catskills, the Catskill Division of the Penn Central (formerly the Ulster and Delaware), follows Route 28 for a substantial distance and then swings north to join the Route 23 corridor.

These routes are related to historic settlement patterns. They were, of course, built in the valleys and thus parallel water courses. Route 28 runs along the Esopus Creek through Ulster County and Route 23 follows the

---

*As of late 1978, there are still no town zoning ordinances in Delaware County but two towns now have subdivision regulations. In Greene County, there are now two towns with zoning ordinances and eight with subdivision regulations. In Sullivan County, 14 of the 15 towns now have subdivision regulations and 10 have zoning ordinances. There has been no change in Ulster County. [Ed.]

Schoharie Creek through Greene County. These water courses are now part of the New York City water supply system. Schoharie Creek has been impounded in Schoharie County, forming the Schoharie Reservoir, before it continues east through Greene County. Waters from the Schoharie Reservoir are conducted by a tunnel underneath the mountains that separate the Esopus and Schoharie watersheds, and are discharged into the Esopus at Allaben in the Ulster town of Shandaken. The Esopus, supplemented by the Schoharie water, has been impounded in Ulster County to form the Ashokan Reservoir. Waters from the Ashokan are conducted by the Catskill Aqueduct across the Hudson at Cornwall, to join the Croton system.

Esopus and Schoharie creeks have been trout streams, part of the rich fishing area that was the birthplace of fly fishing. These streams are still a major recreation resource. Their impoundment and use for water supply purposes have, however, had a profound effect on the aquatic ecosystem. In recent years, a lot of silt has accumulated in the Schoharie Reservoir, in part because of major roadwork along Route 23A. It has been noted that fishing in the Schoharie Reservoir has declined to very low levels—large rainbow trout have apparently disappeared. The silt from the Schoharie Reservoir is carried through the tunnel to the Esopus Creek and thence to the Ashokan Reservoir. Sediment is deposited in the Esopus streambed with negative effects on the aquatic insect life on which the fish feed. Thus, geological and topographic factors, influencing settlement patterns and transportation decisions, interact with urban needs for water to affect recreational fishing adversely, a major economic factor in the Catskill area.

The New York City water supply system also affects fish through its control of water flow. When outflow from the Schoharie Reservoir is reduced during low-water periods, fish may be stranded on the banks of the Esopus. The tunnel can, of course, supplement the Esopus to help sustain its aquatic life during drought periods, but a sudden opening of the tunnel can flush eggs out of breeding areas.

The New York State Department of Environmental Conservation has studied these problems in the upper Delaware River basin (Neversink, Pepacton, and Cannonsville). Although this study covered the portion of the New York City water supply system in the Delaware watershed, west of the area under discussion here, its conclusions are instructive. The DEC found that minimum flows were maintained for too long and that large amounts of water were released too quickly, causing rapid changes in river states, flow velocities, and water temperature. It concluded that "these operating practices have upset stream ecology, caused severe damage or destruction of downstream fisheries, interfered with recreational use of the streams, prevented stream quality standards from being met and generally reduced the value of the most significant stream resources in the basin (New York State Department of Environmental Conservation, 1974).

Water consumption could be cut substantially in New York City, thereby reducing demand on the system and permitting greater flexibility with respect to water releases (cf. TSCWS, 1973).* Just as actions in New York City, such as water metering and leakage control, could influence the impact of the New York City water supply system in the Catskills, decisions in the Catskills can have an adverse impact on this system. Increased population, resulting in increased liquid and solid waste, can degrade the water quality of an area to the point where a water supply system begins to require treatment. An example of this is the Croton component of the New York City system in Westchester County, where treatment studies are now underway. An early warning of the emergence of the problem in the Catskills is illustrated by the experience at Deerfield Acres, a subdivision of 24 homes in the Town of Olive in Ulster County, just off Route 28 near the Esopus Creek and less than half a mile above its entry into the Ashokan Reservoir. As with almost all subdivisions of less than 50 dwellings. individual septic tanks and leaching fields were utilized for the disposal of liquid waste from the Deerfield homes. Such septic tanks must be approved by the Ulster County Health Department (exercising powers delegated by the New York State Department of Health) and the New York City Department of Water Supply. There appears to be some question whether the septic systems in this subdivision were ever inspected by the Ulster County Health Department. There is no question, however, that a majority of the systems are not working properly and that raw sewage from the homes, in addition to being most unpleasant for homeowners, finds its way into the Esopus Creek and the Ashokan Reservoir. The chief engineer of the New York City Department of Water Supply stationed at the Ashokan has confirmed the existence of the problem and stated: "Of course this is a problem common to any watershed but the effluent from just one area cannot pollute the entire reservoir. It would take a little bit from a number of places to have any effect on the quality of the water" (Anonymous, 1972a; cf. Anonymous, 1974a).

The effect of development on water quality is cumulative and, up to a point, the volume of water in a system is so great that pollution from human sources is diluted to an acceptable level. There is no question, however, that the quality of New York City's water depends on the nature and extent of

*The experience of the Jamaica Water Supply Co. shows the impact of metering. The state DEC and PSC ordered the company to install meters in about 100,000 homes that had paid a flat rate for water usage. After installing 5800 meters the company notified the PSC that it was suspending the program because it could not afford the resulting loss of revenues. The water bills of converted customers had declined by 30 to 40%.

development in the watershed and the quality of liquid waste treatment. It is equally certain that the average resident of New York City is totally unaware of any interest that he may have in land use planning in the Town of Olive in Ulster County or in the efficiency of the Ulster County Health Department. *

4.4   Suburban Area Services

Water Supply

In the metropolitan New York area the major water supplies are ground-water, in Nassau and Suffolk counties, and surface water in New York City and the suburban counties of Westchester, Putnam, Dutchess, and Orange. The exception in New York City is the operation of wells by two private water companies in Queens.

In small developments, where the supplies are almost entirely from wells, there has been difficulty in the operation and maintenance of these facilities. They are often neglected and sometimes abandoned by the companies that built them. The larger water supply systems generally have been satisfacto-rily regulated by state and local health departments for quality, and by the Public Service Commission for setting rates of private operations. The major problems in the metropolitan area relate to volumes and treatment.

Nassau County is projecting a daily deficiency in supply by 1984. The droughts of the 1950s and 1960s have shown that there is a deficiency in supply capability of the New York City system during drought periods. This deficiency is aggravated by required releases of water for the Delaware River from the New York City Reservoir at Cannonsville, and by the widespread unmetered service within the city. Additional sources need be developed to serve the region.

The quality of both groundwater and surface water has been good. As development continues in the watershed, however, the quality will decline. This is the actual experience in the Croton Watershed, which supplies 300 million gallons a day (mgd) [114 million liters a day (mld)], out of a total 1200 mgd (455 mld) delivered through the city aqueduct system. The City of New York has considered construction of a water treatment plant within the city. This would require communities in Westchester to provide treatment for the water they get from the Croton system. The Temporary State Commis-sion on the Water Supply Needs of Southeastern New York recommended a

---

*Since this chapter was written, the problem of effluent from Deerfield Acres has been resolved with the reconstruction of the defective disposal systems. [Ed.]

regional benefit corporation as the supplier of water to the suburban counties and New York City (TSCWS, 1972).

Distribution, storage, and pumping facilities for the delivery of water to the consumer are generally in good condition in the New York area. The problems of low pressure and low volumes can be solved; the chief difficulty is the lack of financing needed to make improvements.

Wastewater

Within the metropolitan area, wastewater disposal systems range from individual septic tanks to large treatment facilities in the cities and counties. Within this range there are individual small systems serving several homes or commercial developments such as shopping centers. Municipal systems are similar to these but larger; they are usually city owned and have a treatment capacity on the order of 500,000 gallons per day to 1 million gallons per day. For almost the first half of the century, treatment facilities other than septic tanks and cesspools in fact provided no treatment, but merely removed floating material, rags, and grit. During the 1930s, a number of small communities, aided by public works programs, built primary treatment plants; however, the significant construction of wastewater treatment plants started in the 1940s.

The facilities built during the 1940s, 1950s, and 1960s provided primary treatment. This went beyond mere grit removal and usually provided a 30% reduction in BOD, a 60% reduction in suspended solids, and chlorination of the effluent prior to discharge into a water course.

The collection system that brings the wastewater to the treatment plant—if there is a treatment plant—is usually under local control. It is often a combined system, and is generally in need of improvement and reconstruction. Newer systems in recently developed areas are substantially better but are still subject to the problems of stormwater overflow and infiltration.

In the mid-1960s, New York State passed the Pure Waters Bond Issue. The federal government was empowered to repair some of the damages of pollution in the nation's waterways with the Federal Water Pollution Control Act (PL 92-500) passed in 1972. The Act provided funds on a matching basis for construction of wastewater treatment facilities. It also prompted the regulatory agencies to insist upon upgrading treatment and improving treatment facilities in general. The U.S. Department of Housing and Urban Development instituted a parallel program for the construction of treatment facilities and collection systems in small communities, but it has had little or no impact.

From 1965 to 1972, comprehensive studies, feasibility reports, and detailed designs and specifications for sewage facilities were prepared in suburban New York. At the same time, however, the failure of the federal government to fund its part of the program created a shortage of money. To keep the program going, New York State decided to prefinance the federal share with the expectation of being repaid. After 1972, the program slowed down. Projects were not processed to allow construction to proceed. There were sporadic bursts of activity, such as filing new applications and discussions, which occasionally helped a project. Unfortunately, these were the exceptions.

In the latter half of 1972, there were amendments to the Federal Water Pollution Control Act that significantly broadened the federal government's scope of control through the Environmental Protection Agency. The Act also increased the number of municipalities eligible for grant participation from 55 to 75%. The concept of the Act changed as well. Much broader requirements were instituted, instead of merely mandating that the quality of treatment be upgraded. The applicant for grant funds must now address himself to the problem of stormwater in the system, the effect on the environment, the cost of the facility as related to alternative projects, and other considerations. Again, the availability of federal funds has been less than the amount authorized under the Act. Thus, there are two elements which have slowed the program to a near halt: lack of money and new requirements. *

There are operating problems relating to wastewater treatment facilities and collection systems: those concerning human health, disposal of the sludge created in the process, control of odor, and aesthetics. The single most pressing problem is sludge disposal. Ocean disposal is generally no longer acceptable, and an alternative must be found. The choices of land disposal or incineration create problems of possible toxicity to the land area or air pollution in operating burning plants. The cost of a system providing total oxidation for disposal of sludge would add another 30% to total construction budgets. These facilities are also costly to operate.

Certain actions to alleviate the present impasse in wastewater treatment can be recommended: first, accelerate the construction of the plants as they are now designed, and second, develop a program to study sludge

---

*This section was written in the aftermath of the funding impoundments instituted by the Nixon administration. The flow of federal funds has increased since then, although appropriations are still below authorized levels. In addition, the states and local governments have gradually adjusted to complex federal grant requirements. There were further amendments to the Federal Water Pollution Control Act in 1977 (P.L. 95-217). These did not simplify the funding process, but they did allow localities greater flexibility in the technologies used to solve pollution problems. [Ed.]

disposal—a national problem that is most severe in metropolitan areas where land is scarce and air pollution is already a problem. A solution to sludge disposal may be found in the search for a solution to solid waste disposal.

Stormwater

In the metropolitan New York area, the average annual rainfall varies from 42 inches (107 cm) in Nassau and Suffolk to 48 inches (121 cm) in Westchester and Rockland. The variations, however, are severe. During the drought periods in the mid-1950s and later in the early 1960s rainfall was as low as 31 inches (79 cm). On the other hand, the total precipitation in Westchester in 1972 was 67 inches (169 cm), and in 1973 it was 52 inches (133 cm). Historically, the disposal of stormwater has been considered a matter for public works departments. In earlier times it was done merely by providing open drains. As areas become more developed, these drains were replaced by pipes and culverts. The systems may be separate drainage systems or, as in New York City and Yonkers, they may be combined systems. Other cities and communities have separate collection of sanitary wastewater and stormwater. However, the separate sanitary systems have developed into combined systems. This has come about because the carrying capacity of the sanitary system has been used to handle overloads on the storm drainage system. Large volumes of stormwater are introduced into so-called separate sanitary systems through building downspouts and through structures with water problems in basement areas.

Stormwater is delivered to streams, lakes, rivers, bays, or the ocean for disposal. Stormwater does not become a problem until there is flooding. Floodwater builds up in river valleys or other low-lying areas, and then backs up through the disposal systems to local streets. The need to limit construction within floodplains has been stressed, but further emphasis is necessary. In the suburban New York area, early construction considered the problem of flooding; subsequent development of uplands and drainage basins caused the present problem. As building progressed in the area, streets were placed, sidewalks were installed, and shopping areas with large parking lots were constructed. These actions accelerated runoff time for precipitation and substantially reduced the area of land capable of absorbing the precipitation.

In Westchester County, the river valleys are the north–south corridors for roads, railroads, parkways, and commercial development. Flooding in these valleys often closes the parkways and street systems, inundates structures, and causes a possible health hazard in areas where sanitary wastewater is included in the flooding.

Attempts to correct the flooding have not been successful because the scope of attack has been small. Improvements in stream-channel depth and increased stream velocity in one community will aggravate the flooding problem downstream. Local communities—villages, towns, and counties—do not have the authority to take corrective measures beyond their boundaries. The agency most involved in dealing with the flooding problem on a basin scale is the U.S. Army Corps of Engineers. It has had spectacular success in some large river basins but has not yet solved the problem in smaller rivers in and around the New York metropolitan area.

Another aspect of stormwater, one usually not considered, is that stormwater is itself a source of pollution to receiving waters. Rainfall on an urban area washes dirt, organic material, and animal wastes into the collection system. The present effort to deal with this problem is through wastewater treatment plants, but it does not address itself to all of the problems of stormwater.

Possible solutions to the problem of flooding in urban areas may be found in the use of retention basins, the clearing and maintenance of floodplain areas, and tunnel disposal of large volumes of stormwater. In Nassau and Suffolk counties, because of soil conditions, stormwater is often disposed of locally in sumps, which then collect the stormwater and allow infiltration into the soil. This process obviates the need for extensive drainage systems to carry the water to Long Island Sound. In addition, it has the benefit of replenishing the underground water supply. The pollution caused by stormwater is a problem of such scope that it might better be considered the second phase of the ongoing pollution abatement program rather than an aspect of drainage.

Solid Wastes

Within the New York metropolitan area, the disposal of solid waste has been accomplished using a variety of methods, including ocean dumping, landfills, and incineration. Sea disposal was stopped because the material was being washed back on shore. Two other methods for the major volume of disposal have run into serious problems. Incineration usually reduces the volume by about 70%, but there is still considerable residue. In some cases, because of the operation and the aging of equipment, the residue contains organic matter that encourages rodent and insect infestation. Trucking refuse to the disposal site usually brings resentment on the part of the residents and the commercial establishments within the area. Furthermore, the delivery trucks have both liquid and solid spillage and must wait to discharge their cargo, causing odor and noise pollution. Incinerators are unattractive and require high stacks, often as high as 250 feet. Also, the operating process itself introduces ash, sulfur, and nitrogen compounds into the air, causing an air pollution problem. Overall, incinerators have caused problems in the areas of aesthetics, odor, and air pollution.*

Electrostatic precipitators and scrubbing devices have been installed in attempts to correct some of these problems. They are reasonably effective but are expensive and unlikely to meet new standards. During the past several years, a number of reduction processes have been developed and put into experimental use. Some of these seem promising. The Eweson Process is basically a kiln employing heat generated by bacteria. It does not, however, solve the problem of bulky items and is being used on a small scale. Another process is pyrolysis, which New York City is experimenting with on Staten Island. A third reduction process, developed by Union Carbide, is called the Purox System. The waste is introduced into a furnace and reduced by burning with pure oxygen. There is a usable gas residue that could be used to generate electricity, steam, or heat. The waste residue is a slag. Reduction is on the order of 96 to 98%. The process is experimental and the first unit of 250 tons (227 metric tons) per day is being constructed in West Virginia. There are, of course, numerous conventional furnaces, and research is proceeding on removal of particulate matter and gases from the exhaust of their burning processes. However, it will be 4 to 5 years before new facilities can be constructed with reasonable assurance of satisfactory operation.†

The other major method of disposal is landfill. This has been the least expensive. It has the benefit of reclaiming swamplands and the adverse impact of destroying valuable fresh and saltwater wetlands. The areas for landfill, particularly around the city of New York, are almost all utilized. In Westchester County, the larger tracts of land are on watershed areas of the Croton System and have the potential of polluting the water supply. New York City and Nassau County have both developed recreational facilities from the reclaimed land.

There are serious drawbacks to landfill operations, however. As with incineration, there is a potential for rodents and infestation; resentment of the residents along the route to the landfill and adjacent to it is also a problem. Precipitation on landfill may result in leaching into nearby bodies of water or groundwater. Only more recently recognized is the damage landfills do to

---

*As of 1978, New York City is planning to close three of its six remaining incinerators. The other three will be retained and upgraded with electrostatic precipitators. [Ed.]

†The Staten Island experiment was later carried out in Baltimore. It was not successful and the system is no longer being marketed. As of 1978, however, the Purox system was being considered for a site at John F. Kennedy International Airport in a joint study by the Port Authority and the Brooklyn Union Gas Co. New York City itself has decided to move forward with a proposed water-wall incinerator to be constructed at the former Brooklyn Navy Yard (Wegman, 1977; Koch, 1978). [Ed.]

wetlands, which are breeding grounds for fish and fowl, and help to cleanse the waters they abut.

Studies have been made recommending compaction and rail-haul of solid wastes out of the metropolitan area. These proposals, however, have generally been resisted. The recent proposal to rail-haul New York City wastes to abandoned mine areas in Pennsylvania was vigorously opposed by the State of New Jersey, through which the material would be hauled. The U.S. Supreme Court disallowed a New Jersey statute banning such transshipment, however.*

The agencies dealing with solid waste disposal problems range from small villages to the federal government. On the one hand, the villages, towns, cities, and counties attempt to provide a public service by disposing of, or being responsible for, solid waste. This service has been basically a collection and disposal system. The disposal element is the present problem. In attempting to resolve the matter, these government bodies have tried the conventional methods. Recent events show these solutions to be unacceptable at this time. Therefore, local governments with limited areal jurisdictions must look for help to units with larger jurisdictions and greater resources. In May 1974, Westchester County assumed responsibility for its solid waste problems precisely because the local government units were unable to solve the problems on their own.

The most natural place to seek help is from the regulatory agencies, which have set the standards and criteria that have made the present systems of disposal unacceptable. The New York State Environmental Facilities Corporation (EFC), under DEC, has expanded its activities. Its projects to date have not been particularly innovative, but studies by EFC began to incorporate new trends. The newer "look" means separation of materials, recycling of metals and glass, and compaction to reduce volumes. These methods in themselves do not completely solve the disposal problem but they do reduce volumes. EPA has provided funding for experimental projects and the incentive (money) for the private sector to develop hardware to help villages, towns, cities, and counties provide the service within the new standards of the regulatory bodies. The various health departments—local, county, and state—sometimes find themselves in the uncomfortable position of first requiring the waste disposal service and then attempting to close the facility that provides the service because it is substandard. The operation of such systems, including collection and disposal, stops at the city and county level. Although a regional solution to the problem has been suggested, it may not

---

*City of Philadelphia et al. v. State of New Jersey et al. 425 U.S. 910. While there are now no legal barriers to the rail-haul proposal, it is no longer being considered as an alternative by New York City for economic reasons. [Ed.]

be the answer. The smaller communities are looking to county government for a solution to the problem—Nassau County is working on it; Westchester County has it; and New York City is involved in various experimental activities. In the interim, time is needed. The lead time to put a waste disposal facility on the line is about 7 to 8 years. It is apparent, then, that until the new technologies are proven, and until plants utilizing them can be put into operation, creative approaches using conventional methods for handling disposal must be effected.

4.5 Environmental Services in the Capital District

The Capital District of New York is the northern node of development in the Hudson Basin. Albany, Rensselaer, Saratoga, and Schenectady counties include an area of 2216 square miles. The population of the Capital District is about 730,000, most of which is concentrated in the urbanized area that centers on the confluence of the Hudson and Mohawk Rivers. The four counties contain 78 town, city, and village governments that have direct responsibility for local affairs.

Environmental services in the District are usually provided by local governments. Each municipality ordinarily organizes itself to provide the institutions, facilities, and financial capability necessary to make environmental services available to its inhabitants. But as in other regions, this model does not hold for all municipalities. Many towns are completely rural and do not provide any public environmental services. Individual wells supply water; septic tanks or cesspools are used for liquid wastes; solid wastes are burned or otherwise disposed of on the individual property. This situation is not limited to farms. As developers have leapfrogged their residential subdivisions into the rural fringe beyond the reach of public systems, individual wells and septic tanks may serve single-family homes, or private water supply and wastewater systems may be installed by developers to serve individual subdivisions.

In the urbanized area of the region, many municipalities have their own environmental services and facilities. Others, however, have arranged with neighboring municipalities to purchase water at wholesale rates and to distribute it locally. Wastewater is also conducted to treatment facilities elsewhere. Municipalities may have regular water and sewer service departments, or they may have organized one or more special districts to serve particular areas within their jurisdictions. More recently, counties have organized large districts for the collection and treatment of sewage, which is conveyed to main interceptors by local systems. Water supply systems, except for such large networks as those of Albany and Troy, are mostly small in scale and serve limited populations. Environmental services in the Capital District have been carefully surveyed under the auspices of the Capital District Regional Planning Commission (CDRPC).

Governmental Institutions for Environmental Services

Each of the environmental services reports prepared for the CDRPC included an analysis of the institutional aspects of service delivery and suggested alternatives for change. The 1970 Sewer and Water Facilities Analysis (CDRPC, 1970) noted that, as of the period of its inventory, water and sewerage planning were limited to countywide studies rather than oriented to regionwide development and land use goals. Regionalization of environmental services planning implies institutional changes to consolidate construction and management responsibilities.

The 1971 report on the Regional Water Supply and Wastewater Disposal Plan and Program (CDRPC, 1971) did take an areawide approach to the water supply and sewerage problems of the Capital District, and it considered the administrative and organizational aspects of its proposals. Regional coordination of planning and administration is just as important as physically combining individual water supply and wastewater disposal facilities. Three alternatives were identified: intermunicipal cooperation, regional authority, and county districts.

Intermunicipal cooperation is authorized by Article 5G of the General Municipal Law. This may take two forms: under a contractual agreement, one municipality may buy a service from another; or two or more municipalities may jointly finance, construct, and operate environmental services facilities. There may be advantages in either of these arrangements from economies of scale in construction and management. However, there are also disadvantages. The consumer municipality becomes dependent on the supplier municipality. Growth in either or in both may require expansion of facilities that the supplier may not be willing to undertake. Seasonal or secular climatic changes may restrict water supply to the disadvantage of the dependent community; and the monopoly position of the supplier influences rate negotiations. Even jointly owned or operated systems may experience policy or administrative problems resulting from disagreements among the participating parties. Continuous consensus is necessary to the success of such undertakings.

A regional authority may provide the full range of financing, construction, and operations for environmental services. It must be created by a special act of the legislature, however, and it has a financial disadvantage. Since an authority has no power to levy taxes, it must finance its capital and operating costs from service charges and revenue bonds. It must therefore maintain a substantial liquid reserve to ensure its ability to market revenue bonds for capital improvements. For a metropolitan area of the size and characteristics of the Capital District, the authority appears to have no compelling advantages over an alternative institutional arrangement such as the county district.

Under Article 5A of the County Law, county governing bodies may establish sewer or water districts without regard to local political boundaries. The county legislature appoints the administrative body of the district and assumes all financial responsibility for it. County districts are financed by property taxes and general obligation bonds are secured by the taxing power of the county government.

County districts are relatively easy to establish; they provide economies in financing and operations; and they are adaptable to areawide development. Costs are assessed uniformly throughout the district, and all consumers have a uniform rate structure. A permissive referendum is required before a county district may be established. Such approval has been gained in Albany, Rensselaer, and Saratoga districts, where sewage treatment plants and interceptor lines are already under construction.

The county district is the institutional structure for environmental services recommended in the Regional Water Supply and Wastewater Disposal Plan and Program report (CDRPC, 1971). It appears to be most suitable for the Capital District, and its acceptance has been demonstrated in three counties. This acceptance is limited to wastewater disposal, however. Water supply systems continue to be fragmented into small districts. County districts could also have jurisdiction over water supply, and if voter approval were obtained, they could assume responsibility for all environmental services. There are no technical or administrative obstacles to the consolidation of water supply, wastewater disposal, stormwater drainage, and solid waste disposal in the same county districts.

Stormwater Drainage

Because political boundaries do not conform to the boundaries of drainage basins, it is not possible for individual municipalities to manage storm drainage effectively. Streams in the Capital District carry runoff from numerous local jurisdictions, and stormwater draining from upstream municipalities affects drainage and flood conditions downstream. Comprehensive evaluation of flood plains and watershed characteristics is best performed on a regional basis.

The report of the Regional Storm Drainage Study (CDRPC, 1974) recommends county drainage agencies (which may be established under Article 5A, Section 252 of the County Law). They may plan, finance, construct, and manage drainage and flood control facilities. Financial resources are available from county tax revenues and general obligation bonds. County agencies in the Capital District may also enter into cooperative agreements to attain regionwide objectives. They may also collectively support a central technical unit for regional planning and engineering studies. The report suggests that CDRPC could perform this role.

Solid Waste Disposal

Consolidated sanitary landfill operations are recommended by the Comprehensive Solid Wastes Planning Study (New York State Department of Environmental Conservation and CDRPC). Instead of each municipality attempting to dispose of solid wastes within its own boundaries, multimunicipal landfill operations under county management are recommended. Specific sites are identified for use by groups of municipalities in each county. Consideration of the recycling of wastes for resource recovery and their use as a fuel for power generation was not included in this study. However, recent developments in recycling technology and power generation have aroused local interest in these methods, and CDRPC and the City of Albany are now studying their potential application to the region and the city. *

Consensus on County Institutions

All of the technical studies of environmental services in the Capital District recommend county management. But as separate studies were done for each of the different services, the recommendations point to four agencies in each county—one each for water supply, wastewater disposal, stormwater drainage, and solid waste disposal. A more comprehensive evaluation of environmental services in the region would suggest the establishment of one agency in each county responsible for planning and management of all environmental services on an integrated basis.

This form of organization is not a likely prospect for the immediate future, but there is no present crisis requiring such action. County sewer districts have already been established or approved in three counties of the region. It is not beyond the realm of possibility that these agencies may in time also be assigned responsibility for other county environmental services. As there is state legislative authorization for intercounty cooperation, there would appear to be no advantage to the alternative of a regional authority. Large metropolises, such as New York, may require a superagency to deal with their environmental problems; the Capital District's needs for environmental services, on the other hand, appear to be manageable by county institutions.

*The City of Albany and the New York State Office of General Services are cooperating in a plan to use municipal refuse to provide energy for heating and cooling a group of state office buildings. The refuse would be burned in an existing OGS power plant. The refuse processing facility, to be owned and operated by the City of Albany, was under construction as of 1978. [Ed.]

Intercounty cooperation and the technical and political leadership in CDRPC appear adequate to meet the need for regional coordination and integration.

The Environmental Facilities Corporation

The Environmental Facilities Corporation is a public benefit corporation empowered by New York State law to assume any or all of the responsibilities for environmental services that may be undertaken under any of the institutional alternatives outlined in the preceding paragraphs. Under an appropriate fee structure, EFC can design, finance, construct, or operate these services for municipalities, counties, or the whole region. As of March 31, 1973, EFC had entered into contracts for 64 projects across the state. These were mostly for small, individual municipalities. It has one project in the Capital District, a $1.8-million turnkey sewerage project for the Village of Scotia in Schenectady County.*

Constraints on the Provision of Environmental Services

Physical

The physical bounds within which one must act in providing services are readily understood, although the services of reputable engineering firms are required to delineate the precise possibilities and the feasibility of proposals in any specified area. If the topography will not permit intergovernmental cooperation, no matter how eager municipalities may be to participate, the system proposal must be abandoned. Engineering feats can build systems under rather adverse conditions, but cost factors reduce the likelihood that certain projects will become realities. The proposal of intermunicipal agreements that cross major physical barriers, such as the Hudson River, indicates that many aspects of intergovernmental cooperation between Rensselaer County and the rest of the Capital District have at least been discussed.

Financial

The financial constraints on the construction and operation of environmental service systems cannot be overemphasized. Virtually every proposal,

---

*As of 1978, EFC has been involved in approximately 120 projects throughout the state, primarily in water pollution control and solid waste management. In about 20% of the projects, EFC's role is limited to financing. However, the Corporation has also entered into 35 construction contracts, 15 operation and maintenance contracts, and about 50 contracts involving the provision or management of professional or technical services. In addition, in 19 cases, the Corporation has contracted to design, build, and operate an EFC-owned facility to serve a specific municipal client. A 1978 amendment to its enabling act authorizes EFC to construct and operate facilities for hazardous industrial wastes. [Ed.]

including those recommended as most economical, has a price tag beyond the financial capability of the average municipality. In every community government officials and citizens alike are likely to complain of a project's high cost, and many are opposed to the higher tax rates and user charges that such systems require. Some communities conclude that they simply cannot afford to undertake an environmental service system without federal and state aid. Even with such assistance, some jurisdictions are still hard pressed to ensure a viable program.

In the Capital District, some communities in Rensselaer County have commented on the inadequacies of present aid formulas. A town supervisor complained that the regulations punish communities that take the initiative to remedy serious environmental system deficiencies without external assistance. The town is now more interested in intergovernmental cooperation to improve its position on the eligibility list for aid. The mayor of Castleton-on-Hudson noted a problem in the aid formulas that affect his community: the area immediately adjacent to the village needs sewerage service badly, but the village cannot annex the area and provide the service without losing federal aid—which will be provided only if the project remains intermunicipal.* If the area is not annexed, New York State will not provide aid for operating costs for this part of the system. There is no way this problem can be resolved logically. He further complained of the constantly changing requirements for aid, which have delayed the treatment plant construction considerably. Although these changes are probably always for the better, they raise havoc with local officials who are just trying to get an application completed so they can begin to solve the problem.

The general lack of appropriations for many types of aid, as well as restrictions on eligible projects, further constrain local government initiative in solving environmental problems. An example is the Town of Sand Lake. It voted to participate in Rensselaer County Sewer District No. 1 because 52% of the septic systems in town were considered inadequate. The town subsequently found that aid was easier to obtain where there is public pollution. The need for collection sewers to alleviate private pollution has a lower priority, and there is a critical lack of funds for such projects (Kestner, 1974).

Financial problems often crop up when costs for an intermunicipal system are allocated among its various users. One of the major problems with the contract method of obtaining environmental services is the lack of control over rates charged by the supplying jurisdiction. Even within municipalities, differentials between various districts or service areas can present obstacles to system development.

---

*The federal "bonus" for intermunicipal projects is no longer in effect. For additional information on the Castleton case see Volume 2, Chapter 7, pp. 67-70.

Legal–Institutional

Controlling intermunicipal contract agreements for services is a problem. A possible solution would be to place authority to review such agreements under the auspices of the State Public Service Commission, which could resolve problems of equity and determine the rights of individual participants.

The degree to which politics is involved in the process of intergovernmental relations for providing cooperative public services is not known. Whether the issues are partisan or whether they merely reflect traditional differences within or among municipalities, or among various levels of government, again cannot accurately be measured. These conflicts do, however, exist within Rensselaer County, and they certainly limit effective relationships for the efficient administration of environmental services.

One area that needs attention is voter education on alternative ways of providing environmental services, and on the effects of each proposal. The current concern for the environment has partially remedied this situation, but evidence indicates that many residents still do not understand the real impact of these problems or of proposals to manage them.

Services in Albany County—An Example

Present New York State law provides several alternative forms of environmental service arrangements applicable to Albany County: special districts, town or countywide special districts, intercounty districts, and public authorities. All of these arrangements exist or are proposed for Albany County.

The trend in the Albany area is to provide services through the creation of special districts, which enable a locality to retain control over the services its residents demand. As urbanization spreads into suburban towns, urban services must be provided, particularly water and sewer services. Greater efficiency and economy would probably result from large, rather than municipal units.

Recently the towns in Albany County began to consolidate their sewer and water districts. These consolidated district proposals, however, have met opposition at the local level. Although the law provides for public hearings and referenda on the proposals, the towns too often act independently of the municipalities. The result has been greater opposition on the part of the locals to future consolidation plans.

Countywide districts are an alternative to the multiplicity of small special districts. Most towns in the Albany area now have sufficient water supplies, so that there is little need to move into cooperative agreements. Similarly, most towns have ready access to riverfront or creek land, thereby ensuring a site for the disposal of treated sewage. Thus, there is little incentive to push for consolidation of districts.

The Albany County sewer system was established to provide sewage treatment for city residents. The extension of that system into the Pine Bush area of the city enabled nearby towns to join the county system at relatively low cost. There has been resistance to incorporation into the county system, but most residents advocated incorporation, because they would have incurred higher cost had they not been included. The consolidation of districts at the town and, later, at the county level can be a viable alternative to fragmented water and sewage services in the Albany area.

Service districts larger than the county—multicounty or regional—have been proposed by members of the legislature. Although appearing to be reasonable alternatives on paper, these large units encounter great problems in practice.

Substate–Regional Arrangements for Environmental Services

The New York State Joint Legislative Committee on Metropolitan and Regional Areas undertook a comprehensive study of its subject in 1969. It reported (NYSJLC, 1971) that existing regional agencies lack both the necessary authority and the tools for a coordinated response to urban pressures. Strategies on regional approaches to metropolitan problems have, in the past, encountered political opposition. Government action now merely consists of the aggregate of the policies of all local governments within each metropolitan area. Because there is no coordinating mechanism, this political structure can yield neither an adequate public service program nor a coordinated economic and social development strategy.

The State of New York adopted legislation for land use control in the 1920s. This legislation was to enable municipalities to protect their neighborhoods by controlling growth. However, the enabling legislation was developed on a piecemeal basis, and can now be found throughout the state's town law, village law, general city law, and municipal law. Among other things, it relates to zoning, subdivision regulations, official maps, and appeals. Each set of statutes has been amended many times over a period of 50 years and is thus replete with ambiguities, inconsistencies, and omissions. Each municipality still makes its own decisions on the control of land use.

Too often resources are wasted: incompatible water and sewer systems are sometimes built; facilities are often duplicated; a sprawling pattern of development, which makes public services more expensive, is often generated; regional concerns, such as air and water, go unprotected (Advisory Committee on Intergovernmental Relations, 1973). Regional coordination can sometimes prevent such wastefulness by performing a surveillance function. If, on the other hand, it is assumed that reducing fragmentation through regionalization also reduces the effectiveness of the service delivery system, then the approach cannot in itself be effective.

Growing federal and state concerns about the need for effective multijurisdictional approaches, and the absence of authoritative multifunctional areawide institutions, have led to the development of districting substitutes for such comprehensive bodies by the federal and state governments. In the 1960s, the federal government supported a policy of initiating and shaping regional responses to problems. Through areawide planning, review, districting requirements, and incentives, federal agencies began to fill the institutional void at the substate level. Some federally supported, multipurpose, areawide procedures—such as the A-95 review procedure—have been major steps toward the establishment of more authoritative areawide decision-making bodies by local and state government; others, such as the encouragement of limited-purpose substate districts, have hindered the prospects for achieving major institutional reorganization (Advisory Committee on Intergovernmental Relations, 1973).

Basically, two different federal substate districting strategies seem to be emerging: one for the generalists (A-95 type) and one for the specialists (multijurisdictional mechanisms). Multijurisdictional special districts theoretically offer many advantages. They are relatively easy to establish; they maintain the status quo, since they do not change the existing local government bodies; they provide an ad hoc approach to a problem; they can act as an agent for regional government rereorganization; and they provide clues as to which functions are most properly areawide in nature. On the other hand, it is argued that such agencies often show a lack of cooperation with general-purpose governments, are remote from the local citizenry, and tend to erode minority political power.

At the regional multicounty level in the Albany area, cooperation is limited. CDRPC serves a review function on proposals in which there is federal involvement. It provides some cooperation between counties, but control over CDRPC is exercised by the mayor of the city of Albany. CDRPC had great difficulty in operating until the mayor's power was recognized and accommodated.

Regional Councils of Governments (COGs) are generally defined as multifunctional, voluntary associations of elected local officials or of local governments represented by their elected officials. The COG is an organizational device to bring together representatives of an area's local governments to discuss common problems, to exchange information, and to develop a consensus on policy questions of mutual interest.

COGs embody a confederation-type approach to areawide coordination. They have no governmental powers or operating responsibilities. No COG, however, has been able to solve any problems of a highly controversial nature. Here the representativeness is counterproductive. Local citizen interests are represented, yet debate on matters where costs and benefits are not balanced has effectively halted any action (Advisory Committee on Intergovernmental Relations, 1973).

Other than CDRPC, there has been little cooperation, historically, among the counties in the Albany metropolitan area. Each county is almost a distinct entity, offering widely divergent forms of city and county governance. Regional councils can be useful as agents for new governmental cooperative organizations. There are several other proposals of governmental reorganization coming to the fore. Two-tier or three-tier arrangements, involving regional councils as well as the county and local units, are examples. The basic unresolved question is the proper relationship between generalists and specialists to ensure effective regional public service districts.

Public authorities are created by a special act of the legislature. Although each of the Albany County towns and cities has its own industrial development agency, a county authority could remove land from city and town tax rolls through condemnation. An Albany Republican senator has opposed such a county agency on the ground that it could be used by the Albany Democratic organization to exert pressures on suburban towns and other cities in Albany County.

State Level Arrangements for Environmental Services

One of the major obstacles faced at the New York State level by proponents of the various county and regional approaches to reorganization of sewer and water districts is the traditional upstate–downstate political rift. Upstate, there is a move to larger units (county and region), whereas New York City's trend is the reverse. The city is moving away from the larger units toward a neighborhood approach to governance. Upstate, it is more efficient to reorganize the existing service arrangements. It is, however, necessary to arrive at some optimal size of that service district. It cannot be too small, since this would result in fragmented, unifunctional arrangements; if the districts are too large, responsiveness suffers, and it becomes difficult for local citizens to influence policy.

New legislative proposals for institutional arrangements have resulted from studies on both the state and federal levels. Former Governor Rockefeller saw the importance of the regional approach to environmental service institutions. Unfortunately, many citizens throughout the state reacted negatively to regional planning bills. Other problems faced by proponents of reorganization are those of definition. If the state wishes to step in and impose regional arrangements, it must first define what constitutes a region. After that, it must ensure that all regions are comparable; what applies to one region must apply to all.

Is an approach to the problem such as government fragmentation politically feasible? If so, would a solution mandating formal cooperation be accepted? Of course, the most acceptable solutions are not necessarily the most effective (NYSJLC, 1971). But in most cases, considerations of political feasibility and ease of implementation have dictated approaches to solving areawide service problems. Local decision-makers generally find it more expedient to act on a function-by-function basis rather than to establish a substate district or an independent special district. This is so in Albany County, where even functional cooperation is opposed by some suburban towns.

Conclusions

The study of environmental services in the Capital District illustrates the difficulties encountered in providing environmental services in a medium-sized metropolitan area. However, that study suggests some actions that may be generally helpful to communities facing problems in providing environmental services:

1. Improved federal and state aid formulas and requirements for a comprehensive approach in assisting local governments
2. Establishment of controls for intergovernmental service agreements to guarantee equitable contracts for all participants
3. Extensive analysis of the structure of local government to investigate possible arrangements if state controls were modified
4. More effective communication between governments and between levels of government in their cooperative efforts to solve environmental service problems
5. Improved public information and programs to acquaint residents with various proposals and consequences if environmental service problems are not resolved
6. Increased emphasis on technological development of alternatives to present environmental systems in an attempt to reduce cost and to improve effectiveness in solving municipalities' problems

4.6   Environmental Services for New York City

Water Supply

Sources

New York City is probably the world's largest supplier of water. On an average day it furnishes 1500 mgd to 7.3 million people (Albert et al., 1974).

The city's water supply area is, in fact, a regional water supply resource for southeastern New York and northern New Jersey.

The New York City municipal water supply is basically a surface water system. Water is impounded in upland areas and fed through aqueducts to the Kensico Reservoir, the control reservoir in Westchester County. At the Kensico, the waters are brought together, blended, and fed into the major distribution network through Westchester County (Fig. 4-3).

Although New York currently has no problems in connection with finances or personnel in the supply and distribution of water, the city will soon require an additional source of supply. This will probably be the Hudson River. The question of a new source immediately raises the question of jurisdiction. It is believed in some concerned state government circles that the existing upstate watersheds will eventually be considered regional resources.

Agencies

Three city agencies share responsibility for New York City's water supply. These are the Board of Water Supply, the Department of Water Resources, and the Bureau of Sanitary Engineering in the Department of Health. The Board of Water Supply is responsible for the development of new sources of water supply. It designs and constructs new reservoirs, aqueducts, treatment plants, and other facilities. As each project is satisfactorily completed, it is entrusted to the Department of Water Resources, which is responsible for operating and maintaining the water supply system for the city. This department must furnish water of adequate quality to meet all the city's needs. It makes and enforces rules governing and restricting the use of water, and it fixes prices for the supply of water subject to approval of the Board of Estimate.

The Bureau of Sanitary Engineering also maintains quality control checks over the city's water supply through a bacteriological sampling program. This Bureau is also responsible for investigating complaints pertaining to the water supply. The Bureau of Laboratories also does bacteriological and fluoridation analysis.

Quality

Water from New York's three major surface systems meets drinking water standards. However, a slow but steady deterioration of the quality of all three systems is apparent. This is due to agricultural activities and suburban and industrial growth throughout the watersheds. The Croton systems will probably require treatment facilities in the immediate future. The point from which water may be taken from the Hudson River generally meets most of the Public Health Service drinking standards. Efforts over the past few years

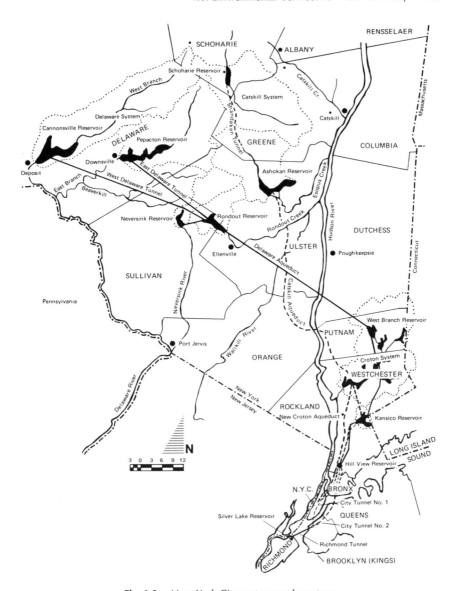

Fig. 4-3. New York City water supply system.

to reduce water pollution have improved the quality of the river, but some of the industrial pollutants that are appearing upriver are not treatable by conventional water or sewage techniques.

Sewerage

The New York City government itself has built and maintained sewers for only sixteen years. Previously, sewer construction was handled separately by each borough, and property owners were assessed directly for such improvements. There were no citywide standards, inadequate sewer capacities in some places, limited expansion and, at times, poor workmanship and alleged fraud. When the city government took over the system in 1962, about 100 square miles of the city remained unsewered, and much of the existing system was inadequate or in need of replacement. It was estimated that several billion dollars of capital outlay over a 10- to 20-year period would be needed to correct these inadequacies. This money is not available from federal or state sources and is not exempt from the New York City debt limit.

Pollution Control

The first water pollution treatment plant for New York City was located at Coney Island and began operation in 1953. From then through 1970, a dozen other plants were constructed. About 75% of the wastewater generated daily in the city receives some form of secondary treatment. The rest, mostly from Manhattan's West Side, spills into the Hudson River as raw sewage. This describes dry weather conditions.

Additional facilities are now under construction, along with expansion of existing plants. One new plant is on the Hudson River and another at the old Brooklyn Navy Yard site. The city will then have sufficient facilities with adequate capacity to meet all anticipated dry weather demands. However, there is still the problem of stormwater overflow when excess water is poured into the system.

Urban Drainage

Even a light rainfall can cause New York's sewers to overflow. Queens is often flooded because of inadequate drainage. Prior to the mid-1960s, the stormwater of New York's combined sewer system carried raw sewage into recreational waters along the city's 575-mile waterfront. One to 3 days were required to dilute and dissipate the storm and sewage water in the receiving waters after a rainstorm. Some beaches were frequently closed owing to this side effect of the combined sewer system.

In 1964 the city began a pioneering effort to correct this problem. The Marginal Pollution Control Program was instituted to eliminate beach pollution. The city's Bureau of Water Pollution Control built tanks to hold stormwater, to chlorinate it, and to return it to nearby sewage treatment plants. The program covers three drainage areas: Jamaica Bay, Eastchester Bay, and the upper East River. The Jamaica Bay project consists of six stormwater detention plants, as well as storm and sanitary sewers for the Rockaway treatment system. It carries a price tag of $65 million (Anonymous, 1964).

Sanitation

Each day in New York City, 25,000 tons of refuse are generated. The tonnage increases each year and collecting and disposing of this waste is one of the city's most difficult problems. About one-third of the refuse is incinerated in six plants located throughout the city. The remainder of the solid waste is buried in landfills, mainly the Fresh Kills on Staten Island. These landfills are becoming saturated, however. The city had planned to increase its incinerator capacity to 18,000 tons per day by 1975, but the new plants have been delayed by the city's continuing fiscal problems.

The expense of handling and processing solid waste is mounting steadily. Satellite systems of automatic collecting, preliminary processing, and mechanical handling of residue would assist the city. These local systems could be encouraged or even required for all large new developments. Without these systems, the city may not be able to afford collection at its present level.

The Future

The population of New York City should be rather stable throughout the remainder of the century. But increasing affluence will not stabilize the problems the city faces in environmental services. If present trends continue, water consumption and concurrent sewage loads will increase, along with solid waste. The already stringent water and air pollution standards in the New York area will, if anything, become more restrictive. These problems of growth, in the face of obsolete or nonexistent plants in many areas, present challenges to the city's administrators and engineers.

4.7   Conclusions

When the four major environmental services are viewed overall, their interrelationships become apparent. Water is first a supply for human consumption, but also is a vehicle for sanitary waste disposal. The resulting wastewater requires treatment, and the degree of treatment affects the quality of the receiving waters. Receiving waters may be used for fishing, recreation, and possibly water supply for another community. The sludge from the wastewater treatment process needs to be disposed of, and such disposal may affect air quality, water quality, and the general health of the public, depending on the system used. The residual of grit, rags, and grease actually is part of the solid waste stream. Sludge may be added to solid waste for disposal. Stormwater overburdens sanitary systems, drainage systems, and wastewater plants. It is a source of pollution and causes physical damage to property.

In regulating and providing environmental services, the apparent interrelationships have led to "superagencies." The intention of these agencies is to provide an overall view and coordination of effort, perhaps to the mutual benefit of several of the systems. Examples of this type of agency are the U.S. EPA, the New York State DEC, and the Suffolk County Department of Environmental Control. But it is not practical or effective for a single agency to provide and regulate environmental services. It would be unusual for an agency to criticize its own operation.

The decision-making by these agencies is ultimately determined, in large measure, by those personalities that are most articulate and forceful. Thus, where operating departments are competing (water supply, wastewater, solid waste, stormwater disposal), the strong department head will generally prevail in policy and funds. In the area of standards and regulation, usually the strictest attitude will prevail for the same reason.

Some "superagencies" have a dearth of operating people and a plethora of "concept people." The communities and agencies attempting to solve problems and to construct facilities do not have a workable liaison with the decision-making people in the superagencies. Superagencies often respond to questions with, "we are waiting for clarification from higher up."

The superagencies lack accountability. Decentralization of their authority and responsibility is needed to ensure accountability. If DEC shifted responsibility to the regional level, the regional administrator would be compelled to pursue projects and problem-solving for his or her area. The administrator would be more likely to follow the status of projects and problems, pushing for answers and continuing progress with superiors.

One of the task group members, who daily must work with local officials and the mechanics of environmental service systems, expressed the opinion that existing units of government are able to provide these services and to confront the problems connected with them. Rather than creating new bodies, the existing government departments and agencies need to be reoriented. In some cases, their powers need to be broadened or their areas of responsibility redefined.

A task group member familiar with the technology of environmental services stated that in the very near future—say, within 5 years—new methods and processes will be available to improve these services. With the development of better basic services, local agencies must be able to implement them. A responsible and concerned local administrative structure would do much to facilitate the use of advanced techniques and provide adequate delivery.

The Role of Environmental Service Systems in Development

It was mentioned earlier, and is worth repeating, that civilized communities cannot survive without adequate environmental services. Potable water and sanitary disposal of human and other potentially disease-producing wastes are unavoidable requirements for high-density development. Another requisite for land development is access. Systems for environmental services and transportation may, therefore, be designed and constructed by area governments to foster a predetermined pattern of urbanization. The pattern itself may be depicted in a land use plan. Municipal governments are authorized by state law to enact local zoning ordinances, subdivision regulations, and an official map. These legal controls on development, when combined with municipal planning for environmental services and transportation systems, may effectively channel private development to conform to the land use plan. A new generation of land use controls is now in the making, embodied in the Model Land Development Codes of the American Law Institute.

Although the legal and technical tools are available for land use planning and regulation, they are often not used effectively. There are many reasons for this, but perhaps the most serious constraints on metropolitan land use planning are economic and political. Land use regulations are more readily accepted in urban and suburban areas, where they are seen as protecting the values of existing development. In the surrounding rural fringe, however, property owners object to restrictions on the market in land that might limit their opportunities for speculative capital gains. Political constraints on land use planning and control are partly ideological within those local jurisdictions where voters and property owners object to restraints on private initiative. A more serious political constraint is the fragmentation of local government and the variations in the exercise of statutory land use planning powers by municipalities in metropolitan areas.

There are 78 municipal jurisdictions in the Capital District, for example. Many have enacted land use controls, but fragmented planning seldom produces a coherent or efficient regional pattern of urban development. The Capital District Regional Planning Commission is preparing a metropolitan land use planning proposal. It will not be completed until the summer of

1974,* and in any case it will have to go through the process of public scrutiny and political evaluation before it will have any great impact on the regionwide development process.

Metropolitan transportation planning is largely determined by the New York State Department of Transportation (DOT), although there are opportunities for inputs by county and municipal governments. But much of the financing of transportation and environmental services construction is made available by the federal government. Therefore, the preparation of a comprehensive metropolitan development plan that integrates land use, transportation, and environmental services requires technical and political coordination among many local jurisdictions and between county, state, and national governments.

Given the economic and political constraints on zoning and other land use regulatory measures, regionwide planning of transportation and environmental services could exert a strong influence on the future physical structure and development patterns of metropolitan areas. Planning coordination by county and state agencies, especially DOT and DEC, together with regional planning boards, could effectively guide development to conserve environmental values, reduce energy consumption, reduce air and water pollution, and economize governmental operations.

Control of development through environmental services has recently taken the form of moratoriums on sewers or on buildings. These have included freezes on new sewer authorizations (the extension of trunk lines into currently unserviced areas); on new sewer hook-ups; on the issuance of new building permits, or a class of building permits, such as multifamily; on the approval of subdivisions; on rezonings or zonings to higher densities; or a slowdown or quota allocation for any or all of the preceding within an affected area (Rivkin, 1974).

There appear to be two principal motives for sewer moratoriums. When facilities are inadequate and public health questions are involved, the police power may be invoked to reduce or stop development. Money, or rather the lack of it, is the second motive. Until recently, capital investment in sewerage facilities had been a comparatively small proportion of total public investment. But popular concern about the environment and the Federal Water Pollution Control Act and subsequent amendments have put pressure on local governments to undertake large capital programs for the collection and treatment of sewage. Federal and state governments have legislation to set and enforce water quality standards. Inadequate disposal of municipal sanitary wastes is an important source of water pollution. Communities are

---

*The CDRPC's Regional Development Plan was completed in 1977 and has been officially adopted by the Commission and the four Capital District counties (CDRPC, 1978). [Ed.]

under pressure, therefore, to build or improve wastewater treatment facilities.

Sewer moratoriums have been imposed by federal and state, as well as local governments. According to a 1973 HUD survey, thirteen states imposed one or more sewer moratoriums, acting under state water quality standards mandated by federal legislation (Rivkin, 1974).

Occasionally, water supply problems have also been the cause of building moratoriums. Nevertheless, freezes on building permits, rezonings, or utility connections and extensions are a simplistic method of dealing with the complex problems of metropolitan development. They have had undesirable side effects, such as a speed-up of construction by developers before the moratoriums take effect, hardship for the small-scale builder, discrimination against multifamily housing, obstacles to production of low and moderate income housing, and leapfrogging of development to metropolitan fringe jurisdictions not covered by environmental and land use controls.

Urgent analyses of environmental factors should be taken into account in determining a desirable land use pattern and the formulation of a plan to guide the physical accommodation of future population and economic growth. It is hoped that municipal, county, state, and national government agencies concerned with urban planning and development in the Hudson Basin region will coordinate their efforts with regional planning agencies to optimize development, public services, and environmental conservation.

Whereas direct regulation of settlement patterns appears simple and desirable, historical precedent gives little reason to believe that adequate measures are politically feasible. At best, progress in this area will be slow. Indirect controls appear more promising. Approaches for consideration include the following:

1. Public investment in the construction and operation of water supply and sewage treatment facilities to those areas where population now exceeds a particular number and density should be limited.

2. There should be a moratorium on the construction of new roads with public funds and a discontinuation of the acceptance of dedications of private roads or streets.

3. Agriculture near population centers should be encouraged, thereby providing opportunities for constructive utilization of sewage and reducing the need for chemical fertilizers.

4. Consumption of water should be tied to its price, with an initial per capita amount for residential purposes at low cost and sharply higher rates for use in excess of that amount. Reduction of per capita consumption of water would, of course, reduce the volume of liquid waste requiring treatment, though not the quantity of pollutants.

5. Solid waste, too, should be regulated by cost to the extent possible, with excise taxes imposed on packaging materials that create disposal difficulties. Properly separated residential wastes could be purchased at a price sufficient to encourage separation but not high enough to encourage use. An example is the Oregon returnable container statute. Separation would permit increased recycling as well as simplify the use of combustible wastes for fuel.

Strategies such as those indicated are necessary if environmental service systems are to be planned and operated more rationally. Although such systems are considered "public goods" and therefore are not subject to the same economic laws as "private goods," this distinction has created several of the problems outlined in this task group report. Ways must be found to inject economic benefits and burden into the public's actions with respect to the consumption of water and other natural resources and the production of sewage and solid waste. The costs are now too remote and subject mainly to decisions taking place within a political context. When they are brought to bear more directly on an individual's actions, when an individual must pay for himself or herself, then development behavior will be modified. Settlement can be rechanneled to reinstate and preserve the clean environment and plentiful resources once taken for granted by inhabitants of this planet.

Chapter 5

ENERGY SYSTEMS

5.1 Introduction

Energy availability greatly increases the work-performance capability of the Hudson Basin. It makes possible a high-quality lifestyle and also leads to extensive degradation of the environment. Those incompatible consequences can be reduced significantly by applying the technical and economic resources of the region. However, modification of present lifestyles also is necessary for attainment of society's quality-of-life objectives.

Continued growth of the region's energy demands is forecast for several decades. Impacts on the environment and on community development are being challenged as excessive costs for meeting energy demands, and demand estimates also are being challenged. Energy systems have lost the confidence of the public.

Per capita energy consumption in the Hudson Basin is lower than the United States average, particularly for industry and transportation uses. For those reasons, and also because of the relative affluence of the region's

Members of the Energy Systems Task Group: Peter Borelli, James G. Cline, Eugene D. Eaton, Robert E. Ford, and Richard G. Stein.

population, energy stringencies are likely to impact less severely on the Hudson Basin than on the United States as a whole. For the next 10 to 15 years, although public and private management may abate the adverse impacts of energy stringencies, it is unlikely that energy demand growth will be significantly lower or that supplies will be augmented substantially.

For the near future, energy stringencies may have some effect on consumer economics, on transportation, and on housing and settlement patterns; however, such effects probably will be limited. For the longer term, population size, affluence, and lifestyle (including transportation) practices will determine the character of Hudson Basin energy systems to greater degree than other factors, with the exception of possible major technological advances, possible war, or other catastrophes.

Existing and improved technologies will diminish polluting emissions and certain other environmental damage. But for other forms of environmental degradation, ameliorative technologies are less well advanced. Environmental protection costs will be substantial, and the adoption of ameliorative technologies will depend on the readiness of energy users to accept the costs, including reduced energy availability. Government sanctions will have to modulate economic restraints.

Central to decision-making in the public interest is strengthening procedures and techniques for the development and expression of public consensus. Current progress encourages expectation that the decisions now emerging in the Hudson Basin will move it toward socially acceptable cost–benefit balances that take proper account of environmental and community development values.

The functioning of energy industries and the public regulatory agencies in energy management must become both more accessible to the affected public and more responsive to societal objectives—especially regarding protection of the environment and community development. Innovative management procedures must be adopted to mitigate current practices that make massive commitments of environmental and financial resources to energy system development. State agencies, in consultation with cognizant federal agencies, should provide continuing appraisals of the state of the environment, energy requirements, and energy system capability.

The need for a lot more information and knowledge calls for continuing programs of research, development, and demonstration regarding problems of technology, ecology, public administration, and energy-systems management. Although many of the Hudson Basin problems will be dealt with in programs of nationwide sponsorship, regional and local programs are also needed, particularly in adapting and demonstrating the practicability of energy-conservation and environmental measures.

5.2   Functioning and Problems of Hudson Basin Energy Systems

The Present Situation

The Hudson Basin energy systems are generally comparable to those of the nation, characterized by continuing increases in requirements coupled with increasing difficulties in providing energy supplies, and now exacerbated by foreign control of major petroleum sources. The emergence of this dilemma has been apparent for a number of years, but only recently has it been publicly acknowledged, and the sudden onset of energy stringencies threatens to disrupt individual and societal well-being. The Hudson Basin energy systems are networks of highly developed physical facilities, management operations, and financial structures. They now provide about 3500 trillion Btu per year for the 20 million people of the region, thereby increasing their work-performance capability 10,000-fold.

That enhanced work-performance capability makes possible an abundant lifestyle (although it is not equitably shared by everyone), including pleasant homes, high levels of nutrition, health care, and amenities. But it also causes air and water pollution and ugliness in urban and rural environments. More importantly perhaps, it changes the way people live—witness the automobile–exurbia syndrome, for example.

Regional per capita energy consumption, 175 million Btu per year, is less than three-fourths of the United States average. The relatively low per capita energy consumption in the region is due to lower use for industry (about one-fifth of the national average) and for transportation (about three-fourths of the national average). The latter is related to the concentration of 90% of the region's population in the densely settled metropolitan core where travel distances are short and use of public transit prevails.*

Fuels for heating and cooling, for transportation, and for generation of electricity constitute, in about equal amounts, over three-fourths of regional energy consumption. In the 1960 to 1970 decade, the growth rate of residential use of energy was only slightly greater than the 11.6% population increase. However, during that period, total net energy consumption in the region grew about 30% (40% for gross consumption). Commercial uses grew at about the same rate. Fuels consumed for electricity generation dou-

---

*The energy supply and consumption estimates used in this report are crude approximations derived from variety of sources, especially from the Regional Plan Association 1974 study of energy consumption in the New York urban region. That region is generally similar to the Metropolitan plus the Middle Hudson areas of the Hudson Basin Project. However, the frailties of these estimates are attributable solely to the Energy Systems Task Group.

bled. Transportation energy uses grew by more than 50%, with automobiles being the most energy-intensive mode of surface travel—6500 Btu per person-mile in comparison with 3100 Btu for subways and about 2500 Btu for trains and buses.

Virtually all energy used in the Hudson Basin is converted from sources that originate outside the region, thus permitting this region to enjoy the benefits of energy availability and to avoid many of the direct social costs. Because of its precarious dependence on low-sulfur crude oil from the Middle East there is strong incentive for nuclear-fueled generation.

The general structure and functioning of the energy systems of the region conform with nationwide patterns. In the Hudson Basin, as elsewhere in the United States, they are private-sector entities organized predominantly by energy mode (electricity, gas, heating oil, gasoline, and other highway fuels). They are managed by complex mixes: large corporate producers and suppliers of energy fuels, with variously sized enterprises for distribution to end users.

The profit maximization objectives of energy systems are tempered by government regulation in order to represent public service responsibilities. Existing mechanisms, however, are not yet effectively providing for the public interest in this regard, especially for the attainment of the least net-social-cost of supplying energy and of overall efficiency in meeting user requirements.

Impacts on the environment and on community development are being challenged by the utilities and fossil fuel industries as excessive costs for meeting energy demands, and the demand estimates are also being challenged by environmentalists, civic groups, and other critics. There is pervasive loss of confidence and skepticism about the functioning of energy systems as stewards of the public interest.

Trends and Implications

For the longer term, fundamental and far-reaching developments may change the technology, the economics, and the social posture of energy systems. Fundamental technological changes that could affect their functioning include coal gasification and liquefaction; nuclear breeder and fusion electricity generation; tidal, geothermal, and solar energy; and possibly even more radical technologies. There are also potentials in system design and management, such as dispersed conversion facilities, salvage of rejected heat, and district total energy systems. However, long lead times (10 to 15 years and longer) and large expenditures must precede major alterations of existing practices. Although there is a stated national commitment to substantial supply augmentation, the magnitude, character, and timing of the supplies ultimately available will be strongly influenced by both public and private decisions. It is unlikely that there will be substantial effects within the next decade from even the massive programs now being mounted to augment energy supplies and to encourage conservation.

In the near term, management practices will mitigate but not eliminate the hazards of fuel shortages for the automobile operator as well as for the utility company. A large share of recent energy problems resulted from the sudden onset of stringencies, and such adverse impacts on energy users may be alleviated by distribution arrangements, e.g., by improved highway fuel allocation or by rationing.

Large commercial and residential complexes, like industrial plants, will begin and will continue to adopt fuel conservation measures. Initially, they will mainly be relatively inefficient retrofit devices. In a somewhat longer time frame, significant energy conservation results should be achieved from site and structure design.

Single-family homes and private passenger autos will be slower in adopting conservation practices because of greater investment costs as well as the persistence of custom. In time, energy-intensive autos will be replaced with smaller ones having more efficient engines.

Energy stringencies may dampen migration from city cores to exurbia, and population increase may be housed mainly by infilling existing settlements. More fundamental changes in settlement patterns associated with enlarged public transit require greater commitments, politically and economically, than may be forthcoming.

In the near term, substantially increased prices for energy may affect marginal commercial enterprises—especially those associated with recreation and resort development. Low-income workers may also be affected, especially those in rural and exurban areas who have large gasoline requirements. For the larger, more affluent share of the population, energy prices may have a relatively small effect on consumption, although increased expenditures for energy will exert pressure to curtail other purchases. Higher energy prices, in conjunction with uncertainty of supply, may discourage acquisition of a second home. Increased energy costs in conjunction with increases for labor, materials, and debt service may affect the market for commercial buildings and single-family homes.

For the next 10 or 15 years, the huge social investment in energy facilities and their interrelationships with other societal systems will be a conservative force resistant to change. For the longer term, population numbers, affluence, density of settlement, and travel practices will be determinative of energy consumption and thus of the character of energy systems. Energy stringencies, however, will impact on the Hudson Basin less severely than on the United States as a whole because of the relatively high per capita income of the region and its low use of energy for industry and transportation.

Existing and improved technologies will diminish the impacts of polluting emissions such as sulfur dioxide, particulates, and rejected condenser heat—but at substantial costs, including reduced energy production. Less readily amenable to present technologies are control of automotive emissions and the visual blight of transmission lines. These too may be subject to technological amelioration in the near future, although at very high costs. In some other areas, ameliorative technologies are less well developed, notably those with aesthetic content, such as site and structure designs. There can be confidence, however, that such technological competence will develop.

Crucial to the application of ameliorative technologies will be the readiness of energy users to accept higher costs and/or reduced availability of energy supplies, particularly the latter. Because the provision of energy supplies is subject to the economies of competition, government sanctions are needed for environmental protection. Ongoing experimentation (e.g., variances from air quality standards versus improvement of stack gas scrubbers) will determine the extent to which environmental protection will be effective.

It may be possible to provide for future Hudson Basin needs for thermal-electric generation capacity without occupying any new sites along watercourses. This may be accomplished by enlarging existing installations, employing various types of cooling systems, and utilizing derelict industrial sites.

5.3   Toward Accommodation

The New York State Power Plant Siting Act

With the passage of the New York State Power Plant Siting Act (generally referred to as Article VIII) in 1972 the Legislature of the State of New York accorded equal importance to environmental protection and electricity supply. It provided that approval of power plant siting proposals shall be based on the public need for the facility and on the nature of its probable environmental impact through authoritative determination of whether the facility represents the minimum adverse environmental impact, considering the available technology and the economics of alternatives, as well as aesthetic and other environmental values and public health and safety; is designed to operate in conformance with applicable laws and regulations; is consistent with long-range planning for electric power supply; will serve the public need for power, and the public interest in protection of the environment.

In this regard, the New York statute is consonant with the declaration of the National Environmental Policy Act:

> It is the continuing policy of the Federal Government, in cooperation with State and local governments, and other concerned public and private organizations, to use all practicable means and measures . . . in a manner calculated to foster and promote the general welfare, to create and maintain conditions under which man and nature can exist in productive harmony, and fulfill the social, economic, and other requirements of present and future generations of Americans.

Decision-Making in the Public Interest

Government involvement in energy-related decisions is becoming more extensive. Decision-making in the public interest should seek a balance of benefits and costs to society. As said in the *Calvert Cliffs* decision, it must be a finely tuned and systematic balancing of all relevant concerns on a case-by-case basis. Public confidence in, and acceptance of, energy-related decisions requires that they be arrived at through open and consistent procedures exercised by persons with credible public-interest credentials. Societal institutions charged with the performance of these functions must be strengthened and improved.

Federal and state agencies deal with public health and safety aspects, and with engineering and financial feasibility, but they are not well suited to deal with regional and community development. As a consequence, those aspects of energy system development have been slighted until recently.

Progress is being made now in strengthening the mechanisms and in improving the techniques of public consensus on energy-related issues. The strong impetus that has been and continues to be supplied by citizen groups, as in the Cornwall and Indian Point issues, is being transformed into formal procedures for public participation in decision-making, notably pursuant to Article VIII.

The first stage of public involvement in such decision-making is appraisal and evaluation of the social benefits and costs of alternative courses of action—information basic to rational choices. Orderly analytic procedures ensure that account is taken of the significant effects of supplying and using energy, of doing so only partially, or of not doing so at all. There are many technical difficulties and much work involved in assembling such information, but the environmental impact statement that the National Environmental Policy Act requires provides such analyses. Federal agencies, notably the Atomic Energy Commission, have adopted procedures for comprehensive accounting. Although impact analysis procedures are still in a developmental phase, there has been enough experience with them to confirm that they are practicable and that they warrant wide application.

The second stage of public involvement is the exercise of choice. It is at the core of decision-making and, in many respects, it is not amenable to rigorous procedures. Engineering and economic analysis of all benefits that are quantifiable can select the course of action that is most socially cost-effective, yet it would miss important but unquantifiable societal values. How many cold tenement flats are offset by a lovely landscape? Are 10,000 megawatt hours of pumped-storage energy worth the ruin of a mountain stream? Questions such as these cannot be answered categorically. Each situation is a unique combination of social, economic, ecological, and amenity values and hazards. Experience suggests the following guidelines for decision-making in the public interest.

In considering proposed energy system actions, account should be taken of all significant economic, social, and environmental costs and benefits. In addition to demonstrating engineering feasibility, there should be a reasonable showing that (a) provision of the proposed energy supply is the least net-social-cost means of meeting public needs; (b) the proposed action complies as fully as is feasible with responsible expressions of regional and community development objectives; and (c) the proposed action will include all feasible measures for protection of environmental, ecological, aesthetic, and amenity values and for avoidance of irreversible damage to the environment.

Because the impacts of an energy system action may have significantly different consequences in different environmental situations, and because the differences in the societal value systems of the various regions and communities may affect the acceptability of the proposed action, approval of it must be considered on a case-by-case cost–benefit evaluation.

Because of the diversity of interests affected, and because of public concern about unfamiliar or unknown hazards of indeterminable probabilities, cost-benefit evaluations should be conservative (e.g., for nuclear reactors).

The functions of intervenors should be embedded in the decision-making process; and although appeal to the courts should not be foreclosed, legislative hearings are better suited than judicial hearings for considering all affected interests. Decisions are best arrived at by discussion and negotiation among members of a board, rather than by a mere tallying of votes.

Institutions are now functioning for case-by-case decision-making on energy-related issues. A major deficiency, however, is that local communities, the impact sites of environmental degradation, generally are inadequately equipped and organized to be effective participants in the decision-making process. Creative leadership will have to devise means for remedying this shortcoming.

Incremental Commitments

Although the energy-related issues that arise in some situations can be resolved adequately by reliance on existing knowledge and informed judgment, the consequences of proposed energy-system actions frequently cannot be gauged in this manner. For example, at present (and probably for some decades to come), many energy-related decisions must consider the degree to which they involve irreversible processes. Formerly, construction of an energy facility might have been acceptable because unforeseen adverse consequences could be detected and arrested before irreparable damage to socially important values was done—a low-head log weir for hydropower is an example, and another is strip-mining coal in level terrain of low acidity.

With the increasing size, service life, and cost of facilities, reversibility considerations have become correspondingly more important. Especially because of attractive economies of scale, new energy facilities are so large, intricate, and costly that their abandonment or substantial modification may be impractical. It is also because of their size and durability that many of their second- and third-order impacts may be difficult to detect, much less foresee. In fact, many of the massive long-term commitments involved in present-day energy-system development plans exceed our knowledge base for appraising their probable impacts on humans and on the environment.

This is not to argue for complete knowledge as a prerequisite for proceeding with energy facilities. In many situations the damaging effects of not having system capability when it is needed may be too high a price for omniscience. It is possible, however, to devise prudent decision strategies even in situations whose consequences are of high uncertainty. One such strategy is to subdivide massive long-term commitments into units that can be undertaken incrementally, and to monitor the consequences of each successive commitment. That strategy permits identification of peril points while there is still an opportunity to modify facility design before incurring massive damage.

Such incremental staging of a facility has a higher first-cost than construction at the most efficient engineering rate. The amount of the additional cost will vary according to the character of the increments and the rate of progress. Conventional methods can be used to calculate those additional costs of various incremental commitments. Conventional incremental steps decrease the risk of damage. Strategies of this sort provide a rational basis for decisions about the costs and hazards of energy facilities and systems.

While incremental-commitment strategy is compatible with much of the engineering and management of energy systems, its effectiveness could be materially enhanced by suitable changes in design and practice. Innovations for that purpose may be among the greatest opportunities for improving the social efficiency of energy systems. They would also further guarantee public participation in decision-making.

Monitoring and Appraisal

The importance of energy systems to society requires that decisions affecting them be based on informed perceptions of three societal concerns: the state of the environment, the requirements for energy, and the capability of energy systems. Appraisal of those aspects of energy production must be developed from continuing monitoring and evaluation. New concepts as well as new techniques must be developed for those tasks. Because such appraisals involve large regions, they should be made by state agencies in consultation with appropriate federal agencies.

Concern over present energy requirements is sharpened by demand forecasts. The projected 3.5% annual energy growth rate means that supplies will have to be doubled in the next two decades, and that construction of massive facilities must be initiated now and more facilities added for years to come. Although unending exponential growth is an unrealistic concept, no limit has been adopted, and mounting environmental and financial costs are an alarming prospect.

Somehow society must determine and make explicit the tolerance limits of the environment. The assessment must be broader and more comprehensive than mere compilation of local damage episodes. It must appraise the viability of heterogeneous biomes that include man and many other species. The tolerance limit cannot be an absolute that is determined once; rather, it should be a continuing appraisal of the capacity of the environment to sustain development without unacceptable degradation.

At present, energy is provided to anyone willing to pay for it, and energy systems gauge energy requirements by the prospects for marketing at a profit. However, because of the limitations of marketplace economics in taking account of the societal costs of energy supply and utilization, that metric is unsuited to public-interest concerns. For example, conventional marketplace economics is inappropriate for determining the allocation of natural gas as boiler fuel. Public decision-making must consider energy requirements under various alternative policy options. Furthermore, if energy supplies and requirements are considered in their entirety, rather than on the basis of individual energy companies, needs could be met by the most efficient mix of energy fuels.

Electricity brownouts, long lines at gasoline pumps, and heating oil shortages bear witness to the shortcomings of energy systems. Often those breakdowns of service are alleviated by channeling public support and resources into the energy systems, e.g., by diversion of military petroleum supplies, relaxation of air quality standards, and public subsidy of utility companies. Almost always, the deficiency is revealed suddenly and public assistance is provided inefficiently on an emergency basis. With increasing societal dependence on energy and increasing stress on energy systems, breakdowns in services could be seriously damaging. Independent periodic examination of energy systems would provide timely warning of facility or financial deficiencies, and should also reveal opportunities for technological and/or managerial improvements.

5.4 Energy Systems' Needs for Information and Research

As is true nationwide and worldwide, the effective performance of energy systems in the Hudson Basin is impeded and curtailed by the phenomena of increasing demand for energy coupled with limited energy supplies. Even for the short term, and emphatically for the longer term, satisfactory management of energy systems requires more information and more knowledge to enlarge the range of technological options, evaluate their probable consequences to human and environmental well-being, and appraise their social acceptability and feasibility. Contemporary studies and reports are identifying the wide range of needs for physical, life, and social science research, development, and demonstration (RD&D) to provide the required knowledge.

Energy Technology

With respect to the physical science and engineering aspects of energy problems, a national commitment is emerging for RD&D programs whose scope and magnitude will match the problems. Because of the character of those fields, the results of research in them has wide transferability. The knowledge gained can be applied generally throughout the nation with only (but by no means negligible) technological adjustments to regional and local conditions. Thus, the technology problems of the Hudson Basin energy systems will be dealt with largely through national RD&D programs, and they are not treated in this chapter. As is noted in the following sections, however, modifications of energy technologies to ameliorate their adverse consequences must be developed jointly by energy engineers and other experts in health sciences, ecology, regional planning, and related fields.

Energy–Health Relationships

Knowledge of energy systems' relationships to human health is of crucial importance in determining energy-related societal actions. Those relationships are both beneficial and adverse: beneficial in making possible a wide range of high-quality nutrition, working and living conditions, medical care, and stress-abating amenities; adverse in creating harmful emissions, safety hazards, and stress-inducing environments. The information and research needs in this field initially are the proper concern of the Human Health Task Group. At later stages, there will be need for interaction with the Energy Systems Task Group to examine opportunities for ameliorative modifications of energy technologies.

Ecological Impacts of Energy Systems

The knowledge needed for dealing with the ecological aspects of energy-related problems is amenable to generalization in only a limited degree. Design criteria suited to ecosystem tolerance of heat loadings or heavy metals in Puget Sound may not be applicable to the California coasts, Narragansett Bay, or Lake Michigan, much less the Mohawk River. For practical purposes, ecological RD&D must be site-specific, at least until the understanding of ecological processes is greatly amplified. Pending the acquisition of such greater knowledge, the composition of Hudson Basin ecosystems, their tolerances, and their recuperative capabilities must be researched within the basin. Ongoing ecological studies, while probably warranting expansion, are believed to be well designed. Although those questions are appropriately treated by other task groups, ecologists must participate with energy engineers in designing modifications of technology that will be compatible with ecological constraints. To be effective in such joint endeavors, ecologists and engineers must understand the rationales of both fields.

Regional and Community Planning

While the nation engages in formulation of national energy policies and programs to resolve problems of supply inadequacies, demand restraint, resource allocation, energy pricing, cartelization, foreign trade, and international relations, the impact of energy systems on Hudson Basin people can be dealt with only at the local level. By and large, while they want abundant supplies of energy, the people affected are dissatisfied with the energy systems—their impacts on lifestyle, on the environment, and on community and regional development. At the present time, society's institutions for coping with such dissatisfactions are not functioning effectively, and that deficiency reduces the efficiency of the energy systems as well as their social utility.

The impact of energy systems on community development is a major focus of dissatisfaction and frustration. Intricate advance planning precedes installation of energy supply and delivery facilities such as electric generating plants and transmission lines, natural gas pipelines, and petroleum refineries and depots. Although such planning generally is of a high caliber technically, it rarely, if ever, adequately considers whether the proposed facilities and/or the energy supplies that they will provide are acceptable to the people of the region and of the affected communities. To a considerable degree, the energy industry's planning is inadequate in this regard because of the failure of societal mechanisms for the formulation and expression of public consensus. In fact, societal mechanisms are not effective even in identifying what the issues are. The resulting last-minute contention, losses to the energy industries, and damage to the public interest are well known.

In a number of states, mechanisms exist for public consideration and decision-making regarding proposed energy-supply facilities, especially thermal-electric generating plants and transmission lines. Generally, those mechanisms provide for adequate advance disclosure of intention to construct facilities; the public need for them; their probable health, safety, and environmental consequences; and a comparative analysis of alternative courses of action. Such disclosure is followed by public hearings at which intervenors may present dissenting views for consideration by the state regulatory agency. Whereas recourse to judicial processes is not foreclosed, the intent is to obviate it as much as possible through accommodation of the public interest in open administrative procedures.

The limited experience to date with this approach is encouraging, and argues for strengthening and perfecting it. There is need, for example, for better assurance that all relevant information is considered, that analyses are objective, that conclusions are valid, that cost–benefit evaluations are consonant with societal values, and that decisions are in the long-term as well as the short-term public interest. Other needed improvements are related to ensuring adequate public information (including identification of the issues) and with formation of a public consensus. Improvements along these lines can be devised by joint endeavors that involve a diversity of competences ranging from the sciences and engineering to public administration and law. Although the effort required will be large, it is warranted by expectations of significant contributions to democratic government.

Energy Uses and Conservation

Until the end of this century, and probably longer, the United States will have less energy than it is accustomed to having—less per capita, less per dollar. Stringencies in the physical availability of energy supplies (and higher prices) will affect every sector of the nation: industrial and agricultural production and employment, transportation, homes, and individual lifestyles. The consequences could be deeply damaging—serious unemployment, food shortages, inflation—but perhaps they need not be. Prudent private and governmental management may modulate the transitions to less energy-intensive modes without disruptive strains. Such benign transitions are unlikely to be automatic; they will depend on a long-continuing series of wise private and public decisions based on relevant information.

Energy conservation technology—i.e., the hardware, the engineered processes, and the government regulations to conserve energy—will generally be of nationwide applicability. But energy-conserving practices will have many elements that are specific to a region. For example, energy conservation practices in transportation, in architecture, and in recreation may tend to have regional patterns. Private decisions may be significant determinants of those patterns. Basic to wise private and public decisions is information on how individuals, agricultural enterprises, and industrial and commercial firms respond to energy stringencies, and where energy stringencies generate damaging strains. Probably much of the needed information can be derived from data now being routinely secured by the energy industries, especially the electric and gas utilities and petroleum distributors. Acquisition and analysis of such information are first-priority needs for coherent decisions and actions at regional and community levels.

Demonstration

Improved practices and innovations can be tested and perfected at pilot-study scales, but they will be widely adopted only through demonstration. This is true for energy conserving practices, such as those related to transport of persons and goods, building insulation, and industrial and domestic equipment.

The purchase of equipment or the utilization of services is determined mainly in private decisions (although government may be influential through taxes, subsidies, or regulations). Adoption of energy conservation measures generally requires modification of behavior patterns and attitudes, including the calculation of the question, Is it worth the trouble and expense? Marketing experience, from industrial machinery to groceries, confirms that demonstration is essential for adoption of a changed process or product.

To be effective, demonstrations must be tailored to the target audience. For most energy conservation practices, the tailoring specifications should be for targets no larger than the Hudson Basin. Involvement of community leadership in planning and designing demonstrations is important for their success. Demonstrations, perhaps of somewhat different design, are particularly necessary for successful establishment of innovative advances in energy systems management by private enterprises and public regulatory agencies, and in public participation in energy decision-making.

Chapter 6

LAND USE / NATURAL RESOURCE MANAGEMENT

6.1 Introduction

Stresses Placed on Extensive Resource Uses by Urbanization

The resource uses assigned to this task group for consideration have one thing in common: they occupy the land that is left by urbanization. Where they are not the residual claimants for resources, it is only because of very strong institutional arrangements to protect them. Industry, commerce, and residential uses easily outbid all but the most unusual extensive resource uses, both in the market and in the other institutions of resource allocation. As for the super user—the regional jetports, super highways, large shopping complexes, and bigger factories—little stands in their way. This in itself is reasonable enough, but the inefficient, inequitable, and perhaps dangerous way that the transition comes about is unreasonable in many respects.

Technically, we probably have the capability to put almost any two land uses next to each other and, at a cost, to keep them from causing each other serious problems. But conflict between new and old land uses is nearly the

Members of the Land Use/Natural Resource Management Task Group: David J. Allee, George D. Davis, Frithjof M. Lunde, Paul Marr, and Carl Mays.

rule rather than the exception. Our institutions are not capable of avoiding many of the effects of one activity upon another. Where the cost of avoiding the problem is low, it is often not required. And where the cost is high, there is little incentive to avoid it, either by locating elsewhere or by finding new technology to cut the cost. Therefore, the challenge to our institutions to provide rational resource management is substantial.

Uncertainty blankets the management of natural resources. With massive urban growth, such as that experienced in the Hudson Basin region, that uncertainty is compounded many times. The effect extends over an area that goes well beyond the dimensions of our study area. The result is a diminishing commitment to the extensive natural resource uses, both by individual owners or operators and by the institutions that serve and support the extensive resource use industries. Agriculture and forestry are based on time-consuming biological processes. Conservation-oriented land uses involve a heavy component of service orientation with many of the benefits extending beyond the time of the immediate and direct use. For the most effective management of these extensive uses of natural resources, the people involved make a significant personal commitment; nothing less than a way of life is involved.

The speculator is the ambiguous symbol of the uncertainty caused by urbanization. He has a very legitimate role in that he anticipates the coming of change and facilitates it. In return, he is lured by the capital gains associated with intensification of resource use. It is here that the ambiguity of his role begins. Although more than a few farmers and forest producers become speculators, few speculators have any commitment to the extensive industry.

It is not just a matter of changing the land to make it ready for the new use and of having an owner ready to sell at the right price. Public actions are also usually required to facilitate the change. The speculator is not in a position to be politically neutral, and the prospect of change will pervade the entire community. Main street merchants and local officials will link themselves with the change. Indeed, the status of those who remain associated with the extensive resource uses will fall in the eyes of the community.

Obviously, with the growth of urbanization there is a need for change. The point is that the speculator psychology extends far beyond what is required to provide for that growth, and the result is a wasteful undermining of the extensive uses of natural resources in a very large area.

The Land Market: Is It Out of Control?

Tradeoffs between those values that can be reflected in monetary terms and environmental values, which cannot, are at the heart of many issues that come under the label "environment." Indeed, economists usually explain environmental problems as social values that are not fully reflected by prices in the relevant markets and thus do not provide adequate incentives for socially desirable decisions. Prescriptive analysis then becomes the search for means to adjust the incentives expressed in the market. That adjustment can be most painful when the economic stakes are as large as they are in shifts from extensive to intensive land uses.

Pressures That Follow from Prospective Capital Gains and Tax Base Changes

Whatever analytical framework is used for environmental problems, it is clear that the workings of the market play an important part in resource management. Obviously, with a large, mobile, and growing population base, the prospect of selling some land, at some time, for an intensive use exists almost everywhere. But in a relatively large part of the area, such prospects are not sufficient to remove completely the incentives to manage the land for its inherent resource capability in farming, forestry, wildlife habitat, and other extensive uses. Recognizing that land increases in value an average of tenfold in the transition from rural to urban uses, and that such changes occur in a most scattered pattern, it is not difficult to see why landowners in areas of strongly perceived urban prospects have been compared to roulette players. The probability that any particular parcel of land will be required for a higher value intensive use in the near future may be quite low. The costs of holding land idle also may be significant over time, but the perceived payoff is so high that severe stresses are placed on incentives to continue extensive land uses.

Sprawled, inefficient, and environmentally deficient urban development—and the ensuing pressures on resource management—have been convincingly attributed to the uncertainty and natural monopoly aspects of the transfer process. The market is thin—few buyers and sellers are active in it at any one time. Information about public investments and development trends is poor and is skewed in its distribution among participants in the market. Various tax, zoning, and other factors tend to limit the availability of land for sale. Most influential are the expectations of existing owners about the prices they will one day obtain. An occasional sale for a lower price often does little to deflate these expectations, since more land to sell at that price cannot be produced and brought into the market except by buying from other roulette-playing owners. Finally, the costs of overcoming distance have fallen relative to other location factors. Whatever the exact causes, there is an overwhelming pressure for scatteration of development, and the amount of land being held in anticipation of transitional capital gains is many, many times the amount that is actually put to urban uses each year. In fact, the inventory of idle land is increasing more rapidly than is the land in actual urban use.

Local Dominance in Land Use Management

In New York State, cities, towns, and villages (but not counties) have the option of adopting various land use controls. These include zoning, subdivision regulations, building codes, utility extension rules (to encourage efficient and equitable cost charges), and others.

The potential for, and interest in, the assertion of a public interest in the use of land is considerable. But equally clear is the very heavy pressure of the potential for capital gains and other development profits to keep such controls from constraining the owner. Furthermore, the influence of property taxes and an apparent acceptance of the notion that almost any development is better than none mean that local governments often act in ways that reinforce some of the negative incentives in the land market rather than correct them. A fear of the uncertainty of other than local controls discourages support for changes from the financial and land development industries. The immediate neighborhood effects of development are sometimes effectively contained by local controls. Those of uniquely regional significance are rarely recognized. Just as there are far more parcels of land held in anticipation of urban development than will be needed, and held for prices well over those that can be paid by nonurban users, so are there many local governments anticipating, even seeking and planning, for levels of development that are inconsistent with regional prospects and regional interests.

The burdens on a community that has had a small amount of rapid development are particularly revealing. Suddenly, there are demands for all sorts of public investment; schools, roads, and hospitals cry out for expansion. The local government, heavily dependent on property taxes, is caught between those who need more services and those who cannot see why they should pay more for services they have always received. Encouraging still more development becomes irresistible, sometimes regardless of environmental effects, particularly if it is thought that it will produce more new taxes than service costs.

Local governments play a "dog-in-the-manger" role in land use controls. They have a strong self-interest to protect. Institutional changes to provide increased representation of county, regional, state, and even multistate and national interests must consider and build upon this reality.

6.2 People, Resources, and Issues

Trends and Issues in Natural Resource Use

Wilderness and Wildlife

Despite its accessibility, the Hudson Basin retains vast tracts of semiwild and wild lands. More than half of the region is forested, but true wilderness is exemplified in the Adirondack and Catskill forest preserves, which are protected by the "forever wild" clause of the New York Constitution. With good management, even the privately owned "suburban forests" of the middle and lower Hudson Basin are socially valuable and productive wildlife and recreational areas.

In the case of publicly owned natural lands, the most important challenge is the overuse of the more popular areas. These areas, open to all at little or no cost, are increasingly accessible. But they also include ecosystems that are easily upset by the repeated pounding of human feet. As a result, we face the possibility of losing the very environment that people come to enjoy. An example is the High Peaks area of the Adirondacks.

Wilderness areas are also challenged by encroachment of more intensive uses, ranging from scattered vacation homes to large-scale second-home developments, commercial recreational facilities, mining, and public utility projects.

The problem is not so much the loss of scattered individual parcels of natural areas as it is the impact of more intensive uses on adjoining fragile natural areas. This is particularly a problem in the checkerboard public and private ownership pattern of the forest preserves in New York.

For fish and game, the need for effective habitat management programs simultaneously grows more urgent and more difficult. Man cannot help but alter the "natural" environment, if only by his very presence. Habitats have continuously been altered in the Hudson Basin as fields were cleared, transportation links built, shorelines developed, and water polluted. Some species have perished or suffered heavy setbacks, especially some of the more important predator species. Other species have expanded as a result of man's intrusion, either because of the reduction in predators or changes in habitat.

Along with these man-made changes, there has developed a need for man to manage more actively the determinants of the status of wildlife in the region. Fish hatchery programs can help to offset the loss of natural spawning capability, for example. On the other hand, when man removes natural controls on species buildup, such as predators, he surely has an obligation to keep wildlife populations within the supportive capacity of their habitats by means other than starvation.

Some of the basin's most serious problems, as well as its greatest opportunities in wildlife management, occur on private lands. Wildlife seldom respects artificial boundary lines. The benefits of good wildlife management accrue to many, and results are impressive only when a number of individual landowners make the effort to improve wildlife habitat on their respective parcels.

There are several groups of private landowners who could play an especially important role in improved wildlife management. Contrary to commonly held ideas, the most productive wildlife regions are not necessarily "wild." Farm areas, with their woodlots, hedgerows, and leftover crops, provide special management opportunities for many forms of wildlife. Forestry practices also make a large difference. Some species are helped by minimal human intrusions and selective timber harvesting. Others, such as deer, seem to respond to harvesting that leaves only the immature, healthy timber, thereby opening up the forest cover.

The point is that both of these classes of landowners have a large impact upon wildlife habitat. Yet we have no way of compensating farmers and forest owners for the widespread social benefits of improved wildlife management. In fact, we often do the opposite. As larger fields have become more economical for agricultural production, we have subsidized the removal of hedgerows without seriously considering the need to compensate farmers for leaving some hedgerows intact for the sake of wildlife management.

Forestry

There are more trees in the Hudson Basin and New York State today than there were 50 years ago. As technology and regional competition have affected farming in the state, millions of acres of former cropland and pasture have reverted to weeds, brush, and eventually to trees. The U.S. Forest Service has documented the increases in forested land in New York. Between 1950 and 1968, "commercial" forestland (any land physically capable of producing crops of wood and not committed to other uses) increased by 14% in New York to more than 14 million acres. The volume of timber on this land increased even more rapidly, rising by 20% between the 1950 and 1968 surveys. If we include the public forest preserves, private Christmas tree plantations, and forested lands of very low productivity, about 56% of New York's 30.6 million acres were forested in 1968.

Although trees have become more plentiful in recent decades, the timber harvest in New York has either declined or held its own. Estimates show that the annual timber harvest declined by more than 20% during the 1950s and began to show a modest increase only in the mid-1960s.

One serious obstacle to the continued expansion of the forestry industry in the Hudson Basin region is the declining quality of the forest resources for timber harvest. This is true for both sawmill and pulpwood uses. A comparison of the findings of the 1952 and 1968 New York forest surveys shows that a declining average size of harvestable trees is a continuing problem, despite the increases in total volume of timber. The vast majority of New York's timber resources are made up of seedlings, saplings, and small-diameter trees. Trees large enough to be classified as saw timber were found on only 30% of the state's commercial forestland in 1968.

Today one out of every four trees in New York's forests is classified as either too rough or too rotten to be potentially harvestable. The quality of saw-timber trees has fallen dramatically. In 1950, 30% of the hardwood saw-timber volume could be classified as top quality. By 1968, only 15% of the saw-timber resources were of this grade.

Under current ownership objectives, the forestry industry will be forced to use new methods if it is to improve either the harvest intensity or the quality of timber resources. The forest industry itself owns only 9% of the commercial forestlands in New York State. Another 6% is controlled by the public sector. The rest, a whopping 85%, is controlled by other private owners. Farmers own slightly more forestland today than 20 years ago, but the significant fact is that the great majority (59%) of all of the potentially harvestable forestland in New York is owned by nonfarm private owners, including rural residents and absentee owners.

If the wood-using industry is to expand along with the suburban and exurban forests of the Hudson Basin, it will have to learn much more about this new class of forest landowners. It will have to learn to understand their varied and noncommercial objectives and find ways to cater to their needs if it is to harvest their trees. It is quite possible that services that add to, rather than subtract from, visual amenities, wildlife habitat, and access could be successfully featured instead of consciously avoided. Group arrangements that feature these services might have a chance of success in the suburban forest; those that focus only on logs will not.

Outdoor Recreation

Recreation is a significant use of land in the Hudson Basin. The various levels of government, local to federal, provide a wide range of facilities from ball parks to ski centers and national recreation areas. The private sector offers complementary facilities, from grand resort hotels in the Catskills to marinas and "storybook towns." In addition to these opportunities, there are individual activities in the form of hiking, fishing, boating, and hunting wherever permitted in either public or private areas.

The upward trend in recreational usage has numerous effects on rural resources and communities. It brings a limited amount of year-round population into rural areas, provides new sources of rural income, and may greatly increase value of rural properties. However, a recreation-based economy typically provides relatively low average incomes, is notoriously seasonal, and is highly susceptible to things such as recession, inflation, the weather, and fuel prices. If farming is not intensive and highly viable, purchases of land for recreational use will drive land prices and taxes beyond the reach of existing farmers and take additional farmland out of production prematurely.

The continuing interest in water-oriented recreation will mean more use of waterfront parks and marinas and more demand for public access to shores, even where few organized facilities exist. The North and South shores of Long Island can be expected to increase in popularity, straining the existing recreation sites in this area. There is significant potential for water recreation in the Hudson and Mohawk rivers and in the State Barge Canal system. The extensive water pollution abatement program now under way will eliminate the dumping of raw sewage and other wastes into these waterways. In particular, the construction of secondary treatment plants has already decreased pollution in the Hudson River and increased fish runs.

The most critical outdoor recreation needs in the Hudson Basin are in the New York metropolitan region. Capacity deficiencies and the very high use of existing facilities were emphasized as major problems in the New York State comprehensive recreation plan, "People–Resources–Recreation" (New York State Office of Parks and Recreation, 1972). Deficiencies in the Capital District are less severe and can be reduced by expansion, improvement, and the limited development of new sites.

The overuse of existing facilities is a problem facing most public recreation agencies throughout the Hudson Basin. It is most severe in metropolitan areas, where many inner-city poor and aging do not have adequate access to urban fringe facilities. Facilities now served by mass transit are among the most heavily patronized. The extension of mass transit service on weekends and holidays can alleviate overcrowding at some sites only to exacerbate already high user rates at other locations.

Other serious problems center around the declining recreational access to private lands. Landowner surveys carried out at Cornell University on the factors surrounding the posting of private lands in New York are most instructive (Brown, 1973). By 1973, 43% of the privately owned land in New York State was posted against trespassing, compared to 25% only 10 years earlier. Access seems to be most restricted where recreational demands are the greatest, i.e., near large urban centers.

When asked why they had decided to post their land, more than 97% of the posting landowners cited at least one reason that implicates the behavior of recreationists they have come in contact with or have heard about. Hunters and snowmobilers accounted for a large majority of the bad experiences. However, landowners who post and those who do not post their lands in New York have very similar attitudes about the value of hunting and snowmobiling as recreational activities. In fact, those landowners who post are just as likely as nonposting landowners to be hunting, fishing, and snowmobiling participants. What most clearly separates posting and nonposting landowners is their image of the behavior of recreationists in general. For example, in the New York survey, 71% of posting landowners, as compared with 26% of nonposting landowners, felt that hunters are generally irresponsible. The comparable figures for attitudes toward snowmobilers were 65 and 44%.

Attitudes are hardening rapidly. If the trends of the past 10 years were to continue for only another two or three decades, virtually all private acreage in New York State and the Hudson River basin would be posted against public recreational usage. But effective methods of arresting and reversing the trend will be difficult. When New York landowners were asked whether they felt they should receive a fee for recreational use, only about 10% agreed. Clearly, landowners are more concerned about their property and personal safety than about remuneration. However, the leasing of lands from cooperative landowners for hunting, fishing, or snowmobiling might relieve other landowners of some of the pressure that is causing additional posting. In New York a cooperative hunting program offers some protection for the landowner in exchange for full public access. A program for the purchase of fishing-access easements on New York trout streams provides for payments to landowners, but it also stresses the protection and control provided for the landowner over how his land will be used. Both programs are ripe for further study and possible expansion.

Second-Home Development

Concentrations of second homes often help support the economy of areas suffering from farm abandonment or those areas traditionally reliant on seasonal tourism. In addition, much of the past and present development of second homes places little, if any, additional stress on the environment. The present controversy about second homes is essentially centered around the impact of large-scale developments. Some of these have been carefully designed to blend into the rural landscape, but more often they are platted at densities that violate the natural setting and overload local resources and public services. The degree of concern depends on factors such as the adequacy of the available water supply and sewage facilities, and the impact of the development and its residents on the natural landscape. There are also social effects. These include the increased demand for services such as highway improvements and police and fire protection. And as second homes are converted into year-round residences, additional classroom space will be needed.

The critical impacts of second-home developments are often on water resources. Outdoor recreation is substantially water-oriented, and second-home developments are very often associated with natural or artificial lakes, stream modification, or seashore sites.

But access is the key to the enjoyment of the "public" water body. Typically, homes and cottages are built on privately owned lots in a thin strip along the immediate shoreline. Lots are typically small because the demand for access is large and its price is high. As a result, the area that should be the least intensively developed for maximum enjoyment appears even more developed than it actually is because all of the development is concentrated on the immediate shoreline. Development here is highly visible to all users, but the individual seldom considers this when designing and building his dream cottage.

Traditional shoreline development also has other detrimental effects. Water pollution from inadequate sewage treatment is a frequent problem. Intensive development at the water's edge also affects the physical and biological resources of that important land–water interface. Marshes are filled, soil and beach material are washed into the water, and fish feeding and spawning areas are permanently disturbed.

Unfortunately, many rural jurisdictions have had insufficient experience in assessing the desirability of second-home proposals. The expected benefits are presented by the developer with the proposal, but the economic and environmental costs are typically diffused and hard to predict. For example, the expected increase in tax revenues may not offset the cost of public services that will have to be borne by the existing local community, but opinions will vary on this. Sizable developments may completely change the character of the existing community, but this may not be foreseeable at the time.

Mining

A variety of mining operations are carried on in the Hudson Basin. Essentially all of them use open pit methods that often have severe environmental effects. The most significant mining activities are sand, gravel, and crushed rock quarries situated in the vicinity of the New York and the Capital District metropolitan areas. Between these two centers are the Portland cement plants based on limestone outcroppings overlooking the western bank of the Hudson River from Ravena south to Kingston. Other mining activity is scattered and includes the slate quarries of Granville, dispersed limestone and dolomite quarries, the largest garnet mine in the world at North Creek, and magnetite and titanium operations at Tahawus near the headwaters of the Hudson River.

The imprint of these activities is noticeable and lasting. Steeply cliffed quarries customarily are worked and abandoned without a program for reclaiming these sites for subsequent use. This is a particular problem in suburban areas, where formerly isolated quarries are encroached upon by residential development. Important scenic features are sometimes threatened, such as the Palisades, where crushed rock quarries continue to mine the reverse slope. In addition, where ore concentrating processes are used, they may leave huge slag heaps that are no less difficult to reclaim than open pits. Besides visual effects, the impact on water quality can be severe.

These mining impacts persist, despite a growing public awareness and concern, because of the heavy economic incentives to the mine operators and the long time-spans involved. Effective public action will, therefore, have to be forward-looking as well as strong. Largely preventive programs are often suggested, including the bonding of mining operators to ensure reclamation. Another alternative is the public acquisition of properties that are becoming a serious hazard, and restrictions on new mining operations to ensure that they meet environmental standards. It should be recognized that, in some instances, reclamation requirements may not be economically feasible, even for society as a whole, in that the cost is far greater than the value of the improved view or water quality. This is, however, a question that can be resolved only by an impartial, case-by-case analysis.*

A tempting solution for many of the problems associated with the surface mining of sand and gravel is the mining of these materials from the ocean floor or from Long Island Sound. But here again, there are economic and ecological problems that may prove too difficult to overcome. An alternative that deserves more attention is the recycling of urban rubble. While the sorting and storage of materials are expensive, quarrying and transportation costs are also rising and considerable environmental harm could be avoided. Recycling could provide a partial solution to the growing demand for crushed rock, sand, and gravel.

Agriculture

Since the 1940s more than 60 million acres have been taken out of crop production in the United States. In New York State alone, about 200,000 acres of farmland currently are passing out of farming each year from a total farm area of less than 11 million acres. This long-term decline in the use of land for farming can be explained as two quite different processes: land that is going out of production at the urban edge and the obsolescence edge.

The Urban Edge   New York is considered to be a highly urbanized state. Yet only 10% of its land area is currently in urban use, including transportation. It will be a long time before that figure reaches even 20%. Within the Hudson Basin region, the figure is slightly higher because of the effects of the New York metropolitan region and major urban centers in the Capital District. Yet we must remember that the Hudson Basin is a highly diversified region, evidenced by its inclusion of both the largest metropolitan agglomeration in the United States and the wilderness areas of the Adirondacks.

The effects of urban expansion on agriculture are covered in the section on urban expansion. However, it bears emphasizing here that farmland need

---

*Since this chapter was written, New York has enacted a Mined Land Reclamation Act. It requires a reclamation plan to be filed for any land from which more than 1000 tons of material will be mined in any 12-month period. The mine or quarry owner is required to post a surety bond or provide other evidence of financial ability to carry out the reclamation plan. [Ed.]

not be close to an expanding urban area to be affected. About 15,000 acres of New York farmland are removed each year for conversion to urban uses. Perhaps several times that much is idled because of the effects of urban expansion and scatteration. In addition, many times that much is under-utilized by the more indirect effects of urbanization, including land specula-tion. The urban edge is not a sharp cutting edge. It is a much duller and broader edge, perhaps better compared to a shadow.

In these days of a fast-growing world population and resulting burgeoning demand for food, the premature conversion of farmland and loss of agricul-tural production are a case for concern in itself. But farmland conversion occurs simultaneously with a wasteful pattern of urban expansion. Thus, there is perhaps even more at stake for the urban dweller than for the food-producing sector. Many feel that the existing pattern of urban expan-sion produces unnecessarily high-cost lots and housing in a limited range of choice, and therefore reduces the possibility of meeting the housing needs of the poorer half of the population. Scatteration ensures that public utilities will be expensive because they will be spread out to serve scattered new residences.

The Obsolescence Edge   Although the transfer of land to urban uses has serious long-term effects on the urbanizing areas where it is concentrated, the vast majority of land that leaves farming today is in more rural areas. Since 1950, more than half of the counties of the United States, practically all of them rural, have declined in absolute population. Even in a highly urbanized state such as New York, out of the 200,000 acres of land that leave farming each year, the vast majority have reached the obsolescence edge of today's farming. Probably more acres of farmland have been dis-placed by this process than by erosion or poor conservation practices.

The story of how farmland reaches the obsolescence edge involves both technology and the more indirect effects of urbanization. On the technolog-ical side, both farmers and farmland have been replaced by people who still work to help produce agricultural products, but who work in factories to produce the manufactured inputs, such as fertilizers and machinery, that substitute for farmland and labor. Another important factor is that all land is not created equal, or at least not equally responsive to the new agricultural technology. In general, the advances in agricultural technology have ena-bled substitution for some natural shortcomings of the land and enhance-ment of the importance of other good qualities. Chemical fertilizers have lessened the importance of natural fertility at the same time that the advent of increasingly mechanized equipment has stressed the advantages of the flatter, larger fields. Of course, there are many other examples.

Many lands have become so disadvantaged by changing technology that they have been pushed out of farming by technological obsolescence alone.

They fail to provide a satisfactory income even if the land has no alternative use or value. But during the past three decades, various "pull" factors have helped to speed up the process greatly. Improved roads, the private car, and mobile industries in search of labor have brought almost all farmers in the Hudson Basin within commuting distance of alternative jobs. Also, general trends toward increased urbanization, higher incomes, and expanding leisure time have helped to create a new, expanding market for those farms that are close to the point of technological obsolescence. Marginal farms are increasingly transformed into country homes, vacation homes, and private recreational lands. It takes a surprisingly small number of otherwise urban-oriented people to provide an active market for such land. For example, if the 200,000 acres of farmland that are released annually in New York State were sold in parcels of 40 acres each, it would take only 5000 nonfarm families out of a state population of 18 million entering the market each year to transfer it all.

It is true that future trends in farm employment and land use are not entirely predictable. During the recent remarkable resurgence in farm prices and incomes, farm employment has stopped declining, even stabilized, and many acres of previously idle land have been put back to the plow. But it is improbable that the export demand for foodstuffs will be enough to ensure the continuation of this turnaround in farm employment, especially in the Hudson Basin. In the long run, it is likely that farmland that is suited to the technology of another era will continue to revert to brush and woods.

There are unique displacement problems and policy issues for those farming regions that find themselves moving closer to the obsolescence edge. As the surrounding year-round farm population dwindles, communities often find themselves with a shrinking base for their community services and organization. For those communities that are suitably located, the shift of land to recreation and open country residences provides an opportunity, but it is not without its problems. If it is too successful, the open-country environment that attracted development in the first place will be lost. Also, a local economy based on commercial recreation commonly displays even more seasonal and annual variation than farming, and may provide average incomes only slightly more desirable. But of course for many of these communities there may be no better alternative available.

Public Lands

Public lands in the Hudson Basin include municipal, state, and federal holdings, but the scope of land and water resources over which there is at least a limited public control is far broader. Public utilities, for example, may have their land management policies and programs reviewed before public hearings, and the state is technically responsible for the management and protection of the lakes, streams, and rivers which it holds as a public trust.

The ways in which these public resources are managed are as varied as the agencies or municipalities involved. In some instances an agency, such as a municipal park department, manages a land-oriented program that is subject to annual review by the local legislature and is constantly under direct public scrutiny. In contrast, land holdings by various state authorities are often managed with little response to public pressures or to the desires of other agencies for the multiple use of resources.

The primary interest here is in state lands and the lands indirectly subject to some degree of state regulation. Most municipal lands are of local significance and are situated within the political limits of their own jurisdictions. There are a few exceptions, and these are notable—for example, the considerable holdings of the New York City water supply system, which extend north into the central Hudson Basin. Unlike other states, federal land holdings in New York are limited by the state constitution. The principal federal holdings are selected recreation sites, national monuments, defense installations, and office structures. The types of extensive federal land holdings found in most other states—public forestlands, major public parks, Indian reservations, and waterway facilities—are managed by state agencies in New York.

Lands and waters that are the responsibility of the states include those under direct supervision, those held by regulated entities, and public water bodies under less intensive or even passive management, such as lakes, streams, and rivers. In New York, state properties directly supervised include those held by line agencies, such as the Office of Parks and Recreation, the Department of Environmental Conservation, and the Department of Transportation. Specialized noneline state agencies also hold extensive and highly valuable properties. These include the authorities for transportation, electrical power generation, and ports.

Public utilities, such as power, telecommunications, and railroads, are subject to state review of their policies and programs. Through these regulatory powers and public hearings, it is now possible to effect socially desired changes on the management of utility properties. For example, the New York State Public Service Commission, through its Office of Environmental Planning, is actively working with utilities to ensure that environmental standards are adhered to and enhanced when in the public interest. This includes analysis of transmission line routings, power plant siting, and the environmental programs of electrical utilities. Recent changes in public service law require that private electric utilities submit their long-range plan annually to the Commission. These plans are reviewed at public hearings where the utilities can be questioned on their environmental policies.

The basic problem for public land management in the Hudson Basin is the lack of common policies for the use of the extensive land holdings of the many specialized public and quasi-public agencies. Extensive tracts of land are held for a single purpose without serious consideration of their use for other purposes. Single-purpose authorities may acquire important properties, such as the former Stewart Air Force Base, and plan for large-scale development without extensive review of the implications for local communities.

Problems such as these suggest the need for a clearly defined state policy for the management of lands and waters. (They also validate the need for SEQR, the state-level equivalent of NEPA, enacted in 1975 and now being implemented.) Such a policy would result in increased multiple use of resources often reserved by single-purpose agencies for overly restricted uses. This can lead to a significant increase in public access to lands and waters for recreation and education. It may also generate additional revenue from resources that are now underutilized.

Urban Expansion

Urban expansion in the Hudson Basin region continues to be dominated by the spreading edges of the New York metropolitan area. To be sure, the middle and upper basin communities, including the dominant Albany–Schenectady–Troy metropolitan area, are experiencing significant urban scatteration. However, the aggregate effect of all of the middle and upper basin urban areas on their surrounding communities, agricultural lands, open space, and forests is far less than the urban impact of metropolitan New York on its environs.

Urban areas can expand in many ways, even with a given level of population increase. In a Cornell University study of the conversion of land to urban uses in New York, it was found that the amount of land used to accommodate urban expansion varies greatly with the existing density of settlement and other factors (Allee et al., 1970). In the towns studied for the project, the conversion of land ranged from 153 to 357 acres per 1000 population increase. This information illustrates that the problem for most urbanizing areas is not one of an overall lack of land for urban expansion. The Hudson Basin has sufficient space to accommodate urban expansion, open space, and a viable agricultural industry, but we need to pay more attention to the location of each.

The most common complaints about the present pattern of urban expansion can be summed up by the term "urban sprawl." Marion Clawson has found two striking parallels between today's expansion of urban land uses and westward land-use expansion in the nineteenth century:

> First, settlement did not move smoothly across the country; rather, it moved somewhat fitfully, leaping across or around large areas. Scattered settlement was far more typical than solid or orderly settlement. Second, it was marked throughout by large scale speculation in land. (Schmid, 1968)

Scatteration of uses of widely differing levels of intensity has become a trademark of urban fringe areas. Urban expansion occurs not in a solid wave but as a splattering of relatively intensive land uses upon a landscape that is otherwise farmland, open land, or idle land. Strip development along existing roadways is a common type of scatteration.

Scatteration is denounced by taxpayers and planners alike for the way in which it escalates the cost of public services by creating the need for long water and sewer lines to reach the scattered developments. Figure 6-1 shows the contrast in utility systems when development is scattered and when it is

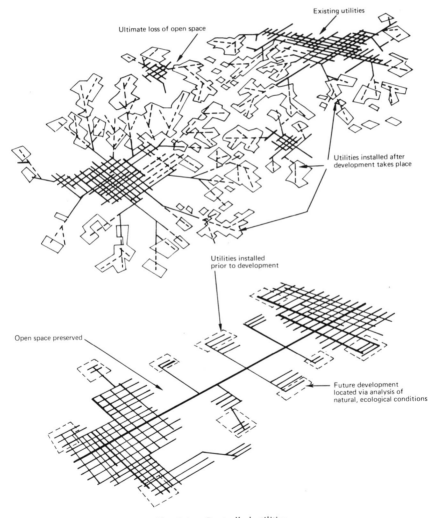

Fig. 6-1. Controlled utilities.

not. A more compact form of development could result in lower per capita costs for schools, highways, and personal commuting.

Conflicts are inescapable whenever widely differing uses rub up against one another. For the rural homeowner, these "edge effects" can mean unwanted smells and noises, and spray drift from neighboring farms. At the same time, the farmer is likely to become concerned about the increased possibilities of vandalism, nuisance litigation, and taxes for public services that he does not need. Conflict will always exist, but a scatteration of urban uses means that there are more edges to rub together.

Land speculation is as ubiquitous on the urban frontier as it was on the western frontier. Its presence has led this task group to ask whether the land market is out of control. It is a speculation that reaches far out into the countryside to land that is still years away from the potential jump in earning power associated with a shift to urban use.

Speculation is, of course, fueled by the expected windfall of large capital gains when the land is actually desired for a more intensive use. Although estimates of the magnitude of the typical capital gain vary widely, we are safe in assuming that it is large relative to the farm, forest, or open space value of land.

Urban sprawl is associated with considerable inefficiency in the form of underutilization and premature idling of land. A number of studies undertaken in various areas of the United States and Canada show that at least as much rural land is idled by the urban conversion process as goes directly into an urban use. Even more rural land is seriously underutilized because the expectation of future urban use makes it impossible to employ the land profitably in its most efficient and desirable long-term use. In total, the area affected by urban pressures is much larger than can reasonably be expected to be converted to urban uses in the next few years.

It might seem that one advantage of urban scatteration is that it results in an abundance of open space available for use by the scattered urban-style residents. But the developed areas are often so located that the undeveloped parcels are better characterized as idle land than as usable open space. Whatever open-space function this land provides, it is invariably unintentional and undependable in the future.

Economic Considerations in Land Use

Some economic activities are attracted to a particular location by a ready local market, and others by a ready supply of inputs—especially those that process bulky natural resources. But a large and growing number of employment-generating activities are quite footloose, able to locate more in response to the whims of management than the amenities of the community.

Of course, many are attracted by the previous decisions of others. With the automobile and the telephone, the superhighway and the airlines, the snowplow and the state-supported rural school, the scope for choice in both residential and employment location has greatly increased. Program after program in the last half century has been organized to equalize the delivery of public services. Transportation investments and consumer preference have long favored the more ubiquitous mode—the automobile. The result is that the location of many primary jobs has been liberated from the old confines of urban centers. Equally important, commuting and recreation patterns have also been liberated.

None of this has changed the locations of the natural resources themselves, but the significance of that location has changed in at least two ways. First, competing producers of the same products are economically much closer—fresh produce for New York can come from virtually anywhere. Second, a wide variety of potentially competing users for the same resources can and do exist.

Of course, the location of employment activities has never been a completely passive and one-sided affair. While every community has members who are actively interested in cultivating more and better paying employment opportunities for their community, not every community is equally endowed with inherent economic growth potential. Emerging factors such as environmental considerations, public investment, community attitudes, and community amenities, however, have produced important changes in the character of economic growth potential.

The result is pressure for a greater mixing, a loss of the homogeneity of land use that once seemed to work naturally out of the incentives that existed in the system. The neat, homogeneous areas of the once-fashionable master land use plan may never have been very realistic. But the message is that the region, to some degree, is facing all of the problems to be faced anywhere.

The environmental problems that stem from a heterogeneity of economic activities pose many challenges, but especially for regions that, for some reason, need to be kept relatively homogeneous. The Hudson Basin region includes many areas where it can be argued that, if the "best" long-term use of the natural resource base is to be made, some of the scale and mix of economic activities in these areas must be either limited and/or a special effort must be made to manage the associated environmental impacts. Mountain wilderness recreation areas and prime agricultural areas are examples.

This is not to suggest that such areas need to forego general economic health and welfare for the sake of some specialized interest, but rather that to achieve both may well require some special efforts.

Social Characteristics, Environmental Perceptions, and Organizations

The Hudson Basin region is as socially diverse as any comparable region in the world. Its full range could not be explored in this study. However, a concurrent study of the perceptions of local leaders in 20 of the New York counties north of New York City provides considerable insight into the variation in capacity to deal with environmental problems in the region.

Relationship of Environmental Issues to Other Issues*

What is the overall priority that people give to environmental problems compared with problems such as inflation, taxation, and crime? Because most of the respondents to this question were directly involved with environmental issues, their answers in part indicated the degree of support respondents were receiving in their respective counties.

Nearly half the respondents ranked the general importance of environmental issues below that of other issues in their county. Only 13.9% of the 296 informants ranked environmental quality as the most important. The results suggest that Hudson region residents are concerned over a variety of environmental issues. All informants (taken as a group) indicate that water pollution (23.6%); land use (19.6%); solid waste disposal (16.1%); and natural resources, parks, and open space (11.9%) were the most commonly perceived issues. Indeed, these four categories of issues alone accounted for over 70% of the issues mentioned across the entire region.

Population size and urbanization were mentioned as a relatively important environmental issue in Dutchess County (16.4%), Orange County (11.3%), and Ulster County (12.4%)—three counties directly in the path of the urban sprawl of the New York metropolitan area. Informants from the counties already a part of the New York metropolitan area—Rockland, Westchester, and Putnam—did not mention population size and urbanization as often, suggesting that these counties have adjusted to urbanization.

Other issues that have moderate regional ratings but high ratings in selected counties are air pollution and noise pollution. Air pollution was mentioned more often in the more urban counties—Albany (10.1%), Rockland (10.4%), and Schenectady (10.7%). But noise pollution was mentioned relatively more often in the very rural counties—Fulton (9.5%), Hamilton (9.8%), and Montgomery (11.0%).

Of all the issues mentioned in the region, 8% were land use issues related to the siting of public projects. However, in Schoharie County, proposed as the site of a pumped-storage generating facility, 43.1% of the issues men-

---

*See Capener et al. (1973), pp. 16–29, from which this discussion was extracted and in which details and definitions are presented.

tioned involved public project siting. In Columbia County, land use issues connected with public projects were not mentioned at all.

It is evident that the voluntary (unofficial) environmental organizations, such as the Sierra Club, Audubon Society, Scenic Hudson Preservation Conference, were quite visible to the informants over the whole region. The informants looked to this category of organizations more than any other for leadership in the environment. Official governmental environmental organizations were the second most common set of organizations mentioned in the entire region. Local agencies, however, were mentioned more often than were state and regional agencies, which suggests that the state and regional agencies are projecting a rather low profile except in the specific county in which their offices are located.

Organizations considered only moderately popular in the region as a whole, but considerd quite important in one or more counties, were planning boards (5.1%), general government organizations (3.3%), business associations and private research organizations (3.1%), health organizations (2.7%), and agricultural organizations (2.7%).

As in the case of issues, the percentage distributions of organizations for any given county may differ greatly from the distribution for the 20-county region as a whole. In most counties, for example, health organizations accounted for less than 3% of the county total, but in Columbia County 25.7% of all organizations mentioned as involved in environmental issues were health organizations.

How does the social structure of a county impinge upon the residents' perception of and response to environmental issues? This necessitates the construction of a variable which reflects the overall intensity of concern in a county with environmental issues. This variable could then be correlated with indicators of social structure.

Environmental Issues Correlated with Social Structure

Although many relationships could and should be investigated, only a few of the more immediate ones were explored (Table 6-1). For example, three variables—the number of inhabitants in the county in 1970, the number of people per square mile in the county in 1970, and the percentage of the population living in an urban place in 1970—were correlated with the "intensity of concern about environmental issues" dependent variable. The results were as follows: population size correlated at 0.53, density at 0.49, and urban at 0.47. All three were significant statistically (at or beyond the 0.05 level of confidence) as well as substantively.

Some investigators have suggested that the environmental movement is an upper middle class phenomenon, and perhaps even a function of wealth generally. From the limited data of this study, a significant correlation of

TABLE 6-1. Zero-Order Correlations between Issues and Organizations with Selected Independent Variables for the Twenty Counties of the Hudson River Region

Independent variables	Issues (DV1) (r)	Organizations (DV2) (r)
Population size (X_1)	0.533*	0.010
Population density (X_2)	0.490*	0.037
Percentage urban (X_3)	0.466*	0.264
Percentage of family incomes, $12,000+ ($X_4$)	0.573*	0.147
Dependency ratio (X_5)	−0.550*	−0.374
Percentage from different county (X_6)	0.069	−0.180
Percentage born in another state (X_7)	0.613*	0.183
Percentage living in same house, 1965–1970 (X_8)	−0.276	−0.019
Percentage renters(X_9)	0.553*	0.298
Medical specialties scale (X_{10})	0.811*	0.418
Median family income (X_{11})	0.537*	0.105
Local government revenues (X_{12})	0.487*	−0.049
Total bond indebtedness(X_{13})	0.534*	0.329
Percentage with 12+ years education(X_{14})	0.495*	−0.011
DV1 Issues standardized	—	0.678*
DV2 Organizations standardized	0.678*	—

*$P < 0.05$.

0.57 between intensity of concern and the percentage of families in the county who reported incomes of $12,000 and more was observed. Counties with fewer persons in the high income brackets will have less support for doing something about the environment but may still have the "need" in terms of outsiders' perceptions.

Other aspects of social structure were also examined. Specifically, it was hypothesized that some relationship probably existed between a county's overall intensity of concern with environmental issues and the county's general ability and willingness to deal with social and physical problems facing it. Accordingly, the correlation between the aggregate value of revenues of all government units in the county and the issue variable was 0.49, which is both statistically and substantively significant. Similarly, the aggregate value of bond indebtedness of all government units in the county correlated at 0.53 with the issue variable.

A scale of availability of health and medical services in the county was constructed, on the assumption that as a county acts in this regard, so might it act with regard to environmental problems. The correlation between this scale and the issue variable was 0.81, which makes it an excellent predictor. It must be cautioned, however, that this simple relationship may be heavily influenced by wealth, and this would have to be considered in a more detailed analysis.

The proportion of residents in a county who may have had an experience with a contrasting environment might provide a basis for evaluating environmental issues. The 1970 census tabulation of the percentage of the county's population who were born in another state was used; it correlated with the issue index at 0.61.

To summarize, the overall intensity of concern with environmental issues appears to be related to population size, density, degree of urbanization, ability and disposition of local government to deal with social problems, and family wealth.

Environmental Organizations Correlated with Social Structure

Most of the relationships established between the extent and intensity of environmental issues and the selected social structure variables were also expected to exist with the organization variable. However, this expectation was not supported by the data, as is demonstrated in Table 6-1.

Neither population size and density nor the percentage of the population living in urban areas was significantly related to the number and frequency of organizations mentioned by the informants. These correlations indicate that the response to environmental pollution as measured by the organizations mentioned is *not* related to the population size of the counties, the density of their population, or their degree of urbanization.

Certain factors usually associated with the presence of organizations— income, education, stability, leisure or dependency, government revenues and indebtedness, and having contrasting experiences—need the catalyst of intensive environmental issues before the response takes the form of recognizing the role of organizations. Further evidence of this hypothesis is the correlation between issue intensity and the organization variable, $r = 0.68$; the correlation is statistically significant (beyond the 0.05 level of confidence). This relationship lends support to the notion or theory that organizations are created because of the intensity of issues in the area.

6.3   Interdependencies with Other Policy Areas

Questions on natural resource management and associated land use issues have direct bearing on all of the issues being addressed by the other nine task groups. In a sense, natural resource management is the infill between the other subject areas, and the matrix upon which the other issues are played.

To identify interdependencies with other policy areas, the term "resource management" must be viewed in its broadest sense, i.e., including both public and private action and involving the full range of public policies, public values, and goals as they relate to material resources. If that is accepted, then some of the key interdependencies between natural resource management and the other policy areas are as follows.

Land Use/Human Settlements

Nonurban uses (i.e., those based on natural processes) cannot compete in the free land market with more intensive uses, and are prematurely and needlessly idled by the scattered encroachment of intensive uses. Some form of intervention in the free land market is required. Therefore, one of the key issues that the human settlements policy area must address is the kind of intervention that would enable nonurban uses to better resist urban encroachment. In addition, natural lands are often a drain upon the tax base. The only way to resist price pressures on these areas may be to enfold them into the public domain.

Ways of compensating the various nonurban land use "losers" by means other than the tax route should be considered. Means should also be found to preserve and encourage the continued use of high-value agricultural lands on the urban fringe by protecting them from excessive and premature speculative pressure. The Agricultural District Law may or may not be an effective answer. Human settlements policy should also look very hard at the ad valorem real estate tax and its impacts on public and private decision-making.

Inasmuch as the change of land use on the urban fringe is characterized by incremental shifts, it is necessary to strike a balance between comprehensive planning and the cumulative effects of incremental action. Achievement of this balance depends upon a more positive direction of urban growth and some degree of intervention in the free land market.

To do any kind of comprehensive planning at the state or regional level, there must be some form of local control of incremental decision-making in land use planning, while allowing higher authority to deal with regional and statewide issues. Therefore, human settlements policy should approach the questions of defining the thresholds of regional impact and criteria for identifying decisions of critical regional concern.

Since it is equally true that a region is but a collection of settlements, one of the issues to be addressed in human settlements policy is that of dominant regional character. To preserve the values of diversity, aggregations of settlements (i.e., regions) should consider and agree upon those elements that define regional character and that typify the best environmental values to be found in the region.

Human settlements policy should concern itself with the creation of an institutional capacity that will permit local communities to fit into the hierarchy of environmental planning and regulatory agencies at all government levels. This assumes that comprehensive planning at statewide levels will come into being within the decade.

In a similar vein, municipalities need to be able to better integrate special purpose districts and special purpose agencies into their own procedures. As is illustrated in some of the case studies in this report, these districts and agencies are now too autonomous for the municipal government to deal with effectively.

Energy Systems

Energy has never been conceived of by its own agents, by its regulators, or by the general public as a growth-directive force or a force for comprehensive planning and development. Limitless energy deliverable at any point on the map has been the rule to date, and pricing policies have discriminated little by location or pattern of development. This is especially true for electric utilities. If energy were viewed instead as a growth-directive force, many changes could ensue. One such change might be a complete overhaul of the energy rate structure.

The siting of additional energy facilities has become a most emotional decision-making process, with local resistance hardening in the face of physical and biological effects on local natural resources. Better ways of accommodation, even compensation, must be found along with less environmentally damaging technology. But in addition to these questions, energy siting decisions should also consider the effects on regional character, settlement patterns, and the linkages or corridors that bind them together.

Last, energy systems should be examined for opportunities to maximize return to the region from lands dedicated to energy networks through increased multiple use of the rights-of-way.

Environmental Service Systems

Environmental infrastructure should also be viewed as a potential control function in addition to a service function. Systems for water supply, sewage, drainage, and waste disposal have decisive effects on regional carrying capacity and the limits to community development, in addition to individual land use decisions and capital gains. It is customary to assume that service systems follow development rather than lead it. This premise should be reexamined.

Service-system engineering has reached the point where it is possible to construct simplified, yet dynamic, regional models of wastewater, water supply, nutrient build-up, and other factors which bear upon the capacity of the land to absorb or be limited by environmental services. The ability of the terrain and of the water courses and water-bearing substrate to absorb nutrient build-up, to ameliorate pollution, and to disperse nutrients in beneficial ways varies enormously from place to place.

With regard to nutrient build-up, it is time to reexamine the criteria for permits to install individual waste disposal systems, as opposed to collective systems. Research to determine these thresholds should not only focus on the immediate absorptive and regenerative capacity of the site of the individual system, but also view their effects on regional differentiation, regional diversity patterns, and regional limits to growth in conjunction with other community growth factors.

Solid waste disposal poses especially vexing problems for natural resource management. Of prime interest is the practice of treating municipal trash and sludges as pollutants to be buried underground or dispersed in the oceans, rather than treating them for the nutrients they are and the energy source they could be. Also, there is the question of institutional means to bring about such a change—means that would be responsive to different population densities and, therefore, to different amounts and kinds of solid waste.

Transportation

Transportation systems are now cast in a new light because of the recognition that energy is no longer boundless. Transportation is one of the largest users of energy and competes with other energy-using sectors. It is essential that transportation planners reexamine energy and land use relationships, workplace/residence relationships, transport corridors, and transport shifts— all within an energy-conserving ethic. The efficiency of energy use, measured in per capita miles and per ton miles, must be a factor in planning shifts in transportation facilities.

Transport planners need to be more concerned with preserving and up-grading existing transport facilities rather than focusing on new facilities. The railroads are a prime example of an energy-conserving means of transport that has been neglected in favor of highway and air transport, partly through effects of public subsidy.

With energy as a new factor, water transportation requires a new appraisal. The Hudson River is on the threshold of a possible renaissance. The comparisons between the Hudson and the Rhine are now couched in scenic terms. It would further enhance the potential of this great river if its use for water transportation were to rival its European counterpart.

Improved access to natural areas brings not only more people, but also more intensive land uses, which can be so disruptive to these natural systems. Transportation planning should be very sensitive and responsive to this fact. Poorly planned transportation improvements can destroy the backbone of virtually any extensive land use, including forestry, farming, and open country uses, by bringing in scattered, more intensive uses and the widespread land speculation that precedes them.

Biological Communities

Those concerned with development of the physical environment for man's use are not sufficiently armed with either the incentives or the knowledge to consider the effects of their actions on natural systems. Planners require more simplified tools for synoptic analysis of environmental quality with respect to biological communities.

In addition, decisions on land uses that affect these natural systems must stand the test of legal challenge and fit into the hierarchies of social concerns in a more cogent fashion than is now possible.

In seeking such an analytical system, the goal should be the preservation of a full spectrum of regional ecosystems so that the entire heritage of the region's natural communities is identified and protected. It is particularly important to maintain a sufficient number and size of parcels, including buffer zones, so that the natural systems to be preserved are kept truly intact.

The scientific and civic community concerned about biological communities should provide the planners with means to help define a regional character with regard to natural systems. To do this, discrete habitats should be mapped as land uses in the zoning sense. This task should include the mapping of aquatic as well as land use zones.

For the body politic, it is necessary to identify the biological communities of critical regional and state importance. This is a first priority task to make available the qualitative judgment of the concerned human community on the relative priorities for preservation at the regional and state level.

Human Health

It is perhaps not too uncharitable to say that the human health field has been dominated by the concept of epidemiology, the prevention of community health disasters, rather than a positive action approach to maintain robust and healthy human communities. From the standpoint of social policy it would be very useful to conduct social research directed toward establishing a heirarchy of regional goals and mechanisms for viable community life. Programs, although not necessarily the methodologies, of the kind represented by the "Choices for '76" program of the Regional Plan Association, come to mind. It is possible to devise a sampling mechanism to obtain a valid consensus on a number of public health and human health questions. Surveys using statistical sampling techniques could delve into questions such as the value of landscape diversity. Similarly, it can be assumed from common sense that there are health effects related to density, but there seems to be little social research available to guide the planning process. Although a certain amount of social–physical research has been done in the strictly urban scene, there is not a comparable body in rural sociology that deals with the qualitative side of life.

What is being discussed here is the prospect of establishing levels of habitability, dependent upon various densities and mixes of land uses. This concept has been initiated for confined environments by architect Danforth Toan and further explored by NASA, but insufficient work along these lines has been done on the environment at a large scale.

Leisure Time and Recreation

To establish interdependency with natural resource management, it can be assumed that leisure time and recreation refer primarily to outdoor recreation in all of its forms. In this regard, it appears that we are finally beginning to recognize fully the possibility of recreation saturation in many of our outdoor playgrounds. At our beach fronts and shorelines, in the lakes of the basin, and in Long Island Sound, we have passed the point of diminishing returns in many instances. Therefore, a key issue in leisure time and recreation is the establishment of quantitative and qualitative thresholds of recreational saturation and the optimum levels of recreational density for various activities in various natural settings. This would help to define dominant regional character and to work toward its enhancement and preservation.

Clearly, a closely linked matter involves further research to determine the compatibilities and incompatibilities of recreational uses with uses such as forestry, agriculture, fishing, wildlife preservation, and others. In all of this, water has a key role. Therefore, in thinking about leisure time and recreation, preventing the deterioriation of presently clear and free-flowing waters must be stressed. Land use practices are coming to be recognized as closely related to water quality.

Some recreation areas have deteriorated much like central cities, and the reversal is just as difficult. One device that might be explored is that of a recreational development authority charged with rehabilitation (in the same sense as urban renewal) of decayed recreation areas. These would include lakeside "slums" and eutrophied lakes and streams. One of the principal tasks of such a body would be to establish access points to open water bodies and other important natural assets, such as escarpments, summits, and ravines. It would be concerned with the compatability and integrity of the whole mix of land uses in a recreation region.

Another important challenge would be the development of acceptable surrogates for the destructive activity that is degrading natural environments used for recreation. Ways need to be devised to take the pressure off the backpacking trails, the outdoor recreational vehicle routes, and the points of boating congestion. It may be necessary to limit some of these activities, as is currently being discussed, even on water bodies as large as Long Island Sound. But perhaps attention should also be given to substitute development. For example, increasing the capacity of the barge canal for hikers and boaters should relieve the pressure on more fragile mountain trails and lakes.

At state, regional, and local levels all parties of interest need to establish definitive maps locating resource "edges" of various levels of quality so that these important junctures between natural forms and existing uses can be taken into account in the planning process. A shorelines act, or perhaps a shorelines renewal act, setting forth recreational preferences over single private uses, bears investigation as a tool for recapturing a high proportion of privately held shorelines for public use.

Water Resources

The abundance of water traditionally associated with the humid Northeast can no longer be taken for granted. Spot water shortages due to heavy use and low rainfall have been experienced in the Hudson Basin in the past. As water demand continues to grow, such shortages presumably will be more frequent and more serious.

One of the powerful new forces in water demand is the burgeoning requirement for cooling water in power generation. Therefore, in planning for future water demands, society must answer whether and in what circumstances to use water as a cooling medium for power generation.

Another key question is whether the watershed reserves needed to meet future demand can be provided without "locking up" land and water bodies for this single purpose, as has been done in the past. The same attitudes of epidemiology that govern thinking about public health have dominated potable water supply engineering. Indeed, it can even be asked whether there should not be some balancing of regional supply pools to distribute water resources among regions more equitably.

6.4   The Management Process

Technical Considerations

Carrying Capacity as a Limit to Growth

The biological sciences have long used the concept of carrying capacity to estimate the number of individuals that a given land area can sustain. This concept is based on the needs of an individual species, such as food, cover, and water, but the concept also recognizes the natural psychological limits to population density. In more recent years, efforts have been made to apply this concept to environmental analysis for resource management. For instance, estimates have been made of how many people the existing resources of the earth and the existing state of technology can sustain at the present standard of living. Although there is a theoretical maximum human population based on the basic requirements for life, such a maximum is not desirable unless factors that protect the quality of life can also be integrated into the calculation.

The physical and biological limitations on human development are dictated by the land and its associated resources. The identification of these limitations as individual elements is well understood. A whole range of factors, including soil, water, topography, flooding frequencies, wildlife communities, vegetation, and air, affect and may limit various types of development. With respect to coastal areas, the ability to extract groundwater without saltwater intrusion may be a limiting factor. The interactions between and among physical and biological resource communities and the ripple effect of adding to or subtracting from the resource base are not so well understood. For example, pollution of groundwater might not adversely affect humans, yet it may change a nutrient cycle, alter the vegetative cover, and disrupt both plant and animal communities, thereby impacting surrounding areas. The axiom that everything is tied to everything else is becoming recognized; but the nature of the ties and the potentialities have not been researched enough to be applied. Yet these interactions can and do affect the land's carrying capacity.

The human carrying capacity of land, as modified by provision for a quality life, is difficult to quantify. Land use patterns, the availability of diversity within the community, and the availability for diversity within a reasonable travel distance are elements of the land's carrying capacity when defined with a goal of preserving a quality environment and an enjoyable life style. These social elements must be identified and included in any land use plan designed to regulate and control growth and development.

The social factors related to the carrying capacity concept can be summarized as follows: a social definition of dominant regional use; density limitations and concentrations; service infrastructure; and constraining interregional linkages. A definition of the desired dominant regional use is the most basic social consideration in land use planning and regulation. The means of determination will be different for different levels of control and different regions, but in each case it must be a conscious social and political choice if it is to be effective. Each region must recognize the constraints imposed by larger regions and the needs of the population as a whole in establishing regional use goals.

Analytical Techniques

The analytical techniques available for comprehensive land use planning and natural resource management can be broken down into the following general categories: single-factor resource analysis, single-factor statistical analysis, constraint analysis, and amenity analysis.

The first of these techniques, which analyzes a single resource on a geographical base, encompasses many well-established methods of analysis. For example, in water resources, such single-resource analytical techniques might be concerned with aquifers and aquifer limits; groundwater recharge zones; stream flow and its seasonal limits; flood limits at various levels of flood frequency; or an analysis of these interrelated networks of water resources along with their capture, distribution networks, and pressures. A similar single-factor analysis technique that deals with land is the eight-class system of agricultural soil-capability mapping used by the U.S. Soil Conservation Service.

Single-factor statistical analysis comes in many forms, dealing with population and density, existing land utilization (as in the case of the New York State LUNR System), and other factors. The various techniques for the analysis and prediction of traffic flows are also examples of single-factor statistical analysis.

Constraint analysis is concerned with the limits on land use development. It is based upon the examination of natural resource processes and natural limiting factors. Two examples of constraint analysis developed to a relatively high degree are the engineering interpretations contained in the standard county soil surveys prepared by the Soil Conservation Service and the geotechnical constraint mapping now being done by engineering geologists concerned with both the deep substrate and the surface soils. It is now possible to predict flood limits with a reasonable degree of accuracy, including the calculation of flood limits of various expectancies, from seasonal to 100-year floods. The detection of fault zones, substrates, solution cavities, mine subsidence possibilities, and collapsing soils are all new tools in constraint analysis that should provide sufficient analytical power to enable planners and users to avoid some of the major mistakes of the past. Even relatively simple constraint analysis techniques can be highly useful and effective. Mapping slope by categories of degrees of slope is now commonplace. The usefulness of this particular tool is hampered, however, because the various slope classes have not been standardized for the purposes of aggregating data on a regional or statewide basis.

The methodology of analyzing the special constraints inherent in fragile ecosystems, such as the existence of the habitats of rare and endangered species, is still not as well quantified or formulated as some of the above.

Amenity analysis is finally reasonably well established. There has been much experimental work done on landscape classification, both in the establishment of generic typology and in the measurement of landscape perception. More recent efforts have focused on the determination of amenity levels on something other than a personal and intuitive basis. The work done by Ervin A. Zube provides one example. Zube's work on the relationship of visual and cultural environmental values to resources planning, published as Appendix N of the "North Atlantic Regional Water Resources Study" (NAR, 1972), is a seminal study in landscape amenity analysis.

In the area of shoreline analysis, architect–planner Frithjof M. Lunde, a Hudson Basin Project member, in association with coastal scientist, Dr. John M. Zeigler, and augmented by urban planner Edward Echevarria, have collectively developed techniques for the calibration of beaches for recreational and tourism capacity, based in part on visual amenity considerations as well as other physical and cultural criteria.

In addition, optimum recreation densities for natural and wilderness areas are currently being studied. Visual amenities and the establishment of critical thresholds at which aesthetic satisfaction is lost are important factors in these studies.

Political Considerations: Illustrative Cases

The Adirondack Park Agency Experience

The increasing recognition of society's broad concern with, and legitimate role in, the use of land as a finite resource is perhaps nowhere more evident than in the history of the 6-million-acre Adirondack Park. In the Adirondacks, the citizens of New York State have clearly shown a desire to protect the existing character of an important and unique natural resource area and to have the opportunity to evaluate major changes in land use carefully. Political changes can clearly be made even in an area as fraught with emotion as the home rule issue, but change is most likely when a strong, legitimate, regional, or statewide concern can be demonstrated.

The citizens of New York State are the largest landowners in the park, with approximately 2.3 million acres in state ownership. Using this information and the area's designation as a park in 1892, the 1973 State Legislature adopted a Land Use and Development Plan regulating the use of the park's remaining 3.7 million acres of private land. This plan was designed to allow appropriate private development within the park while at the same time protecting the park's resources.

The plan was based on an intensive study of existing land uses, available services, physical and biological resource limitations to development, and alternative methods of protecting the open space character of the park. The evaluation of these parameters led to a Land Use and Development Plan that channels development to the vicinity of those existing developed areas that are most capable of sustaining and providing services for intensive uses. At the same time, the plan identified approximately 87% of the private land within the park as valuable open space. It limited building to one house per 8½ acres on 34% of the private land and one house per 43 acres on approximately 53% of the private land. Despite these seemingly restrictive density limitations, the plan still allows for up to a tenfold increase in the present park population of approximately 210,000 permanent and seasonal residents.

Concurrent with the adoption of the Adirondack Park Land Use and Development Plan, the State Legislature authorized the Adirondack Park Agency to regulate development to prevent undue adverse environmental impacts on the park's unique scenic, aesthetic, wildlife, recreational, open space, historic, ecological, and natural resources. The legislation provides for a permit requirement for any development of a regional scale or any development located in critical environmental areas .

The Park Agency's Land Use and Development Plan and regulatory mechanisms place it in the vanguard of land use planning and control throughout the United States. However, it is recognized in both the plan and the legislative mandate that special physical and social factors are vital elements in the successful implementation of the program.

The political pressures to create a state agency to control private land within the park came predominantly from the citizens who resided outside the park. Most of the residents of the park were opposed to state controls that would restrict the use of private land. Outside the park, the debate did not focus on whether the state's citizens would support state land use controls throughout the state but rather in one particular region. Furthermore, much of this widespread social support stemmed from the psychological value of a 6-million-acre open space reserve. Just the knowledge that such an area exists is of as much concern to many of the residents of the Hudson Basin as the immediate need for actual use and enjoyment of the park.

The other social concerns reflected in the legislative mandates and in the implementation mechanisms are the needs of the park's 120,000 permanent residents. This is one of the most economically depressed regions in the state. The two major employing industries are recreation and forest products. Both are heavily dependent on open space and resource production lands. Unemployment rates of 20% are common within the park. Even for those fortunate enough to be employed, the seasonal nature of employment in the recreational industry is a perennial problem. One of the goals of the state's land use control program is to enhance the economic potential of the region while at the same time not degrading its unique and fragile natural environment. Although difficult to achieve, these goals are not necessarily incompatible.

The Hudson River Valley Commission Experience

The Hudson River Valley Commission (HRVC) was created by the legislature in 1966 to develop a comprehensive plan and to review physical development projects within the narrow limits of the Hudson River corridor in New York State. The commission's role was advisory, and implementation of its recommendations relied upon action by a multiplicity of public and private agencies that play a role in the physical development process.

A valuable contribution of the HRVC to the current environmental effort was its operational application of a definition of the term "environment." The Commission viewed the environment as a complex system of interrelated resources—natural, man-made, and social. To this end, the HRVC fashioned an interdisciplinary staff, structured by the components of its concept of the environment, that was capable of understanding and contending with the entire spectrum of environmental concerns.

The task of the commission was to achieve an environment in which both natural and man-made components were sympathetically related. The law specified two means of accomplishing this objective. The first was comprehensive planning, delineating regional resource-use policies for the river corridor, and suggesting a pattern for development. The second was project review, involving assessment of changes in the environment that would result from specific project proposals and, where problems were evident, proposing better solutions. The critical part of the commission's mandate was the review process, where it was confronted by the realities of planning and design promulgated by both public and private sponsors. Comprehensive planning provided the broad environmental framework upon which the review process was based.

The commission was not content with the negative role of assessing project impact. It was more concerned with stimulating good development in the right location. Procedures were devised to identify projects with the potential of bringing about significant change in the environment and also to identify areas significant to both the development and the protection of the environment of the river corridor. In this capacity the HRVC offered a high degree of leadership and commitment.

The HRVC also initiated a relationship with the project sponsor at the earliest possible date, preferably before the sponsor authorized his consultants to prepare final project plans. Although this approach requires considerable staff resources, there were several advantages in making a staff input at an early stage:

1. The state's concern for the protection of the resources of the river corridor could be expressed in a positive manner, using the expertise of the HRVC staff.
2. The affected locality could benefit by staff advice at no cost.
3. The project sponsor need not waste time and money in developing plans for a project that would result in the impairment of resources.
4. The HRVC staff was able to discuss the project concept at the peer level with the sponsor's consultants.
5. And scope for interest accommodation was at its greatest. Positions of opponents, supporters, and other agencies (whose acquiescence would be necessary) were still fluid, not publicly set, and thus could be influenced by the intervention of the commission.

The HRVC brought a comprehensive view of environmental management into a field already crowded with other players. A key to the creation of the HRVC and to the development of its role was finding an aspect of environmental quality that was not already recognized as the province of other well-established agencies. Visual aesthetics provided such an opportunity. The "turf" of the commission was tied to what could be seen from the river itself. Whereas this may seem to be quite limiting, some such legitimizing mechanism in the interagency and intergovernmental struggle for budget, support, and recognition is necessary. It should be noted that, with the collapse of budgetary and political support for the commission within the state administration, the visual dimension in environmental management of the Hudson region is again effectively vacant.* If a regionwide management agency is to be attempted again, the problem of identifying a legitimate turf must be once again faced.

Second-Home Developments in the Adirondacks

The political pressures that can arise from major proposed changes in existing land use patterns are illustrated by the recent trend in large-scale second-home developments in the Adirondack Park.

*The Hudson River Valley Commission was abolished as an independent agency in 1971. Reduced in budget and powers, the commission and a small staff continued to function for a few years, first within the Office of Planning Services (itself now defunct) and then within the Office of Parks and Recreation. The HRVC now exists only on paper, its remaining functions having been assumed by the Department of Environmental Conservation. [Ed.]

Development more or less bypassed this mountainous region until recently. But as more people became affluent enough to own second homes, and an interstate highway was completed from New York City to Montreal, development pressures in the Adirondacks mounted. As usual, changes appeared very slowly, resulting in a gradual erosion of the park's character. Much of the change was a result of more and more people purchasing lots and building second homes in the Adirondacks. This steadily increasing pressure on the fragile natural resources of the park did not go totally unnoticed. In 1967, an Adirondack Mountains National Park was proposed. Many citizens of New York disagreed with this proposal, but it forced them to ask how the park's open space character could best be preserved, in view of the present checkerboard pattern of public and private ownership. In 1968, Governor Nelson A. Rockefeller created a study commission with broad mandate to recommend policies for the proper use and protection of the Adirondacks. After 2 years of study, this commission presented 181 recommendations to the Governor. They ranged from specifics such as the reintroduction of the timber wolf to the Adirondacks to a broad but strong recommendation that a semi-independent agency be created to control development on private lands within the park. The latter recommendation was partially justified by emerging proposals for a new type of second-home development within the park. The first example was a proposal by Ton-Da-Lay Limited to create a massive second-home community of between 4000 and 7000 units near the Village of Tupper Lake. Shortly after the commission's report, Horizon Corporation of Tucson, Arizona, announced plans for still another second-home community of approximately 9000 units in a presently undeveloped portion of the park.

The public reaction in the face of such unprecedented pressures on the hitherto sparsely developed park was almost immediate. In 1973, state legislation was enacted, creating the Adirondack Park Agency to plan the use and development of the private lands within the park and to ensure that the state's interest in the area would be protected.

Thus, it was not the gradual erosion of the park by small second-home developments as much as the threat of massive second-home communities that resulted in a demand from the public that the area be preserved. Furthermore, pressures developed not so much from the readily identifiable threats to specific factors, such as potential pollution from large numbers of individual septic systems, but from the threat of a drastic change in the character of the area.

Mining Operations

Mining operations pose numerous land use problems that have been reviewed in a variety of forums. To date, however, no effective mechanism has been devised to control the ultimate disposition of the mining site. Plans for the future use of mined lands and for allocating the burden of reclamation costs must be established. Furthermore, the question of defining what rights go with prior uses of land, and to what extent they apply, has seldom had greater potential economic or environmental impact than in the case of mining operations.

The Tahawus ilmenite mine near the headwaters of the Hudson illustrates both the difficulty of an answer to the prior-rights question and the need for terminal plans.

N-L Industries owns approximately 11,000 acres in the heart of the Adirondack Park at Tahawus. The company mines ilmenite, a moderately magnetic oxide of iron and titanium, by open pit methods. Two open pits occupy a surface of about 115 acres. There is one inactive pit 3000 feet long, 1500 feet wide, and between 300 and 700 feet deep; and one active pit 3000 feet long, 150 feet wide, and 125 feet deep. This mine is the largest titanium mine in the world. Over 300 people are employed at Tahawus, in an area of chronic unemployment. Under present economic conditions it is felt that the mine will be able to continue operation for possibly 50 more years.

Iron ore had been intermittently mined at Tahawus since the nineteenth century. As an ilmenite mine, it dates back to the early days of the Second World War, when titanium oxide was in great demand for paint products for military use. The opening of the mine and the building of the extraction plant were financed by the United States Navy.

Abandonment of individual pits, acres of tailings, and discharge of water used in the operation present potential environmental, safety, and aesthetic problems. To date only the aesthetic problem has been serious.

The mine is located in a "peninsula" of private land jutting into the Adirondack's largest unit of state-owned land designated as wilderness—the High Peaks Wilderness. The operation is visible and audible from many of the scenic mountaintops in the Wilderness. The northern portion of the N-L property is narrow, contains two scenic ponds, and abuts the High Peaks Wilderness on three sides. Although this portion has not yet been mined, it may contain economically viable ore deposits that the company may some day wish to extract. Mining here, if it is by open pit, would have serious impact on the state's largest wilderness and might well jeopardize the surrounding area's wilderness classification from a practical standpoint. Only underground mining and long-distance hauling of the tailings could avoid a major confrontation of environmental and economic interests should the company desire to mine the northern portion of its holdings.

Under the requirements of the type of mine reclamation legislation moving through the United States Congress at this time, this kind of open pit mine would not be subject to early regulation. Even if it did become so subject, as an open mine there would be no attempt to restore it to the status quo ante, because that is not the intention of the proposed laws relative to strip mining.*

The entire ownership, but particularly the northern 320 acres, would be a logical state acquisition to protect the existing state forest preserve holdings. Others feel that it is open to question whether prior use ensures any mining company the unilateral right to continue to extend its operations into the very heart of the High Peaks Wilderness. Because the original conditions of national emergency are long since behind us, some feel that the state should preempt this possibility.

Such an acquisition or taking, however, might be a serious blow to the economy of the surrounding, economically depressed area. This concern must be given due weight. Considering the diverse interests involved, a middle ground of accommodation that will allow the mine to operate but only with stringent environmental and aesthetic regulation, perhaps coupled with state acquisition of the northern 320 acres, must be reached.

The second question is whether or not the state can now begin to impose forward reclamation planning upon mining operations so that, as they continue, there will be a systematic plan for the ultimate use of the mined-out property. This might include the determination of the final water level of the exhausted mine pits and the preparation of the lands adjacent to the ultimate shoreline level so that when the open pits ultimately fill with water, the shoreline vegetation and general condition will be amenable to future public use.

The need for reclamation of mined-out areas is not limited to large operations such as Tahawus. The sheer number of sand, gravel, and other borrow pits that are scattered throughout the region make them of perhaps even greater concern in the regional land use context. Programs to minimize their aesthetic and other environmental impacts during operations and reclamation programs that provide for beneficial future land uses are increasingly necessary. However, "beneficial use" does not necessarily mean only sanitary landfills. The current fashion of considering abandoned open pits as prime candidates for sanitary landfill sites will increasingly be called to question, especially as potential landfill materials are increasingly thought of as reclaimable resources to be "mined" for their value as recycled fuel, metal, or plastics.

Regional Sanitary Landfills

Any sanitary landfill is an environmental and political problem of large magnitude, and a regional facility is just so much more so. The problem of

*Mine reclamation acts have been enacted at the federal and state levels. [Ed.]

joint municipal action is a political decision problem of the most vexing kind. Under present incentives, who wants the regional dump next to him? Yet all need a dump, and a bigger dump is easier to manage. The Croton Point regional landfill is a prime example of these problems within the basin.

By order of the courts, Westchester County has been required to analyze the impact of the Croton Point landfill upon the water resources of the Hudson River and upon the public uses of Croton Point, which is also a county park. As a park, it is of unique regional value with a high recreation potential. The biological and hydrological investigations mandated by the courts have found that leachate from this landfill, which is essentially the only large landfill available to communities in Westchester County, is indeed polluting the Hudson.

The current state of the art does not offer an immediate solution to the leachate problem; however, the hydrologists involved in the study propose that the leachate be contained by a series of expensive well-pointing systems on the periphery of the groundwater discharge slope, and then treated in a manner similar to municipal sewage. Other schemes are being considered that would render the surface land over the terminated landfill less permeable, thereby lessening the leachate concentration and making it more feasible, economically and technically, to contain the leachate.* The nearness of the landfill to a major swimming and picnicking area is an especially unfortunate historical accident and the source of acute political and technical problems. Westchester must now consider exporting its solid wastes—but who wants them?

Storm King

The history of the Storm King pumped-storage electric generating facility proposed for Cornwall, New York, underscores the inability of existing private and public management processes to cope rationally with major land use decisions of a complex nature. This proposal, heralded by its sponsor, the Consolidated Edison Company, as the ideal solution to the intermittent electric power needs of the New York metropolitan area, was first announced about 16 years ago. To date, the project remains locked in litigation and has provided the issues for lengthy confrontations between the utility company, various levels of government, and private conservation groups representing various national and local interests.

The project involves the creation of a water storage reservoir at the top of Storm King Mountain, which rises from the west bank of the Hudson River

---

*Since this chapter was written, the county has installed a series of collection basins from which the leachate is recirculated through the fill. This system has greatly reduced the amount of leachate entering the Hudson. Nevertheless, the existing landfill area is under a federal mandate to close by 1981. [Ed.]

about 50 miles north of New York City. Water from the river is to be pumped to the reservoir and upon its release will activate electric-generating turbines located at the base of the mountain. The power needed to operate the pumps will be produced by existing generating plants located in New York City when the demand for electricity does not utilize the maximum generating capacity of these facilities. The power to be produced by the pumped storage plant is to be used solely to augment existing generating capacity during peak-use periods when such capacity is inadequate.

The utility company contends that this method of electric power generation will not have an adverse effect on the environment of the region and will make more efficient use of the existing capital investment in present generating facilities by utilizing off-peak generating capacity. It has been estimated that this technique requires about three units of energy for every two units ultimately delivered to the final user.

The project has been criticized by private and public conservation agencies, who question the impact of the project on fish life in the river, especially on endangered species whose habitat is up to hundreds of miles from the project. The City of New York has expressed concern for the safety of its Catskill Aqueduct, which furnishes a large portion of the city's water supply. The aqueduct runs under the river near the project site and could be damaged by the blasting needed to construct the storage reservoir. City residents have stated that additional air pollution within the city will result from increased use of the existing generating facilities needed to power the reservoir pumps, which otherwise would be used less intensively.

The utility company also proposes, as part of the project, to develop a recreation area for local residents and a sight-seeing overlook that will attract people from outside the locality. But the impact of the project and its ancillary recreational facilities on the state and local road pattern, as well as the need for additional recreational resources in this area of vast state park holdings, has not been assessed. At the same time, the project represents a large tax windfall to local government—a windfall to be paid for indirectly by utility customers outside of the area.

The major issue, although not widely discussed, is the public benefit of a decision made by a private company with a single public function to perform. A unique natural resource has been proposed to be used for this single purpose. The means of evaluating the public benefit of this purpose, compared with other uses, is not yet available.

It is obvious that present public management procedures are inadequate to the task when issues so vital to many governmental agencies and the public are still unresolved after 16 years of review and litigation.*

*At this writing the project is no longer in litigation but is still awaiting further hearings before the Federal Energy Regulatory Comission. Con Edison plans to have the project in service by the mid-1990s. [Ed.]

Rockland County Transmission Line

This case illustrates the inherent inability of a single-purpose public agency to respond to other aspects of public need. The issue concerns the public benefit to be achieved by the use of state parklands for a portion of a major interstate power transmission line traversing the length of Rockland County, New York.

The fixed points of the proposed transmission line were a Hudson River crossing tower and a substation, located 15 miles away, that also receives power from generating facilities outside of the state. The Palisades Interstate Park Commission, a park agency of the states of New York and New Jersey, maintains the lands west of the crossing tower and south to the substation, which lie outside the park jurisdiction. A well-defined escarpment provides a natural line of demarcation between the park and the private lands below.

The route proposed by the sponsoring utility company had the transmission line gradually ascending the escarpment for almost the entire length of the line, and terminating at the substation on the other side of the escarpment. This would result in a highly visible scar across the heavily wooded hillside, which provides the backdrop for an intensively developed area of the county.

An alternate route was devised by a countywide study committee created by the County Board of Supervisors to resolve the objections to the visual blight resulting from the proposed alignment. The committee suggested that the route follow the base of the escarpment from the crossing tower to a break in the escarpment where the line could be elevated with the least visual disturbance and then continue through a small section of the park to the substation. This proposal would lessen the portion of the line that would be visible to the thousands of nearby residents and eliminate the need to mar the escarpment.

The area of the park proposed to be crossed by the study committee's transmission line route is heavily wooded and all but inaccessible to most park users. The number of persons able to view the line through the park would be a fraction of the number of persons who would view the line daily from their household.

The Palisades Interstate Park Compact states that the lands owned by the commission shall be used only for park purposes; however, the commission does have the power to grant easements when, in its opinion, such easements will not interfere with the use and enjoyment of the park by the public. When the commission was confronted by the Study Committee's request for an easement through the park to implement its transmission line route, the commission deemed that such request would interfere with the enjoyment of the park by the public. In this manner, a solution to an important public need was denied by the ruling of a governmental agency unable to respond to any public concern other than the purpose for which it was created.

Political Consideration: Some Problems

Is Home Rule a Reality for Tomorrow?

New York, New Jersey, and Connecticut are rapidly urbanizing states; however, their local governments are largely the remains of a system originally devised to serve the minimal needs of a rural society. Each local government has decision-making powers that can influence the total environment, yet no local government's jurisdiction or expertise is adequate to allow comprehension of the total environment.

Highly competitive local governments can ignore harmful effects external to their own boundaries just as well as any private decision-maker. They are, after all, elected to take care of their own constituents' problems, not those of neighboring political units. In so doing, local governments always have to consider the effects of their policies on their main source of local financial support, the ad valorem real estate tax. As a result, both public and private decision-makers are led to treat the region's common property resources as if they were limitless.

Local governments do not exist in a vacuum, of course. State and federal programs also affect resource use, often with some linkage to the local community. Among them are county soil and water conservation districts, fish and wildlife management boards, and regional planning commissions. But, despite all of these programs and linkages, the student of natural resource management has to conclude that, although we may be making progress, we have not yet learned how to put it all together.

There are some interesting straws in the wind. Under New York's Department of Environmental Conservation, explicit authority has been given to consider the total environmental impact in the granting of permits, even when the more restricted purposes of the permit may have been satisfactorily met. Environmental regulations and permit procedures are a means whereby the state level provides incentives and "back stiffeners" for local decision-makers. Grants-in-aid and cost sharing for various projects are another widely used approach.

Is home rule a reality for tomorrow? Few would suggest that the many functions performed by local governments should be shifted to the state. However, any coordinated decision-making process for land use, the division of control among local, county, and state governments, should vary according to the fiscal and professional capabilities of the local governments. For example, many think that counties should be given more authority in land use control. In a sparsely settled area, such as the Adirondacks, counties could assume controls presently vested in towns and thereby strengthen the local input by consolidating resources. Other areas of the basin, such as Long Island, have the capabilities to continue strong, effective land use regulation at the town level. The bulk of the basin would lie somewhere between these two extremes. The state's role can be exercised through regional areas to ensure that variables between regions are properly reflected and the dominant regional use is given highest priority. Furthermore, the state's responsibility and authority should vary not only by the potential impact of the decisions to be made but also by the state interest in the region. Certainly the state interest in the Adirondack and Catskill parks is greater than in most other portions of the basin as a result of the large state land holdings and the park designations. Land use decisions must be fully explored in a public forum, and entrusted to agencies that are responsive to a wide variety of concerns and interests. This also means that land use decisions must not be left entirely to agencies responsible for creating or promoting the activities being evaluated.

To ensure that all legitimate concerns are properly identified and evaluated in the decision-making process, state agencies should be created or strengthened to coordinate land use planning. Another possibility (complementary to a state agency) is the creation of regional planning and regulatory bodies, such as the Adirondack Park Agency, to cover all regions of each state. The chairmen of the regional agencies might sit collectively to make land use decisions affecting more than one region. This group would also need a central staff, but it should be limited to truly interregional decisions, such as jetports and major highway exchanges, and leave the bulk of the decisions to the regional and local units. With this type of system, however, accountability to elected officials is essential at each level. Indeed, the likelihood of appeals over the heads of such officials is so great that close contact with the elected final arbiters is probably inevitable if the process is to be effective.

Maintaining Flexibility in Land Use Regulation

It is usually agreed today that some form of social control over land use decisions is desirable. But local zoning, as conceived and practiced from the mid-1920s until this decade, has also created static land use documents. The ideal form of land use regulation will also maintain as much freedom as possible for both government action and entrepreneurship. Before this can happen, however, the numbers of devices that can promote flexibility must be expanded from the present few.

Present devices include Planned Unit Development ordinances, the "density averaging" procedures as provided for in Section 281 of the New York Town Law, and the options available under the New York Agricultural Districts Law and the Fisher Forest Act. New Jersey is currently considering a method for the transference of development rights. Experimentation is actively continuing, but there clearly is room for other means of promoting flexibility. For example, one alternative might be some form of "buffer-zone option" regulation. This would contain specific criteria that would permit zoning changes, but only after consideration of the constraints imposed by the natural system within specified guidelines.

The Single-Purpose Agency

Too often environmental problems are seen as the "public" being forced to protect itself from the single-mindedness and tunnel vision of profit-motivated private individuals and business firms. Little reflection is needed to recognize that all organizations simplify complex situations by ignoring many, if not most, relevant considerations. Decision-making is hard enough even then. Single-mindedness and tunnel vision are the cause of major environmental problems created by public as well as private actors. But making and enforcing rules of good environmental behavior on public agencies pose some special problems and opportunities.

Is "the public" also "a developer"? Should a public agency, when it proposes to build a facility, have to consider the same restrictions imposed on a private developer? Flood risk may call for raising construction to higher elevations. Waste discharges load the receiving air and water whether they come from private or public projects. Problems of traffic and parking, visual and noise effects, and other environmental impacts can be generated by public as well as private undertakings. But if a public agency is taking environmentally significant action, it is usually guided by a very different set of rules, rule makers, and enforcers than the private entrepreneurs.

The most fundamental reason for the environmental problems of single-purpose agencies is that there are limits to the agency's mandate, mission, authority, expertise and specialist mix, and its funding. Therefore, it should come as no surprise that there are limits to its results.

The mandate of the single-purpose agency is partly a question of the enabling act and legislative history of the agency over its life span. It is also partly a question of the quantity and quality of support by the electorate, legislature, and succeeding administrations. Summed up, this means that the real and perceived mandate of the single-purpose agency is well defined and, by that very fact, limited.

Although an agency's mandate is reflective of its purpose, its mission may be a different matter. In part, the mission, as perceived by the agency, may be grounded in the enabling acts and other regulatory devices that control its life, but it can also be a reflection of the succession of personalities who have governed the agency through its life span. This is particularly true when the mandate of the agency is general and not fully defined by law. The degree of autonomy of the agency is also important.

The third limit to the actions of the single-purpose agency is its authority, which is at least of two kinds. There is its *real* authority, its "clout" in the popular vernacular, and its jurisdiction or *apparent* authority. Some agencies possess apparent authority which is not real or lasting. For instance, the late, lamented Hudson River Valley Commission temporarily achieved a great deal of influence over development in the Hudson River corridor, primarily through its use of technical expertise and persuasion and the efficacy of the techniques by which it chose to make its limited authority felt. Planning agencies in general provide good examples of illusory authority—i.e., they appear to have great power but in fact have relatively little. An unfortunate example of this is the Office of Planning Coordination of the State of New York with respect to its preparation of the State Development Plan—a plan that was subsequently lacking in legislative support and for which there is no present or prospective means of implementation.

Conversely, there are agencies that, at first glance, do not appear to have any substantive power but which in fact have a great deal. Some of the best examples here are the various public health bodies at the state and lower levels of government. These agencies, through their control of the permit procedures for subdivisions and private-dwelling water supplies and sewage disposal, have very substantial impact upon land use patterns throughout the state but keep an extremely low public profile.

Allied to an agency's authority is its influence. There are many agencies whose influence extends beyond its authority, its mandate, or its mission. When the influence is real, but not precisely backed by law, it often relates to the persuasive position of a powerful agency within the hierarchy of lesser agencies of a state or other unit of government.

Another characteristic of an agency, and a very important one, is its kind and level of expertise and specialist mix. This tends to be limited by law but is also influenced by the needs of the agency, as perceived by those who prepare and grant its funding. It can also be heavily influenced by the rise of a practitioner group associated with its specific kind of expertise, as for instance the American Society of Highway Officials, the American Institute of Planners, the National Council of the States for Building Codes and Standards, and other specialist groups. The kinds of talent that an agency can afford are related to the justification that the agency can mount for a particular kind of expertise to accomplish its mission. The point here is that it is very hard for the single-mission agency to justify a need for multidisciplinary personnel, and this is a characteristic of such agencies that tends to limit their outlook and practices.

Last, some of the most critical limits on a single-purpose agency relate to the extent of its funding and how it goes about acquiring financial support. Very often, adequate funding is due to the skill and persuasiveness of the agency's leadership in garnering public legislative support, as well as support over time by a series of administrations. Furthermore, agency funding is not always a reflection of the real social priorities but may be strongly influenced by the existence of a substantial constituency as well as by vested interests that depend on the funds flowing through the agency to the private sector.

It is for all of the above reasons that the single-purpose agency is not able to solve or even to become involved in multipurpose problems of great magnitude and complexity. The fatal flaws include the obvious tunnel vision associated with the limited expertise and the failure of the staff and leadership of the agency to appreciate other values, other forms of consideration, and the conflicting missions of other agencies. This is not to say that there is no recognition of the importance of multipurpose cooperation and planning. However, because of their limits, single-purpose agencies *claim* to be willing to participate with other agencies in comprehensive planning more often than they actually do.

It is often difficult to recognize any real differences between the behavior of "private" and "public" concerns. This is particularly true for the quasi-private and quasi-public agencies. In terms of land use resolution and other aspects of comprehensive planning, the quandaries which these agencies pose are numerous. Consolidated Edison, for example, is ostensibly a private corporation, yet it is the sole purveyor within its service area of an important public service—electric energy. It is "private" only so far as it can maintain its stance as a public stock corporation able to meet its financial and capital growth requirements within the private sector. As is now clearly evident, when it no longer appears to be able to keep that capability, it will quickly revert to a quasi-public status and will seek funding by subsidy or other aid from the public sector. The Port Authority of New York and New Jersey was, until recently, a quasi-public agency that was totally autonomous in its activities. The Port Authority pursued a course just as single-minded as any private company. In the process, it neglected other considerations that might properly have come within its purview simply because it chose not to enter those arenas, as for instance, mass transit.

The single-purpose public or quasi-public agency has great difficulty in achieving a balance of the public good vis-à-vis other agencies. Much like a private business concern, the single-purpose agency tends to follow its own limited mandate and pursue its own mission, without full regard for the impact on other areas of the life of the state, region, or community.

To cite an example, one can examine the electric utility company. The credo and, in fact, the franchise of this utility mandate that it will supply electric power, anywhere, anytime, and in any amount within its service area at a price that reflects only its average costs. The tradition of the electric utility company throughout the world is that it is proud of its record in achieving that goal. The esprit de corps of its dedicated professional group is based on having achieved this kind of growth and of having matched the rate of growth of urbanization and electrical demand on a one-for-one basis, with reserve capacity to spare. The electric utility company would find it odd to be charged with the massive impact on land use which, in fact, it does have. The indiscriminate availability of electric energy at any time and any place helps to make possible important changes in land use, including the scatteration of urban growth. Yet the utility does not question the social value of this effect. Indeed, it takes pride in facilitating this freedom. It cannot begin to achieve balance with regard to other land use demands and socially optimum land use control because it does not recognize them as subjects of its concern.

The fact that the electric utility stands willing and able to provide service that promotes disorderly growth means that electric rate-payers as a whole help to subsidize sprawled growth. They pay the total electric bill, which includes the extra costs due to scatteration. There is seldom any differentiation in utility rate structures for the location of the user, but only for the class of user. Rate structures favor the large user regardless of the location of that user.

The balance needed between electrical energy availability and orderly land use would be achieved if the utility, through the control of its own distribution system, were somehow made an agent for the orderly growth of urbanization, rather than one of the agents facilitating indiscriminate growth. If it could concern itself with the phasing and forward planning of distribution networks related to overall land use as well as individual customers, the provision of electric energy could be integrated with truly comprehensive planning. By simultaneously making available electricity and other elements of public infrastructure, such as water supply and sewers, this integration would also reduce the distribution costs of electricity. But it is clear that mountains of law, habit, and perception of mission will first have to be scaled to achieve such an integration.

In summary, the ability of the single-purpose agency to approach land use and natural resource management in a comprehensive way is limited by all of the elements cited. The ability of a single-purpose agency to claim sole jurisdiction over its own area of expertise should be doomed as the need for multipurpose planning increases. Government must learn to deal with the interagency problem effectively and to provide the necessary incentives that will create a true spirit of cooperation between agencies. This is something that will be difficult to achieve. Without the framework of a dynamic planning system and comprehensive development plan for land use control against which to guide and direct such agencies, it might be impossible.

Balancing the Access of Particular and Diffused Interests

Environmental problems usually involve a public or private actor responding to a particular set of incentives, seeking a limited objective, and not taking into account the impact of the actions involved on other values. Typically, if the third party effect—the externality caused by the primary activity—is important to a group that easily identifies its interest, there will be a potent political base from which to seek mitigation. The worst problems arise when the externality affects many people but means little to any one of them—a poorer basis on which to organize. The sum of the effect may be large, but the diffused interests are at a disadvantage if the cost to avoid it is immediate and significant to only a few, even though the cost is far less in sum than the benefit. The diffused effect may also be more conjectural, uncertain, long-range, and intangible—therefore less amenable to quantification.

Improving the information available about diffused effects, and easing access to public redress for those who represent such interests, is an obvious approach to improving environmental management. The environmental impact statement and the associated review process are steps in this direction—environmental management councils are another. Means should be sought to strengthen and increase such devices.

The Environmental Data-Base Problem

"Earth Day" 1970 spawned a concern for ecological systems with emphasis on biological communities and their well-being. Professional ecologists were quick to point out that we had in hand only a fraction of the understanding required to manage such systems rationally. As one conflict situation after another has come, and only occasionally gone, it is apparent that we usually lack the analytical tools and the data base to judge what impacts have resulted or will result. Research is moving rapidly—if not fast enough—to provide the analytical tools. But biological phenomena call for monitoring and data collecting with different spatial and time dimensions than for other phenomena. All this applies in its own way to evaluating the social impacts of environmental changes.

Biological processes are obviously affected by differences in the seasons. "Natural" changes have a way of showing themselves in shifts over the years, not the months. Thus, a few observations over the period needed to study and design a project can never adequately characterize the ecological processes involved unless it is possible to tie into a long-term data base.

Environmental problems are not restricted to biological phenomena. Social effects, from taxes to juvenile delinquency, pose many of the same kinds of data problems. Cause and effect cannot be related, even crudely, unless there are both analytical techniques to estimate them and data that go beyond those which can be collected by the project-design activity. Research can solve the problems of technique, but only organizations to monitor and collect the data can solve the problem of the data base.

6.5 Incremental Changes to Consider

The following are some suggested institutional changes that could improve natural resource management in the basin through relatively incremental changes in existing programs and policies. These changes would largely facilitate the expression of values and resource-use objectives that are not easily achieved now.

Possible Innovations in the Near- and Mid-Term

Agricultural Districts

In New York State there is a strong interest in protecting contiguous tracts of agricultural and other open space land from premature urban influence. In the last 60 years, about 12 million acres—more than half of the farmland in the state—has gone out of farm use. However, approximately one-third of New York's 30.6 million acres are still in farms.

Urban expansion has played an important role in the viability of agricultural areas. Each year about 10,000 to 15,000 acres of cropland are directly converted to urban uses in New York. But several times that much are either idled or underutilized because of scattered development resulting in speculation and land use conflicts.

The concern for the plight of agricultural areas under urban influence has led to a series of policy efforts in the state during the past decade. Special farm assessment bills, similar to a New Jersey law that provides for present-use assessment of farmland, were passed by the legislature twice in the middle 1960s but vetoed by Governor Rockefeller. But interest in preserving agriculture was growing. Shortly after the two vetoes a Governor's Commission on the Preservation of Agricultural Land in New York was created. This temporary commission later led to the creation of a permanent Agricultural Resources Commission.

Meanwhile, other people were looking to the possibility of extending the use of the police-power approach to deal with agricultural preservation, along with many other regional and state-level land use concerns. With the planning efforts of the New York Office of Planning Coordination in the late 1960s, the preservation of viable commercial agriculture became, for perhaps the first time, a major concern of planning in New York.

To implement the goals for improved land use, OPC proposed a large-scale revamping of the planning and land use control laws of the state. The proposal included a shifting of many functions from local jurisdictions to the counties and the state, and from lay people to professional planners. In particular, areas of critical state concern would have been created, including the major farmlands of the state. Within these areas, state zoning could have been used, if necessary, to stop the further expansion of urban uses.

OPC never had the chance to try its approach. The 1970 legislature instead reduced OPC's budget by more than half and changed its name to Office of Planning Services without even voting on the omnibus land use proposals. Opposition to the threat of state zoning was especially intense in these rural portions of the state where many of the farm districts would have been located and where even local zoning did not exist.

The agricultural districts under present New York State law are best understood as a compromise approach that grew out of these experiences. First, they are a compromise in terms of the property tax provisions. Not all land qualifies for a present-use tax assessment. Farms outside agricultural districts can apply for present-use assessment, but under terms that not all landowners will find attractive. Even within a district, open land does not automatically qualify, but only farmland for which the owner can show that he sold an average of $10,000 worth of agricultural commodities during the past 2 years. Also, owners are subject to a 5-year tax rollback on the exempt tax if the land is converted to a nonfarm use.

Property tax considerations for commercial farms are only one of six major provisions that apply within agricultural districts. The others are that (a) local governments may not restrict or regulate farm structures or farming practices beyond the requirements of health and safety; (b) state agencies must modify administrative regulations and procedures to encourage the maintenance of commercial agriculture to the extent compatible with health, safety, and any applicable federal regulations; (c) the right of public agencies to acquire farmland by eminent domain is modified, though not removed, and these agencies are required to consider alternative areas; (d) the right of public agencies to provide municipal funds for facilities, such as sewer and water, that would encourage nonfarm development is also modified; and (e) the power of public service districts to tax farmland for sewer, water, and nonfarm drainage is restricted.

Agricultural districts represent a break with the traditional police-power approach to public influence of land use. They are essentially nonauthoritarian, although they do include a mixture of voluntary and mandatory provisions. The goals are simultaneously to encourage commercial farming as a living entity and to discourage the entrance of nonfarm uses.

Agricultural districts are initiated by local landowners of at least 500 acres who submit a proposal to the county legislative body. A proposed district then moves through a cumbersome series of county-level reviews, public hearings, and review by state-level groups such as the DEC, OPS, and the Agricultural Resources Commission. In the end, however, the successful formation of a district depends on landowner initiative, certification from DEC, and approval by the county legislature. Once through these hurdles, the district boundaries may not be changed by either landowner or county actions for at least 8 years.

Once an agricultural district is formed, there is no guarantee that the land in it will remain in agricultural use. The task of public agencies in acquiring land by eminent domain and providing municipal funds for sewer and water facilities within agricultural districts is made more difficult by DEC review (a possible 60-day holding period and public hearings), but the right to proceed is hardly removed. It is true that special public service districts are prohibited from taxing farmland for sewer, water, lighting, and nonfarm drainage improvements. There is, however, no restriction on building for nonfarm uses with septic tanks and wells, nor of taxing for municipal services after the conversion to urban use has taken place.

Agricultural districts have proven popular among rural landowners. To date, more than 100 districts have been formed in New York. Their 1 million acres represent more than one-eighth of all farmland in the state (Fig. 6-2). A large proportion are located in the Hudson Basin, with an especially large concentration in the mid-Hudson, less than 100 miles from New York City. This popularity is all the more remarkable considering the landowner initiative required, the cumbersome procedure for forming districts, and the very low incidence of requests for the tax-break provision of agricultural districts. In short, agricultural districts do seem to be much more acceptable to rural landowners than zoning. Agricultural districts do try explicitly to meet the needs of an extensive land use that have remained virtually ignored by traditional planning and zoning approaches.

But popularity among landowners does not necessarily mean that agricultural districts will be effective in protecting viable farming areas from urban influences. In areas where speculation is strong and there is a possibility of urban intrusion within 8 years, agricultural districts have not been formed. It is significant that, despite the overall popularity of agricultural districts, none have been proposed for Long Island, even on its eastern tip. In this regard,

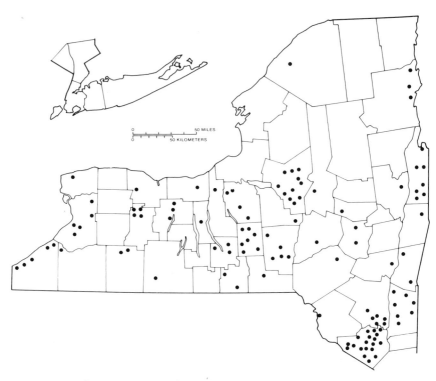

Fig. 6-2.   Location of agricultural districts, November 1, 1973.

one wonders just how permanent agricultural districts will be and whether the present ones will last 8 years. Some argue that agricultural districts are mainly a temporary tax reprieve for the farmer who is not yet ready to retire.

It appears from the limited experience to date that agricultural districts will have to be strengthened or combined with other tools if farming is to be preserved where the incentives of possible capital gains are strong. The possibility of pooling the development rights of landowners within an ag-ricultural district is but one tool that could be investigated further. In this way, the capital gains from the conversion of any particular piece of land would be shared by all landowners, thereby avoiding the overwhelming finan-cial incentive for the individual landowner to convert to a nonfarm use without fully considering the impacts of his action on surrounding landowners.

If farmland is to be preserved in many areas, agricultural districts will have to be included in a more general strategy of land use management. It is doubtful that the residents of Suffolk County would be willing to spend millions of dollars for agricultural preservation just so the nation will be assured of the continuation of a commercially viable potato industry on Long Island. What they would like to see is the preservation of large contiguous tracts of open space land that will enhance expanding urban areas. Clearly, one of the important challenges ahead in modifying agricultural preservation policies will be to provide for a stronger role for the local urbanizing area in policy determination so that preserved agricultural land can still be farmed commercially. One avenue for doing this might be to modify agricultural districts so that it is easier for counties, for example, to buy or lease development rights from landowners inside the districts.

Rural Land Districts for Nonfarm Landowners

Agricultural districts offer a starting point for the protection of the integrity of farm areas. But many rural areas are not farmed, are not occupied by commercial recreation activities, and do not necessarily have many public access lands or recreational facilities. They do typically have residences, some on large holdings, more on 5- to 100-acre parcels and a surprising number of houses on small lots.

The proportion of seasonal residences varies with the commuting distance to a job center or with access to water. The open country environment is itself a man-made resource that is created, shared, and enjoyed by all. The landowners around a common property resource, such as a lake, may recognize their common interest and organize into an association. But public services are generally provided by the town and county, and few are tailored to the special needs of these various property owners. There are numerous untapped opportunities here for providing special services that can simultaneously enhance the ability of the natural resources to meet the needs of existing resource users and protect those resources from incompatible development. A complex example from which insights can be drawn are some of the large land-holding clubs in the Adirondacks. Here, most of the land may be owned in common by the cottage owners, and everything from stocking fish and selling timber to installing the tennis courts and operating the bar are done in common. At the other extreme, a number of individual agencies have tried to organize groups of landowners for much narrower purposes or have offered them particular services. Owners of small-scale forest parcels have been approached to engage in joint harvesting and marketing schemes. Wildlife habitat seems to be a semicollective product that is best enhanced when a number of individual property owners simultaneously carry out edge maintenance and food plant enhancement efforts. Cooperative hunter management schemes have been attempted to discourage posting. A few special-purpose districts have been formed to provide extra police or fire protection or trash collection. County soil and water conservation districts have provided technical assistance for pond construction and other conservation measures on the individual properties.

There is an opportunity here, borrowing from this and other experiences and from that of the New York Agricultural Districts program. Special improvement districts at the town or county level could be designed to serve the special needs of particular open-country, residential neighborhoods.

A lake district might improve the outlet structure, manage weeds in a main channel, provide a clubhouse, and contract for extra police services in the off-season. Owners in a wooded area might form a district to harvest timber subject to environmental considerations, to pool wildlife habitat and trail maintenance efforts, or to build a common swimming pool. To encourage such multiple-purpose resource-management entities, property owners might be offered some of the benefits available to farmers in agricultural districts in exchange for some joint action that has a wider value. Tax relief or other publicly provided consideration might be the quid pro quo for scenic easements, public fishing, public hunting, or public trail access. Such entities could be formed through the initiative, or with the assistance, of environmental management councils, soil and water conservation districts, planning boards, and the like.

Obviously, rural land districts for nonfarm landowners could try to do many things. It is unlikely that any program would attempt all of the points listed above. But opportunities do exist that would aid in the preservation of rural land.

Freshwater Shoreline Management

Shorelines of lakes, ponds, rivers, and streams have unique physical, biological, and aesthetic values. They serve as prime attractions for seasonal and permanent residential development. Their importance is increased through their interrelationships with surrounding environments. Changes on shorelines can affect not only the shoreline itself, but also adjacent water bodies and the aesthetic character of the entire area. For these reasons, scarce natural shorelines must be protected from the kind of development that can cause unnecessary, and often irretrievable, loss and degradation of existing shoreline qualities.

Undisturbed shoreline vegetation serves the important functions of maintaining bank stability, filtering out particulate matter before it can enter the water, providing shade to keep water temperatures cool, and providing food for aquatic organisms. For human inhabitants, the vegetation provides privacy and noise filtration, and modulates strong winds, sunlight, and other climatic factors. Other shoreline types, such as natural beaches, bedrock outcrops, and cliffs, can provide unique recreational opportunities and aesthetic qualities.

The water side of the shoreline includes some of a water body's most critical aquatic habitats. Littoral zones are important as fish spawning areas. Weed-bed areas are important food source areas and serve as a refuge for small fish. This area is also an important habitat for many species of birds, mammals, reptiles, and amphibians. Shorelines are important aesthetic resources, both because of their visual and biological diversity and because they are visible from so many different points on the adjacent water body and on the opposite shore.

Construction activities of various types, filling and excavation, and storm drainage runoff can cause unsightly and destructive shoreline erosion and sedimentation on the water bottom. Clearing of vegetation can increase sunlight and water temperatures, increase local climatic variability, and remove potential screening. Construction of buildings, boathouses, parking areas, lawns, and other activities can all have an adverse aesthetic impact, the magnitude depending on the site's visibility and landscaping, and on building design, color, and construction materials. Docks, rafts, and boat launching sites and other shoreline alterations can also have adverse aesthetic impacts, and can adversely affect fish spawning areas and other key aquatic habitats. Operation of motorboats, especially on smaller lakes, can cause erosion of shorelines, conflict with other water uses, such as swimming and fishing, and create unwanted noise. Dam regulation of water levels can also cause shoreline erosion, expose large areas of lake bottom, and make access to the water edge more difficult.

Perhaps the greatest problems for many lakes are from on-site septic tank disposal systems. These systems are frequently improperly designed, located, constructed, and maintained; the result is often contamination of surface and drinking water by bacteria and viruses, and various taste- and odor-causing substances. On lakes and ponds, increased eutrophication rates result from the additional input of plant nutrients such as phosphorus and nitrogen. Discharges into lakes from sewage treatment plants may also cause the same problem.

Another problem related to the layout of subdivisions is that of shorefront access. Many developers divide their entire shorefront into as many high-priced lots as possible, leaving no access to shorefront for people buying back lots. Furthermore, the shoreline becomes developed and the setting is drastically altered, thus limiting the water's value as a community asset or attraction and often lowering surrounding land values.

Techniques are available for avoiding or mitigating the above problems. These techniques can take many forms: subdivision regulations; sanitary, building, and aquatic-recreation codes; zoning ordinances; permit systems requiring detailed project review and determinations by local and state planning, health, and conservation agencies; use of covenants and deed restrictions; creation of property owners associations; and creation of groups to operate dams and regulate water levels. Basic restrictions are the establishment of minimum shoreline lot widths and lot sizes, minimum setbacks of buildings and individual septic tank disposal systems (at least 100 feet), and restrictions on cutting shoreline vegetation. The specific numbers used should reflect the intensity of development desired and the sensitivity of the local environment. These restrictions should be flexible enough to encourage the clustering of lots.

If this approach is used, the land most suitable for building would be built on, and the remaining land would be preserved as open space. Community shoreline areas should be provided with adequate beach, docking, and boat-launch facilities for back lots and shoreline lots. These facilities should be provided for shoreline owners on the basis of not more than one set for every five to ten lots, and covenants should prohibit them from individual sites. Where they are proposed, in subdivisions and on single isolated lots, permits should be required from a local or state regulating body. In the case of those extremely overcrowded and dilapidated shorelines that are best described as recreational slums, a shoreline renewal program is a distinct possibility.

Ideally, undeveloped freshwater lakes of less than 100 surface acres should have their shorelines kept in a natural condition. Development should be kept out of sight of the lake and the lake preserved for the use of all. Where there are special problems of fragile shorelines, susceptible aquatic life, water quality, or conflicting recreational uses, local governments or property owners associations could adopt various forms of water-use restrictions, even general use-zoning of the water surface. These can limit the size of motors allowed, maximum speeds, and the time and area where motor-boating will be allowed.

Disposal of sewage is a major problem in many shoreland developments. It is advisable to provide a central sewage system and community or municipal treatment plant for as much lakeshore development as possible. If the discharge would significantly affect lake or pond eutrophication rates, these plants should provide tertiary treatment for the removal of plant nutrients, particularly phosphorus. Subsurface discharge into sand beds can be another effective method of disposal. At the least, discharge should be located at the outlets of lakes if possible, so that it can flow into running water courses that have greater self-regeneration capacity.

Saltwater Shoreline Management

The federal program to encourage coastal zone management is an important and necessary step, but only preliminary to an effective management program. Coastal planning, like conventional land use planning, is a derivative of state powers, but it has been customary for states to delegate land control to local governments. Now the states are being asked by the federal government to draw back this delegation of authority selectively, so that the development of coastal resources will not be dissipated by decisions based only on local and short-range objectives. This next step in the formation and implementation of a state coastal planning program is a difficult one. The coastal states must proceed with respect for existing prerogatives. If local governments become unduly alarmed at the shift in planning powers, they can cripple or kill a state coastal program.

The need for political caution, however, should not overshadow the necessity for proceeding with determination in the task of directing and coordinating the use of coastal resources. This includes the regulation of resources that are not usually within the purview of planning agencies and the effective coordination of the actions of government agencies—including those at the federal level. As defined by each state, the geographical jurisdiction of coastal zone commissions may include the shores of rivers, estuaries, and swamps wherever there is an admixture of saline and fresh water. The zone extends seaward to the 3-mile limit. A commission's powers can include regulation of the traffic on the water surface, as well as the use of the floor and resources below.

A coastal zone study is now being done in New York State to develop recommendations for a coastal management plan and the means of implementing the plan. This study will be an important new step in integrated land, water, and resource management. It will be a departure from the land orientation of most present planning, helping to clarify a complex and overlapping array of responsibilities. The greatest challenge, though, will be working with local governments to help them clarify their coastal policies and to encourage them to broaden their views of land and resource use.

Revitalized Small Watersheds

The small watershed movement was largely spurred by the small watershed protection program of the U.S. Soil Conservation Service, with its heavy emphasis on structural flood protection for farmland. Projects that involved other benefits, such as recreation or urban flood protection, are disadvantaged. The Water Resources Development Act of 1974 authorized at least 80% cost sharing for any flood-risk reduction measures such as floodproofing, relocation of buildings and activities, purchase of wetlands, and development easements. It remains to be seen whether the traditional bias against urban flood risks will be continued in the SCS program. Changes in the Federal Flood Insurance Act mean that every flood risk area of significance will at least be identified. This should lead to more local awareness of the problems of resource management that are flood related. In any case, it is time to take a new look at small watershed projects.

More to the point is the opportunity for counties to use the small watershed as a unit of public management. Any government has problems providing more control of a resource use in one part of its jurisdiction as compared to another. Counties in the New York portion of the region have few such opportunities, but the small watershed protection district is one of these. The enabling legislation emphasizes flood-risk management and other problems of water quantity. Water quality questions should be considered for inclusion. Not the least of these is the problem of nonpoint sources of pollution, including silt.

Multiple Use of Water-Supply Reservoirs

Water-supply reservoirs of metropolitan cities, such as New York, are often regarded as single-use preserves. However, the idea that public water sources need to be protected by excluding all other uses from their environs is based on the epidemiology of a prior day, and on the water-treatment and engineering knowledge of that time. It is clearly possible, within the present state of the art, to open up these large water bodies for much greater public use, including swimming, picnicking, camping, and boating, without endangering public health.

The famous canard about the number of times the River Rhine passes through German and Dutch bladders is not completely absurd. Many cities, small and large, rely on highly polluted water as the raw material for a quite potable supply. There is ample proof that the pristine quality of the water maintained at the Rondout, Ashokan, and Pepacton reservoirs and the entire Croton Reservoir system may be a luxury from which the people of the State of New York can well afford to trade off a small amount of quality loss—if any—in exchange for multiple use. A phased program of added amenity areas and uses could be made available in the New York City reservoir systems, as well as in the reservoir systems of Newark and the upstate New York communities, while a monitoring program could easily detect any approaching contamination.

It may be that this change is linked, in practical terms, to the creation of a regional authority to develop further water-supply capacity. The drought of the 1960s showed the limits of existing capacity. Subsequent studies have shown the advantages of a regional, intermunicipal, and, perhaps, interstate approach. Multiple use of existing and future facilities may be an important element in reaching agreement among the many parties involved. Upstream communities should be more willing to see a regional water-supply agency created even larger than the New York City Board of Water Supply if it is charged with enhancing the multiple use of facilities that now provide so little to the recreation industry of the upstream region.

Multiple use of water-supply reservoirs is technically feasible. It will add a needed recreation resource, reduce overuse of other bodies of water until that problem can be addressed, and, finally, may be the key to agreement on a new institutional arrangement to solve the water-supply problems of the basin's urbanizing areas.

6.6 Selected Structural Changes in Programs and Policies

Major structural changes do occur in our policies, programs, and other institutions for managing natural resources, though more slowly than any advocate for reform would wish. It is useful to have both a sense of the larger trends in institutional change and a sense of some of the larger goals toward which our institutions should be evolving.

As professionals from several fields, the participants in this study are committed to knowledge-based analytical and design techniques as a basis for public and private action. Just as the courts are not recognizing regional effects of land use decisions as a reasonable basis for land use controls, we have long felt, individually, that more effective use should be made of analytics that consider a wide scope. This means that land use decisions must become more shared and must shift somewhat away from a local focus. Local decision-makers should be able to see more effectively how state and federal programs can and should fit together to best serve the needs of their areas. As more federal and state programs evolve, the local coordination role will become more important. At the same time, regional and statewide impacts must be more effectively taken into account. With more people, more wealth, and more activity, the scope for extra local efforts will also be greater. Thus, in this section we seem to be pleading for more capacity at the local level to make sound choices that, at the same time, take into account more effectively the interests of the larger community. This will require some reforms that we can see quite clearly and others that are only questions in our minds at this time.

Reforming and restructuring of government follow some cyclical patterns, which the professional and academic community should take into account in its examination of resource management. There is a kind of natural history of change that starts with a growing awareness of a problem. Those who would speak for the diffused interests in an issue become more articulate and their case is more widely understood. A climax is reached and policy changes are made. The reformers have achieved less than they wanted but enough to relax for a time. The more particular interests soon become almost the only active nongovernmental participants until the next wave of reform is triggered.

Students of public programs must recognize that it is largely during these periods of interest that there is a market for their wares. It is then that there is a need for comprehensive understanding and articulated images of what the future could be like. Of course, that is also when resources for research become available, often only to produce results in time for the next cycle of issue examination. We speak to the problem of speeding up this cycle in Section 6.7. Here the cycle is significant because we anticipate that a climax is not far off and that the elements we have developed may be ready for consideration.

Matching the Level of Government to the Situation

Traditionally, land use control has been exercised at the local level of government, although the authority exists at higher levels. This tradition, commonly referred to as home rule, has in many cases been a stumbling block to the emerging interest in regional, state, and federal participation in land use planning. Today's sprawling transportation systems, growing environmental awareness, and massive development proposals with wide-ranging social impacts emphasize the need to regulate land use at the unit of government closest to those people who will be most directly involved with the potential impacts. Home rule, in other words, should be more nearly based on the "home" likely to be impacted.

Land use controls at higher levels of government should complement local land use controls. For example, knowledge that the state is going to regulate the land use will often encourage local governments to do their own land use regulation. In one method of encouraging local ordinances sensitive to nonlocal interests, the state may impose land use controls directly with the provision that, as local governments develop their own controls protecting state, regional, and local interests, most of the land use regulation authority shifts back to the local level. In this strategy, the state would eventually retain only a monitoring role and perhaps control over projects whose scope is too large for local regulatory capabilities.

Defining the proper role for each level of government based upon the impacts of potential land uses can become a complex matter. Impacts most often vary inversely to the distance from the project site and, therefore, there is room for argument about when the impacts become so insignificant that a definable area of impact cannot be determined.

This task group feels that the federal role should be primarily confined to the establishment of national land use goals and objectives and to coordinating decisions on projects that cross state boundaries. A further federal role might be the establishment of general criteria for state land use planning and control and the provision of incentives for the states to consider more fully national goals and objectives in their own regulatory activities.

The states must make the basic determination of whether their land use control program should operate within a central state agency, or be delegated to regional authorities, or to some combination of the two. Regardless of the decision, such agencies and authorities should be interdisciplinary. They should have a sufficiently broad base to incorporate all legitimate concerns into both the decision-making and planning processes. After the adoption of a generalized state land use plan, state control and review of projects should be limited to those of truly state concern. It is not clear what criteria should be used in choosing these. State-level concern might be defined by project magnitude, such as acreage or potential population; or by location, such as projects involving critical environmental areas of importance to a widespread population; or by type of project, such as transportation complexes.

The Adirondack Park Agency experience in New York State is one experimental effort that will provide an improved basis for the evaluation of a partnership arrangement between state and local government. This program distinguishes between projects of strictly local concern and projects of state concern. It also includes a middle ground for projects that are, based on their size or location, of lesser state concern but that may still produce impacts beyond the immediate locality. In these cases, an attempt is being made to broaden the typical local government review process to bring in elements more common in a regional planning and review process. The success of this program will be a good indication of the potential of such intergovernmental working relationships, as well as of the capability of local units of government to consider objectively impacts that may reach well beyond their own political boundaries.

Financial and Fiscal Reform

Fiscal impact is the single most powerful incentive in shaping land use decisions. In fact, it may be said that assessed valuation is the major criterion for granting or denying zoning changes by local government. Zoning ordinances are now being devised that give the widest latitude to nonresidential uses, in the hope of attracting tax ratables with low municipal service costs in contrast to a far more limited scope for residential uses with their greater need for community services. To further this policy, low-density, large-lot residential zoning is encouraged, and without adequate concern for natural resource allocation or accurate assessment of municipal costs to income.

The fiscal position of local governments in the region has been changing over the years. Much like the difference between the myth of constitutional protection for private profits in land and the reality of the court interpretations, there is probably a myth and reality problem here. Local governments have been rapidly moving away from dependence on the property tax. The outlook is for that dependence to decrease even further. Other pressures for reform exist, and it behooves those concerned with environmental and resource management to add their concern to that of others. It would be a shame to have a major shift occur—and we are on the brink of one—without the environmental arguments for reforms being considered.

New Jersey, under court order to change the basis for funding education in that state, has adopted a state income tax. In New York and Connecticut the seeds of change have been planted and cultivated. The arguments being heard in the courts note the wide differences in funds spent per child and the relationship this has to the tax base per child, even under state-aid formulas that are supposed to correct such inequities. The equal protection clause of the Constitution is involved.

We may be on the brink of a major change in local government financing, but like most such brinks in governmental affairs, it is one more in a series of incremental changes. By 1962, New York school districts collected $616 million in property taxes, slightly less than half of their total revenues of $1296 million. State aid went from $598 million in 1962 to $1786 million in 1972, but by then real property taxes had also increased to $1726 million—almost the same proportions as a decade earlier. Federal aid, it should be noted, moved from $10.8 million to $161.1 million. Enrollment in this period changed far less than expenditures, rising from 1.8 million to 2.4 million. By 1962, schools had already established a dependence on state funding and increased it by 1972, in absolute if not relative terms, to the property tax.

From 1962 to 1972, local governments in New York moved even more rapidly away from the property tax. In 1962, total property-tax collections, including school taxes, were $2.37 billion in total revenues of $5.2 billion. By 1972, real-property taxes had more than doubled to $5.4 billion, but total revenues had more than tripled to $17.1 billion. State aid went from $1.3 billion to $5.1 billion while federal aid rose even more steeply from $253 million to $2.62 billion. Local governments have been the "growth companies" of American governments. In the New York portion of the Hudson Basin this has been accomplished with a declining relative dependence on the property tax.

How are these trends—increased dependence on sales taxes, federal revenue sharing, and cost sharing of local services by state and federal government—affecting the provision of necessary services and the achievement of other goals? Clearly the property owner has an obligation to pay his fair share of taxes. Traditionally, a "fair share" has been based upon a mix of ability to pay and services rendered. We would add another consideration—the incentive for socially desirable actions on the part of both the individual and the community in environmental and resource management.

The real property tax suffers on all counts in many of its applications. If true market prices are used to set tax valuations—and the trend is to do this more strictly—then the bias in the market to value more land than is needed for intensive purposes puts substantial pressure on those who would use it for extensive purposes. At the same time, the capital gain on land when realized as income is taxed at a preferential rate—half the rate on income from most other sources. This alone encourages inflating of land value. Frequently, tax districts to extend public services, such as sewer and water, charge on an average-cost basis for operating costs and on an assessed-valuation basis for facilities. On the one hand, this arrangement does not charge the hard-to-service customer enough; on the other hand, it charges the developed land too much to the benefit of the undeveloped land. For the extensive-resource user, any such charges will be for services not needed for the extensive activity and will discourage its continuance.

Changing the basis for local government finance in areas where extensive uses of natural resources are to be encouraged should, in our opinion, be a high-priority issue for future long-term structural change in public policy.

Achieving State Agencies That Will Reinforce Local Government

Studies of one type of environmental conflict situation, that arising downstream or downwind from many modern poultry houses, can indicate directions for administered solutions to other environmental problems in open-country, low-differentiation, local jurisdictions.

In many rural communities, an informal voluntary industry committee approach can be as effective as any other approach in bringing together necessary technical expertise and social regulatory mechanisms. Although more formalized regulatory mechanisms are certainly conceivable, many rural areas do not have the administrative or political resources to support them at an effective level.

Rural people have traditionally been relatively tolerant of the odors and wastes that result from what are considered normal farming operations. A person of urban background is often less tolerant of such practices. Since the proportion of urban to rural people is increasing in the open-country portions of the Hudson Basin, the external effects of agricultural wastes, for example, could be increasing even if the actual volume of odor and waste leaving the farm were not. Mechanisms that rely on the role of self-esteem and community esteem may still be enough of an incentive to incur waste management costs as long as the effects are only noticed by neighbors, there is good neighbor-to-neighbor communication, and costs are not too large relative to net returns. But all of these conditions are changing in the direction away from effective control.

A frequent response to waste management problems is to organize an industry committee. The poultry-waste problem will be used as an example here, but the analysis would be similar for many other waste-management problems. A typical local poultry-waste committee would include poultry industry leaders, representatives of local industries that support agriculture, and those, such as county extension agents, who have access to the latest in waste management technology. Such a group is able to improve communication between rural and urban neighbors, present a solid front to the various groups and agencies who may get involved, and channel authoritative suggestions for reducing costs. The result is that conflicts are dampened, and the limited resources of local governments are not taxed. Something is done to meet the problem without forcing a choice between urban and rural constituencies.

The committee's usefulness rests on its virtual monopoly of technical knowledge about poultry operations. At any stage in a conflict, the complaining parties face the question, How can the poultryman alleviate the problem, short of discontinuing his business? Such a committee's informal approach to settling conflicts case-by-case also emphasizes a restoration of "neighborly relations." This approach was followed in the first major court case involving poultry wastes in New York State. A committee visited both the poultryman and the offended landowners nearby. It is important that neighborly relations had existed between the two for a long time before the dispute which resulted in a court fight. The recreation enterprise had apparently lost faith in its poultryman neighbor with the changes in the poultry operation over a period of years. The committee's problem was one of repairing these relations.

An industry committee obviously is an appropriate approach to many rural situations. But unless waste-management technology is developed that has less impact on net returns than anything apparent to date, it cannot be expected to provide a completely effective, long-term solution. What can we expect in its place? To answer that question, we must recognize that rural governments, under pressure from rising urban populations and/or urban interests, are the main candidates for the problems envisioned here. They are typically very short of administrative and political resources—at least by urban standards—to deal with what are really problems of life style.

In the poultry cases that have been studied, when an offended resort operator or resident felt that personal consultation with a poultry operator had failed, his next action was likely to be an appeal to local authorities. Complaints may go directly to the health officer or to the supervisor or other member of the town board, in which case it may be referred back to the health officer.

But the health officer's ability to cope with the poultry-odor problem, or any other waste-management problem, is severely limited. Health regulations, after all, have very limited applicability to these cases. Health officers serve as consulting experts to the town boards rather than as enforcement officers. Sanitary inspectors can function as enforcement officers for town boards. However, the town boards, like the health inspectors, are limited to the legal remedies that exist in their town ordinances. They do, however, speak with authority as the elected legislative body of the town and are empowered to act as boards of health. They have the authority to write new regulations potentially punitive to the poultry or other waste-producing industry, and they have used this power with some effect in the past.

Local governments may adopt various forms of regulations in the attempt to solve the problem. In the case of poultry wastes, some towns in the Hudson Basin have been experimenting with special poultry ordinances and zoning ordinances that would restrict the construction of new poultry operations to specific areas. This makes existing operations outside the poultry zones "nonconforming uses" with restrictions on expansion. However, the difficulties of administering such regulations in these towns, where government tends to be on a rather personal basis, make the effects of such ordinances very unpredictable.

When the urban-oriented groups become sufficiently strong to press for some kind of more effective administered solution, what character might it take? Urban zoning tools can be modified to allow for a conditional land use permit in an agricultural zone where certain performance standards are laid down, such as limits on odor emissions or waste discharges. Or specifications about the way problems are to be dealt with can be called for in an application to begin or enlarge a land use. But these approaches call for judgments and actions that the local government is not well equipped to make on either technical or political grounds.

Deciding what standards should be set, and then whether or not they have been met, obviously calls for reasonably sophisticated staff support. But the bigger task is to marshall political support for decisions that are between an arbitrary yes and an arbitrary no. In many situations of strong conflict, where the opposing parties are a significant part of the constituency involved, it may be easier to satisfy completely one side or the other. The consequences for the officials of leaving both sides strongly dissatisfied are too great to take the risk.

Although it may be difficult to foresee acceptable solutions to the conflict problems raised by agricultural, forestry, mining, and other "rural" wastes developing independently at the local level, more significant measures are developing at the state and federal level. For example, it is instructive to note the effect that New York State's Pure Water Program had on the Long Island duck-wastes problem. For many years, this has been cited as an example of pollution caused by farming—usually perceived as atypical. Even the advent of substantial urban influence over county government had very limited effects; but with a new statewide effort, the tools for more rapid change were at hand. Vigorous state-led action has produced very noticeable changes in waste management by these producers. It should be noted that, in the meantime, the agricultural establishment had put some effort into the development of waste-management technology specifically tailored to duck production. But when a technical solution was finally imposed, it was drawn from the inventory of conventional processes.

Perhaps the worst possible outcome would be regulation by a state agency whose clientele is narrowly urban, whose technological base has no linkages with the institutions of resource management expertise, and which acts independently of local governments and has no communication channels with local groups. One expectation then would be a period of ineffectiveness in achieving more intensive environmental management, because the requirements the agency sought to impose would be so unreasonable that industry objections would undercut political support for the program. A more likely outcome is an awkward period in which a number of operators are forced to undertake waste-management investments that may later be shown to be ineffective or more expensive than other effective means.

It is a fairly well-accepted principle of public regulation that performance will be colored by the clientele of the agency involved. This clientele includes the interest groups that support it and those whom it has been regulating for a sufficiently long period that interchange of staff and executive personnel and other strong interactions have developed. It also includes the professional groupings and research agencies from which it draws its staff and new technology. Regulation will also be colored by the kind of technical knowledge built up before regulation takes place.

Society and the extensive-resource industries would be better off if regulation were facilitated by an agency with clientele in both rural and urban areas, which drew staff and technology from professions and agencies that serve both. But it is not clear that the agricultural-waste problem by itself, for example, is a sufficiently broad base for such a unique arrangement. More likely this could come about by the modification of existing state or regional agencies. For example, a shift of water pollution programs out of a public-health-oriented agency into a multi-interest resource agency has been a step in this direction. The development of an agency charged with the management of all the problems of urban growth into rural areas might be another. But whatever the vehicle, there is a need for state-level agencies that can help rural, local governments to deal with problems of natural resource management and conflict resolution effectively.

Elements of a Model State Land Use Law

The elements that should be embodied in a model land use law include the following: comprehensive statewide planning, including the establishment of an office and professional cadre; an orderly means for determining the point of state intervention; the ability of the state to establish the existence of overriding public interest in private land use decisions; an orderly methodology to deal with the process of comprehensive statewide planning and its dissemination to the local level; provisions for the state to "watch" the state, as well as for the regions and municipalities to watch the state; regional mechanisms and regional planning bodies, including means of resolving interregional conflict; direct addressing of the "taking issue"; adequate public funds for the acquisition of areas of critical state concern; and public exposure and visible decision-making in land use and natural-resource management at the state, regional, and local levels.

All of these are addressed in the American Law Institute's "Model State Land Development Code," a formidable document still being deliberated by concerned members of the legal profession and interested bodies in the several states. It is a code which this group feels is well suited to the needs of states in the Hudson Basin region.

There is, however, one additional issue not addressed in any current land use law, except peripherally—a measure recently defeated in the Vermont legislature—that is, the conscious control of the public infrastructure. No one has yet proposed, at the state level, the regulation of the public infrastructure, including the energy infrastructure, to influence the timing of the provision of distribution facilities at the local and regional level. This is a potential device of great import in the entire matter of effective state and regional land use control and orderly community growth policy.

The notion behind the current attitude toward energy infrastructure is that it should be the ever-present, unfailing resource, available any time and at any place. The provision of electric energy to an outlying location is a subsidy to that property in the sense that the extra expense of providing energy to a remote point is under a rate system based only on electrical usage borne by the rate payers collectively. Of course, this hidden subsidy is ultimately reflected in land values in the outlying locations. This is unfortunate at a time when speculation is already so disruptive of rational land use patterns.

In the light of the new economics of energy and the need for energy conservation, it may be time to question the unilateral right of the public utility company to extend its services as it sees fit. Is it not within the realm of possibility to create an energy district similar to the mechanisms for administering sewage and water facilities? Such an organization at the local and regional level would work with, yet be in a position to govern, the electric utility in the provision and timing of energy facilities.

Transferable Development Rights

The land market currently operates in a way that unreasonably encourages the property owner to expect large capital gains. At the same time, it produces great uncertainty about where those capital gains will be realized. Private landowners naturally resist any controls that reduce their chance of having rain from that silver-lined cloud fall on their land. Local governments, with an eye to their tax base opportunities, similarly resist controls from above. And perhaps their expectation of the net benefits of community expansion are just as inflated as the private owners' expectations of capital gains. The net result is urban sprawl and much more land denied to extensive uses than is efficient. This effect extends to the farthest reaches of the Hudson Basin region, including the forest and wilderness areas of the Adirondacks, and the potato fields and salt marshes of the tip of Long Island.

What to do? Will incremental changes now underway be enough? Can structural "cures" for the operation of the "unregulated" land market ever be designed that will be convincingly better than the disease? We believe there is no alternative but to try.

A wave of recent efforts has focused on preserving farmlands, wetlands, floodplains, fisheries, or historic sites as land uses that have a value to society for which a present owner cannot charge a rent. Certainly such efforts must and will continue. But is there a mechanism that could be introduced into the land market that would meet the following criteria? It should be available for a variety of purposes and resource-use objectives. Uncertainty should be reduced about where development will take place. The need to appeal to the public purse for funding should be realistic, not massive. The number of land-market "roulette players" should be reduced and other measures to influence resource use publicly should be facilitated.

The following discussion summarizes the situation in Suffolk County, where experimentation is proceeding on ways of altering the land market in two related ways. In a recent decision, Suffolk County has embarked on a plan to attempt the preservation of its rapidly dwindling farmland and open space by the county purchasing development rights for suitable land. The Town of Southampton, also in Suffolk County, has carried out its own experiment by incorporating the transfer of development rights between private parties into its local zoning ordinance. Although not foolproof, both of these approaches offer potential opportunities to mitigate the windfalls or wipeouts from public actions that could greatly help to facilitate a more rational land use control system.

The Present Situation in Suffolk County*

Suffolk County is the fastest growing county in the nation. Its population increased from 161,055 to 1.2 million from 1931 to 1973. The open space and rural charm sought by these urbanites has virtually disappeared. Today, they can find only 2000 acres of farmland and 81,000 acres of vacant land in the western part of the county, most of which is scattered in a random fashion. In the five towns of eastern Suffolk County, there are about 57,980 acres of farmland and about 202,580 acres of vacant land left.

Existing farmland is mainly found in three towns: Riverhead, Southampton, and Southold. It is not scattered but in rather large contiguous tracts. Because of their superb physical properties, the soils of these farms have excellent potential for use as either housing lots or farmland. They are large, cleared tracts owned by only one or two persons, as contrasted with vacant land that is mostly brushland or wooded and whose ownership is fragmented.

The 60,000 acres of farmland are predominantly in potatoes. There are 262 potato farmers who own a total of 24,260 acres. Nearly 50 farmers have 200 acres or more. About 150 acres is a sound acreage for growing potatoes, and those who have less must rent land. Since real estate taxes range from $35 to $60 per acre, a farmer has to pay up to $7500 for 150 acres. This tax burden is extremely high because potato farming in this area requires large amounts of capital investments in irrigation and machinery, since the hiring of seasonal labor is almost impossible.

The market value of an acre of land in eastern Suffolk in 1973 was between $3000 and $15,000 with most land in the upper part of the range. A farmer who owned 150 acres with a value of $10,000 per acre was, according to the

*This discussion draws upon material prepared by Johan B. W. Scholvinck, Department of Agricultural Economics, SUNY, and College of Agriculture and Life Sciences, Cornell University, Ithaca, New York.

Internal Revenue Service, worth $1.5 million. His heirs would have to pay 34% of this amount, or $510,000. Thus, sale of the farm is the only alternative even if the heirs want to continue farming, since the market prices cannot be paid from farm income. Most farmers have to rent land from a nonfarm owner to have enough acreage to grow potatoes economically. The rent they pay about equals the real estate tax paid by the nonfarm owner. Renting is risky because the speculator can sell the land at any time to a developer.

Suffolk County's Plan for the Preservation of Farmland

Preservation of these outstanding farmlands became a major concern of County Executive John V. N. Klein soon after his election in 1972. He established an informal Agricultural Advisory Committee consisting of 12 farmers, two agribusinessmen, and the county extension administrator.

In March 1974, this committee decided on the following solution: that the county should be authorized to purchase development rights on approximately 50,000 acres of farmland on a voluntary basis. Neither the landowner nor the county would be required to sell or to purchase the rights. Once the development rights on a property had been acquired they could not be marketed by the county unless the sale was authorized by a general referendum.

It is estimated that the agricultural value of the land is about 20% of the real estate market value, or from $600 to $3000 per acre. The difference between the real estate market value and the agricultural use value will be the price of the development right.

The Agricultural Advisory Committee also considered recommending that the county purchase the fee ownership and lease the land back to the farmer. However, the committee discarded this solution for the following reasons: (a) The farmer would have no guarantee that he could continue to rent the same land after the expiration of the lease. Because of the competitive bidding, the highest bidder for the rent would get the land. This uncertainty would discourage farmers from making any long-term investments in land that are so necessary in modern farming. (b) The government as a landlord is considered by many to be highly inefficient. The bureaucratic administrative system works too slowly and is not necessarily acquainted with farming activities. (c) The farmer could stop farming any time that he wanted to if conditions became bad. The land could then become idle and be vandalized. (d) The land would disappear from the tax rolls.

The Suffolk County Legislature recently acted on the proposal of the Agricultural Advisory Committee by authorizing the county acquisition of either the fee title or the development rights for appropriate farmland in the county. Both will be done on a voluntary basis, presumably over a number of years. To finance this program, $45 million was included in the county's capital budget. *

Transfer of Development Rights

The program that exists in the Town of Southampton also treats the right to develop land as separable from any particular land parcel. The development right is only one of the total bundle of rights that ordinarily go along with land ownership. The right to develop land may be bought and sold, just like land itself, if a proper market is created for the rights. In this case, the local zoning ordinance was used in an attempt to create both a supply and a demand for development rights.

Unlike Suffolk County, which plans to create a market for development rights solely for the purpose of transferring them to the public where they will not be used at all, the Southampton plan attempts to make development rights transferable among individuals. The creation of a market for development rights works as follows. The supply of rights comes from lands that are arbitrarily denied through zoning regulations, the right to develop to the level reflected in the land market. The demand for those rights comes from landowners who are awarded higher densities in certain areas than would otherwise be allowed, provided that they must first purchase additional development rights. In this way, growth can more easily be channeled from one place to another because the zoning game "losers" are compensated for their depreciated property value. The transfer of the development rights concept also considers a part of the total bundle of rights as transferable to other land parcels.

At first glance this concept appears attractive because of low costs to the community as a whole and almost no government participation. This might indeed be the case for the preservation of certain landmarks in a city, but when the objective is preservation of large contiguous tracts of extensive resource uses, the simplicity of the idea disappears for the following reasons:

1. Preservation of open land on a large scale will not be accomplished unless virtually every municipality mandates development-rights transfers. When municipality A has this concept, but adjacent municipality B does not, the chances are great that a potential developer will go to B because it is cheaper to develop there.

---

*In December 1974 the county solicited bids for the sale of development rights on 1800 parcels of farmland totalling 56,000 acres. After the receipt and screening of bids, the county legislature authorized a development-rights acquisition program covering about 14,000 acres. The first phase of the program, involving 3800 acres at a cost of $21 million, was about 50% complete in December 1978. The cost of the development rights has ranged between 60 and 80% of full market value. [Ed.]

2. A sufficient market will exist only if there is an incentive for the developer to build in the desired districts. The dual-density system can only create this incentive if the allowable residual density is low.

3. Besides the fact that the residual density has to be low, there must be enough development rights available. Although the transfer district may be designed to absorb exactly the amount of development rights freed by the designation of the preserve, there is no guarantee that these rights will indeed be available. The landowners in the preserve might want to wait, expecting that the value of these rights will increase. Purchase by government or condemnation are possible tools for overcoming this problem, but then political feasibility and financial problems arise immediately.

4. The opposite situation is possible if the landowners in the preserve offer their development rights while there are no buyers for these rights, Because of the mandatory nature of the preserve, the government would then have to buy these rights to sell them later to developers.

These are only some of the problems with applying the transferable development rights concept, but they are sufficient to illustrate why the transferable development rights tool has remained virtually unused in Southampton thus far.* There are, however, important potential advantages in the use of the development rights concept, including the following: (a) The landowners in the preserve will get a substantial, immediate tax break and will not be forced to sell the land to meet inheritance taxes. (b) This tax break creates a tax loss for the local community, but this can be compensated by the increased taxes paid by owners of land and buildings in the transfer district plus a real estate transfer tax that could be paid by the landowners in the preserve on their development rights. (c) The "windfall/wipeout" phenomenon would be mitigated because landowners in the preserve would be duly compensated as opposed to what would occur under exclusive zoning. Property owners in the transfer district would not obtain large capital gains because of public actions. (d) The so-called externality costs would be charged to those benefiting from the development process instead of to the whole community. (e) Development-rights transfer fits nicely with existing zoning techniques such as cluster development and planned unit development.

---

*Southampton authorized transfers of development rights (TDRs) as part of a new zoning ordinance adopted in 1972. So far the device has been used only once, to transfer rights from an awkwardly shaped 36-acre parcel to another property owned by the same developer. Both parcels had been zoned for 2-acre lots. The resulting 35-home subdivision was under construction as of December 1978. The parcel from which the rights were transferred has been acquired by the town as a groundwater-recharge area. [Ed.]

Suffolk County is an attractive place to apply the transferable development rights concept, partly because the size of the agricultural preserve is small and partly because the land values are high. However, the plan of county acquisition of development rights proposed may fail because of its voluntary nature, the high proportion of agricultural land owned by nonfarmers, and the high value of the development rights. Perhaps the $45 million already authorized by the county legislature might better be used to start a development-rights pool than to buy these rights and put them forever "in the freezer."

6.7 Strategies for Establishing Research Priorities and Utilizing Existing Knowledge

Strategies for Using Existing Knowledge

Do we need more knowledge about environmental problems? Certainly! But as the farmer is supposed to have said to the land grant college extension agent, "I only farm half as well as I know how now."

No students of environmental and resource management problems fail to be impressed by how little we know about the linkages between resource uses, about how to make the carrying capacity concept operational, about the effects of land use controls and the like. Yet most are somewhat bitter about how little of the experts' knowledge is really put to work.

Reasons for this are not difficult to hypothesize. Unfortunately, too little research is available on this topic for us to do much more than speculate. Lindblom's argument that fragmented, incremental decision-making, with its serial and disjointed character, actually makes the best use of available knowledge, is certainly worth reflection (Lindblom, 1959). The comprehensive planning model is so attractive to most experts because it fits the interrelatedness and size of the systems to be managed, makes great demands upon our models, and demand for our experts, too. Lindblom argues that the models and the experts have not, to date, been able to compete; that they cannot predict consequences with enough precision for acceptance. Bureaucrats and elected officials scattered through competing levels of government, each divided into competing agencies, are able to predict more convincingly the consequences of small, accommodating, bargained moves away from the status quo.

But from time to time it is possible to achieve a rather major readjustment in the structuring of our institutions in response to a new problem set. Such restructuring is undoubtedly aided by the images and analyses extended by those who are in a position to be comprehensive. Anyone studying environmental problems, almost because of any definition of what an environmental problem is, concludes that our comprehensive environmental management institutions need strengthening. One approach to this is to be found in improving the use of existing knowledge. We present several strategies here that illustrate some of the necessary steps.

The Mechanical Access Problem

Earth Day 1970 spurred interest in computerized data banks, not to mention handbooks, checklists, information guides, monitoring kits, and games, all intended to instruct in the principles and details of environmental management. But it is the computer that offers the most promise of making manageable the flood of environmental data. Hundreds of environmental impact statements, thousands of books and monographs, tens of thousands of articles, millions of bits of geographically located descriptive data, add up to an intimidating total for anyone who would be comprehensive. Their position is greatly improved by having access to computerized searches of bibliographic data, and to data banks that can provide manipulations of land use data, water quality observations, and measures of business activity.

Much progress has been made in software and data formulating. The New York Land Use and Natural Resources (LUNR) inventory of the New York State Office of Planning Services and Cornell University is one of the few, if not the only, fully operational statewide systems in the country.* Of greater interest to other environmental topics than that of this report are systems that store data on air and water quality.

Literature-search systems can provide the person just turning to a new technical topic with summaries of the latest articles and reports keyed to his need. The computer provides in minutes what would have required hours in many libraries. But not all topics are equally well covered, either in the basic literature or in the data bases. Regional planning agencies have access to such systems. But perhaps the question to be asked is whether these are *really* available to many of the local government officials and private organizations that could make use of them.

Information can affect a decision because of its content and because of the attributes of those who put it into the system of decision-makers. Obviously, not all participants have equal capacity to adapt information to their point of view. Thus, one way to change the results of decisions that affect the environment is to change access and adaptive capacity.

---

*The Office of Planning Services has been abolished. Responsibility for LUNR at the state level has been shifted to the Department of Commerce. The inventory itself is still maintained at Cornell University. [Ed.]

Adaptation of Information

A frequent complaint about data systems such as LUNR is that many potential users cannot use them. LUNR, with its square kilometers described in over 100 characteristics, is a good case in point. All that information about land cover and land use, water bodies and soils, wetlands and parks, ought to be, and is, relevant to many environmental decisions. But how can this information be synthesized so that all the computer capacity serves a specific purpose? A specialist is needed who not only knows how to manipulate the data base but also is knowledgeable about, and sympathetic to, the problem and point of view. Some participants in environmental decisions have no difficulty in finding the means to obtain such assistance. Other points of view find it difficult to organize such technical assistance without help from a public or philanthropic agency.

Some of the earliest, and probably still the most successful, examples of such technical assistance are agricultural extension and research programs. Farmers as individual businesses are usually too small to do their own adaptive research. And what one farmer might develop would be easily copied by another—dissipating much of the incentive to develop it in the first place. This is much like the position of the small woodland owner in the basin, or the landowner who would improve wildlife habitat, or the local conservation group concerned about litter or open space, or the local official wondering about recycling as an adjunct to trash collection, or the chamber of commerce wishing to expand tourism in its area.

Technical assistance programs are most efficient and effective when they can relate to individuals who see enough common interest to organize into private or official groups. Thus, the Extension Association, the Fish and Wildlife Management Act boards, the Soil Conservation Districts, the local and regional conservation councils and commissions, planning boards, and the like become logical targets for an environmental education effort. But by their very nature these groups have their own limited range of legitimized interests and are in the orbit of particular single-purpose agencies.

Also note that many of these provide management assistance at the individual landowner level and thus appeal to a relatively strong set of incentives to use information. The challenge is to move this existing system of technical assistance and adaptive research into more effective management of resource areas and environmental systems. This can be done by both making the agencies already involved more concerned and by adding new linkages in the interorganizational system.

A further element in effective land use planning and control relates to the development of a true land ethic. A comparison of the European countryside with the American countryside shows a distinct difference in the treatment of land. Land must be recognized not only as a market commodity but also as a basic resource whose use can be accompanied by serious harmful effects. Our existing knowledge about land, its uses, and the social effects of those uses could be utilized more effectively in an educational effort. In fact, an intensive and continuing educational program geared to the development of a land ethic would be a valuable long-range contribution to the American way of life.

A word of caution, however, is necessary in the case of education to achieve changes in values, such as the adoption of a land ethic. Values tend to be associated with positions on issues. Those who try to extend something such as a "true land ethic" run the risk of being identified as advocates of a particular point of view. If they are at the same time attempting to extend the use of technical information, the creditability of that technical information may be reduced. This risk may be inevitable in any educational work touching upon environmental issues. There are, nonetheless, approaches to public education and involvement that reduce the risks and maintain effectiveness.

Enhancing the Public Will to Use Knowledge

The practitioners of muddling through—that is, virtually all public decision-makers—often make decisions by ignoring as much relevant information as possible. Consequences that are not certain or that will not result in immediate penalties, as well as alternatives that are not familiar or that must be carried out by someone else, can be ignored. If it can be ignored chances are it will be ignored. Providing a way to share decisions among those who have a stake in them, with that sharing to be roughly proportional to the stake, is an important element in the better use of knowledge. But how do we achieve such sharing?

Interagency coordination procedures and public participation requirements are becoming more common; regulatory bodies to protect the public interest have been in use for years. Such arrangements help, but as many studies have shown, they have limitations and need constant attention. Comprehensive planning programs, particularly those that serve multiple jurisdictions, are also a means of bringing knowledge to bear on decisions. But an educational process, as distinct from a planning process, may be a necessary complement to these other approaches. The objective is to speed the policy-development cycle whereby an issue is identified, proposals made for change, support recruited, and opposition accommodated until a change is instituted. And then, after a period of adjustment, the cycle begins again. A series of educational events, if appropriately structured, can speed up the cycle, broaden participation, and increase the use of knowledge.

One approach of a university-based experimental program is instructive. With the encouragement of a regional development organization, Cornell University employed two community education specialists for the Syracuse region to emphasize public problems of a rural–urban nature. They experimented with a number of techniques to improve lateral communication between agencies, units of government, and community leaders. Perhaps the most successful approach involved using the planning of an educational event as a means of bringing together those with a stake in an issue and those who might not otherwise communicate effectively.

A broad issue area would be identified. Then the obvious public and private leaders would be contacted to help define the issue more precisely, to identify the audiences that should be reached, and to spell out their need for information. Differences would soon appear, and the formation of an informal planning group to work them out would follow naturally. At such discussions, the agenda always included a review of who was affected and how his stake should be taken into account. Since the purpose was to plan an educational activity, bringing knowledge of alternatives and their consequences to bear on a problem was a natural focus. Although the emphasis was put on simply understanding all aspects of a problem, the planning and carrying out of several educational events provided opportunities for interest bargaining and accommodation, and for information gathering and exchange, that otherwise would not have existed. While this occurred to one side of the normal decision-making structure, it was nonetheless in the open and in an atmosphere of high purpose.

Obviously much of the public activity that affects resource management has a very local focus. Approaches that broaden the effective community to match the real region of impact are necessary. The state, multistate, and national areas can be influenced by other strategies that make use of a knowledge base. This study is an example of such a strategy. An elite group is assembled to study a problem. It brings to bear expertise of every relevant kind and the view of the public interest which experts have. Its recommendations and analysis provide both authority and understanding for changes in public decisions. Although it would be surprising if we did not endorse this process, we feel we can do so with special relevance to the environmental problem. Almost by definition, environmental problems come about because of the diffused nature of the effects of environmental degradation and the very particular burden that is usually associated with avoiding degradation. Diffused interests need help whenever they can get it, and elite study groups are more likely than not to call attention to measures that would work in favor of balanced environmental management. Also, such study groups extend and reinforce the idea of the comprehensive planning and decision-making processes which need to be strengthened if environmental problems are to be solved.

Another strategy for using environmental knowledge that should be considered is the strengthening of the environmentalist interest group. Knowledge is one of their weapons in the political and legal battles to correct environmental insults. Many understand the taxes that a modern sewer plant requires—reminders come with each tax bill. But few understand its impact on a fishery, and fewer still appreciate the need for skilled, well-paid technicians to operate a biological process. It would seem that placing the resources to extend such understanding into the hands of those who have an interest is one way to correct some of the imbalances that lead to poor environmental decisions.

A final strategy for the use of knowledge that must be addressed more effectively is related to the problem of increasing the capacity of government, particularly at state and local levels. The capacity to choose implies a balance of authority and support that makes each alternative politically real. This requires intergovernmental and extragovernmental arrangements of many kinds. But within a given level of government perhaps no simple change would mean so much as increasing the resources available to our legislators. Executives can call upon the agencies, and judges upon the litigants, but legislators often depend largely upon the lobbyist. Lobbyists are an efficient, if not too balanced, source of information. They extend ideas about alternatives and their consequences not only in technical terms (i.e., will it work and what will it cost) but also in political terms (i.e., who cares and what are they apt to do about it). Legislators have been negligent in not providing themselves with staffs that can give them both technical and political information in environmental problem areas. Legislators need access to their own planners and program analysts.

Indeed, a state planning agency might well report to the legislators rather than to the governor in some cases. Adjudication between interests is certainly a central part of the process of better resource management. Appeals over the head of an agency charged with resource management are so common and likely that such an agency must be closely linked to the point in government where final arbitration is likely. Likewise, a regional management entity must be linked to sources of political decision-making if it is to be effective.

At the state level, New York has successfully experimented with a science advisor for the Assembly and an expanded central staff. Academic and nonacademic sources of knowledge are effectively mobilized, although further refinement and development, particularly among the universities, is called for.

New York is enjoying a particularly vigorous period of regional commissions and study groups. The Adirondack experience has made many hopeful that such regional accumulation of knowledge and specification of problems will move them toward more responsible resource management. There is little doubt that resource regions have different needs and requirements. Commissions and study groups help keep these needs and requirements from being lost to the natural tendency of state and federal agencies toward uniform application of the law.

Land Markets, Incentives, and Taxation

Effective land use planning and land use regulations are a necessity in the near future if we are to allocate our natural resources wisely and to improve the quality of life. If we are to be successful in this effort, we need to attack our resource management problems at the most basic point. This task group has identified the potential capital gains involved in the conversion of land to more intensive uses as a major force that is highly disruptive to both socially acceptable private land management and the attempts by local government to regulate private land use. There is need for continuing research on the operation of land markets and the land conversion process, especially as it operates on the urbanizing fringes. The structure of these markets is still not well understood, and their behavior over time is barely touched upon by current research efforts. In particular, the influence of landowner characteristics and expectations, speculation, and public utility expansion deserve increased attention.

Land use controls that severely restrict allowable uses or intensity of use may depreciate the value of the land. This is especially important where the land is developable but, for reasons affecting society as a whole, the land is deemed better suited for low-intensity uses. On the other hand, certain lands are essentially undevelopable, such as very steep lands and some wetlands, and these lands are seldom depreciated in value by zoning restrictions. One of the most important missing elements needed by land use planners and regulatory agencies is a legally supportable method to balance the windfall gains that accrue to certain landowners and the losses in value of other landowners. To fill this gap, studies should be made by an independent task force under the auspices of a private foundation or a quasi-independent government agency such as the Council on Environmental Quality. Because of the difference in state laws, such task forces might have to be established on a state-by-state basis.

It will continue to be difficult to express adequately the social concerns in land use decision-making through regulation and control if public controls continue to have such a potentially disruptive effect on private land values. Our present system of zoning illustrates the unhappy results of this route. In future research on suitable public policies for land use control, it is imperative that potential methods of stabilizing the private economic impact of public policies be fully investigated. For example, the possibility of compensating the "losers" in land use control (such as those who will have to put up with a locally higher density of development for the sake of saving socially desirable open space) seems to have merit and would make many more local land use control decisions possible.

In addition to the inherent characteristics of the land parcel and the effects of public controls, land use and value are also highly dependent upon a wide range of services that have little to do with the natural characteristics of the land itself. Yet we know far too little about either the effects of public and private services on land use or about the potentials of changing the process of providing these services so as to encourage land use patterns that are more socially optimal.

Many of these services, such as transportation systems, water and sewer, flood control, and fire protection, are publicly provided. How they are provided and charged for can have large impacts on land values, especially if new, outlying users do not pay the full additional cost that they cause the system to incur. There are other forms of public infrastructure, provided by essentially "private" concerns, that may also exert a large influence on land use patterns. Yet the interest in this research question appears to be only beginning. The example that comes to mind is that of the electric utility industry discussed earlier. Research is needed to determine the effects of all forms of public infrastructure and their rate policies on land uses and values, as well as the possibilities of regulating all forms of public infrastructure so that these side effects are fully considered.

Sound land use policy is also affected by the mix of taxes used to support local government activities. All taxes have unintended and undesirable side effects, but the property tax, capital gains tax, and other taxes can act as strong disincentives to rational land use in both individual resource decisions and public decisions. There is a definite need for research that deals with the probable impacts of alternative changes in the financing of local government activities.

This effort is especially timely now, when governments seem ready to consider some major long-term changes in taxation methods at the local level. This reexamination has been brought about largely by pressures outside of land use effects: by the courts' concern for the equity of property taxes in financing education, and by the increased importance of revenue sharing.

The Biological and Physical System

A few observations made over the period required to study and design the engineering of a project or a land use conversion can never adequately characterize either the biological or the social effects of the change without the availability of a long-term data base. Whether the impacts involve taxes and crowding or disturbed spawning beds and water temperatures, many of the same kinds of data problems are involved. Impacts are diffuse and hard to trace. Changes occur over long periods and it can be extremely difficult to associate cause and effect. Because of these and other problems, adequate incentives do not exist for project-oriented data collectors to obtain the full story on biological and social impacts. Therefore, there is still a largely unfilled public need for further development of organizations to monitor and collect data for a truly long-term data base.

Dealing with the external effects of land use changes has been especially perplexing because of the paucity of sound analytical research directed toward the particular externalities of land use. This is partly because the external effects emanating from land use are so pervasive, cover such a wide range, and can be so hard to identify positively.

Many of the reasons for society's need to improve its environmental monitoring and predictive capabilities are now widely understood. This is especially so in those cases where undesirable impacts are widespread, long-term, and perhaps even irreversible. But today there are new reasons. For example, if the public regulation of private land use is to become more socially acceptable, society's sense of fairness to the individual will result in the increased need to establish, in advance, explicit criteria for environmental review. This is not a simple, mechanical task. We know far too little about how to identify, measure, and define the threshold values of all of the components of an acceptable quality environment, let alone the best way to reach that goal.

Closely related to the previous concerns are the needs associated with the use of the carrying capacity concept. Many factors influence the ability of a land parcel and its surrounding environment to support intensified development—ranging from the physical limitation of surface area to the adequacy of water supply to more nebulous limits, such as the negative impacts on the surrounding land uses. But carrying capacity can virtually never be expressed as absolute limits to growth. As the word "development" implies, it is possible to substitute partially for limits on land's natural capacities. Buildings can rise above the ground or go below it, or they can be made more efficient in their use of floor space. Water supplies can be augmented from offsite sources, much as many other commodities are imported. Irritation to the neighbors' ears can be partially reduced by insulating, landscaping, and screening.

The point is that there are thousands of factors that theoretically can limit the carrying capacity of land, virtually none of which demonstrate a clean and absolute break-off point. Many of these limits will be fully considered by an informed individual because they impinge directly on his ability to use the land. But the greatest problems are created when it is the carrying capacity of the neighboring land or the common property resource that is affected by one man's development—when the wilderness character of the Adirondacks is disrupted or the area's groundwater supply is depleted. It is in these cases where there is the greatest need to translate the theoretical concepts of carrying capacity into workable and acceptable materials for directing local resource policies.

In sum, while research should continue on how an individual deals with the limits in the use of his resources, we would give major priority to understanding how one user affects the ability of another user to enjoy a resource. In particular, the tradeoffs between public management and use limits in regulatory terms should be highlighted. The key point is where public management techniques become ineffective in increasing carrying capacity and regulation must be stressed instead. Until this phenomenon is widely understood, regulation, as zoning has so often shown, will not be effective.

Understanding Integrated Resource Use Areas

Over the decades, contiguous areas of a particular economic activity have grown up around features of the natural resource base—fruit orchards in areas of special climate, second homes in those areas that are both accessible and pleasantly open, and shoreline development along the numerous lakes, rivers, and coastal areas of the region. But moderately extensive resource use areas can be very fragile. Productive fruit areas have been shown to be especially sensitive to the disruptive effects of even scattered intensive development. In the case of resource use areas heavily based on a common property resource, such as shoreline developments, most problems are created from within. The common water body is subjected to excessive use and a thin strip of shoreline is intensively developed to the detriment of all.

There is a need to recognize the importance of maintaining the integrity of extensive resource use areas so that negative externalities are minimized and positive externalities are maximized. To accomplish this, particular types of resource use areas need improved monitoring, understanding, and, eventually, management as an integral system. With regard to their management, there is a need to understand better the thresholds of combinations of resource uses and policies that will allow selected extensive resource uses to maintain their integrity.

Agriculture is one example of land use for which the maintenance of integrity is important. This is especially true for those types of farming, such as dairy and fruit farming, which require a complex system of support services and extensive long-term capital investments.

For many decades, marginal farmland in the region has been abandoned (actually converted to other extensive uses) because of technological change and regional competition. This process has been well documented, but there is room for more study of the effects of long-term farmland abandonment on regional economies and public services, and the special needs of communities which are undergoing the shift from an agricultural economic base to some other dominant land use.

Today the integrity of many farming areas in the region is being attacked by the direct and indirect effects of urban expansion and scatteration. The importance of farmland demise due to such expansion, as opposed to the traditional "abandonment," needs further investigation.

Integrity is also important in the case of commercially harvested forested areas. Under present incentives, these lands are typically harvested in large tracts, and forest management is important to their long-term productivity. But the integrity of areas used for commercial forestry is vulnerable because of their inability to compete effectively in terms of land value with most other uses. One of the most important problems for the future of forestry in the region today has to do with ownership patterns, since most of the forested land is today privately owned in small- to medium-sized tracts for diverse objectives. The problem is not one of trees but of harvesting and managing those trees for increased wood and fiber productivity. Often this is physically possible to do while improving the suitability of the land for other uses, such as wildlife management. Therefore, there is a definite need for research on ways of providing incentives for increased wood fiber productivity on privately owned forested lands.

Wilderness areas represent a special type of forested area for which the need for preservation is especially acute. Means have to be found to deal with the overuse problem in many of the most popular publicly owned natural areas before public overuse destroys the very natural system that people came to see in the first place. In addition, more attention should be given to the methods of determining just what combinations of land uses, both within and on the border of natural areas, can be permitted without damaging the wilderness area.

In areas where second homes are, or could be, the dominant land use poses special problems. Further research should deal with the various effects of second homes, both those constructed individually and in large-scale developments. Second homes bring various temptations and costs to the local area. Therefore, such research should deal with the effects of second homes on the local economy, local taxation, local public services, and the surrounding natural resource base as well as the regional impacts.

Traditional shoreline development too often simultaneously results in restricted public access, intensive and unsightly development along a thin strip of water frontage, and detrimental effects on the natural qualities of both the fragile shoreline and the water body. This task group has identified two priority research areas to deal with some of these problems. First, research should analyze the possible methods of preserving the natural qualities of shorelines. This would include an economic and environmental comparison between shoreline development plans that provide an undeveloped shoreline strip and those more traditional patterns which promote intensive development along the immediate shoreline. Particular attention should be given to the effects on nonpoint pollution and the user capacity of the adjoining water body. Second, further attention should be given to an analysis of the possible ways of dealing with the problems of excessive use and conflicting uses of water bodies. In particular, the possibilities of water-surface zoning should be explored.

Of course, there already are existing programs and policies that help to shape the incentives for the management of all of the extensive resource uses previously mentioned. There is a need, however, to investigate more fully the incentive effects of all existing policies on the management of extensive resources.

Entirely new policies and major changes in existing policies will be required if we are to deal with ecologically integrated areas effectively. Various specific proposals will need to be researched thoroughly. For example, there is a need to investigate the legal, economic, and political feasibility of pooling development rights and capital gains on land, since this is increasingly suggested as a way of altering the private incentives that make it so difficult to maintain the integrity of extensive resource uses.

Alternatively, research could usefully center on potential changes in the design of the zoning tool so as to better handle ecologically integrated areas. Such research would focus on how to classify areas designated specifically for extensive uses and how to get the lines on the zoning map to mean something in practice.

Social Systems, Environmental Values and Perceptions, and Intergovernmental Relationships

Environmental problems, particularly those encompassed in the topic of land use and natural resource management, bring into bold relief the problems of governance that have been a special American struggle for years. This is not the place to rewrite the Federalist Papers—even if we were so endowed. But it is a place to suggest some lines of research that should be pursued so that we might better design government to deal with these and other problems.

We recognize that the American approach to solving the need for central authority produces problems itself. Three or four levels of government, each of which is, in fact, responsible for everything, plus four branches of government (constitutions usually neglect to include the agencies as a fourth branch) look to many like an unwieldy mess. The conventional wisdom is to consolidate and simplify. Yet practice is to do the opposite, perhaps because practice reaches to the problems, not theories, of government. Yet theories of government that really deal with the way this nation does and should organize itself seem to be in very limited supply. The principles articulated by Woodrow Wilson many years ago have been under sustained intellectual attack, but only a few attempts have been made to replace them with a new set of integrated concepts.

How does one bring the broadest public interest to bear on decisions? How can vocal and special interests be offset properly? How can the autonomous single-purpose agency be given incentives to accommodate other legitimate and conflicting interests? Surely there is something better than the public hearing as a way to meet requirements for due process and fair treatment. Government by referendum, by general election, is often not as responsive as some would wish, yet town meetings are not practical. When leaders do try to act in an enlightened manner, how can they protect themselves from the ignorance of the masses? How can one educate if people do not care? If any conflict is sufficient grounds for dumping an official, how can he be expected to act as a statesman?

These and similar questions arise from many public issues, but because of the way environmental problems arise, they have special meaning here. In almost every case environmental problems seem to appear as external effects of particular actions. The negative effects of those actions are spread over many people. The externalities are diffused in time and space, are often indirect and hard to identify, and to understand and perceive. On the other hand, the burden of avoiding the action is usually very specific and direct, involves a tangible and well understood cost, and is very well perceived. Those with an environmental stake find it hard to organize and sustain the representation of their interests. Earth Day 1970 may have been a peak in environmental awareness, but we still do not seem to have effective support for long-term environmental monitoring systems. It is not at all clear, for example, whether or not our water quality programs are working. The processes by which environmental interests express themselves in public decision-making need more study and evaluation. The linkage between public perceptions of environmental problems and political decision-making needs special examination. Indeed, the systematic evaluation of perception as a political datum may have considerable value.

It is clear that local governments have a strong role in influencing land use and resource management through the operation of what are legitimate local governmental functions—extension of public utilities; provision of roads, schools, fire, police, and other services; zoning, taxes, and other fiscal arrangements. Yet it is clear that the capacity of local governments to manage these services with an adequate accommodation of regional interests is in serious doubt. There is a need for research on how intergovernmental relations can be established so as to expand the local capacity to choose, to provide incentives for local governments to take regional impacts into account, and to evolve both stable and efficient methods of shared decision-making. An important step would be research that examines the nature and operating characteristics of interagency and intergovernmental coordination mechanisms.

Local governments differ in capacity in part, it would seem, because communities differ in their social structure and makeup. Differentiation—the capacity of a community to respond to messages and opportunities from the outside—is a concept that needs more research. Public programs such as wastewater management, agricultural districts, or wetlands preservation operate more successfully in some communities. We need to understand such phenomena and learn how to design state and federal programs that adjust for these differences.

There is a need for research to appraise the possibilities of the comprehensive management of regional resources, including both private and public decision-making. Comprehensive models and plans that stress environmental interrelatedness obviously are quite foreign to many decision-makers. We need a better understanding of how such management models can, in fact, be brought to bear on the shared decision systems that exist and are likely to evolve.

Social impacts of environmental management decisions obviously feed back through the political process and help frustrate many efforts. Much of this might be avoided if, first, the social impacts were more accurately estimated instead of guessed at and, second, if we designed specific measures to mitigate negative social effects.

Compensatory and mitigatory social features for environmental programs open up a whole new dimension in policymaking that should be explored. The problem is an extension of the taking issue. When an individual loses property to the government, he is compensated. Use of the police power by the community on the individual is circumscribed by the taking clause of the constitution. But what is the corresponding protection for that community; for example, whose future economic prospects are limited because it is in a protected wilderness region? Pragmatic political considerations suggest that this should be explored. Should the Adirondacks and the Catskills, or some communities surrounded by agricultural districts, receive special consideration in state aid formulas for schools or general local governmental services? How are the social impacts of environmental decisions felt, and which ones should be compensated?

The "Multi–Multi" Problems

This report has taken the single-purpose agency to task. Tunnel vision in decisions is decried. Observing that everything is related to everything else is commonplace. Planning must be multipurpose because natural resources can and should be managed to serve more than one use at a time. Multiple objectives must be considered in evaluation because otherwise those values that easily translate into dollar measurements may have an undue advantage. Participation in decision-making must be multiagency and multi-interest to ensure the appropriate tradeoffs and, through accommodation, to reach decisions with less wasteful conflict. And planning and research must be multidisciplined because the dominance of one discipline, however enlightened, cannot hope to deal adequately with all the intricacies of environmental problems.

The above dicta seem to be emerging as a kind of new conventional wisdom. But behind each there is a thread of needed research. Each needs to be verified and refined.

For example, there is a lot of publicly owned land in the basin, owned mostly by the states but by local governments as well. Add to this the rights-of-way and lands held by public utilities and other quasi-public owners, and the total is impressive. It is managed by many different agencies and the suspicion is strong that the multi–multi problems have not been fully faced. A review of such lands (and waters), including their extent and character, their multiple-use potential, and their potential interrelationships with private lands, seems in order. Then, more detailed research into ways of increasing multiple use as well as improving interagency, intergovernmental, and public–private coordination could stimulate large dividends in improved resource management.

A specific opportunity in the area of game management has been studied enough to suggest that potentials from further work may be great. Habitat management is usually a question of land use management. With the harvesting of trees and clipping of meadows come changes in the mix and quality of deer and small game habitat. Hedgerows may be a waste of land to the farmers but they are a boon to the hunter and wildlife observer. The examples go on and on. But game is no respecter of property lines, and thus the incentive for habitat improvement is lost on the private property owner and many public land managers. The design and feasibility of new incentives for wildlife habitat improvement should be explored.

Habitat management in the two New York wilderness park areas in the basin takes on a special significance. Changing habitat quality on the publicly owned land by direct cover manipulation is prohibited by constitutional strictures. But hunters and wildlife observers are in the forefront of groups that visit and express interest in these areas. Thus, the public interest in habitat management on the private lands in these park areas may provide unique dividends because of its association with the public "forever wild" lands. At this time, however, few incentives are offered for habitat improvement on private lands.

Water resources management provides another focus for research into the multi–multi problems. Water is a ubiquitous resource in that its management potentially cuts across the management of every other natural resource (as does land and air). The point is that a number of management tools have been tried in the water field that should provide useful insights into resource management problems of a different nature. Indeed, some of the old institutional forms tried in water agencies might well be viewed as the nucleus for broader resource management initiatives.

The Hudson Basin and the states of which it is a part have experimented with both watershed or basin approaches and statewide mechanisms for interagency coordination and resource management. In the past, the meaningful linkage of water quality management and water quantity management has been stoutly resisted by the agencies involved. Recently, it has been only somewhat more successfully argued that water quality is more properly linked with air quality and solid waste problems. Whatever the merits, the question of a comprehensive water resource agency would provide a research focus for the general problems of managing the multiple aspects of the single-purpose activity, dealing with land on a comprehensive basis, etc. Likewise, it should be fruitful to explore the potentials and experience of strengthening the watershed and the basin as units for resource management. Again, past orientation has been largely in the direction of dams and channels, riverbanks and shores, because other aspects such as water quality and even recreation have been the "turf" of agencies other than those leading the watershed or basin efforts.